Fisheries ecology of floodplain rivers

Robin L. Welcomme
Senior Fishery Resources Officer
Food and Agriculture Organization
of the United Nations, Rome

Longman
London and New York

To Valerie, Andrew and Deborah

Longman Group Limited London

*Associated companies, branches and representatives
throughout the world*

*Published in the United States of America
by Longman Inc., New York*

First published 1979

British Library Cataloguing in Publication Data

Welcomme, Robin L.
   Fisheries ecology of floodplain rivers.
   1. Fishes, Fresh-water – Ecology
   2. Floodplains
   3. Fishery management
   I. Title
   597'.05'2632   QL624   78-40147
   ISBN 0-582-46310-6

Printed in Great Britain by
Richard Clay (The Chaucer Press) Ltd, Bungay, Suffolk

Contents

Preface

A certain imbalance has come to exist between knowledge of the fisheries of lakes and those of rivers. Possibly in response to the outburst of major dam construction during the 1960s and early 1970s, attention focused on the newly-created man-made lakes, and considerable literature appeared dealing with the ecology of lacustrine fish stocks. Until very recently a corresponding effort on rivers has been lacking. River fisheries have few of the conspicuous qualities of those of the major reservoirs; they are dispersed in space and frequently only small quantities of fish are caught in any one locality. Nevertheless, a considerable proportion – possibly the majority – of the world's freshwater fish catch is taken from running waters and their lateral seasonal flood zones. In recent years there has been a steady increase in the pressure being put upon rivers and their floodplains. In addition to intensified fishing, a variety of agricultural, industrial and domestic uses have all made mounting demands of the ecosystem, which in many cases have affected the fish communities adversely. A sad history of declining catch, attributable to the deterioration in the quality of the water, has been repeated in many parts of the world. Similarly, modifications to the aquatic environment by drainage, irrigation, dam construction and other land- and water-management practices have led to sometimes catastrophic changes in fish populations. In the face of this environmental degradation due to uncoordinated multipurpose use, the general lack of knowledge of the ecology of riverine fish has placed the river basin manager at a disadvantage in trying to predict and obviate the more extreme of these effects on fisheries.

This book is intended partially to compensate for this lack by assembling information on the way in which the riverine environment and the fish stocks inhabiting it respond to the various demands made of the resource. The subject matter is limited mainly to the 'potamon' reaches of those seasonal rivers of the world having major flood zones, because it is precisely these which support the major fisheries and are at the same time being sought after for a great variety of other purposes. In any case the fisheries of some other categories of river (particularly those of salmonid rivers in the temperate zones) have been covered more than adequately in previous works. I have attempted to survey the available literature as completely as possible and to draw on personal experiences, as well as those of other workers in the field, to give a general evaluation of the limnology, ecology and fisheries of flood rivers, without giving excessive detail on the biology of individual organisms which would obscure the main argument. Unfortunately, for reasons of language, some very valuable sources have been barred to me. For example, much of the extensive literature on the Don, Volga, Amu Darya and other Russian rivers is not included, although it is hoped that this will be eventually incorporated into the general body of knowledge. Uses of the floodplain other than fisheries have been only lightly touched upon in so far as they affect the living aquatic resources. Detailed descriptions of such topics as floodplain agriculture would surely occupy a volume larger than this. The book sets out to be as self-contained as possible, but is complemented by several earlier and contemporary works which are widely quoted in the text. These are *Tropical Inland Fisheries*, C. F. Hickling, 1961; *The Inland Waters of Tropical Africa: An Introduction to Tropical Limnology*, L. C. Beadle, 1974; *Fish Communities in Tropical Freshwaters*, R. H. Lowe-McConnell 1975; *The Ecology of Running Waters*, H. B. N. Hynes, 1970; *River Ecology*, R. B. Whitton (ed.) 1975; *River Ecology and Man*, R. T. Oglesby, C. A. Carson and J. A. McCann, 1972.

Because of the comparative nature of the material presented, the text has to move between river systems and even between continents in the same paragraph. The location of the rivers discussed is sometimes indicated in the text, but to avoid over-frequent repetition a geographic index is provided at the end of the book. Equally, fish species are not always cited in full, but their family and authority are quoted in the *Taxonomic Index*. The system of notation kg hm^{-2} yr^{-1} has been adopted as standard, but for those not familiar with it, it is directly equivalent to kg/ha/yr (hm^2 or square hectometre = 1 hectare).

R.L.W.
June 1978

Acknowledgements

Although published under one name any book of this type is the result of the work of many people. The knowledge has been acquired not only by the scientists working on the topic as an academic problem but also by the fishermen who depend upon their wisdom for the very food they eat. During the course of journeys to tropical rivers I have benefited from the friendship and cooperation of many who work directly with the fisheries described here, and to them I owe an enormous debt. In particular, I am grateful to Mr P. B. N. Jackson, the staff of the East African Freshwater Fisheries Research Organization and Prof. L. Beadle who guided my efforts during my five-year stay in East Africa. I am equally indebted to Mr H. Loko and the fishermen of the Ouémé and Niger rivers in Benin for initiating me into the mysteries of the fisheries of large river systems. The fishery administrators from many countries have contributed considerably to the progress of the work, both individually and through the agency of the regional bodies of FAO, with reports or clarifications on the status of fisheries in their own areas. Much of the stimulus to collect this material and eventually publish it comes from my colleagues, without whose interest and encouragement I would not have been able to proceed. In particular, I would like to thank Drs J. Gulland, H. F. Henderson and R. Lowe-McConnell who read the draft of the manuscript, for discussions and helpful suggestions for its improvement; Mr M. Ben-Yami and Mr D. James for their advice on the section on the fishery; Mr H. Underhill for his comments on the section on hydrology, Dr J. Howard for his assistance with remote sensing and Mr M. Frere for providing data on evapotranspiration rates. My thanks are also due to members of the working Group on River and Floodplain Fisheries of the FAO Committee for Inland Fisheries of Africa, Mr N. G. Willoughby, Mr D. Tweddle, Mr A. Mabaye, Mr R. E. Hastings, Prof. J. B. Awachie, Mr M. Konare and Ms C. Gilmore, for permission to quote unpublished material arising from the discussions of the Group; also to Dr H. Matthes, Dr J. Kapetsky, Mr H. Meecham and Dr I. Dunn for agreeing to my use of information acquired during the course of the field projects in which they were engaged.

I am most grateful to the several persons who have helped in the physical preparation of this book. To my secretary, Ms E. Ronchetti for generally making life easier by taking over many administrative chores and for seeing several drafts pass through her typewriter, to Ms G. Soave for checking the references and to the staff of the Fishery Library for obtaining for me numerous works of reference, and not least to my wife Valerie for her patient support, encouragement and valued corrections to my English and punctuation.

For permission to use previously published illustrations and tabulations I am indebted to many authors and equally to the Institut Géographique National for allowing the use of the air-photographs and to NASA for making available the space imagery.

This work was prepared while working for the Food and Agriculture Organization of the United Nations who have kindly granted me permission to publish and also to quote from the FAO documents listed in the bibliography. The material presented in this book represents my own personal views which do not necessarily coincide with the opinions of the Organization.

Chapter 1

Introduction

The continental land masses of the world are traversed by rivers which bring fresh water within the reach of all but the most arid and desertic zones. Rivers are populated by fish which are exploited at all levels, from the sport of small boys to commercial fisheries by the collective use of complex gear. In this way riverine fish contribute to the protein balance of the world's rural population and provide valuable relaxation in more industrialized societies. The nominal catch of freshwater fish, as given in the *FAO Yearbook of Fishery Statistics* (FAO, 1976) is about 10 million tonnes. Of this a considerable proportion comes from rivers or the seasonally inundated ground associated with them. In Africa, for example, nearly half of the 1·4 million tonnes caught in 1975 was thought to originate from rivers (Welcomme, 1976). Neither Asia nor Latin America have the profusion of major lakes that is a feature of Africa, and therefore a correspondingly greater quantity of the fish catch must be of riverine origin.

From the fisheries viewpoint perennial rivers may be assigned for convenience to two major classes, reservoir and flood rivers. Reservoir rivers, such as the lower reaches of the Zaïre, have a stable flow throughout the year. The lack of major flood peaks allows the stream to be contained within its main channel which is only overflowed in years of exceptional rainfall. The evenness of the flow is usually due to year-round precipitation or to the presence of major lakes or swamps which store water to release it slowly throughout the year. The fish communities of such systems are diversified with trophic specialization and well-defined food webs (Roberts, 1973). They differ widely from the communities of flood rivers, behaviourally and dynamically, in that they tend to resemble the populations of lakes rather than those of seasonally flowing waters. The artificial regulation of flow by the construction of dams, has transformed many former flood rivers into watercourses of the reservoir type.

Flood rivers are those where large seasonal variations in rainfall over the basin are transmitted downriver as a pulse of increased flow. As a result of this, lateral plains have been formed which are submerged by overspill from the main channel. Relatively narrow plains are normal depositional features of the mature or 'potamon' reaches of tropical savanna rivers of modest slope. In some forest rivers, too, alluvial deposits have built up into fringing plains, such as the 'várzeas' of the

Amazonian system. In fact it now appears that many of the present savanna plains were formerly lightly forested and have only recently become denuded through man's activities. In many areas of the world more extensive and complex seasonally flooded features have arisen by geographic accident. In these, large flat plains are transected by rivers which have some impediment to drainage downstream. This causes the water to be retained and to extend over vast areas, some of which are equal in size to the world's largest lakes.

The great fluctuations in level cause a seasonal cycle of flood and drought over much of the area, although a core of permanent water does persist within the main river channels and the low-lying depressions of the floodplain itself. Extreme changes in water chemistry and primary production also occur throughout the cycle, giving rise to a constantly shifting pattern in the variety of ecosystems which make up the river–floodplain complex. Organisms inhabiting these types of systems have had to adapt to spatial and temporal fluctuations which are perhaps unique among aquatic environments. Nevertheless, most floodplain rivers have diverse and abundant fish faunas which support some of the richest of inland fisheries.

The fertility of floodplains is legendary, and many of man's earliest civilizations have developed around them. Since about 5 000 b.p., when the earliest systematic colonization of the Nile, Mesopotamic and Indus rivers occurred (Toynbee, 1976), there has been a concentrated effort aimed at the taming of floods for the benefit of agriculture. This trend persisted until the present, and modern efforts at impoundments and canalization for power, irrigation and flood control are but the latest of a long series of such attempts. However, man's present usage is more intense than ever before, and to the environmental hazards of hydraulic engineering is added the threat of contamination of the waters with a variety of industrial and agricultural chemicals. In addition, bad or non-existent basin management, deforestation and the farming of marginal hill-slope lands has increased erosion and the resulting silt loads of rivers. This silt is usually deposited on floodplains, filling channels and lakes and choking vegetation, but at the same time causing the plains to grow faster than ever before. The rich fish communities of the plains are therefore faced with competing uses which not only modify the environment, depriving the fish of living space and access to parts of the river necessary for the completion of their life cycles, but also change the quality and quantity of the water in which they live. Because of this some long-established fisheries have now disappeared and others are on the way to extinction.

Despite the importance of flood rivers for fisheries, the great academic fascination of their fauna and flora, and the impact of modern developments upon them, relatively few studies have been carried out on such areas. In fact, by comparison with the wave of studies on man-made lakes and their fisheries, knowledge of the fisheries of rivers which they have often replaced is negligible. Possibly the earliest systematic studies were those of Antipa (1910) whose original work on the Danube was continued both by himself and by other workers until its ecology is possibly the most extensively studied of the world's major river systems. This work has been summarized by the Academia Republicii Socialiste Romania (1967) for Roumania, by Balon (1967) for Czechoslovakia, and a more general overview has been given by Liepolt (1967). Antipa's general conclusion that the fisheries production of the Danube is directly proportional to the extent and duration of the floods (Botnariuc, 1968) has proved to be equally applicable to all other flood rivers investigated. The work on the Danube has further demonstrated that the plain cannot be considered in isolation but must be treated as part of the larger river system (Botnariuc, 1967; Balon, 1967) – an approach that has been maintained in this work.

Systematic study of the fisheries ecology of tropical rivers began on the Niger, when a laboratory was set up in the Central Delta (Blanc *et al.*, 1955) whose output through the numerous publications of Daget clarified much of the taxonomy and biology of the fish of this river. At the same time the Jonglei Investigation Team (1954) explored the Nile Sudd in the southern Sudan, and work on the limnology of the area was continued by the Hydrobiological Unit of the University of Khartoum throughout the 1960s. More recently other African floodplains have been under investigation. Intensive but short-duration studies on the Kafue river by the Universities of Idaho and Michigan *et al.* (1971) did much to shed light on the growth and mortality rates of certain species. Elsewhere, workers have been gathering information on the fisheries and general ecology of the Shire river, the Okavango delta (Botswana Society, 1976), and the Yaérés floodplain of the Lake Chad basin.

In South America most of the major river systems have been investigated to some extent. Bonetto (1975) has given an overview of the Argentinian studies of the Paraná river, while Godoy (1975) has summarized a life's work on the Brazilian Mogi Guassu tributary of the same river. In the Amazon the findings of the Instituto de Pesquisas de Amazonia in conjunction with a team from the Max-Planck-Institut für Limnologie, have been presented in broad perspective by Sioli (1975a, 1975b). Work on the Orinoco system has been more restricted, and although Mago-Leccia (1970) and more recently an FAO project have carried out some investigations, understanding of this system is still minimal. Some smaller river systems have been investigated in more detail, including the Rupununi by Lowe-McConnell (1964) and more recently the Magdalena by an FAO project.

Studies on Asiatic river systems are more restricted. A series of workers, from Chevey and Le Poulain (1940) onwards have observed the fishery of the Mekong river. These observations have provided the basis for detailed information on migration patterns, but otherwise little has been published of the biology of individual species or the dynamics of their populations. Some studies have been carried out on the Indian sub-continent which have been summarized by Jhingran (1975).

However, the waters of many Indian rivers have been modified by dams, consequently work has been concentrated on the reservoirs and their stocking needs.

Chapter 2

The environment

2.1 General morphology

At first sight floodplains appear flat and relatively featureless. However, slight variations in the elevation and slope of the terrain lead to great differences in the time of immersion of any locality on the plain and in the patterns of flow of the water covering it. The constantly shifting bed of the river, and the silting of old features and cutting of new ones, lead to the maintenance of the characteristically flat plain, while producing constant modifications in the detailed geography of the area. Sedimentary material brought downstream by the river is deposited at various places, and material is eroded by the lateral migration of the river channel in its valley and by the scour arising from flow over the surface during floods. These two processes proceed simultaneously in such a manner that over a number of years the net inflow of sediments equals the net outflow.

According to Leopold *et al.* (1964) such a plain will typically include the following features:

1. The river channel.
2. Oxbows or oxbow lakes representing the cut-off portion of meander bends.
3. Point bars, loci of deposition on the convex side of curves in the river channel.
4. Meander scrolls, depressions and rises on the convex side of bends formed as the channel migrates laterally down-valley by the erosion of the concave bank.
5. Sloughs, areas of dead water formed both in meander-scroll depressions and along the valley walls as flood flows move directly down-valley scouring adjacent to the valley walls.
6. Natural levées, raised berms or crests above the floodplain surface adjacent to the channel, usually containing coarser materials deposited as floods flow over the top of the channel banks. These are most frequently found at the concave bank. Where most of the silt load in transit is fine-grained, natural levées may be absent or nearly imperceptible.
7. Backswamp deposits, overbank deposits of finer sediments deposited in slack water ponded between the natural levées and the wall or terrace riser.

8. Sand splays, deposits of flood debris usually of coarser sand particles in the form of splays or scattered debris.

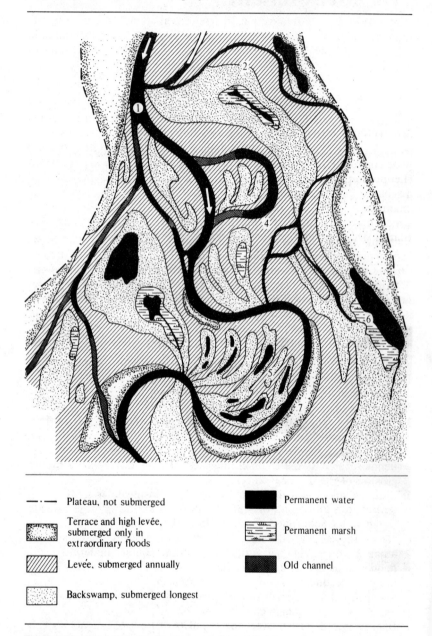

— · — Plateau, not submerged	■ Permanent water
Terrace and high levée, submerged only in extraordinary floods	Permanent marsh
Levée, submerged annually	Old channel
Backswamp, submerged longest	

Fig. 2.1 Diagram of the main geomorphological features of a tropical floodplain; numbers refer to description in text.

These features, which are illustrated diagramatically in Fig. 2.1, determine the quantity, distribution and flow of water in the system throughout the year. Most of them are readily distinguishable in moderate-sized floodplains, but in smaller valleys are obscured by the rapidity with which changes occur. Individual features of the floodplain are briefly described below [numbers in (parentheses) in text refer to Fig. 2.1].

Channels – the lotic component

The main channel (1) or channels of the river and its anabranches (2) usually retain water, but not necessarily flowing water, at all times of the year. As the river enters its alluvial plain it starts to meander, forming wide convoluted channels whose curves are proportional to river width (Leopold *et al.*, 1964). At slightly steeper slopes for the same bankfull discharge the river tends to follow a more direct course, but braided channels arise. These consist of many anastomosing anabranches, which may themselves meander, winding among sandy or vegetated islands which are exposed at low water and flooded at high water (Fig.

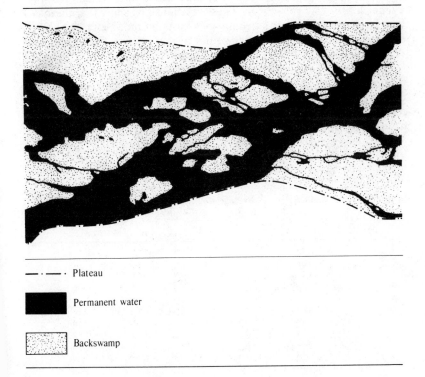

— · —— · Plateau

[■] Permanent water

[▦] Backswamp

Fig. 2.2 Typical braided channel; the example shows a portion of the Niger river.

2.2). In some larger rivers, the Amazon and Zaïre for example, the islands form levées with depression lakes at their centre. Where braided channels occur the lateral floodplain is sometimes limited in width and its whole extent may come to be contained within the main channel. In these instances the islands are analagous to the lateral floodplain and fulfil a similar role in the biology of the fish (Svensson, 1933; Gosse, 1963).

The dendritic arrangement of the channels of a river throughout its drainage basin is well known. Several suggestions for ranking streams forming this type of pattern have been proposed. Horton (1945) suggested the concept of stream order, where first-order streams are those with no tributaries, second-order streams those which have as tributaries only first-order streams, and so on. In this classification the longest tributary of each order is considered to extend headwards to contribute to the length of the main channel of the river. Strahler (1957) revised this system so that all streams of each class have the same rank. Horton further noted that the number of streams of different orders in a watershed decreases with increasing order according to a logarithmic relationship of the form, *number of streams* $= a.b^{stream\ order}$. The length of the streams increases with increasing order in a similar manner, *stream length* $= x.y^{stream\ order}$. These relationships show that there is a very large number of small tributaries whose combined lengths make up a considerable percentage of the total of any system. For example in Africa, Welcomme (1976) calculated approximately $12 \cdot 8 \times 10^6$ km of streams of which $6 \cdot 7 \times 10^6$ are in first-order streams using the equations, *number of streams* $= 1 \cdot 971\ 9 \times 10^7 (0 \cdot 21^{stream\ order})$ and *stream length* $= 0 \cdot 695\ (2 \cdot 301\ 4^{stream\ order})$ (Table 2.1). Low-order streams are often of a torrential nature, whereas large floodplains tend to be concentrated around higher order rivers.

Table 2.1 Estimated theoretical number and length of various orders of river channel in Africa (after Welcomme, 1976)

Order	Number	Average length (km)	Theoretial total length (km)	Typical river in class
	'A'	'B'	(A×B)	
1	4 166 969	1·6	6 667 150	
2	870 615	3·7	3 203 865	
3	181 900	8·5	1 540 693	
4	38 005	19·5	741 097	
5	7 940	44·8	356 347	
6	1 659	103·3	171 358	
7	347	237·4	82 492	Moa
8	72	547·1	39 392	Ouémé
9	15	1 259·1	19 013	Volta
10	3·2(3)	2 897·8	9 273	Niger
11	0·7(1)	6 669·0	4 668	Nile
Total			12 835 346	

In addition to the main channel or channels of the river, floodplains have a network of channels and creeks which penetrate the levées to connect the main river with the backswamps and meander scroll lakes. Such channels may or may not retain water at all times of the year, but they represent the main path of water and fish movement during the earlier periods of rising water and later phases of falling water.

On many floodplains naturally occurring channels are supplemented by artificial canals constructed for navigation, irrigation, drainage or even fishery purposes.

Standing waters – the lentic component

Permanent or semi-permanent standing waters are left by receding floods in the form of sloughs in oxbows (4) [numbers in (parentheses) refer to Fig. 2.1], meander scroll depressions (5), backswamps (6) or the residual channels left by the former course of the river (3). These water bodies expand and contract according to the annual flood cycle (Fig. 2.3), and during the highest floods tend to merge into a continuous sheet of water covering the whole plain.

Distinction is often made between lakes, lagoons or pools on the one hand and swamps on the other. Although the terms lakes, lagoons and pools have been used interchangeably in the literature, and refer more or less impartially to bodies of water of some depth and slight to moderate vegetation cover, there is a useful distinction to be made between lakes, as large features of a floodplain system which persist relatively unchanged over a number of years, and lagoons and pools as more transitory open-water features. Lagoons remain connected to the river throughout the year, whereas pools are usually smaller and more ephemeral bodies of water which become isolated and have a tendency to dry out in the dry season. The term 'swamp' is applied to those depression wetlands whose soil remains saturated or more or less permanently covered with shallow waters and which, as a result, support characteristic growths of vegetation which dominate the environment.

Permanent standing waters of the floodplain are generally shallow, rarely exceeding 4 m, and may be in communication with the river. Alternatively, their deepest point may lie below the water table of the plain enabling them to remain wet throughout the year.

Water bodies on the floodplain lose water by evaporation and to a lesser degree by filtration throughout the dry season. This results in the contraction and eventual drying out of many water bodies with a concomitant concentration of dissolved substances. In most river systems this does not produce any appreciable result, as concentrated solutions are rapidly washed out by the next floods and the average conductivity of the water remains low. However, in some regions of high salinity or one-way flow, temporary brackish pools or salt pans can result. The most extreme example of such an area is perhaps the 1 million hm^2 Plain of Reeds of the Mekong delta, where there are extraordinarily high concentrations of alum.

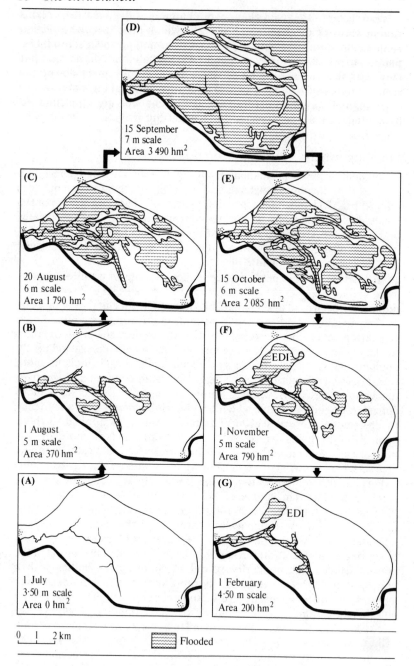

Fig. 2.3 Annual cycle of flooding of a typical floodplain depression of the Senegal river (Vindou Edi). (After Reizer, 1974.)

Very large lakes or groups of lakes are associated with some floodplains. These are sometimes distinct entities geologically, but ecologically they are usually completely integrated into the river–floodplain system. The greatest of such lakes, the Grand Lac of the Mekong (Fig. 2.4), floods an area of 11 000 km^2, most of which was forested, but which is reduced to about 2 500 km^2 of open water in the dry season. It is connected to the main river by a broad channel with reversible flow, the Tonle Sap.

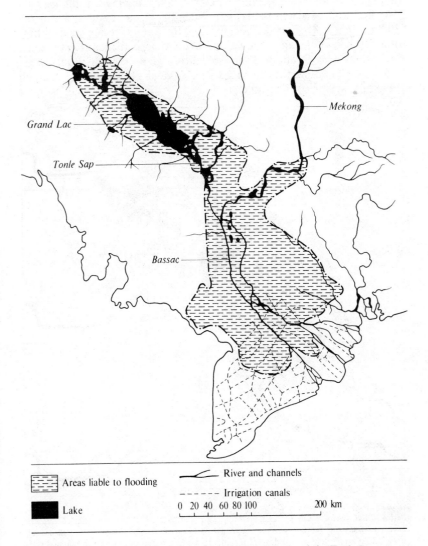

Fig. 2.4 The delta of the Mekong river with the Grand Lac and the Tonle Sap.

A similar but smaller feature is found in the Senegal river valley where the Lac de Guiers is connected to the main channel by the river Tawey. The lake has an extreme dry-season area of 120 km² and expands to twice this when flood waters flow into it through the Tawey in August and September. The lake district of the Niger Central Delta (Fig. 2.5) forms part of the general flood system at high water, but breaks up into 18 major lakes with a combined area of 2 400 km² at low water. The 11 000 km² Kamulondo depression floodplain of the Lualaba contains some 50 permanent and semi-permanent lakes, having a total area of 1 545 km² and of which the largest, Upemba, has a dry-season area of 530 km². In the Magdalena river (Fig. 2.6) the waters are confined within some 800 lakes ('cienagas') of varying size and permanence at low water. Their total area is about 3 400 km², although some individual water bodies, for example the Cienagas de Zapatosa (119 km²) and Ayapel (123 km²), are of considerable size.

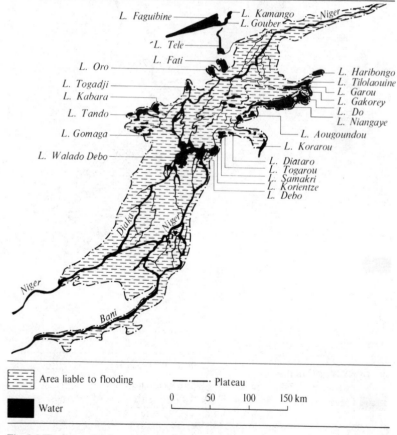

Fig. 2.5 The internal delta of the Niger river and its tributary the Bani, in Mali, showing the numerous lakes at the northern end of the plain.

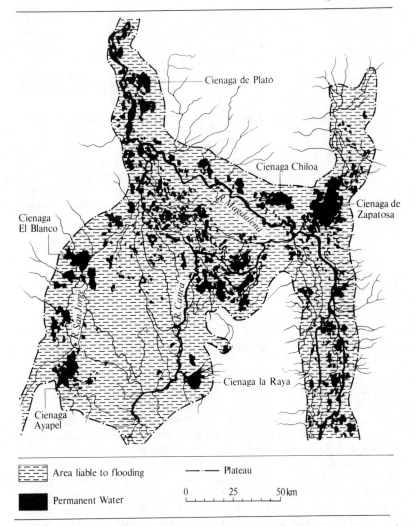

Fig. 2.6 The internal delta of the Magdalena river at its confluence with the Cauca and San Jorge rivers in Colombia; note the numerous floodplain lakes (cienagas).

The 'várzea' floodplain of the Amazon is similarly interspersed with lakes, some of which are very large. There are 20 lakes of over 50 km² and the Lago Grande do Curuai covers 630 km². While these resemble the floodplain lakes found in other systems, a special type of water body is also found in the Amazon. The clear-water tributaries to the lower and middle reaches of the river have large widened mouthbays formed originally from drowned valleys. Such 'river-lakes' are the site of sedimentation at their upstream ends where new várzea-type floodplains are formed from the deposits (Fig. 2.7).

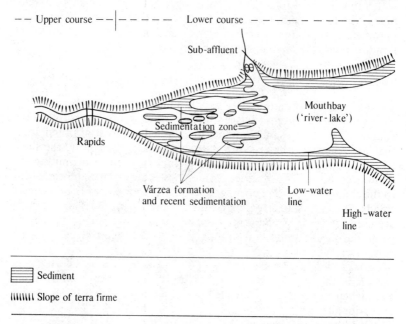

Fig. 2.7 Diagram of the morphology of middle Amazonian affluents. (After Sioli, in Whitton, 1975).

The individual water bodies of the floodplain usually persist over long periods during which they age, although particularly high floods can produce sudden changes through scour and deposition. The ageing process consists of a natural succession from open-water lake to dry land, via the intermediate stages of shallow lagoon and swamp ecosystems. Botnariuc (1967), in particular, has studied the processes involved in the transformation of the lakes of the Danube floodplain. Here the transition from lake ('ghiol') to reed-grown pond ('japse') is caused mainly by the growth of emergent vegetation which slows water currents and accelerates siltation, thus allowing a further extension of the vegetated area, although the process is partially reversible when higher floods may scour deposits and vegetation from the lake bottom. Similar siltation can be detected in the deposition of new várzea in the mouth lakes of the Amazon, or in the change in form of lakes and channels viewed as a time series by remote sensing. Side-looking radar, and satellite imagery show floodplains to be littered with the remains of old floodplain features now silted over. The succession may also be reconstructed from series of lakes such as those described by Green (1972a) for the meander complex of the Suia Missu river in Brazil. The disappearance of older features of the floodplain in this way is compensated for by the generation of new bodies of water by the constantly changing course of the main river channel. The speed with which this occurs is related to the discharge of the river and its silt load, but it is to be supposed that, given relative constancy of these parameters, the ratio of open-water bodies on the plain to total area remains relatively unchanged through time.

The floodplain

The alluvial plain of the river can be divided into two main zones. Firstly, the levée regions (7) (see Fig. 2.1), which more or less follow the course of the river channel and its former beds, consist of raised areas that are flooded for the shortest time annually. Secondly, the flats, which extend from the levée to the terrace or plateau delimiting the plain. Exceptionally high levées sometimes occur immediately adjacent to the channel. These are only occasionally submerged by the highest of floods. Such areas, together with the raised terraces bordering the plain are used for human habitation, or give island refuges for cattle or wild game during the flood season. Levées may be much reduced or even completely absent in rivers carrying very fine silt. Because coarser material is deposited early after the slowing of the flow as a river enters the plain, there is a tendency for the raised areas bordering the river channel to diminish in height downstream. In river basins with exceptionally high silt loads, for example the Chao–Phrya delta in Thailand (see Fig. 2.8), deposition raises the river channel and levée high above the surrounding plain. In some areas of the world both the levée and the terraces are covered with dense gallery forest (see Figs. 2.27 and 2.28), but other floodplains are occupied only with sparse scrub or are denuded of trees altogether (savanna plains). The flats which make up the greater proportion of the plain show slight differences in relief owing to old depositional features. More depressed parts are interspersed with standing waters of various types. The edges, adjacent to the terrace or valley wall delimiting the plain, may be more deeply excavated where locally increased flow scours deposits to form lagoon or backswamp complexes (6) (see Fig. 2.1). Irregularities may also be formed where inflowing tributaries deposit alluvial fans.

Proportions of floodplain features

The proportion of the floodplain which remains permanently under water is generally as difficult to establish as is the total area submerged at the peak of the floods. There is for the most part a lack of reliable maps showing floodplain features, and even where they do exist the period of mapping rarely coincides with the period of minimum water. However, newly developed techniques using satellite imagery present possible solutions to this problem (see Appendix, p. 267). Further complications arise from the temporal instability of floodplain features and the changes wrought by man himself. In most populated areas the floodplain and its hydraulic regime have been

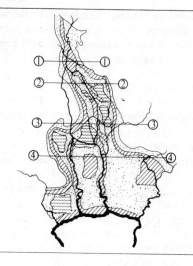

☐ Above flood level
▢ Covered only by highest floods
▨ Covered by average flood

▦ Flooded each year, main area for garden rice
▤ Deeply flooded each year

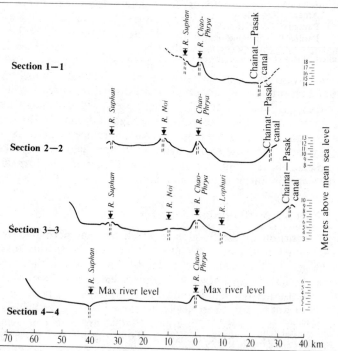

Fig. 2.8 Plan and cross-sections of the Chao-Phrya delta, Thailand, showing channels raised within levées above the level of the surrounding plain. (After Ohya, 1966.)

considerably modified by the digging of canals, the raising of artificial levées and the levelling of depressions. Some information on relative areas is available from the best studied floodplains in Africa (Table 2.3), and from a smaller selection in Latin America (Table 2.2). As flood regimes vary in the intensity of both their flood and dry-season components, values for high-water and low-water areas fluctuate about a mean. The figures quoted in Tables 2.2 and 2.3 should be treated as such averages, being only approximations derived from relatively small-scale maps.

Table 2.2 Areas at peak flood of some Central and South American floodplains

No. Fig. 2.10	Floodplain	Area at peak flood (km²)	Authority
1	Grijalva San Antonio R. – delta	8 000	USAF*
2	Atrato R. – delta	5 300	USAF
3	Magdalena R. – delta	20 000	Pardo (1976)
4	Catatumbo R. – delta	5 000	USAF
5	Orinoco R. – Apure–Arauca internal delta	70 000	Matthes (pers. comm.)
6	Orinoco R. – coastal delta	20 000	USAF
7	Rupununi R. – Internal flood zone	6 500	USAF
8	Amazon R. – central delta	50 000	Sioli (1975a)
9	Amazon R. – coastal delta	25 000	Sioli (1975a)
10	Paraguay R. – Gran Pantanal	80–100 000	Bonetto (1975)
11	Paraná R. – fringing plain	20 000	Bonetto *et al.* (1969a)

*United States Operational Navigation Chart – scale 1:1 000 000.

Table 2.3 Characteristics of some African floodplains

No. Fig. 2.11	Floodplain	Area at peak flood (km²) 'A'	Area at low water (km²) 'B'	$\frac{B}{A}\times100$	Authority
12	Senegal R.				
	coastal delta	7 970			
	fringing plain	5 000	500	10	Lessent (pers. comm.)
13	Niger R.				
	– Central Delta	20 000	3 877	19	Raimondo (1975)
	– fringing plains:				
	Niger	907	270	30	FAO/UN (1971a)
	Benin	274	32	12	FAO/UN (1971a)
	Nigeria	4 800	1 800	38	FAO/UN (1970a)
	Benue R.				
	– fringing plain				
	Nigeria	3 100	1 290	42	FAO/UN (1970a)
14	Ouémé R.				
	– coastal delta	1 000	52	5	Pers. observations
15, 16	Chari and Logone R.				
	– Yaérés	7 000	NI	–	Ali Garam (pers. comm.)

Table 2.3 Characteristics of some African floodplains cont'd

No. Fig. Fig. 2.11	Floodplain	Area at peak flood (km²) 'A'	Area at low water (km²) 'B'	$\frac{B}{A} \times 100$	Authority
17	– Total system	63 000	6 300	10	Blache (1964)
18	Zaïre – Mbandaka	No information		–	
19	Zambezi R. – Barotse	10 752	537	7	FAO (1969a)
20	Okavango – internal delta	17 000	3 120	20	Cross (pers. comm.)
21	Pongolo R.	100	26	26	Coke and Pott (1970)
22	Kafue R. – Kafue flats	4 340	1 456	27	Gay (pers. comm.)
23	Shire R.				
	– Elephant and Ndinde marshes	665	200	30	Hastings (pers. comm.)
	– Total system	1 030	480	48	
24	Laupula R.				
	– Kifakula depression	1 500	NI		
25	Lualaba R.				
	– Kamulondo depression	11 840	7 040	59	
26	Nile R. – Sudd	92 000	10 000	11	Rzóska (1974)
	Volta R.				
	– fringing plain Ghana	8 532	1 022	12	Vanderpuye (pers. comm.)
	Ogun R. – fringing plain	43	25	59	Dada (pers. comm.)
	Oshun R. – fringing plain	37	20	73	Dada (pers. comm.)
	Masilli R. – fringing plain	15	2	13	Barry (pers. comm.)

In Africa the area of permanent water ranges from 5 to 59 per cent of the total flooded area, with a pronounced mode at between 10 and 20 per cent. There is insufficient information to judge whether significant differences exist between the flood ratios of the various categories of floodplain and these may depend more on soil type or local climate. It is difficult to describe the simple ratio between flooded and permanent water areas. Indeed, the extent to which the various depositional features of the plain can change from season to season makes such figures of only temporary value, except as indicators. Table 2.4 shows, for some African plains, the proportion of the permanent waters that remain on the floodplain as standing waters and those located in the divers river channels.

There are pronounced differences in this proportion and the smallness of the sample does not permit definite conclusions to be drawn on the possible causes of this. However, it might be expected that on floodplains where agriculture is intensively practised during the dry season, much of the standing water, and particularly the swamps, will tend to disappear through drainage and fill. This in fact appears to be the case for the cultivated Senegal, Ouémé and Pongolo plains as compared with the Niger, Lualaba and Kafue plains, which are used primarily for cattle grazing. The main exception to this is the Shire in

Table 2.4 Composition by area of different types of permanent water on floodplains during the dry season

Floodplain	River and channels	Standing waters			Total area
	(hm²)	Lagoons (hm²)	Swamps (hm²)	Total (hm²)	(hm²)
Niger R. – Central Delta	61 300(16)*	300 400(77)	26 000(7)	316 400(84)	389 700
Lualaba–Kamulondo	29 400(4)	154 500(23)	480 000(72)	643 500(96)	663 900
Kafue–Kafue flats	5 380(4)	10 180(7)	130 000(89)	140 180(96)	145 560
Shire	2 000(4)	5 500(12)	40 500(84)	46 000(95)	48 000
Pongolo	392(14)	N.D.**	N.D.	2 428(86)	2 820
Ouémé	1 402(27)	3 768(73)	slight	3 768(73)	5 170
Senegal valley	28 100(57)	21 800(43)	slight	21 800(43)	49 700

*Percentage of total.
**N.D. No distinction made.

which there is a large area of permanent marsh. In the three floodplains where a breakdown is available, a large amount of the standing water is classified as permanent swamp. Unfortunately, the dividing line between swamp and lagoon is somewhat fine and vegetated areas of lagoons are often placed in this category.

The various floodplain features are sufficiently important in the lives of the peoples inhabiting the main rivers for a particular terminology to have arisen in many languages. While by no means exhaustive, Table 2.5 lists the main names that have been used in the literature by workers from various countries to describe individual features.

Table 2.5 Glossary of terms for floodplain features

Country	Features			
	Levée	Floodplain	Depression lagoon or swamps	Channels and side arms
Benin	Tikpa	Ti		
Brazil		Várzea	Lago de várzea	Paraná
Dem. Kampuchea		Veal	Beng	Prek
Colombia			Cienaga	Caño
India			Bheel	Jheel
Rumania			Ghiol: japse	
Senegal	Fonde	Oualo	Vindo	Tiangol
Sri Lanka			Villus	
Sudan		Toiche		

2.2 Types of floodplains

It is perhaps hazardous to attempt any definitive classification of floodplains. However, three general types can be discerned whose characteristics are sufficiently different that they may influence either the behaviour of the fish populations inhabiting them, or the problems faced by a fishery.

Fringing floodplains

Nearly all tropical and subtropical rivers and many temperate ones have a lateral flood zone. This takes the form of a relatively narrow strip of floodable land lying between the river valley walls (Fig. 2.9). Fringing floodplains are normal developmental features of a river which follow its course in all areas where the slope is favourable. They tend to increase

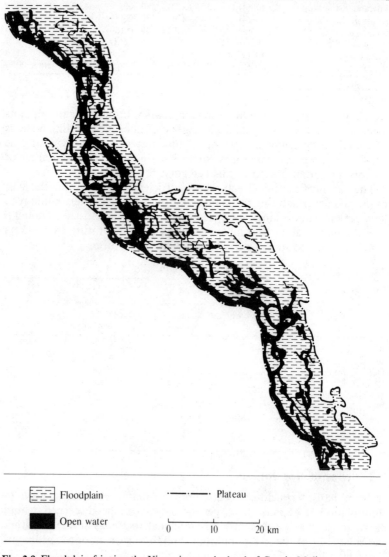

Floodplain   ·——·——· Plateau

Open water

0   10   20 km

Fig. 2.9 Floodplain fringing the Niger river at the level of Gao in Mali.

in width the less the slope of the river, and this generally means a progressively greater elaboration of the floodplain along the river's course to the sea.

Internal deltas

Occasionally, river systems encounter geological features which cause them to spread laterally over very large alluvial plains. Such features may be the site of a former lake filled with alluvium, for instance the Yaérés of Lake Chad, the deltaic discharge of a small river into a larger one, such as is found where the Apure flows into the Orinoco, or the backing up of the aquatic system by an obstruction downstream, the Kafue flats for example. Such floodplains may occur at any point along the course of the river. The main stream usually becomes divided into anabranches which rejoin the main channel below the deltaic area, or several rivers flowing into the same plain may interconnect with complex and shifting channels. In certain parts of the world, the Bahr Aouk headwaters of the Chari system, the Gran Pantanal of the Paraguay river or the Apure–Arauca tributaries of the Orinoco, for instance, the terrain is so flat that enormous areas of land are flooded to a very shallow depth by rainwater as well as by overspill from the river. Such 'sheet flooding' is often dictated by land-form processes other than those created by the rivers themselves, but the network of channels and lagoons that arise by erosion during drainage give such areas a deltaic character.

Coastal deltaic floodplains

The terminal lateral expansion of the alluvial plain and the breakdown of the main river channel into distributaries produces the classic fan-shaped delta. Coastal deltaic floodplains are influenced by the marine environment in that, in the dry season, sea water penetrates the main channels as a saline tongue. Tidal effects are often transmitted far upstream, even beyond the limits of the saline tongue, but little invasion by salt water occurs during the floods, and only the coastal fringe is submerged by tidal action.

Certain floodplains are intermediate between the internal delta and the coastal delta. These occur in those rivers which discharge deltaically into either inland freshwater lakes, such as the Yaérés system located at the place of discharge of the Chari–Logone into Lake Chad, or rivers much larger than themselves. The principal ecological differences between fringing and internal deltaic floodplains on the one hand, and coastal floodplains on the other, are firstly, the greater extent of the water body available to fish in the dry season in the coastal floodplain and secondly, in the penetration of sea-water and marine species into areas adjacent to the sea.

2.3 Brief review of major floodplains

Many flood rivers in the temperate zones have to a certain degree been contained by flood-control measures, although extensive floodplains still exist in some countries. In the United States the 100-year flood area is estimated at 543 000 km², or about 6 per cent of the total land area of the nation (Sabol, 1974) and despite ambitious and long-standing programmes of flood control many rivers still flood regularly. The Danube is the major European river with surviving floodplains (Liepolt, 1967), although these have been much diminished since 1947 by flood control and damming. The total plain area is given as 264 500 km² by Liepolt (1972), but after reclamation only some 5 000 km² are still liable to inundation in Rumania. In the Czechoslovak–Hungarian reach of the river 230 km² are regularly flooded from May to August and 30 km² remain as permanent water. It is the intention to eventually reclaim all floodplains including the delta. Other flood rivers exist in central and northern Asia, for example the Amur and Amu Darya, which are described in the Russian literature. The major seasonal floodplains of the world are now found mostly in the tropical and sub-tropical zones. Most tropical rivers have fringing floodplains for at least a part of their length and these are too numerous to list individually, but some of the major flood zones are briefly described below.

Central and South America *(Fig. 2.10 and Table 2.2)*

A group of morphologically similar floodplains is clustered around the Caribbean. These are internal or coastal deltas, which contain enormous numbers of permanent or semi-permanent lakes, locally termed 'cienagas'. The most important of these plains is that of the Magdalena river (3) [numbers in (parentheses) refer to Fig. 2.10] whose internal delta with the San Jorge and Cauca rivers extends over 20 000 km² of savanna. Most of the plain is well inland, but extends seaward along the Canal del Dique on one hand and down the main river channel to the Cienaga Grande on the other. The whole area of 20 000 km² can be flooded for up to a month, 16 000 km² for between 1 and 3 months, 13 000 km² between 3 and 6 months, and some 4 000 km² for periods varying between 6 and 12 months. When the floods recede completely about 800 cienagas remain with an area of 3 260 km². The Atrato river (2), also in Colombia, extends over a forested alluvial plain for the last 100 km of its course. The plain which covers 5 300 km² is interspersed with numerous cienaga lakes. Of similar size is the 5 000 km² of savanna flooded by the Catatumbo river as it flows into Lake Maracaibo (4). The Grijalva, Usumacinta, San Antonio and San Pablo rivers of Mexico combine near their mouths into a series of anastomosing channels running through a broad flood zone (1) which covers an area of about 8 000 km² at maximum floods. Up to 150 km inland, abundant cienaga systems are located among the main watercourses.

Several vast areas subject to sheet flooding are found on the

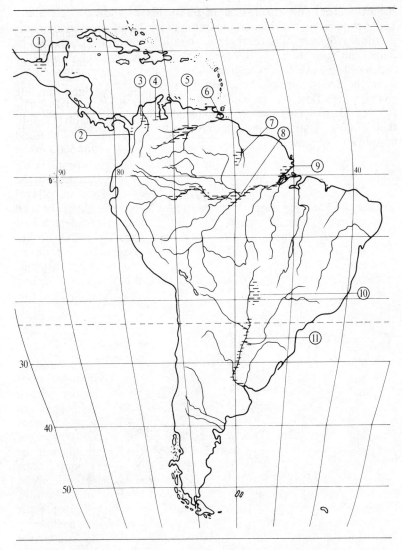

Fig. 2.10 Location of the major floodplains of South and Central America; numbers are referred to in text.

continent. The greatest of these is probably the Gran Pantanal of the Paraguay river (10) whose shallow interconnecting complex of lakes extends over 80–100 000 km² at peak floods. The savanna 'llanos' of Colombia and Venezuela (5) are also subjected annually to shallow sheet flooding. This area is drained by the Meta, Arauca, Capanaparo and Apure rivers which combine into a more deeply inundated deltaic floodplain of over 70 000 km² at their confluence with the Orinoco. The Rupununi river annually floods a very variable area of savanna to a depth of 1 to 2 m (7). In exceptionally wet years the flooded area extends from the headwaters of the Essequibo river to the Takutu and Ireng rivers, which flow via the Rio Branco into the Amazon. These sheet-flooded plains have in common the shallowness and extensiveness of their inundated area, their numerous anastomosing channels and small temporary lagoons.

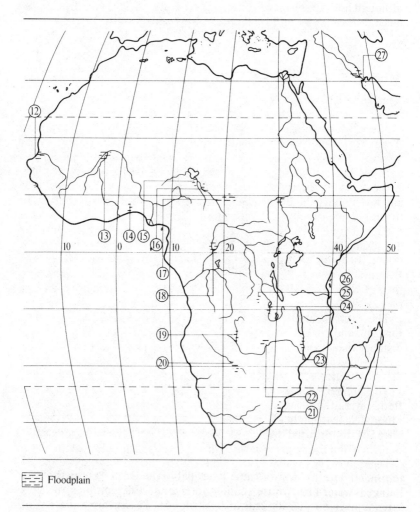

‗‗‗ Floodplain

Fig. 2.11 Location of the major floodplains of Africa; numbers are referred to in text.

The Amazon river and its major tributaries have densely forested floodplains for much of their length. However, the main river channels are fringed by, and enclose, vast alluvial plains up to 50 km wide in the upper reaches and 100 km wide further downstream. The Amazonian flood zone reaches its greatest extent in the central delta (8) located between the confluence of the Amazon and Tapajos. The heart of this area, the Ilha Tupinamborama covers about 50 000 km². A similar combination of fringing floodplain and internal delta is found along the Paraguay river below the Gran Pantanal, and along the Paraná river after its confluence with the Paraguay (11).

Coastal deltaic floodplains are uncommon in South America, although both the Orinoco (6) and the Amazon (9) have densely forested coastal flood areas of 20 000 and 25 000 km², respectively.

Africa *(Fig. 2.11 and Table 2.3)*

Nearly all African rivers have extremely well-developed fringing floodplains of which perhaps the best studied are the savanna plains of the Senegal and Niger rivers. The Senegal (12) [refer to Fig. 2.11] flows through a broad valley which, during the dry season, retains about 500 km² of water confined in 'sloughs' of various kinds (66 km²), as well as in the Lac de Guiers (150 km²) and the main river channel (281 km²). At peak floods the river covers 5 000 km² of the valley. The Niger (13) and its tributary the Benue river, also cover an extensive lateral plain. In the republics of Niger, Benin and Nigeria the Niger itself flooded 5 981 km² at high water, shrinking to about 35 per cent of this area in the dry season. Much of the Nigerian plain of this river has since been lost due to the flood-control effects of the Kainji dam and its reservoir. The Benue river, also in Nigeria, has a very impressive fringing plain, broad for its length. This has a flooded area of 3 100 km² with a dry-season area of 1 290 km².

The Zambezi has two plains on its upper course which flank the river for 240 and 96 km respectively. They flood laterally for a greater distance than usual, penetrating up to 16 km inland on either bank. The combined area of these Barotse plains (19) is over 10 000 km², but only 5 per cent of this area remains wet in the dry season.

The greatest of the African coastal deltas, that of the Nile whose floods were the basis of the wealth of pharaonic Egypt, is no longer inundated seasonally. The fringing floodplains of the river have also virtually disappeared due to the flood-control measures of the series of dams barring the upper course of the river. Savanna deltas occur in the Senegal river (12), where nearly 8 000 km² are flooded annually, and the Ouémé river (14), whose 1 000 km² delta terminates in the 180 km² brackish-water Lac Nokoue. The Niger delta covers 36 260 km², most of which is densely forested, and has a 7 500 km² coastal fringe of saline mangrove swamps.

Internal deltas are common in Africa. The largest of these, that of the Niger (13) (see also Fig. 2.5), occurs where sand blown from the Sahara has resulted in the deflection of the Niger river eastwards near Timbuktu. A depositional plain has grown up behind this with lakes lying in the depressions between rocky outcrops. It extends over 20 000–30 000 km² during the four- to five-month flood season, but its area shrinks to 4 000 km² in the dry season, most of which is retained in the permanent lakes. The Kafue river, backed up by a range of hills, which are now the site of the Kafue Gorge dam, has formed an alluvial plain of over 4 340 km² (22). This is inundated during the rains, but only 1 456 km² of permanent waters remained throughout the year prior to the closing of the dam. The 7 000 km² Yaérés floodplain (15) is the site of the deltaic discharge of the Chari and Logone rivers into Lake Chad through the Logomathia and El Beid rivers. The present lake and the floodplains of the lower Chari occupy the site of a larger Paleo–Chad, now shrunk in size by the progressive desiccation of the Sahara Desert.

The Yaérés are only part of a much larger family of floodplains centred on the Chari and Logone rivers. At least two other groups of plains subject mainly to sheet flooding by rainfall and local run-off are found in the system. The largest of these (17) extends from the Bahr Aouk and Bahr Salamat rivers covering a considerable portion of southeast Chad and some 37 000 km² of northeastern Central African Empire. The second group (16) spreads between the Logone and Chari rivers and eastward along the Bahr Erguig anabranch of the Chari. According to Blache (1964) the Chari–Logone basin floodplains have a combined area of 90 000 km², of which about 70 per cent are inundated at peak floods (September–October) and only 7 per cent remain wet in the dry months of April and May.

Many African flood areas are associated with permanent swamp systems. The most famous of these and the most extensive wetland in the continent is the Sudd of the river Nile (26) (see Fig. A.1). Located at the confluence of the Nile and Bahr el Ghazal, the 10 000 km² permanent complex of papyrus swamp and open-water lagoon swells to over ten times this area when the floods of the Nile arrive from the south. The Elephant and Ndinde marshes (23), which cover 673 km² when flooded, shrink to only 384 km² of swamps and lagoons in the dry season. They form part of the larger Shire river system which covers a total flooded area of 1 400 km² or 480 km² in the dry season. A third large swamp complex is centred around the internal delta of the Okavango river and the 800 km² Lake Ngami (20). These swamps have a residual area of 3 120 km² and cover between 16 000 and 20 000 km² at high water. The Kamulondo depression, one of the few true floodplain areas of the Zaïre, contains lakes and swamps with a permanent water area of approximately 7 000 km², which nearly doubles during the flood season.

There are two smaller plains, resembling in some ways the cienaga floodplains of Latin America. The Kifakula plain, formed by the deposition of alluvium by the Luapula river between the Johnson Falls and Lake Mweru, (24) covers 1 500 km² and is scattered with permanent lagoons. The Pongolo floodplain is even smaller (100 km²), but is of interest in that its upstream end is blocked by the Strydom dam, which has permitted experiments in the discharge requirements for the maintenance of small floodplains.

True forested floodplains similar to the Amazonian Igapó and várzea forests are more or less confined to the Zaïre basin and a few smaller river basins in Cameroon and Gabon. Below Kisangani, the course of the Zaïre broadens to include an increasing floodable area. This culminates in the Bangala swamps, and the vast complex of floodlands at the confluence of the Zaïre, Ubangui and Sangha rivers (18). These areas are subject to bimodal flooding and tend to retain their water to a great extent and therefore differ very considerably from the highly seasonal type of plain. The true extent of this area is difficult to assess and it is almost completely unpopulated.

Asia *(Fig. 2.12)*

The floodplains of Asia are more highly modified than those of Africa and South America. In many cases they have been inhabited for many centuries and two of them have been the cradles of some of the earliest urban cultures. Works for irrigation, drainage and flood protection, have resulted in the disappearance of many of the original features. Coastal deltas are especially common in the region, and in the flooded areas rice culture is almost universally practised. Several thousand years of irrigation in the Euphrates–Tigris floodplain (27) (see Fig. 2.11) have left many traces, but flooding still continues over the 20000 km² delta and over the plains that fringe the rivers' upper courses. A series of lakes lie within the plain, which cover a total area of 9 000 km² at high water and are confluent with the marshes. At low water the lake area is reduced to about 5 000 km². The largest of these lakes is the 5 200 km² Lake Hammar (Al-Hamed, 1966). The Indus river (28), also the site of very early civilization, has a wide braided channel for much of its course. This periodically shifts its bed due to excessive silt deposition raising the river channel and its levées high above the level of the surrounding plain. When it overspills its banks it may spread laterally for up to 40 km, losing water by seepage and evaporation in the otherwise desertic region. The river flows into the sea through a large but infertile deltaic plain. In the virtually rainless areas of Pakistan, the Indus and its floods are essential for irrigated agriculture. Both the Ganges and the Brahmaputra rivers also have unstable beds flowing through braided channels. The main fringing floodplain of the Ganges is over 600 km long and between 16 and 80 km wide. The Brahmaputra has an especially broad channel, up to 12 km wide in places. The two rivers combine to form an immense delta, liable to sheet flooding from rainfall as well as river discharge (29). The types of floodplain classified by the duration and depth of inundation of the portion of the plain lying in

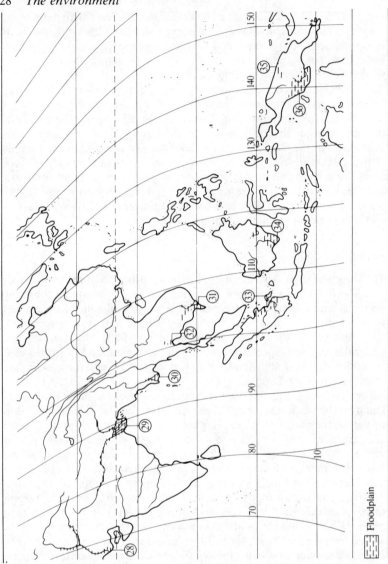

Fig. 2.12 Location of the major floodplains of Asia; numbers are referred to in text.

Bangladesh are shown in Fig. 2.13. In fact most of the active part of this delta lies in this country, as the western region, centred on the Hooghly river in India, is silted and rarely floods through the now dead distributaries. In Bangladesh alone there are 93 000 km^2 of floodable land including 28 340 km^2 of paddy-fields which are inundated for three to four months of the year. In addition, there are an estimated 14 000 km^2 of permanent open inland waters. The seaward parts of the

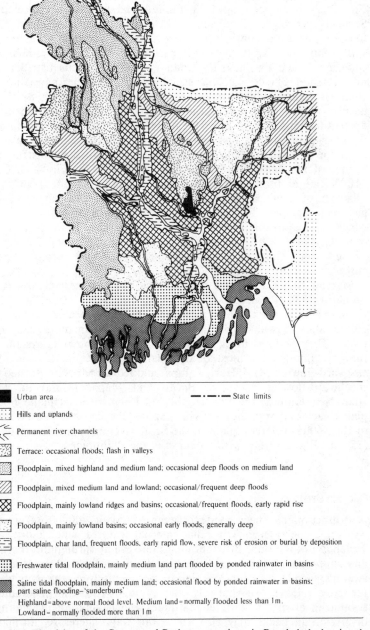

■	Urban area	——·——·—— State limits
▦	Hills and uplands	
⌇	Permanent river channels	
▨	Terrace: occasional floods; flash in valleys	
⫶	Floodplain, mixed highland and medium land; occasional deep floods on medium land	
⧄	Floodplain, mixed medium land and lowland; occasional/frequent deep floods	
⊠	Floodplain, mainly lowland ridges and basins; occasional/frequent floods, early rapid rise	
⫶	Floodplain, mainly lowland basins; occasional early floods, generally deep	
⊟	Floodplain, char land, frequent floods, early rapid flow, severe risk of erosion or burial by deposition	
▤	Freshwater tidal floodplain, mainly medium land part flooded by ponded rainwater in basins	
▦	Saline tidal floodplain, mainly medium land; occasional flood by ponded rainwater in basins; part saline flooding—'sunderbuns'	

Highland = above normal flood level. Medium land = normally flooded less than 1 m.
Lowland = normally flooded more than 1 m.

Fig. 2.13 The delta of the Ganges and Brahmaputra rivers in Bangladesh showing the major land types classified by depth of flooding.

plain have dense brackish-water mangrove forests known as 'sunder-buns' some 5 000 km² in area.

The 31 000 km² deltaic alluvial plain of the Irrawaddy river (30) (see Fig. 2.12) is flooded both by rainfall and upper river discharge. Submergence by local precipitation precedes the arrival of the river floods by at least a month. Artificial levées constructed for flood control will eventually change the whole pattern of flooding. A similar but smaller deltaic plain flanks the Chao–Phrya river and its distributaries in Thailand (32) (see Fig. 2.12, see also Fig. 2.8). Here the main river channels are raised high above the surrounding backswamps which are deeply flooded each year, although recently the construction of an upstream dam seeks to control the timing and extent of the inundation. Another plain that is fast being altered by flood-control measures, irrigation and an ambitious programme of upstream dam construction, is that of the Mekong (31) (see Fig. 2.12, see also Fig. 2.4). Over 74 000 km² in total area, 21 000 km² are never flooded, although 8 850 km of river, canals and irrigation channels take water to every part of the plain. The area of permanent water is only 4 000 km², of which the majority is in the 2 500 km² Grand Lac. In fact, this body of water is one of the regions most greatly affected by the modification of the hydraulic regime of the river as its floods have been drastically curtailed.

Marshy flood areas are common on the Indonesian islands of Sumatra (33), Borneo (34) and West Irian (36) (see Fig. 2.12). Fundamentally very similar in nature, these are located on the flat coastal alluvial plains and submerged and drained by numerous small rivers. They perhaps most closely resemble reservoir river systems as they are flooded for most of the year. In Indonesia there are the eastward-flowing Musi, Hari, Kampar and Rokan rivers; in Borneo the southward-flowing Kahajan, Barito and Mahakan and in West Irian/New Guinea, the Fly, Diguil and Pulan rivers. Upland flood-plains, such as that of the 6 555 km² Kapuas lake district in West Borneo or the 7 500 km² lateral plain of the Sepik river in Papua New Guinea (35) (see Fig. 2.12) are also common in the Philippines.

2.4 Hydrology

A distinction has been made between 'reservoir' and 'flood' rivers. Typically, the reservoir river has internal features which reduce the variability of the flow, distributing it more evenly throughout the year and suppressing pronounced flood peaks. Such features as extensive swamps, forests, lakes or even floodplains themselves, may store water for later release. Alternatively, the cumulative discharge of many tributaries arising in different latitudes and having correspondingly diverse flood peaks may also act in this way. Therefore, the lower reaches of rivers may tend to take on 'reservoir' characteristics, the best example being perhaps the Zaïre river below Kisangani. Even here there are two pronounced flood peaks (Marlier, 1973). The existence of swamp, forest and lakes in the river basin do not by themselves ensure the complete smoothing of flow and many flood rivers have all these features. As this book is concerned with floodplains, little consideration will be given to those rivers which do not have one or more pronounced floods per year.

Characteristics of flood regimes

Flooding originates from three sources: (1) overspill from the river channel; (2) local rainfall; (3) tides.

Overspill from the river channel
Floods have their origin mainly in run-off from the rainfall over the river basin. The retention and release of groundwater contributes less to the spates and tends to smooth out flows, reducing the amplitude but increasing the duration of the flood. The proportion of the rainwater that appears as run-off or as groundwater depends on the type of terrain and its vegetation cover. Local differences in these factors can cause very different flood patterns, even in two adjacent streams. Because of this, and because of the rapidity with which run-off from local rainstorms can affect low-order streams, graphs of water level or flow in the smaller watercourses are apt to appear 'spiky' with numerous rapid changes in flood condition (Fig. 2.14 (A)). In larger channels there is a tendency to even out such purely local variations and generally, the bigger the area drained, the smoother the flood curve becomes (Fig. 2.14 (B) and (C)).

The presence of floodplains also contributes to this smoothing, as the reservoir effect of the water retained on the plain tends to even out short-term changes.

As the flow increases a point is reached where the river channel is no longer able to drain the volume of water. Further rises in discharge above this point (bankfull level) result in overspill on to the plain. Here, because of the flatness of the terrain, increases in volume are achieved by lateral expansion rather than by increases in depth, and the water spreads slowly and diffusely outwards, hampered in its progress by the floodplain vegetation. Such flow is termed 'creeping flow' and is depositional (i.e. silt comes out of suspension on to the plain), as opposed to the erosive flow where a strong directional current is confined within the main channel or along the terrace walls.

Plots of the variation of water level, or flow of a flood against time (flood curves) for large rivers have the appearance of waves (Fig. 2.15). Usually they have a unimodal form, although downstream of the confluence of two systems having differing flood regimes, polymodal floods may occur. The flood wave has amplitude (the total difference in level between maximum and minimum discharge) and duration, the time taken to pass from one low-water stage to the next. It moves

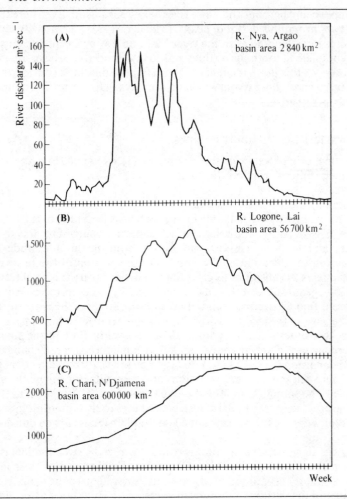

Fig. 2.14 Flood regime of rivers with different basin areas within the Chari–Logone river system showing the increasing smoothing of the flood curve with increasing size of basin.

down-valley at a speed which may depend on many factors, including the slope and degree of enclosure of the river valley, the type of vegetation and the intensity of the flood. In the Niger river for instance (Fig. 2.16 (A)), the flood crest takes over 100 days to move from Koulikoro to Malanville. As this is over 1 760 km, the average rate of travel is about 17 km day^{-1}. Similar speeds of transmission are found in the Senegal, where the 620 km from Galougo to Dagana takes over a month (17 km day^{-1}) (Fig. 2.16 (B)) and the Chari, where the 745 km between Mossala and N'Djamena are traversed in 42 days (Fig. 2.16 (C)). The flood moves down-valley at about 13 km day^{-1} in the Brahmaputra and 29 km day^{-1}

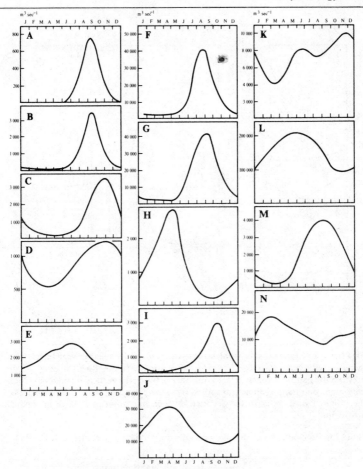

Flood regimes of typical river systems for various continents

A	Ouémé	Pont du Save	1942-66	Orstom	(1969)
B	Senegal	Bakel	1903-66	Orstom	(1969)
C	Chari	Fort Lamy	1936-66	Orstom	(1969)
D	Nile	Malakal	1912-62	Unesco	(1971)
E	Danube	Bratislava	1931-60	Unesco	(1971)
F	Ganges	Hardinge Bridge	1934-62	UN Water Resources No. 29	(1966)
G	Mekong	Kratie	1933-53 1961-66	Unesco	(1971)
H	Tigris	Baghdad	1931-36	Unesco	(1971)
I	Chao-Phrya	Nakohn-Sawan	1905-66	Unesco	(1971)
J	Mississippi	Tarbert Landing	1928-65	Unesco	(1971)
K	Magdalena	Calamar	1965-73	Ducharme	(1975)
L	Amazon	Obidos	1928-47	Unesco	(1971)
M	Apure	San Fernando	1962-65	Unesco	(1971)
N	Paraná	Posadas	1901-63	Unesco	(1971)

y-axis = rivers' discharge $m^3 sec^{-1}$

Fig. 2.15 Flood regimes of typical river systems for various continents.

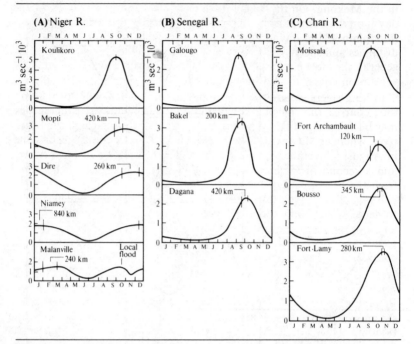

Fig. 2.16 Time taken for the flood wave to traverse the distance between selected points in three African river systems. The time taken for the flood wave to cover the distance between the points is indicated by the distance between the vertical line showing the time of maximum flood and the line transposed from the preceding point upstream as shown in the graph; figures refer to the distance between one point and the point immediately upstream.

Table 2.6 Precipitation at sample locations on floodplain areas (from Van der Leeden, 1975)

| | Annual precipitation (mm) | | | | |
	J	F	M	A	M
Africa					
Mali (Bamako)	–	–	0·4	15·2	37·7
Sudan (Wau)	–	5·1	22·9	66·0	134·6
Botswana (Maun)	106·7	8·7	71·1	17·8	5·1
Zambia (Lusaka)	235·1	190·5	142·2	17·8	–
Asia					
Dem. Kampuchea (Phnom Penh)	7·6	10·2	25·4	78·7	144·8
Thailand (Bangkok)	5·1	27·9	27·9	58·4	132·1
Bangladesh (Dacca)	7·6	30·5	61·0	137·2	243·8
Pakistan (Rawalpindi)	63·5	63·5	68·6	48·3	33·0
South America					
Venezuela (Ciudad Bolivar)	35·6	20·3	17·8	25·6	96·5
Colombia (Cartagena)	10·2	–	10·2	22·9	86·4
Brazil (Manaus)	248·9	231·1	261·6	221·0	170·2
Argentina (Paraná)	78·7	78·7	99·1	124·5	66·0

in the Mekong. On the Kafue plain its speed of transmission is 11 km day^{-1}; on the Central Delta of the Niger 13 km day^{-1} and on the Mekong floodplain 13 km day^{-1}. These figures are averaged over considerable distances and speeds differ within various reaches of the same river. In general, the more expansive the plain, the less its slope and the greater its vegetation cover, the slower will be the velocity of the flood crest.

In long rivers, where the timing of the rains is fairly uniform along their courses, the arrival of the main flood crest in downstream reaches may be delayed until the dry season. Such a delay is typical of the Niger river, where at Malanville (Benin) (Fig. 2.16(A)) two floods occur – one in August–November caused by rainfall and drainage of local rivers, and a second in December–March owing to the arrival of the flood from the headwaters of the river.

As the flood wave passes along the floodplain there is a tendency for it to decrease in amplitude and increase in duration, provided no large amounts of water are added by other tributaries. This process is best seen on a river such as the Niger where the channel runs for a considerable distance through arid and semi-arid landscapes.

Local rainfall
Precipitation on the floodplain itself, or on the basins of the lower-order streams immediately surrounding it, saturates the soil and causes local flooding which often precedes the main flood by some considerable period of time. Early work by Svensson (1933) showed that in the Gambia river certain depressions are flooded only by local precipitation and are connected to the river and other low-lying swamps by a single channel or creek. Such swamps may be unaffected by variations in river height, but fish may migrate to them by ascending the connecting channel. Early flooding of floodplain depressions by rainwater has been

Annual precipitation (mm)							
J	J	A	S	O	N	D	Mean
137·2	348·0	205·7	43·2	15·2	–	–	1 120·1
165·1	190·5	208·3	167·6	124·5	15·2	–	1 099·8
2·5	–	–	–	22·9	5·8	8·64	434·3
–	–	–	–	10·2	91·4	149·9	835·7
147·3	152·4	154·9	226·1	251·5	139·7	43·2	1 391·9
152·4	175·3	233·7	233·6	355·6	45·7	2·5	1 470·7
315·0	330·2	337·8	248·9	134·6	25·4	5·1	1 877·1
58·4	205·7	233·7	99·1	15·2	7·6	30·5	927·1
139·7	160·0	180·3	91·4	101·6	71·1	33·0	972·8
86·4	76·2	18·2	12·9	274·3	226·1	114·3	934·7
83·8	58·4	38·1	45·7	106·7	142·2	203·2	1 811·0
30·5	30·5	40·6	61·0	71·1	94·0	114·3	889·0

noted from several systems. In Africa, in addition to the Gambia river (Svensson, 1933), Carey (1971) has described flooding of this type in the Kafue. The inundation of the upper Chari (Bahr Salamat and Bahr Azoum) appears to be almost entirely by local rainfall (Durand, pers. comm.), and in the Nile Sudd the swamps are filled one to two months before overspill from the river occurs. Extensive areas of the Venezuelan llanos (Matthes, pers. comm.) and the Gran Pantanal or Paraguayan Chaco (Carter and Beadle, 1930) of the Paraguay river flood in this manner. A similar type of flooding has been recorded from the Irrawaddy river in Burma (Ohya, 1966), where submersion by rainwater precedes the main floods by about one month. Flooding by local rainfall differs from overspill in that the net flow of the water is from the floodplain depression to the river rather than the other way round. Furthermore, flooding with rainwater saturates the soil and fills the groundwater so that relatively little of the overspill flood is absorbed by the ground.

Annual precipitation on some floodplain areas is shown in Table 2.6.

Tides

Flooding caused by tidal action obviously affects only those parts of coastal floodplains adjacent to the coast. However, secondary effects are produced by the backing up of freshwater floods by high tidal levels. Volker (1966) divided river estuaries into four reaches (Fig. 2.17): zone (a) where vertical tides produce a reversal of the direction of flow and the penetration of saline water into the river channel, or on to the floodplain; zone (b) where the river water remains fresh but tidal effects and current reversals still occur; zone (c) where the water levels are still affected by the tides giving rise to differences in current velocity, although the flow always proceeds downstream; and zone (d) where water level and flow are affected by upstream discharge only; this zone merges into the main river upstream.

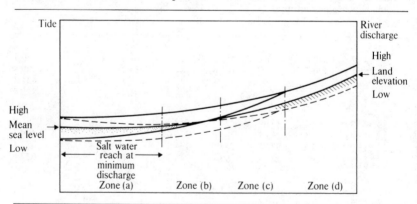

Fig. 2.17 Zones of interaction between marine and fresh waters in coastal deltaic floodplains. (After Volker, 1966.)

Water balance on floodplains

The flood curve at any point in the river, which results from discharge transmitted from upstream, together with precipitation in the immediate area, can be described diagrammatically as in Fig. 2.18 (A). The *x*-axis is time, the *y*-axis may represent any of the indicators of water quantity. The most common of such indicators are water level, discharge rate or storage volume. Although it is effectively a continuous fluctuation in water level the flood can be broken into two parts. In the first, the water is confined in the river channel, and alterations in discharge produce changes in depth and velocity. Changes in volume so long as the flow remains in a confined channel are caused mainly by increases in depth. This phase is delimited by the bankfull stage beyond which the water overflows the channel limits and floods the plain. Thereafter, changes in inflow produce relatively little change in outflow, the excess water being temporarily stored on the floodplain where the volume increases mainly from the extension of the water area. The bankfull level is usually difficult to define precisely, as it varies from place to place in the river and also from year to year. The detailed hydraulics of floodplains are extremely complex and beyond the scope of this discussion. They have been the subject of many studies and attempts at mathematical modelling, such as those elaborated by Weiss and Midgley (1975, 1976).

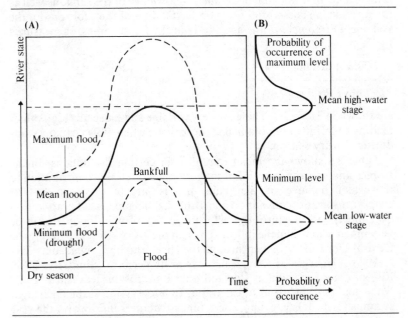

Fig. 2.18 Diagram of (A) a generalized annual flood regime, and (B) probability of occurrence of maximum and minimum water stages.

The intensity of flooding varies from year to year in response to fluctuations in rainfall. Because of this variability, a distribution of the frequency with which any flood height occurs can be established over a· number of years. Such distributions (Fig. 2.18 (B)) may be normal, but are often skewed. The number of years which must elapse on average between a flood of a particular height and the next flood of the same height is known as the return period. The 100-year flood, for example, is that level of flooding which can be expected once in 100 years. The probability of occurrence of any flood is the reciprocal of its return period; the 100-year flood having a probability of occurrence of 0·01 in any year.

Not only does the intensity of flooding vary from year to year, but there is increasing evidence that the variability is of a cyclic nature which is traceable to long-term global climatic patterns (Winstanley, 1975; Bryson, 1974). According to such cycles, years of exceptionally high flooding or of drought tend to be grouped together so there is a good chance of two or more years of intense flooding appearing in sequence, or for one year of low flood intensity to be followed immediately by another poor year. When the latter happens drought conditions can ensue such as were shown in the Sahelian rivers between 1970 and 1974. The grouping of good and poor floods in this manner can have severe consequences on the ecology of the fish as we shall see in the section on the dynamics of floodplain communities (p. 170). The variation in flood level is a normal phenomenon, and a knowledge of the range as well as the mean value is essential to an understanding of the ecology of these systems. Differences in the amplitude of the flood curves, as measured by

Maximum discharge m³ s⁻¹
_____
Minimum discharge m³ s⁻¹

are shown in Table 2.7. These are very variable and especially high values tending to infinity are obtained in those rivers where flow virtually stops during the dry season.

Table 2.6 shows the mean rainfall over certain floodplains. In the tropics and subtropics, rainfall makes only a moderate contribution to the water balance of the plain and is largely exceeded by the evapotranspiration rates shown in Table 2.8. This excess of evaporation over precipitation causes the net outflow from some floodplains to be very much lower than the inflow. Thus, of the $7·11 \times 10^{10}$ m³ entering the Central Delta of the Niger through the Niger and Bani rivers, only $3·82 \times 10^{10}$ m³ emerges at Dire, a net loss of 46 per cent. Similarly, $2·7 \times 10^{10}$ m³ enter the Sudd at Bor and only $1·4 \times 10^{10}$ m³ leaves it at Lake No, a loss of 48 per cent of the water. In a few systems, the Okavango swamps for instance, evaporation almost balances inflow over the year so that there is no appreciable outflow from the system.

The high evaporation rates also means that pools or lagoons, to be

Table 2.7 Mean annual maximum and minimum discharge rates of various rivers (from figures compiled by Van der Leeden, 1975)

	Discharge m^3 sec^{-1}			
	Basin area (km^2)	Mean maximum	Mean minimum	Max. Min.
Amazon (Obidos)	4 688 000	207 400	89 300	2·3
Brahmaputra (whole basin)	580 000	72 460	2 680	27·0
Mekong (whole basin)	795 000	67 000	1 250	53·6
Ganges (whole basin)	977 500	61 200	1 170	52·3
Orinoco (Ciudad Bolivar)	850 000	46 200	7 520	6·1
Indus (whole basin)	970 000	31 200	490	63·7
Mississippi (Tarbet landings)	3 928 000	30 800	7 930	3·9
Paraná (whole basin)	2 039 000	25 130	6 300	4·0
Magdalena (Calamar)	238 000	10 000	3 900	2·6
Oubangui (Bangui)	500 000	9 640	1 070	9·0
Blue Nile (Khartoum)	325 000	5 950	138	43·1
Senegal (Bakel)	218 000	3 430	26	131·9
Chari (N'Djamena)	600 000	3 390	199	17·0
Chao-Phrya (Nakhon Sawan)	110 371	3 363	32	105·1
Niger (Mopti)	281 600	2 820	67	42·1
Danube (Bratislava)	131 338	2 746	1 402	2·0
Tigris (Baghdad)	134 000	2 720	286	99·5
Benue (Garoua)	64 000	1 920	32	60·0
Ouémé (Pont du Save)	23 600	758	0·63	1203·0

permanent, must either be filled annually to a depth greater than the loss by evapotranspiration (between 1·2 and 2·2 m from the data in Table 2.8), or must receive inflow from groundwater.

Table 2.8 Annual evapotranspiration rates from various floodplain regions

	Annual ETP mm	
	Mean	Range
Africa		
Niger delta (Mali)	2 150	1 900–2 450
Sudd (Sudan)	1 900	1 800–2 000
Okavango swamp (Botswana)	1 800	1 700–1 900
Kafue flats (Zambia)	1 650	1 550–1 750
Asia		
Mekong delta (Vietnam)	1 600	1 500–1 700
Chao-Phrya (Thailand)	1 600	1 500–1 700
Ganges delta (Bangladesh)	1 500	1 400–1 600
Indus valley ±30° N (Pakistan)	1 750	1 600–1 900
Indus valley ±25° N	2 000	1 900–2 300
South America		
Llanos (Colombia)	1 400	1 300–1 600
Magdalena ±5° N (Colombia)	1 500	1 400–1 600
Magdalena ±8° N (Colombia)	1 300	1 100–1 400
Amazon river – Manaus (Brazil)	1 300	1 200–1 400
Paraná river (Argentina)	1 250	1 150–1 350

2.5 Chemistry

Ionic composition

The chemical composition of river water depends on a wide variety of physical, chemical and biological features. However, three basic mechanisms control surface-water chemistry: precipitation, the nature of the bedrock and the evaporation–crystallization process (Gibbs, 1970) (Fig. 2.19). In most of the large tropical rivers the ionic composition of the water derives primarily from the rain and the rock or sediments over which the river flows. In rivers flowing through hot arid

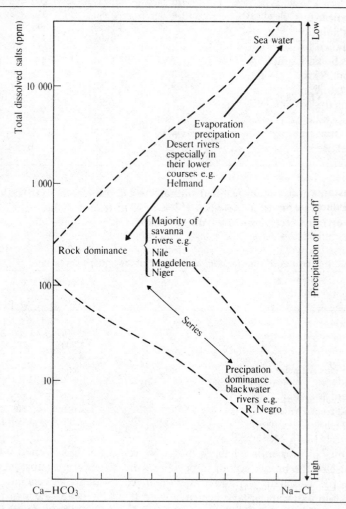

Fig. 2.19 Diagram of the basic mechanisms controlling surface-water chemistry. (Adapted from Gibbs, 1970.)

regions, the rate of evaporation and crystallization of the concentrated salts exerts the main influence, and flood areas located in such zones eventually transform into salt-marsh habitats. Secondary influences on the ionic composition are exerted by macrophytes and phytoplankton, and to an increasing extent by the various industrial, agricultural and domestic human activities.

A particularly widespread and important input from the dry-season use of the floodplain is the dung deposited by grazing game or cattle. It has been estimated, for instance, by Shepherd (1976) that the 3 000 cattle visiting the 1 000 km² Bangula lagoon, Malawi, drop some 500 kg of dung hm⁻² yr⁻¹. This makes a significant contribution to nutrient concentrations, as well as producing localized chemical effects as it enters solution.

Detailed lists of ionic content of tropical rivers are outside the scope of this book. Compilations of such data based on the work of numerous authors exist for Africa (Welcomme, 1972) and Latin America (Ardizzone and Ziesler, 1977). Observations from Asia have not been compiled systematically, but Jhingran (1975) cited data from Indian rivers and Johnson (1967) gave details of the chemistry of some Malaysian rivers.

In those regions where the rocks are impoverished and soils leached, the main supply of nutrients comes from precipitation, such rivers being grouped in the lower right-hand area of Fig. 2.19. In the Amazon basin for instance, the chemical composition of the blackwater streams from the Hylaea, or of the larger blackwater rivers, can resemble that of the rainwater. The frequent similarity of the composition of rain and river waters indicates that such ions as are leached from the soil are balanced by those carried by the rain. Similarly, the chemistry of the headwaters of the Paraná and Paraguay rivers are dominated by atmospheric precipitation (Bonetto, 1975), and in the same area the conductivity of rainwater falling over the Mato Grosso, Brazil, is often higher than that of the streams (Green, 1970). In Africa, Visser (1974) noted that the composition of river and lake waters within a radius of 100 miles of Kampala indicated that rain contributed on average all of the sodium, ammonium and nitrate, over 75 per cent of the chloride and over 70 per cent of the potassium. In the Gombak river, Malaysia, Bishop (1973) considered precipitation as a very important factor determining ionic concentrations.

The rivers of the three main tropical rainforest regions arise on very poor, leached, podsolitic soils. Sioli (1968) described such waters in the Amazon basin as more or less transparent, devoid of significant amounts of inorganic particles, but with very poor light penetration because of the brown colour imparted by dissolved humic substances. Here, pH is usually very low and dissolved nutrient concentrations poor. Similar waters have been reported from the headwaters of the Orinoco (Edwards and Thorne, 1970) and have also been described from both Africa (Matthes, 1964) and Malaysia (Johnson, 1968).

Table 2.9 Description of chemical composition of blackwaters from Asia, Africa and South America*

	Zaïre (Tshuapa R.) (Matthes, 1964)	Amazon (Rio Negro) (Ungemach, 1972)
pH	4·0–6·5	4·6–5·2
Conductivity	24–32 $K_{20}\mu$mhos cm^{-1}	6·8–10·4 $K_{20}\mu$mhos cm^{-1}
TDS	30–65 mg litre^{-1}	
Fe	Fairly abundant	268–535 μg litre^{-1}
+Ca	Very low	232–450 μg litre^{-1}
+Mg	Very low	108–254 μg litre^{-1}
+Na		435–1 358 μg litre^{-1}
+K		235–601 μg litre^{-1}
NNO$_3$	Trace	15–53 μg litre^{-1}
NNO$_2$	Trace	0·035–1·27 μg litre^{-1}
PPO$_4$	Trace	3·2–8·6 μg litre^{-1}
N organic	70–80 μg litre^{-1}	209–478 μg litre^{-1}
Cl		1 800–2 600 μg litre^{-1}
Si		2 000–2 740 μg litre^{-1}
SO$_4$	Absent	Absent

* *N.B.*: These figures are often based on only a few observations and do not therefore necessarily reflect the full range of variations of the parameters measured.

Descriptions and analyses from the three continents are shown in Table 2.9.

Blackwaters from the three continental areas are similar in general composition, except that sulphate is more common in the Malaysian waters than in those of South America and Africa. In South America it is virtually absent and in Africa is present only in those waters flowing from volcanic regions. Johnson (1968) described an aberrant type of blackwater from Malaysia which, by flowing over limestone, acquires higher total ionic concentrations of between 150 and 700 mg litre^{-1}, accounting for the relatively high maximum values in Table 2.9. The 'Gelam'-type waters also had very low pH values of 3·5–4·9, showing considerable excess sulphate. A third series of blackwaters have become enriched by organic pollution and their pH was raised to 6 and above. This series may indicate how blackwaters on other continents will react to pollution from urban sources as human settlement of these areas becomes more intense.

In addition to the blackwaters, the Amazon and Orinoco are fed by clear-water rivers. In the case of the Amazon they originate from the massifs of central Brazil and in the Orinoco from the Guianan shield. These waters are as poor in nutrients as the blackwaters and have similarly low pH values of between 4·0 and 6·6. They do not, however, have the dark staining by humic matter. A third category of Amazonian rivers, the whitewater rivers, more closely resemble the general pattern of other tropical rivers, as described in the rest of this section, and are the main source of nutrients in the basin where, by the deposition of their heavy silt loads, they maintain the productivity of the várzea floodplains.

The lowland equatorial environments of the Amazon and the Zaïre

Malaysia (Johnson, 1967)	Amazonian rainwater (Ungemach, 1971)
3·6–5·9	4·0–5·4
	1·5–20 K_{20} μmhos cm^{-1}
	10–100 μg litre^{-1}
0–1 904 μg litre^{-1}	20–500 μg litre^{-1}
182–17 867 μg litre^{-1}	10–30 μg litre^{-1}
2 092–22 480 μg litre^{-1}	
586–7 429 μg litre^{-1}	
	5–300 μg litre^{-1}
	1–3 μg litre^{-1}
	10–150 μg litre^{-1}
283–30 631 μg litre^{-1}	80–320 μg litre^{-1}
2 000–2 740 μg litre^{-1}	
4 803–216 903 μg litre^{-1}	

give these two rivers many common features. However, there are considerable differences between the two systems arising from the altitude and relief of the basins as well as from the geological formation and the vegetation (Marlier, 1973). The forest is less extensive in the Zaïre and the main channel of the river is divided into quiet and rapid reaches. Flooding is also less severe than in the Amazon.

Temperature

The degree of insolation, substrate composition, turbidity, ground- or rainwater inflows, wind, and vegetation cover, can all influence the temperature of water in rivers and floodplain lakes. Generally, surface-water temperatures follow the ambient air temperature fairly closely, although under dry, hot conditions this is more likely to be correlated with air-temperature minima owing to the cooling effect of evaporation. An annual cycle in which the dry-season temperatures are higher than those in the wet season is common. At low latitudes river temperatures are seasonally and diurnally stable, but at higher latitudes temperatures fall sufficiently to give winter conditions which are cold enough to cause growth checks and even fish mortalities. In the Paraná river, for example, a combination of subzero temperatures and low water caused massive mortalities in 1962 (Vidal, 1964).

Water in the main channel of a river rarely stratifies, as good mixing is maintained by the turbulence associated with river flow. On the other hand, stratified conditions are common in even very shallow floodplain water bodies. Hastings (1972), for instance, recorded diurnal stratification in lagoons of the South Elephant marsh in Africa (see Fig. 2.11 (23)) which were only 1·6 m deep. Similarly, Sánchez Remero (1961)

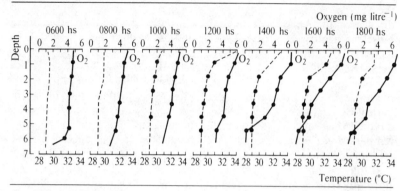

Fig. 2.20 Diurnal cycle of temperature and dissolved oxygen in the Cienaga de Ayapel 24 October 1974 (Magdalena river). (After Ducharme, 1975.)

and Junk (1973) found 1–2 m deep lagoons from the Peruvian and Brazilian Amazonian várzea to be stratified at least temporarily, and Ducharme (1975) (Fig. 2.20), Mikkola and Arias (1976) and Arias (1975) have all recorded stratified conditions from various cienagas of

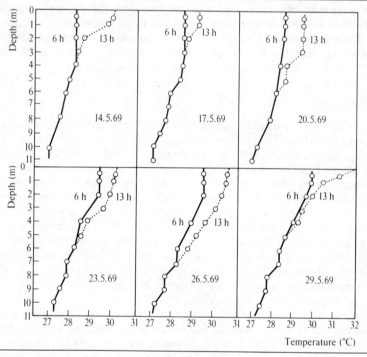

Fig. 2.21 Daytime temperature fluctuations and changes in the stratification of Lago do Castanho within short-time intervals during May 1969 (high-water phase). (After Schmidt, 1973a.)

the Magdalena system ranging from between 1·5 and 6 m depth. In the dry season the Amazonian Lago do Castanho is only about 1·5 m deep, but clear stratification develops on windless days (Schmidt, 1973a). In its flood condition the lake is up to 11 m deep and stratification is more persistent, although the temperature profiles are highly variable from one day to the next (Fig. 2.21) owing to local changes in conditions. The main day-to-day fluctuations occur in waters of less than 3·5 m depth, indicating that only water down to this depth is normally affected by daytime heating. In the Paraná river, which is subject to lower temperatures, especially in winter and during the night, inverse stratification has been noted by Bonetto, *et al* (1969a).

It may be concluded that floodplain lakes not covered by vegetation normally stratify thermally during at least part of the year. In shallower lakes stratification due to surface heating reaches a maximum between 14·00 and 18·00 hours, but tends to disappear at night or under the influence of strong or persistent winds. The difference in density per degree at high temperatures is greater than that at low temperature, for instance the drop in density between 29 and 30°C is about the same as that between 4 and 10°C. For this reason at high temperatures density differences are quite large for even slight differences in temperature, and the resistance to mixing is correspondingly high. In deep lagoons stratification may last for several weeks or even months.

Waters shaded by flooded or fringing forests tend to be cooler and

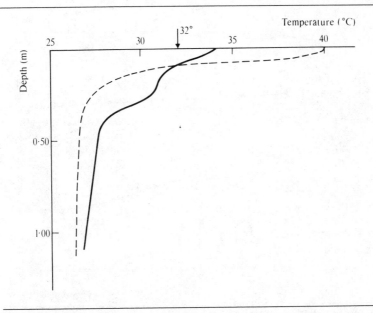

Fig. 2.22 An extreme case of temperature accumulation in the waters under a bed of *Salvinia* at midday. Solid line = open water; dotted line = water under vegetation. The arrow marks air temperature. (After Bonetto *et al.*, 1969a.)

more thermally uniform than those exposed to direct sunlight, although thermal stratification has been described, both from the flooded forest fringing the Tonle Sap (D'Aubenton, 1963) and from Igapó forests of the lower Rio Negro (Schmidt, 1976 and Geisler, 1969). Floating vegetation, on the other hand, gives rise to more varied temperature conditions. Because of the restricted evaporation and high absorption of sunlight in calm areas very high temperatures can be attained within masses of floating vegetation. Bonetto *et al.* (1969a) found exceptional temperatures of up to 40°C in the surface waters of an oxbow lake covered with *Salvinia* (Fig. 2.22). Similar temperatures have been found on the surface of the Lago Calado in stands of *Paspalum repens* by Junk (1973). Temperatures fall off more rapidly than they do in open water owing to shading by the vegetation. Floating mats of vegetation also encourage the maintenance of stratified conditions by damping wind and wave action.

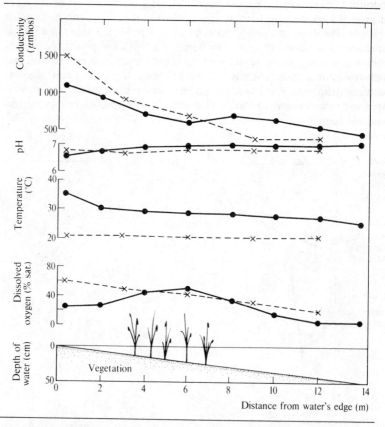

Fig. 2.23 Changes in physical and chemical conditions with distance from the water's edge in a floodplain lagoon: (×--×--×) at 0800h (●——●) at 1200h. (After Welcomme, 1970.)

An important but little-investigated habitat is the shallow open-water littoral at the fringe of the flood zone. At the time of rising water this represents the first contact between the advancing water and the nutrient-rich dry soil. Because of its shallowness, daytime water temperatures may be very high and gradients are set up between the very edge of the zone and the cooler water offshore (Fig. 2.23).

Conductivity

Conductivity is a measure of the total amount of ions present in a body of water and is therefore a useful approximation to chemical richness. In fact, in African rivers differences in conductivity explain about 61 per cent of the difference in fish catch between river systems or rivers of the same system (Welcomme, 1976). As a measure, however, it does not give an indication of the actual ionic composition of the water, and may therefore fail to convey information on limiting factors such as the lack of essential nutrients.

River waters are less variable than those of lakes and the conductivities of most major whitewater rivers tend to resemble one another, with a few exceptions. In fact, variations between tributaries within any one river system are apt to be greater than those shown between different main river channels. This is because the lower-order streams are more sensitive to local geological and vegetational patterns, whereas higher-order channels average the conditions from a range of lower-order ones (Table 2.10).

Table 2.10 Conductivity and pH of some tropical river systems. (These figures are often based on only a few observations and do not therefore necessarily reflect the full range of variations of the parameters measured)

	Conductivity (k_{20} μmhos cm^{-1})	pH	Authority
Asia			
Gombak	29–41	6·6–7·0	Bishop (1973)
Mekong	*c*. 280–630	6·9	Comm. for Coordination of Investigations of the Lower Mekong Basin (1970)
Meklong		8·2	Sidthimunka (1970)
South America			
Magdalena: mouth	490–630	6·2–7·2	Ducharme (1975)
above confluence	131	6·7–7·4	Ducharme (1975)
Cauca	250–500	6·5–7·6	Ducharme (1975)
San Jorge	320–350	6·5–6·6	Ducharme (1975)
Amazon–Solimoes	48·1–83·8	6·8–7·5	Schmidt (1972a)
Maranon	129		Gessner (1960)
Ucayali	150		Gessner (1960)
Negro †	8·4–8·6	4·4–4·7	Schmidt (1972a)
Tapajos ‡	11·9–14·9	4·5–5·3	Schmidt (1972a)
Paraná–Paraguay	90	6·4–8·6	Bonetto (1975)
Paraná	43		Bonetto (1975)
Paraguay	192		Bonetto (1975)

Table 2.10 (cont'd)

	Conductivity (k_{20} μhmos cm^{-1})	pH	Authority
Africa			
Konkoure	22·1	5·9–6·2	Livingstone (1963)
Bandama	90–200	6·7–7·6	Welcomme (1972a)*
Chari	42–73	6·9–7·7	Welcomme (1972a)*
Logone	41–82		Welcomme (1972a)*
Congo–Zaïre	37·1–76·7	5·5–6·5	Gosse (1963)
Ubangi	19·4–56	6·2–6·7	Micha (1973)
Luapula	150–180	6·2	Soulsby (1959)
Ruzizi	828		Marlier (1951)
Lualaba	145–255		
Lt Scarcies	35–55	7·1–7·4	Welcomme (1972a)*
Gt Scarcies	60	7·1	Welcomme (1972a)*
Moa	36	6·6	Welcomme (1972a)*
Oshun	57–96		Egborge (1971)
Niger	31–70	6·7–7·2	Daget (1957a)
Sokoto		6·9–8·1	Holden and Green (1960)
Nile			
White Nile	220–500	8·0–8·9	Hammerton (1972)
Blue Nile	140–390	8·2–9·1	Hammerton (1972)
Kagera	93–99		Talling and Talling (1965)
Sobat	112	7·2	Talling (1957)
Bugungu Stream	245–395	7·1–7·8	Welcomme (1969)
Bahr-el-Ghebel (L. No)	550	7·8	Talling (1957)
Semliki	400–910		Beauchamp (1956)
Orange	159	7·7	Keulder (1970)
Ouémé	60		Welcomme (pers. obs.)
Ruaha	117–136	6·9–7·9	Petr (1974)
Senegal	72	6·8–7·1	Reizer (1971)
Volta			
Black Volta	41–124	6·5	Welcomme (1972a)*
Red Volta	62	6·5	Welcomme (1972a)*
White Volta	119	7·2	Welcomme (1972a)*
Zambezi			
Kariba Lake	50–96	7·4	Coche (1968)
Upper course (Barotse plain)	57–126		FAO/UN (1969a)
Shire	220–450	7·5–8·8	Hastings (1972)
Kafue	130–320	7·5–8·8	FAO/UN (1968a)
Lower course (Mozambique)	108–153	7·7–8·0	Hall *et al.* (1977)

* Welcomme (1972a) compiled data received in response to a circular FAO questionnaire.
† Blackwater river.
‡ Whitewater river.

Within any one system conductivity changes throughout the year. The broad, ionic composition of the water is largely determined by the three processes mentioned in the introductory passage to this section. The concentration of dissolved substances which include organic compounds not measured by conductivity is influenced by four factors:

1. dilution effects, whereby flood or rainwater with weak ionic concentration reduces conductivity;

2. solution effects, the 'shore factor' of Braun (1952), whereby salts locked on previously dry land by decaying vegetation, animal dung, ash from burnt vegetation etc., enter solution as the flood waters extend over larger areas;
3. concentration by evaporation; and
4. absorption by living components of the system.

Normally, these effects combined tend to produce higher conductivities in the dry season than in the wet, both in lagoons and in the river channels, giving an inverse relationship between water depth and conductivity. The same trends have been recorded from the Oshun river (Egborge, 1971), the Kafue river (Tait, 1967a; Carey, 1971; University of Idaho *et al.*, 1971), the Senegal (Reizer, 1974) and the Zambezi (FAO/UN, 1969a) in Africa. Several of these authors have also noted a secondary maximum of conductivity (due to solution effects) as water invades the floodplain, but this is of short duration.

The situation for Latin American rivers is less clear cut. Bonetto *et al.* (1969a) stated that when floods invade isolated floodplain lakes they dilute the dissolved solids that have been concentrated during the dry season. Schmidt (1972a) noted consistently higher ionic concentrations during the dry season in the Amazon river as compared to the rains, and Junk (1973) remarked on a similar fluctuation between high conductivities in the dry season and lower conductivities in the flood in some floodplain lakes. However, both he and Schmidt (1972b) have also described lakes in which the conductivity is minimal during the dry season and maximal during the first phase of river inflow. The explanation advanced for this was that initial flooding by nutrient-rich whitewaters, and solution of salts from inundated lands, gives high ionic concentrations during periods of increasing level. During the non-flood season, water is diluted by drainage of nutrient-poor blackwater from the forest streams and by rainwater.

In the littoral zone of the floodplain, represented by the vanguard of the advancing floodwater, nutrient-rich soil is freshly inundated and the solution of the salts produces a local increase in conductivity. This is undoubtedly of great significance in the productivity patterns of floodplains during the earlier part of the flood phase, when such shallow littoral zones must represent a considerable proportion of the total area of the aquatic system.

Hydrogen ion concentration (pH)

Differences in water type including pH, lead to variations in the fish species inhabiting various waters. In particular, distinctive communities are found associated with the highly acidic waters.

As a general principle, forest rivers with their characteristic blackwaters are slightly to very acid with pHs ranging from 4 to neutrality. Savanna rivers are usually neutral or slightly alkaline (Table 2.10). Because there is decaying vegetation on the bottom of most standing waters of the floodplain, slight gradients with higher pH values at the surface often exist (Bonetto, 1975; Carey, 1971; Schmidt, 1973a). Gradients in pH also exist at the water's edge where the newly flooded soil may produce either a local drop in pH, as in some African swamps, or a sharp rise in others. The sudden rise in the pH of floodwaters on the Central Delta of the Niger, to as high as 8, has been attributed by Blanc *et al.* (1955) to the effects of dung entering solution. Experimental evidence confirmed that cow droppings raise the pH of water rapidly. However, the effects of this are temporary and more acid conditions are quickly restored. Laterite, which is a common soil in tropical regions, and the peaty types of soil found on the surface of floodplains are both capable of reducing pH (Mizuno and Mori, 1970). There is a tendency for swamps to become more acid as the dry season progresses, and Carey (1971) and Holden and Green (1960) particularly noted that pH is lower in swamps than in the river at this time. Drops in pH have also been noted by D'Aubenton (1963) under the floating vegetation mat of the flooded forest of the Tonle Sap. However, conditions in some open-water lagoons can become increasingly alkaline as calcium salts are concentrated by evaporation (Holden and Green, 1960). The lower pH values in swamps usually cause a general drop in pH throughout the system when the acid waters are flushed out by rain or floodwater with poor buffering capacity early in the flood season.

Diurnal fluctuations in pH are primarily associated with the respiratory and photosynthetic activities of the phytoplankton, and a decrease of pH in the euphotic zone during the night, with a minimum early in the morning, is a common feature of Amazonian várzea lakes (Schmidt, 1973a). Similar trends can reasonably be expected to occur throughout the day in the majority of floodplain lakes.

Dissolved oxygen

The distribution of dissolved oxygen within the aquatic system is one of the main factors influencing the distribution of fish. As floodwaters invade the floodplain there is an initial rise in dissolved oxygen concentrations, but these fall swiftly as submerged vegetation begins to decay and only later rise again to the higher levels maintained during the flood season. Figure 2.24 shows the changes in dissolved oxygen concentrations for the earlier phases of flooding in the Paraná river in open water and under floating vegetation. Similar effects have been noted from many other systems, particularly the Sokoto (Holden and Green, 1960) and the Kafue (University of Idaho *et al.*, 1971) in Africa, the Paraguayan Chaco (Carter and Beadle, 1930) and the Magdalena (Arias, 1975) in South America. During the earlier part of the floods, flood or rainwater may flush deoxygenated water out of depression lakes and swamps remaining from the preceding dry season. There is, therefore, a tendency for dissolved oxygen levels to be low during the earlier period when water is rising, although they remain fairly high throughout the major part of the floods. Higher dissolved oxygen levels during the flood season are ascribed mostly to the aerating action of wind and the mixing brought about by turbulence. However, in some deeper lakes stratified conditions with low oxygen tensions near the bottom may persist throughout the year. Vertical oxygen gradients have also been observed in flooded Igapó forests in the Rio Negro basin by Geisler (1969) and Schmidt (1976). In the deoxygenated water, H_2S concentrations may build up through the decomposition of bottom mud and detritus.

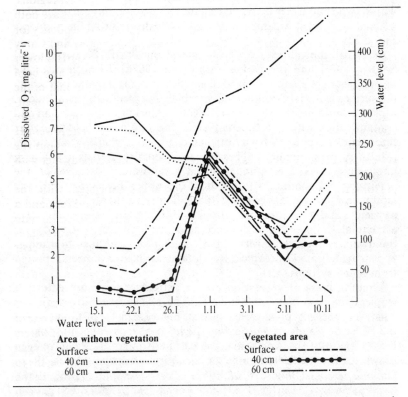

Fig. 2.24 Changes in dissolved oxygen concentration at various depths in open water and under floating vegetation at the beginning of the flood in the middle Paraná. (From Bonetto, 1975.)

In the dry season dissolved oxygen conditions are linked to a number of factors, including the size of the water body, degree of thermal stratification, vegetation cover, phytoplankton development and wind action. In general, there is a tendency for even comparatively shallow bodies of water to stratify with higher dissolved oxygen concentrations near the surface. Wind action is generally insufficient to ensure complete mixing in deeper lakes where strong thermal stratification also exists. In shallower water bodies which lack vegetation cover, wind action may ensure mixing through the whole water column (Schmidt, 1973a). However, resistance to mixing is comparatively high for the reason given in the preceding section. Ducharme (1975) considered that, whereas wind is the major oxygenator in large lakes, dissolved oxygen concentrations in smaller pools are largely controlled by the photosynthetic activity of the phytoplankton. This means that smaller water bodies show greater diurnal changes in dissolved oxygen than do larger ones. Photosynthetic activity raises the oxygen content of the water during the day, particularly near the surface, but dissolved oxygen is withdrawn from water by plants and the biochemical oxygen demand of silt and suspended organic solids, and levels drop during the night (see Fig. 2.20).

Mass fish mortalities have been noted from Brazil (Brinkmann and Santos, 1973) and the Kafue flats (Tait, 1967b). In both cases the mortalities were attributed to sudden reductions in temperature cooling the surface water of floodplain lakes which, coupled with strong winds, caused a rapid breakdown of stratification, abrupt deoxygenation and contamination with H_2S to lethal levels. Mortalities on the Apure river floodplain have also been attributed to deoxygenated conditions (Matthes, pers. comm.). These arise when depressions containing unburnt grasses are inundated with rainwater. Because of the persistence of thermal stratification the upper layers of the water (epilimnion) retain oxygen and the fish survive there. However, the oxygen rapidly becomes depleted in the lower layers and H_2S accumulates. Later the turbulence associated with the entry of river floodwaters mixes the layers, rapidly killing the fish. Such mortalities appear widespread in tropical floodplains as they have been reported from many systems.

Floating mats of vegetation are an extremely common feature of tropical rivers and floodplain lakes. The effects of these are similar whatever species of plant forms the mat. Figure 2.25, for instance, shows the effect of stands of *Paspalum repens* on oxygen concentrations in Lago Calado of the Amazonian várzea, but similar graphs have been drawn for the water column below *Eichhornia crassipes* (Arias, 1975), *Salvinia herzogii* (Bonetto *et al.*, 1969a), *Leersia hexandra* (Junk, 1973), *Cyperus papyrus* (Carter, 1953) and *Vossia* (Tait, 1967a). The general effect of plant cover is to reduce dissolved oxygen concentrations, frequently to zero (Beadle, 1974), with a consequent development and release of H_2S. Because of the large amount of decaying organic matter trapped in the root masses of floating plants, the deoxygenation often reaches a maximum in this zone and sometimes rises slightly with increasing depth thereafter. The degree of deoxygenation below the floating mat depends on water movements, for in strong currents the oxygen gradient beneath the mat may be eliminated. It is, therefore, to be suspected that conditions under vegetation mats are less extreme during the floods, when the constant movement of water may maintain at least some level of dissolved oxygen. The density of the plant cover also influences the extent to which water becomes deoxygenated – the more dense the cover, the less oxygen below it. Plant covers contribute to low dissolved oxygen conditions in two ways. Firstly, a considerable biochemical oxygen demand is created by trapping organic matter and by the decay of their own vegetative parts, thus removing oxygen from the water. Secondly, reaeration of the water is prevented both by reducing wind and wave action on the surface of the water, and by producing shaded conditions unsuitable for phytoplankton growth.

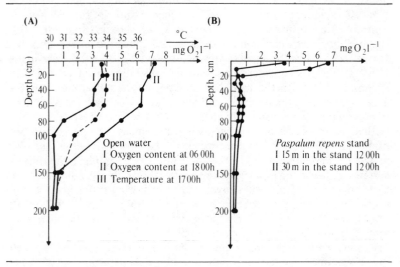

Fig. 2.25 Diurnal changes in dissolved oxygen content and temperature in open waters and under floating vegetation (*Paspalum repens*) in Lago Calado, 8 September 1968. (After Junk, 1973.)

Oxygen gradients also seem to exist in the shallow littoral zone (see Fig. 2.23). Wave and turbulence at the water's edge may here assure a restricted belt of oxygenated water, especially at night, even though the water a little further offshore becomes completely deoxygenated. This effect, if widespread, may be of considerable importance in the ecology of the fish, as many of the juvenile forms are to be found in the zone.

2.6 Primary production

Bacteria and other microorganisms

Little information is available on the abundance of microorganisms in unpolluted tropical rivers and floodplain lakes, although they are obviously of immense importance both in the breakdown of vegetation debris and dung, as well as in the diet of many species of detritivore fish.

Work by Imevbore and Bakare (1974) in the swamps now submerged by the Kainji reservoir, indicated that the distribution of such microorganisms as fungi, actinomycetes and starch, pectin and hemicellulose decomposers, which obtain their energy from organic substrates, as well as aerobic and anaerobic nitrogen-fixing bacteria, were substantially higher in the swamps than in the river. For example a total of $6·3 \times 10^7$ organisms ml^{-1} were estimated to be present in the surface water of the swamps and $5·1 \times 10^{11}$ ml^{-1} were estimated in swamp mud. This contrasts with the $3·5 \times 10^4$ and $1·3 \times 10^{11}$ ml^{-1} found in river water and mud respectively. Fairly constant amounts of bacteria, between $2·3 \times 10^5$ organisms ml^{-1} for the Rio Negro and 5×10^5 ml^{-1} for the Solimões were found in the rivers of the Amazon basin (Schmidt, 1970). Greater numbers were found in the Lago do Castanho, a representative várzea lake. Here total estimates of up to $6·3 \times 10^6$ ml^{-1} were made, although there is considerable seasonal and spatial variation in density (Schmidt, 1969). In the lake, bacterial activity closely follows that of algae, and seasonal maxima of algae are always associated with maxima in bacterial number. Similarly, there is a distinct vertical stratification in both algal and bacterial numbers, with differences in bacterial numbers of between $0·5–4 \times 10^6$ organisms ml^{-1}. Maximum densities occurred at about 1 m depth and at the bottom. These two examples from tropical systems indicate the richness of the bacterial flora in the more sheltered tropical waters. The values present do not in fact differ greatly from those quoted for the Danube by Mucha (1967), where $1·5–2·6 \times 10^6$ organisms ml^{-1} were present in the bacterial plankton in Czechoslovakia and Yugoslavia. In the Soviet portion of the delta $3·2–23·6 \times 10^6$ organisms ml^{-1} have been noted from the river and $3·6–12 \times 10^6$ organisms ml^{-1} from the standing water Killiya arm. The Danube, however, is highly polluted, particularly with organic matter.

Phytoplankton

Studies on rivers and floodplain lagoons from Africa show that phytoplankton density tends to reach a peak in the dry season and to diminish in the floods. Greater concentrations are usually present in the standing waters than in the main river channels. Work by Prowse and Talling (1958) on the Nile near the Jebel Aulia dam indicated the strong correlation between phytoplankton growth and current velocity. The dam slowed the Nile current and produced a rapid increase in planktonic concentrations to a point where nutrient depletion, particularly of nitrates, limited further increases. When the dam was open, the through flow was faster and plankton concentrations dropped. The same trends are shown in situations where the flow of the river is halted by impoundment in backwaters or oxbow lakes. Rzóska and Talling (1966) found phytoplankton to be much more abundant in backwaters of the Nile Sudd. Rzóska (1974) quoted values of between 40 and 140 cells ml^{-1} for the river, whereas densities in lagoons reached from 1 720 to 2 880 cells ml⁻¹, as in a lagoon at river post 12. Differences in the specific composition of the phytoplankton were also common. Blue-green algae such as *Anabeana* and *Lyngbya* dominated in the standing waters, whereas in the river the sparse flora was made up mainly of diatoms, especially *Melosira*. Samples from a small West African river, the Oshun, showed similar trends. Here the main river was inhabited mainly by desmids and diatoms, whereas colonial chlorophycea were the first to colonize backwaters. Egborge (1974) found a good negative correlation in the Oshun between phytoplankton abundance and both water level and current velocity, with maximum abundance at times of low water. Even then the total number of organisms was very low, but more were found in the backwaters than in the main river channel. Good correlations also existed with transparency and conductivity, and a high negative correlation with nitrate concentration indicated that this nutrient limited population in a similar manner to that suggested by Talling (1957). Carey (1971) also found phytoplankton densities to be less during the floods, with dense blooms occurring both in the Kafue river at Nampongwe and in Namatenga lagoon between August and November when the floods had receded. Phytoplankton was generally scarce in the Sokoto river at most times of the year, but was maximal in the dry season between March and June, especially in a floodplain lagoon. Holden and Green (1960) suggested that, although the relative abundance of organisms in terms of numbers per unit volume is lower during the floods, the absolute abundance may well remain the same owing to the dilution of the number of organisms by the enormously increased volume of water in the system.

A similar argument was proposed by Bonetto *et al.* (1969a) who also remarked on the generally low contribution made by phytoplankton to the primary production of the Paraná river. This is particularly small during the floods or in water bodies with dense vegetation owing to high turbidity and shading effects, but may rise in some lagoons during the dry season. Schmidt (1970) also found that the algal population of the Amazon was higher at low water (15 000 cells ml⁻¹) than at high water (3 000 cells ml⁻¹). In a várzea lake the same held true with 500 000 algal cells ml⁻¹ at the period of minimum water level. Much of the rise in the phytoplankton in the river was attributed to discharge of algal-rich waters from lagoons. This cyclic pattern of activity is by no means universal in the Amazon system as the Rio Negro showed a remarkably constant regime of about 10 000 algal cells ml⁻¹, and in Lake Redondo the peak of algal production was reached during the rising waters when the nutrient-rich whitewaters were invading the lagoon (Marlier, 1967). Because of the interaction between the various water types in the Amazon system, the nutrient regimes are likely to differ considerably from the more normal regimes of rivers with only one dominant water type.

One of the major factors limiting phytoplankton abundance and distribution is the transparency of the water. In many Latin American waters, and probably also African ones, the productive zone is limited to a relatively thin layer near the surface. It rarely exceeds 3 m in the Amazonian Lago do Castanho (Fig. 2.26) or 2 m in the cienagas in the Magdalena (Mikkola and Arias, 1976). Limitation of photosynthetic activity during the rainy season occurs when rising waters bring silt into the lagoon. It may be restricted in a similar manner during the period of low waters when wind-induced turbulence resuspends bottom mud. As mentioned above, current and nutrient availability are other factors which act on phytoplankton abundance.

In certain circumstances nutrient concentrations may be greater in the floods, when lagoons are invaded by nutrient-rich waters, than during the dry season when nutrients have been diluted by rainfall or with seepage of poorer groundwaters.

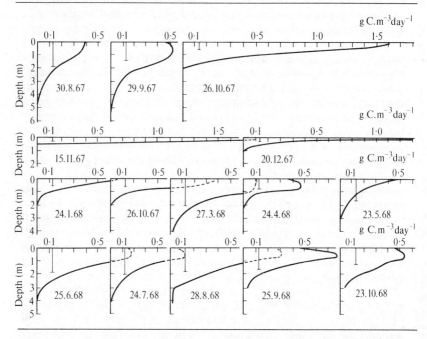

Fig. 2.26 Vertical patterns of primary production by phytoplankton and Secchi disc transparency (vertical bar) in Lago do Castanho from August 1967 to October 1968. (After Schmidt, 1973b.)

Higher vegetation may also influence plankton abundance. In Bangula lagoon in Malawi, the waters within patches of *Nymphaea* supported some $16\,731 \pm 5\,512$ algal units (cells, filaments or colonies) ml^{-1}. Here, shading effects possibly reduce plankton densities. Over submersed vegetation, higher but very variable figures were obtained of $38\,107 \pm 52\,188$ units ml^{-1} (Shepherd, 1976). Reduced phytoplankton densities near emergent and floating vegetation and higher values over submersed vegetation from the Danube have also been remarked upon. The normal cycle of abundance associated with water velocity is shown in the Danube, where in Rumania 0·8 cells ml^{-1} were found during the June floods and 4·0 cells ml^{-1} during the October low water (Szemes, 1967). Similarly, in the slow reaches of the Russian part of the delta, cell counts ranged from 192 cells ml^{-1} in the floods to 2 621 cells ml^{-1} at low water. This pattern was disturbed by heavy pollution in the upper reaches of the river, where in the fast-flowing Austrian stretch 300 cells ml^{-1} were already present. Densities of 10 000–15 000 cells ml^{-1} were attained in the highly polluted Czechoslovakian and Hungarian reaches, where water blooms are common during the autumn, giving a foul taste to the drinking water. Further downstream, in Yugoslavia, cell counts dropped as low as 320–1 060 cells ml^{-1} and continued to fall to the figures shown for the delta. The Danube pattern indicates that when abundant nutrients are available, flow is a secondary consideration in limiting numbers of phytoplankton.

The most extensive work on primary productivity of floodplain lagoons has been carried out by Schmidt (1973b) on the Lago do Castanho of the Amazonian várzea. His estimates of biological production ranged from 2·15 gC m^{-3} day^{-1} at the lowest water level to 0·32 gC m^{-3} day^{-1} during the inflow of new river water. The net annual production was 297 gC m^{-2} equivalent to a gross productivity of 358 gC m^{-2} yr^{-1}. The algal biomass was 1·9 gC m^{-2} or 17 kg hm^{-2} with a gross productivity of 1·1 gC m^{-2} day^{-1}. Production from the Rio Negro was found to be considerably lower, ranging from 0·030 to 0·434 gC m^{-3} day^{-1}, giving a net productivity of 0·063 gC m^{-3} day^{-1} or a gross annual production of 23 gC m^{-2} yr^{-1} (Schmidt, 1976). Other workers have found values between these two extremes. Bonetto *et al.* (1969a) obtained values between 0·050 gC m^{-2} day^{-1} and 1·0 gC m^{-2} day^{-1} from two different lagoons in the Paraná floodplain. Marlier (1967) found productions of between 0·14 and 0·27 gC m^{-2} day^{-1} on the Lago Redondo and Mikkola and Arias' (1976) values for various Magdalena cienagas range from 0·16 to 1·77 gC m^{-2} day^{-1} (Table 2.11).

Table 2.11 Primary production estimates for various Latin American rivers and floodplain lakes*

System	Production	Authority
Amazon: Lago do Castanho	0·82 gC m^{-2} day^{-1}	Schmidt (1973a)
Lago Redondo	0·29 gC m^{-2} day^{-1}	Marlier (1967)
Río Negro	0·063 gC m^{-2} day^{-1}	Schmidt (1976)
Paraná: Lago Los Espejos	0·05 gC m^{-2} day^{-1}	Bonetto *et al.* (1969a)
Lago El Alemán	1·00 gC m^{-2} day^{-1}	Bonetto *et al.* (1969a)
Magdalena: Cienaga Guajaro	0·67 gC m^{-2} day^{-1}	⎫
Cienaga Maria La Baja	0·34 gC m^{-2} day^{-1}	Calculated from data in
Cienaga Carabali	1·77 gC m^{-2} day^{-1}	Mikkola and Arias (1976)
Cienaga Palotal	0·16 gC m^{-2} day^{-1}	⎭

* *N.B.:* These figures are often based on only a few observations and do not therefore necessarily reflect the full range of variations of the parameters measured.

Compared with the values from tropical lakes and ponds of between 2·3 and 29·5 gC m^{-2} day^{-1} tabulated by FAO/UN (1973), the productivity of phytoplankton in rivers is extremely low, although peak production from isolated floodplain pools may temporarily reach this order.

Epiphytic algae

Production by epiphytic algae, especially diatoms, growing on floating and submerged vegetation of the floodplain and its pools, may well be more important than that of the phytoplankton. No quantitative data appear to be available on this community, although several authors have commented on the abundance of such organisms. Rzóska (1974) described the stems and surfaces of emerging, submerged and floating vegetation in the Nile Sudd as being covered with epiphytes, including the red alga *Compsogon*. Epiphytic algae have also been recorded as being very abundant in the Kafue flats (Carey, 1971). The littoral of the Lake Chilwa swamps, which closely resemble those of riverine floodplains, also supports a considerable population of epiphytes on *Typha* shoots and on floating dead plant material wherever there is sufficient light (Howard-Williams and Lenton, 1975). In Latin American waters, Ducharme (1975) and Mikkola and Arias (1976) considered the production of periphyton to be considerably superior to that of the phytoplankton in the cienagas of the Magdalena floodplain. The epiphytic community has also been considered very important in the middle Paraná because of the abundance and density of support in the form of floating and emergent vegetation (Bonetto *et al.*, 1969a).

Although few figures are available it does appear that biological production by epiphytes is very high in most flood zones, especially at the periphery of vegetation masses where light is adequate for growth. In Bangula lagoon, Malawi, for example, the number of cells loosely attached to *Ceratophyllum* was estimated by Shepherd (1976) at $3·35 \pm 2·10 \times 10^6$ g^{-1} fresh weight of *Ceratophyllum*. This gives an extrapolation of $45·21 \pm 17·70 \times 10^9$ cells m^{-2} of lagoon surface which was between 0·8 and 20 (mean 9) times the number of cells of the same organisms found free in the water. There are indications that the density of epiphytes decreases towards the shaded interior of stands and mats of vegetation along with the rest of the 'Aufwuchs' community. Because of the concentrated nature of the periphyton it obviously forms a valuable food source for fish. It also forms the base of a complex community, the 'Aufwuchs' which is associated with the periphytic and perilithic habit. The 'Aufwuchs' community includes many invertebrate secondary producers which are considered in Section 2.7.

Higher vegetation

The distribution of macrophytes in the river and on the floodplains is mostly influenced by the depth, duration and amplitude of flooding, as well as the drainage of the soil and pH (Vesey-Fitzgerald, 1970). Vegetation on floodplains is strongly zoned and various authors have defined major habitats based on the different plant communities. Floodplain plant communities are characterized by relatively few species, many of which are adapted to the seasonal fluctuations to such an extent that they will not support stable conditions. Five main zones can be distinguished on the basis of their flooding characteristics (Adams, 1964). These are:

1. permanently flooded waters with submersed vegetation only (open waters);
2. permanently flooded areas with rooted or floating emergent vegetation;
3. regularly seasonally flooded areas with rooted and floating emergent vegetation;
4. areas that are occasionally flooded (between mean flood and highest flood levels;
5. areas that are not flooded, but whose water table is influenced by the flood regime.

Examples of such zonation have been given by Reizer (1974) for the major floodplain lake (Lac de Guiers) of the Senegal system (Table 2.12), but which applies equally to the valley and delta of this river.

Table 2.12 Summary of principal groupings of littoral vegetation on Lac de Guiers (adapted from Reizer, 1974)

Flood type	Zone	Soil type		
		Light	Heavy	Saline
Permanent water	a	*Ceratophyllum – Utricularia – Najas – Limnophila*		
	b	*Pistia – Lemna – Wolfia – Azolla – Rotula – Spirogyra – Eichhornia – Nymphaea*		
		Echinochloa stagnina – Vossia cuspidata – Ludwigia stolonifera		
		Typha australis	*Oryza breviligulata*	*Phragmites mauritianus*
Seasonally submerged	c	*Ipomoea lilacina*	*Echinochloa colona*	*Brachiaria mutica*
		Cyperus mudtii	*Paspalidium*	*Ipomoea repens*
		Echinochloa pyramidalis		
				Diplachne fusca
				Paspalum
	d	*Chrysopogon zizanioides*	*Acacia nilotica*	*Sporobolus robustus*
		Cynodon		
		Indigofera oblongifolia		
Dry land	e	*Acacia seyal – Acacia raddiana – Balanites aegyptiaca – Tamarix*		

In the Shire river Elephant marshes, Howard-Williams (in Hastings, 1972) distinguished the following zones:

1. Aquatic plant zone: with floating sudd islands composed of

Echinochloa pyramidalis, Ludwigia stolonifera and *Ipomoea aquatica*, together with true floating plants such as *Azolla nilotica, Salvinia hastata* and *Pistia stratiotes*.

2. A swamp zone with water between 50 cm and 2 m in depth which consists of floating meadows of *Echinochloa pyramidalis, Vossia cuspidata* and *Cyperus papyrus*, standing vegetation *Typha domingensis, Phragmites mauritianus*, and interspersed *Leersia hexandra, Ipomoea aquatica* and *Aeschynomene nilotica*.

3. A marsh zone 20 cm to 1 m deep dominated by *Cyperus digitatus, Leersia hexandra, Vossia cuspidata,* and interspersed with floating plants including *Ceratophyllum demersum* and *Utricularia*.

4. Hygrophilous grassland flooded to a depth of 20 cm whose dominant grass *Sporobulus robustus* gives way to *Cynodon dactylon* at its landward edges.

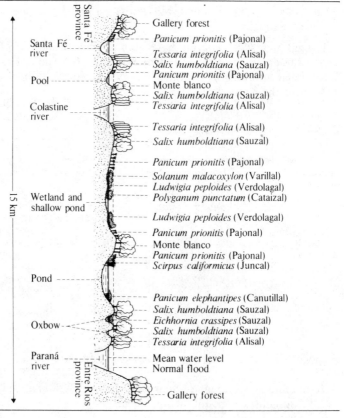

Fig. 2.27 Schematic profile of the middle Paraná valley showing distribution of vegetation. (After Bonetto, 1975.)

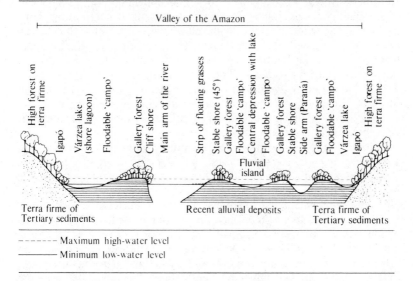

Fig. 2.28 Schematic profile of the Amazon valley showing distribution of vegetation and main floodplain features. (After Sioli, 1964.)

A similar grouping by depth was given by Van Rensberg (FAO/UN, 1968a) for the Kafue floodplain:

1. open bodies of water up to 8 m deep;
2. lagoons and river flanks, etc. flooding from 4 to 6 m with *Vossia cuspidata, Echinochloa pyramidalis, Leersia hexandra, Cyperus papyrus* and *Echinochloa stagnina*;
3. flooded grassland 1·5–6 m deep, mainly dominated by *Oryza barthii*;
4. shallow flooded grasslands and levées with depths of flooding between 0·25 and 25 cm with tussocks of *Setaria avettae* and *Vetivaria nigritana*;
5. floodplain margin regions with *Hyparrhenia rufa, Panicum coloratum, Vetiveria nigritana* and *Setaria sphacelata*.

Detailed analyses of the vegetational zonation of floodplains have also been carried out by Schmid (1961) for the Tonle Sap in Cambodia and Smith (1976) for the Okavango delta, and show relatively little difference in the basic type of zonation.

Profiles of forested floodplains given by Sioli (1964) and Bonetto (1975) (Figs. 2.27 and 2.28) describe the general distribution of the major vegetational zones of the Amazon and the Paraná.

Submersed vegetation

True submersed rooted aquatics are only very rarely recorded from tropical floodplains, although they appear to form a higher proportion of the macrophytes in temperate rivers such as the Danube (Academia

Republicii Socialiste Romania, 1967). This appears to be mainly due to high turbidity or shading by floating meadows and other floating plants in the tropics, which prevent the development of species with no aerial parts. Aquatics with floating leaves are commoner just off the open-water fringe of the floating vegetation or in quiet bays, openings and backwaters within the marsh. Thus, various species of *Ceratophyllum, Trapa, Najas* and *Nymphaea* are widely if sparsely distributed through most of the permanent waters of the world's floodplains, and also appear temporarily in the seasonally inundated area where they are concentrated in the major depressions and channels.

In the floodplain lakes of the Danube *Potamogeton perfoliatus, Valisneria spiralis, Ceratophyllum* sp., *Myriophyllum* sp., as well as *Trapa natans* and *Nymphaea alba* contribute a significant portion of the biomass and total plant production. In Crapina lagoon, for instance, Nicolau (1952) calculated a biomass of *P. perfoliatus* of 1 749 kg hm^{-2}. Estimates in Academia Republicii Socialiste Romania (1967) indicated productions of between 2·52 and 4·55 gC m^{-2} for *Valisneria* and 0·85 and 3·89 gC m^{-2} for *Potamogeton*. Mixed stands, including *Nymphaea*, were estimated to produce between 0·28 and 2·78 gC m^{-2}. Production is high in June–July, but had fallen by September. The lowest values were recorded in December.

Floating vegetation
One of the most conspicuous features of the tropical floodplain swamp communities are the vast areas occupied by floating vegetation; this may take the form of free-floating types or of sudd and meadow-forming varieties.

Free-floating forms   The same types of small free-floating plant tend to recur throughout the world's swamps. Principal among these are *Eichhornia crassipes, Pistia stratiotes, Azolla* sp. and *Salvinia* sp., which form extensive mats which may choke waterways and induce deoxygenated conditions beneath the plants themselves. They are influenced by the wind and current, and Bonetto (1975) has illustrated the manner in which this type of floating vegetation can accumulate at the outlet of depression lakes, clogging normal drainage until released into the main channel as 'embalsados' (Fig. 2.29). *Eichhornia crassipes* can double in number every 8–10 days in warm nutrient-rich waters (Wolverton and McDonald, 1976), but normal production is possibly less than this in the nutrient-poor swamps of floodplains. Dymond (in Westlake, 1975), for example, found a biomass corresponding to 1·4 kg dry weight m^{-2} which is equivalent to an annual organic production of 11–33 t hm^{-2}. There is no doubt from the bitter experiences of regions to which this species and others have been introduced, that its capacity for rapid expansion to occupy the available water space is very great.

Floating meadows   In Africa four species dominate the more deeply inundated parts of the floodplains and regularly form vast floating mats

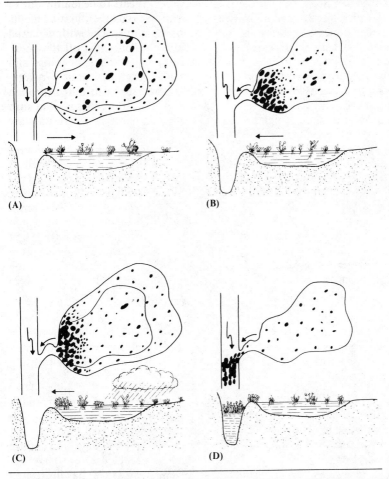

Fig. 2.29 Mechanisms of release of 'embalsados' during the flood cycle: (A) Ponds with 'embalsados' in flood condition; (B) drainage clogged by vegetation after flooding; (C) the same situation during rains; (D) release of 'embalsados' into the river. (After Bonetto, 1975.)

fringing rivers and floodplain lagoons. During the floods, portions of these mats are liable to break up to form floating islands or sudds. These are *Cyperus papyrus, Echinochloa pyramidalis, E. stagnina* and *Vossia cuspidata*. Of these, only *C. papyrus* is dependent on permanent water for its survival.

In the Amazon basin the várzea grasses desiccate during the dry season, although some may be semi-aquatic and have alternative dry-season forms. During rising water there is an explosive growth phase which culminates after four to six months in flowering, followed by

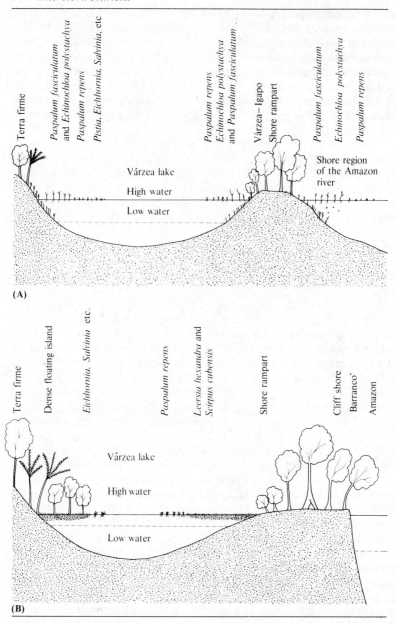

Fig. 2.30 Schematic distribution of vegetation of two types of Amazonian várzea lake: (A) with big oscillations in water level; (B) with small oscillations in water level. (After Junk, 1970.)

senescence and death. During the six-month growing season Junk (1970) estimated *Paspalam repens* to attain 6–8 t (dry weight) hm^{-2} with a production surplus of 3–5 t hm^{-2}. Marlier (1967) estimated a mean standing crop of 96 t hm^{-2} fresh weight, equivalent to 9·1 t hm^{-2} dry weight in Lago Redondo. The flora of Amazonian várzea lakes having high oscillations in water level (Fig. 2.30 (A)), are composed mainly of *P. repens* and *Echinochloa polystachya* which die back completely at times of low water. In lakes with less extreme variations, more permanent islands of *Leersia hexandra* form and these become secondarily colonized with *Cyperus* sp. and eventually small trees and other non-aquatic plants (Fig. 2.30 (B)).

Floodplain meadows
The majority of savanna floodplains are covered with various types of grassland which follow a fairly typical annual course in all but the most highly cultivated plains. Most floodplain grasses are rhizomatous, and after the floods subside the enormous elaboration of wet-season growth is burnt off either naturally or by man-set fires. New growth of the dry-season type is grazed by cattle or by wild game and burning may occur at intervals throughout the dry season. In the floods some of these grasses may take on a wet-season form with floating nodes which themselves develop roots, as in the case of *Vossia* and *Echinochloa*, or may remain rooted in the bottom but increase their stem length. *Oryza barthii*, for instance, stands about 50 cm above the water surface irrespective of depth, even when submerged under 2–3 m of water. Growth is very fast, as much as 1 m in two weeks, and productions of up to 2·5 t hm^{-2} can be achieved in five weeks. Total annual production can be reasonably high, and while dry grassland will not produce more than 2–3 t hm^{-2} yr^{-1}, productions of 10–20 t hm^{-2} yr^{-1} are not regarded as unreasonable for seasonally flooded grasslands by Thompson (1976).

The floodplain grasslands are highly modified, both by the natural flood regime, which selects for flood-resistant forms, but also by burning and grazing which prevent the recolonization of the plain by flood-resistant scrub bushes (Greenway and Vesey-FitzGerald, 1969).

Emergent vegetation
Emergent aquatic vegetation, such as *Typha, Scirpus* and *Phragmites* are widespread but localized in shallow muddy areas, and also tend to colonize sheltered alluvial banks of the river. Certain alkaline soils seem to favour these forms; the Plain of Reeds of the Mekong system where *Eleocharis equisetima* appears in great abundance (Le-Van-Dang, 1970) is a good example of this.

Westlake (1963) placed tropical reed swamps as one of the most productive communities of plants, with organic productions of up to 75 t hm^{-2} yr^{-1}. Analysis of *Cyperus papyrus* has shown it to have about 20 kg total biomass m^{-2} in dense stands, the aerial portions forming 60–70 per cent of the biomass (Thompson in Westlake, 1975), although 3–5 kg m^{-2} were considered more likely over larger areas. *Typha domingensis* reaches a similar total biomass of 4·4 kg m^{-2} with 52 per cent underground. Freshwater macrophytes in Malaysia are only reported as having a standing stock of 370–520 g m^{-2} (Wassink, 1975) – a tenth of the values for African swamps. On the temperate floodplain of the Danube, Botnariuc (1967) recorded 1·2 kg m^{-2} (dry weight) of plants from a marshy pond, and characterized the succession from ghiol to japse as a progression from a primary producton based on phytoplankton in the open-water 'ghiol' to one based on higher emergent vegetation in the marshy 'japse'.

Forest

In the main rainforest zones of South America, Africa and Asia, the floodplains are occupied by dense forests of flood-resistant trees. These may be of two main kinds which are best seen in the Amazon system where the ombrophilous lowland forests occupying the alluvial plains of the whitewater rivers are known as várzea forests, and the tropical evergreen peat forests occupying the floodable zones of the blackwater rivers are known as igapó forest (see Fig. 2.28). Riverside or gallery forests tend to occupy the levées on many wet savanna rivers, and Bonetto (1975) described the Paraná as a corridor by which the Amazonian forest is able to penetrate far to the south of its normal distribution. Dry savanna rivers are frequently bordered by flood-resistant trees and scrub, mainly of the *Acacia* type, but also some palms, especially on dry terrain ridges and levées. Daget (1954) distinguished between non-shaded and gallery-forested floodplain channels in the Central Delta of the Niger. There, the 1 000 mm isohyet separates the two types; the north drainage channels are unshaded and to the south are forested. It is also apparent that many plains that are now savanna were originally forested. The disappearance of tree cover must have had far-reaching ecological consequences and the process can be witnessed at present in such areas as the Apure–Arauca floodplain where deforestation for cattle grazing is in progress.

The role of higher vegetation in nutrient balance

There seems no doubt that the major part of the primary production of the floodplain is concentrated in the higher vegetation and principally in the perennial grasses. These die through desiccation, and by decay, burning or digestion by grazing animals are returned to the dry soil as nutrient ash or dung ready for solution and utilization during the next flood phase. Floating weeds and sudd islands, which are often present in huge amounts, are also a mechanism for the translocation of nutrients within the system, representing a very real loss as they are swept downstream.

The remarks of Howard-Williams and Lenton (1975), summarizing the role attributed to higher vegetation in the littoral flood zone of lakes, can equally be applied to the floodplains and swamp vegetation as follows:

1. the vegetation provides a diverse habitat for animals and plants;
2. it acts as a filter and trap for allochthonous and autochthonous materials which in turn serve as nutrients for the plant communities themselves or for the associated aufwuchs and fish communities;
3. the nutrient pump effect of the emergent vegetation reputedly increases the concentration of elements in littoral areas of lakes and almost certainly does so in newly flooded waters of the floodplain;
4. it contributes to the autotrophic production in that as it decays it forms a rich detritus which is utilized as food by many organisms.

To these may be added the function as a nutrient sink mechanism which, by locking up nutrients during the flood phase and returning them to the soil during the dry season, results in the conservation of salts in the floodplain, rather than their being swept downstream dissolved in the main water mass.

2.7 Secondary production

Zooplankton

Information on zooplankton in tropical rivers is rather sparse. Low densities of about 5 250 individuals m^{-3} of planktonic protozoa, crustacea and rotifers have been recorded from the Mekong (Sidthimunka, 1970). Higher numbers of up to 16 200 individuals m^{-3} were found by Holden and Green (1960) in the Sokoto river, and Rzóska (1974) remarked that small quantities of zooplankton are present in the Nile Sudd. In the Sudd, densities were higher in the dry season (mean of 4 460 individuals m^{-3} from four sample sites) than in the wet (mean of 2 070 individuals m^{-3} from the same four sites) (Monakov, 1969). By contrast, downstream of the Sudd in the Jebel Aulia dam the planktonic fauna reached 75 000 individuals m^{-3}. In the Blue Nile at Khartoum, planktonic crustacea were present at about 20 000 individuals m^{-3} with peaks up to 100 000 individuals m^{-3}, depending on flood conditions (Talling and Rzóska, 1967) and this may have been influenced by the discharge of organisms from the Sennar dam. The abundance of zooplankton in temperate rivers may be seasonally high relative to that in tropical waters. Thus, in the Danube, Enăceanu (1964) recorded only 550 individuals m^{-3} in the winter, but abundance rose to over 1 million individuals m^{-3} in the September peak. This may have been due to enrichment of the Danube waters by 'domestic' and industrial contaminants, as some of the environments studied were designated as polluted.

Because flowing water is unfavourable for zooplankton, populations are on the whole very poor in the main channels of rivers, although numbers can build up in quieter backwaters or in the reduced flow during the dry season. Planktonic organisms may also persist in the discharge from reservoirs or floodplain lagoons, as for example in the Danube (Vranovsky, 1974a and 1974b), where maximum values of zooplankton biomass ranging between 300 and 600 mg m^{-3} occurred in autumn, and where the average amount of zooplankton drifting past a fixed point reached as high as 260 g s^{-1} in 1967 owing to the wash-out of organisms from the side arms. However, numbers usually decrease progressively downstream from the point of release (see Hynes, 1970, for summary).

Zooplankton is much more common in the floodplain pools and backwaters where its abundance per unit volume is usually inversely correlated with the amount of water in the system. Vranovsky (1974a), for instance, found the average biomass of zooplankton to be 14–15 times higher in the Baka side-arm of the Danube than in the main stream (mean of 6·75 g m^{-3} for two years in the river). During periods of low or nil flow, greatly increased biomasses were present, especially in the isolated side arms where values of up to 30 times those of the main river were recorded. Similarly, Sidthimunka (1970) was able to record 131 000 individuals m^{-3} in the Mong river, while only about 5 000 were present in the main stem of the Mekong. In the standing waters of tropical floodplains, too, there is a widespread tendency for greater concentrations of organisms to be present in the dry season, as is the case with phytoplankton. Like phytoplankton, however, the decrease in relative density may only be a dilution effect and the number of organisms over the floodplain as a whole may in fact be higher during the wet season than during the dry. Bonetto (1975) recorded increases in numbers of zooplankton per unit volume, even during the floods of the Paraná, although elsewhere in the system the lowest values were found during the same period (Bonetto and de Ferrato, 1966). Increases in specific diversity often occur simultaneously with increases in absolute number. Rivers subject to marked annual thermal variations tend to have peaks of zooplankton abundance in the spring and summer months (Bonetto and de Ferrato, 1966; Bonetto, 1975), or in the spring and autumn (Ertl, 1966; Osmera, 1973) and these do not always coincide with the period of lowest water. The abundance of organisms varies and considerable numbers are occasionally found in some backwaters. However, these rarely approach the population densities found in permanent lakes. A summary of estimates of zooplankton abundance from floodplain standing waters is shown in Tables 2.13 and 2.14.

Sudden seasonal pulses in total zooplankton numbers seem to arise mainly by increases in rotifers, although the other major components of the zooplankton, the copepods and cladocera, also have characteristic peaks. Nauplii are common and are often washed out of the standing waters into the main channel during rising floods. Rhizopods have also been noted as an important element of the plankton at this time (Holden and Green, 1960; Green, 1963).

Table 2.13 Population estimates of zooplankton organisms in standing waters on floodplains*

River	No. of indi- viduals m^{-3}	Remarks	Authority
Danube			
Erec lagoon	110000	Minimum: December	Ertl (1966)
	4006000	Maximum: April	
Husie lagoon	616000	Minimum: February	
	8493000	Maximum: June	
Dyje: locality 1	10000	Minimum: February	Osmera (1973)
	500000	Maximum: May–July	
locality 2	2000	Minimum: Spring flood	
	10000000	Maximum: June	
Paraná			
Don Felipe lagoon	17000	Minimum: June	Bonetto and De Ferrato
	1200000	Maximum: October	(1966)
Los Espejos lagoon	26000	Minimum: July	
	277000	Maximum: December	
Flores lagoon	12000	Minimum: January	
	830000	Maximum: September	
Sokoto	27500	Maximum: dry season	Holden and Green (1960)
Mekong			
Nong Pla Pak swamp	38500	Random sample	Sidthimunka (1970)
Amazon			
Lago Preto de Eva	738000	Mean	Marlier (1967)
Nile:			
Aljab lagoon	180	January	Monakov (1969)
	3000	May	
Shambe lagoon	600	February	
	3000	May	
Jor lagoon	2700	February	
	12400	May	
No lagoon	8000	February	
	53000	May	
Atar lagoon	59000	April	

N.B.: These figures are often based on only a few observations and do not therefore necessarily reflect the full range of variations of the parameters measured.

Variations in zooplankton abundance have been attributed to a variety of factors. Current, high turbidity and low dissolved oxygen all act to reduce the numbers of zooplanktonic organisms. An FAO/UN report (FAO/UN, 1969a) has also shown a strong correlation between conductivity and zooplankton numbers in vegetation flanking the main channel of the Zambezi river. Here, maxima of both conductivity and zooplankton numbers (110000 Cladocera and Copepoda m^{-3}) occurred during the dry season. Both parameters were minimal, with zooplankton being nearly absent, during the peak flood.

The degree of vegetation also appears critical, and the greatest number of zooplanktonic organisms are commonly found in waters with at least sparse vegetation (Bonetto, 1975). Their density also

Table 2.14 Estimates of biomass of zooplankton organisms in standing waters of floodplains*

River	Biomass g m^{-3}	Authority
Dyje: locality 1	2·0–4·6 (471·6 max.)	Osmera (1973)
locality 2	7·75	
locality 3	7·5	
Baka: side arms	6·75 (mean of 2 yr)	Vranosvky (1974a)
Amazon: Lago Redondo	1·61	Marlier (1976)
Nile Sudd: Aljab	0·001–0·002	Monakov (1969)
Shambe	0·002–0·04	
Jor	0·021–0·049	
No	0·107–0·138	
Atar	0·246	
Magdalena	0·92 (mean for 4 lagoons, April)	
	1·95 (mean for 5 lagoons, June)	Mikkola and Arias, (1976)
	1·53 (mean for 6 lagoons, August)	

N.B.: These figures are often based on only a few observations and do not therefore necessarily reflect the full range of variations of the parameters measured.

increases locally at or near the open-water/vegetation interface, under mats of floating vegetation and associated with submersed plants. This implies that there is a succession of planktonic organisms within the standing waters of the floodplain which corresponds to the general evolution of such bodies of water, from the open-water to the heavily vegetated state, as discussed by Botnariuc (1967). Comparative studies that demonstrate this are few, although Green (1972a and 1972b) has demonstrated such a succession in the floodplain lakes of the river Suiá Missú in Brazil. As the vegetated areas are generally more productive than open-water areas, there is presumably a comparable evolution in productivity per unit area. This would, however, be compensated for by the diminution in size of the individual water body as it progresses through silting from the open water to the marshy state. Work on lagoons of the Danube floodplain by Ertl (1966) and the Elbe floodplain by Novotna and Korinek (1966), indicates that the density of the fish population influences the composition and abundance of the zoo-plankton. Detailed work on ecological interreactions of this nature is unfortunately lacking in tropical lagoons, although it is to be suspected that similar relationships may also be found there.

Zooplankton densities are usually considered to be low in the main mass of water on the floodplain, but the shallow littoral of the flood zone may support considerable quantities of planktonic forms. The higher conductivity and temperature, and local availability of oxygen can support blooms of zooplankton that can be readily observed at the water's edge. Unfortunately little quantitative information supports this as such areas have been relatively little investigated, but the high values for the zooplankton from the Baka and Dyje backwaters of the Danube in Tables 2.13 and 2.14 may be attributed to the fact that these water bodies are mainly littoral in nature (less than 1·5 m deep) with considerable submersed vegetation. In a comparison between littoral and pelagic zones in backwaters, Osmera (1973) showed that mean biomass from the littoral zone was 7·75 mg litre^{-1} as compared with 1·64 mg litre^{-1} in the pelagic zone of the same lagoon.

Survival of the adverse conditions of the flood poses certain problems for planktonic organisms which are readily washed away by the increased flows. Nevertheless, zooplanktonic organisms reappear rapidly when more favourable low-flow patterns are re-established. This has been attributed to reservoirs of organisms in upstream habitats, but Moghraby (1977) considered the 50–100 organisms m^{-3} present in riverside pools of the Blue Nile as inadequate to serve as sources for the regeneration of the population. Instead he produced evidence that the adults or the eggs of many species enter a diapause as temperatures are lowered and silt concentrations increased during the earlier part of the flood. He found abundant pockets of diapausing individuals in various types of bottom deposit, and showed experimentally that they were only released when silt concentrations dropped and temperatures rose to the dry-season norms.

Animal communities associated with floating and submersed vegetation

Floating vegetation supports rich and varied animal communities. These have been studied in most detail in the root masses of the floating meadow grasses *Paspalum repens* and *Echinochloa polystachya* of the Amazon system from where many species of crustacea, insect nymphs, oligochaetes and molluscs were identified. Junk (1973) distinguished three major biotopes according to fauna and flora. The first of these, the flowing whitewater biotope, consists of the stands of vegetation bordering the main river channel. Here faunal densities on the exposed outer fringe were low, possibly due to current, which sweeps organisms away, and to large amounts of inorganic sediment, which hinder feeding. Faunal abundance increased from the fringe towards the centre of the stand or mat, and total abundance at the centre could be as high as 100 000 individuals m^{-2}, although more normally was around 50 000 individuals m^{-2}. Biomass increased from 0·3 g m^{-2} (dry weight) or 1·5 g m^{-2} (wet weight) at the fringes, to 4·2 g m^{-2} (dry weight) or 20 g m^{-2} (wet weight) in sheltered places within the stand. A second biotope, well-oxygenated sedimented whitewater lagoons, undergoes fairly wide annual fluctuations in level which periodically destroy the aquatic vegetation. During the optimal growing period large numbers of individuals occurred, abundance usually ranging between 100 000 and 300 000 individuals m^{-2}, although densities of up to 700 000 individuals m^{-2} were recorded. Faunal density was evenly distributed and biomass varied between 2·5 and 11·6 g m^{-2} (dry weight) or 12–62 g m^{-2} (wet weight). Marlier (1967) found similar values ranging from 3·9 to 13·9 g m⁻² (dry weight) or 18·9 to 39·7 g m⁻² (wet weight) from three samples of floating vegetation in another lake of this type. The third biotope identified was sedimented whitewater lakes with thick stands of vegetation supporting little or no dissolved oxygen. Water regimes are more stable than those of the former type of lagoon. In the peripheral zone of the vegetation mats, faunal abundance was about the same as in the well-oxygenated lake, but various groups of organisms rapidly disappeared owing to oxygen stress, and abundance was very low (0·162—0·29 g m⁻² dry weight), even only a few metres from the outer edge.

This community is also very important in the middle Paraná river, where the abundance and density of *Eichhornia, Pistia, Salvinia* and *Azolla* supplies an ample substrate, (Bonetto *et al.*, 1969a). Mollusca, Insecta and Amphipoda have all been recorded from the roots of floating plants, as have Acarina, Turbellaria, Oligochaeta, Hirudinea, Protozoa, Rotifera, etc. Similar distributions of organisms have been found in African papyrus swamps where the zone close to the interface with the open water was considered the richest habitat in the system (Rzóska, 1974). Many species of oligochaetes, Bryozoa, Protozoa, Crustacea, insects and molluscs have been found among the papyrus, reeds, *Echinochloa* and *Eichhornia* of the Nile Sudd (Monakov, 1969). Few quantitative samples have been taken of this habitat, but five-minute pond net sweeps captured as many as 547 individual crustaceans (Rzóska, 1974). Monakov (1969), who also attempted to quantify the biomass of the Entomostraca, found that the fringe was 10–100 times richer than the open water of the Sudd.

Petr (1968) found between 5 000 and 16 000 individuals m⁻² in the roots of *Pistia* from Volta lake. In the Sudd, Rzóska (1974) found up to 300 individual animals per *Pistia* plant, although densities increased in quiet stretches of the river, notably in the swamps, and reached a peak in river lagoons. Fewer individuals were noted in floating vegetation in Bangula lagoon by Shepherd (1976). Here a mean of 388 individuals of insects, oligochaetes, crustaceans and molluscs were present per square metre of *Nymphaea* and a similar assemblage at 210 individuals m⁻² was found in *Pistia*.

The weight of animals associated with the roots of *Eichhornia* is also high in the cienagas of the Magdalena river, where Kapetsky *et al.* (1977) reported a mean of 35·1 g m⁻² from 17 sample sites in 10 different water bodies. Values ranged from 6·9 to 130 g m⁻².

A particular community has been identified in the umbels of *Cyperus papyrus* (Thornton, 1957). This consists principally of terrestrial forms which pass their lives in this specialized habitat, but which contribute to the allochthonous food supply of the swamp waters.

Submersed vegetation, where present, also acts as a centre of concentration for benthic invertebrates. Examination by the Academia Republicii Socialiste Romania (1967) of 1 550 g of *Potamogeton perfoliatus*, collected from an area of $0.5 \, m^2$, showed 10 489 individuals of insect larvae, crustacea and molluscs to be present. The total weight of $87.5 \, g$ equivalent to $175 \, m^{-2}$ is reasonably high for the benthic fauna of this system, which normally varies around a mean of $20\pm9 \, g \, m^{-2}$. In Bangula lagoon the numbers of individuals present in *Ceratophyllum* was considerably lower, $4 \, 385$ individuals m^{-2}. However, this density was significantly greater than the densities found in *Nymphaea* and *Pistia* quoted above.

Benthos

The literature on the benthos of running waters has been reviewed by Hynes (1970), who concluded that similar elements of the fauna of hard substrates are common to streams and rivers all over the world. Although uniformity is less in larger rivers with softer substrates, certain groups do tend to recur, and the characteristic creatures in such areas are Tubificidae, Chironomidae, burrowing mayflies, and prosobranch, unionid and sphaeriid molluscs. Similarly, Bishop (1973) commented on the similarity of rheophilous rainforest communities in Africa, Sri Lanka and tropical America, to those of the Gombak river, Malaysia, whereas the lowland reaches of the river share many features with other such potamon areas throughout the world. In fact, relatively little information is available on the benthic fauna of slow-flowing, silt-laden rivers associated with floodplains. Such that does exist, indicates a generally poor fauna consisting of a relatively small number of species. Bonetto and Ezcurra (1964), for instance, concluded from observations on the Paraná that the benthic fauna diminishes in diversity and abundance as the current slows. Data from the Amazon (Junk, 1971) also indicates a poor fauna in the main river, although experiments with artificial substrates, where 12 900 individuals settled in four days, showed populations in the blackwater rivers to be somewhat higher than expected. Monakov (1969) also concluded that the bottom fauna is monotonous in the main channels of the Nile Sudd which harbour only small communities of Chironomidae and oligochaetes on a clay or sand bottom. The general biomass ranged between 0 and $0.2 \, g \, m^{-2}$, although Rzóska (1974) has questioned this conclusion on the basis of the small number of samples taken.

Differences in the composition and density of benthic fauna with substrate type undoubtedly occur. Blanc *et al.* (1955), for instance, distinguished between the mollusc faunas of the sandy reaches of the Niger, where rare individuals of *Corbula fluminalis*, *Mutela rostrata*, *Caelatura aegyptica* and *Cleopatra bulminoides* were present, and the muddy reaches, where *Aetheria elliptica*, *Aspatharia*, *Mutela dubia* and *Viviparus unicolor* were abundant. However, the general sparsity of information on benthic faunas from these types of tropical river does not permit any very generalized conclusions to be drawn. For the temperate river Danube, Russev (1967) has described the distribution of biomass according to location and bottom type. These differed considerably with sandy bottoms, which are the least stable, supporting the lowest biomass. The mean biomass in the Bulgarian reaches of the river was 35.22 g m^{-2}, of which 32.49 g m^{-2} were composed of molluscs. Similar mean values of 38.90 g m^{-2} (total) and 34.21 g m^{-2} (molluscs) were obtained in the autumn. Biomass per unit area varied considerably with water level. The mean biomass (without molluscs) was only 0.76 g m^{-2} at high water (April–August), whereas at mid-water it was 1.94 g m^{-2} and at low water 6.34 g m^{-2}. The much higher values obtained as water level decreased were attributed to: (1) the dislodging and transport downstream of benthos at times of high flood, and (2) the dispersion of the benthic organisms over a wider area during the flood period. In the Rumanian portion of the floodplain a similar mean biomass of 20.06 ± 9.35 g m^{-2} was calculated from 12 lakes (Academia Republicii Socialiste Romania, 1967). There are, moreover, indications that submersed or emergent vegetation influence the composition and density of the benthic fauna. In Bangula lagoon, Malawi, Shepherd (1976) found 2 073 individuals m^{-2} in the mud bottom under *Nymphaea*. The major faunal elements here were oligochaetes, molluscs, Coleoptera and Diptera. Under *Pistia* 558 individuals m^{-2} of oligochaetes, Hydracarina and Diptera were present. In *Ceratophyllum* beds 362 individuals m^{-2} of Hemiptera, molluscs and oligochaetes were found. In the open water there were 725 individuals m^{-2}.

Information obtained from permanent standing waters of the floodplain indicate somewhat higher standing crops than in the main river. Monakov (1969) recorded biomasses of zoobenthos consisting mainly of oligochaetes, chironomids and molluscs, ranging from 0.98 to 4.7 g m^{-2}, from five of the floodplain lakes of the sudd. The mean value from his readings were 2.95 m^{-2} for the period of high but falling water, and 2.07 g m^{-2} for the low period. A similar value of 1.75 g m^{-2}, 20 per cent of which is comprised of molluscs, is quoted by Sidthimunka (1970) for the Nong Pla Pak swamp of the Mekong floodplain, at a time when the benthic biomass in the main river was only 0.12 g m^{-2}. Values from the Bangula lagoon ranged between 0.005 g m^{-2} under *Pistia*, 0.06 g m^{-2} in open water, 0.378 g m^{-2} in *Ceratophyllum* and 0.977 g m^{-2} under *Nymphaea*. In cienagas of the Magdalena system, Mikkola and Arias (1976) found wet weights of benthic fauna ranging from 0 to 6.51 g m^{-2}, with a mean of 1.51 g m^{-2}. There were seasonal alterations in the abundance of the fauna attributed to deoxygenated conditions in the deeper water of the swamp. Similar weights were found by Reiss (1973) in temporary lagoons in the savanna floodplain of the Rio Branco in North Brazil. Here, mean values from three lagoons ranged from 0.16 to 0.88 g m^{-2}, but there was some variation with depth and individual samples gave as high as 2.52 g m^{-2}.

The value of 0.25 g m^{-2} (dry weight) obtained from the Lago de Redondo, was considered very low by Marlier (1967), but appears to be consistent with the other published figures. Fittkau *et al.* (1975) for example, found a mean annual weight of between 0·14 and 6·20 g m^{-2} of benthos, and studies by Reiss (quoted in Sioli, 1975a) revealed biomasses also up to 6·2 g m^{-2} in the centre of Amazonian várzea lakes. On the basis of information collected in Lake Tupé, a typical river lake, and some blackwater várzea lakes, Reiss (1977) concluded that the profundal zone of these bodies of water supports the poorest benthic fauna of any Amazonian lacustrine biotope. Values from the littoral zone are higher, reaching up to 104 g m^{-2}. Similarly, while a mean of 1·9 g m^{-2} was found in the open waters of the Magdalena river cienagas, the more sheltered bay habitats had a mean density of 3·1 g m^{-2}. The range of densities from both African and Latin American floodplain lagoons suggests extreme values ranging from 0 to about 6 g m^{-2} and mean values of about 2 g m^{-2}. Rzóska (1974), however, considered that values from such areas should be treated with caution as the cyclic emergences of Ephemoptera, *Chaoborus* and chironomids can profoundly influence the standing crop and biomass. Very dense localized populations of other organisms can also arise where conditions are particularly favourable. Botnariuc (1967), for instance, recorded densities of molluscs of up to 2 657 g m^{-2} in the deep water of Crapina lake of the Danube floodplain. Values are not normally this high, and Russev (1967) quoted Russian work on the 8 580 hm^2 Kiliya arm in the Danube delta, where the mean biomass was 9·45 g m^{-2}. The same work indicated an annual production of 19 235 t (224·19 g m^{-2})from the arm. A high benthic biomass of 400 g m^{-2} has also been recorded from the many tributaries of the Mekong (Sidthimunka, 1970) which again was almost entirely due to a concentration of molluscs. Work by Lellak (1966) on the benthos of Czechoslovakian backwaters showed this to be strongly affected by the presence or absence of fish. Where fish were absent, population densities of *Chironomus* and *Chaoborus* larvae were very high. Similarly, Enăceanu (1957) showed benthic biomass to be higher in enclosures from which fish were excluded (226·12 kg hm^{-2}, mean July–October) than in bottoms freely accessible to fish (70·98 kg hm^{-2} for the same period) in the same lagoon. In floodplain pools where the composition and density of the fish populations isolated by receding floodwaters are likely to vary, differences in benthos are liable to arise as a result of diversity in predation pressures. Although the authors quoted above have noted seasonal fluctuations in the benthos of the standing waters of the floodplain, Bonetto (1975) considered this the least affected of all communities inhabiting such habitats.

On the floodplain itself, where seasonal desiccation occurs, flood-season populations of macro-invertebrates are less well studied. Personal observations have shown enormous densities of pulmonate snails to be present on the bottom and at the water surface of inundated areas. Carey (1967a and 1971) reported Ephemoptera nymphs, Trichoptera larvae, chironomid larvae, Hemiptera and Mollusca to be very abundant and widely distributed in inundated zones of the Kafue river, especially in submerged banks of *Najas* and *Ceratophyllum*. The profusion of molluscs on the floodplain has also been noted on the Central Delta of the Niger by Blanc *et al.* (1955). In the Paraná river, Bonetto *et al.* (1969a) commented on the restricted number of species which contributed to the great biomass. Particularly abundant were Unionacea, which made the most important contribution, despite the low calcium content and relatively low pH. The fact that molluscs can make a significant contribution to the benthos under these conditions is emphasized by their presence in Amazonian blackwaters. Certain of these are, however, so poor in minerals that only small Ferrissidae with conchiolin cases are present (Fittkau, 1967).

In the forest floodplains of the Amazon inundated with whitewaters, benthic organisms are common and have two production peaks, one at the beginning of the inundation and a second after maximum high water in June/July. Reiss' (1977) work on the blackwater river-lake Tupé, also indicated two peaks of abundance for littoral benthos. One peak occurred on the rising flood when 2 559 individuals m^{-2} were recorded, and a second peak occurred at low water when 1 248 individuals m^{-2} were present. Minimum densities during falling water were about 623 individuals m^{-2}. The faunal composition changed completely between the minimum and rising water level peaks. At low water Chironomidae dominated the fauna with minor representation by oligochaetes, Acari and Corixidae. During rising water Chaoboridae and Ostracoda became steadily more important to the exclusion of other groups. However, blackwater-flooded Igapó forests are generally very impoverished; Irmler (quoted by Sioli, 1975a) found a benthic biomass of only 0·2 g m^{-2} in such an area.

In areas of rapidly fluctuating water level which are subject to seasonal desiccation, it is evident that mechanisms must exist to survive the dry season. Fittkau *et al.* (1975) considered three possible mechanisms: migration, dormancy and recolonization. Among larger organisms, such as decapod Crustacea, migration is the principal method. Molluscs may survive the dry period with dormancy, but the majority of insects would seem to depend on recolonization. Hynes (1975) also considered that, in view of the high degree of adaptation required for resting eggs or burrowing and aestivating larvae, recolonization is by far the easiest strategy for drought survival. This implies very rapid growth of larvae, and in fact most larvae and nymphs in the Ghana river studied by him were fully grown after a month. Whyte (1971) has even noted some chironomid species which reached full size in three weeks. Studies on Rhodesian streams liable to seasonal desiccation have shown that the reestablishment of the fauna after the annual resumption of flow can be very rapid (Harrison, 1966). Oligochaetes, crustaceans and insect larvae appeared within 10 days and there was a form of succession whereby the species composition typical of pools was reestablished and stabilized within a month. Harrison's conclusions also indicated that pulmonate snails and oligochaetes survived the drought by aestivating. Some smaller crustacea may have dormant eggs. Most insects recolonized the area by the movement of flying adults from more permanent water bodies.

Decapod crustaceans which form part of the macro-benthic community are a particularly important element of tropical river fauna. In this book, however, these are considered together with fish on the basis of their size, position in the food chain, behaviour and economic importance.

Neuston

The neuston 'community' is little discussed by workers on tropical floodplain ecology. Nevertheless, personal observations have shown the abundance of forms living at the air/water interface. Mosquito larvae and various forms of pulmonate snails are extremely common, as are water striders (Hemiptera and Coleoptera), mites and spiders, particularly in the sheltered water among the stems of the floating vegetation. It is to be supposed that this community expands considerably during the flood season, although as yet there are no recorded observations supporting this assumption.

Material of allochthonous origin

An important input into the aquatic system is the rain of small non-aquatic creatures and organic matter from terrestrial sources. As the floods advance, many invertebrates, especially ants and termites, are caught by the rising flood and incorporated into the aquatic system. There is also a continuous input of insects, seeds, leaves, pollen and other material from flooded forests and grasslands. This either enters the drift in flowing waters, or settles to the bottom where it is decayed by bacterial and fungal activity. The invertebrate communities of papyrus heads have already been mentioned as a source of allochthonous material, and the aerial portions of other floating floodplain meadow plants are probably similarly colonized. The amount of material entering the aquatic system from this source is presumably linked to the extent of flooding and the maturity of the meadows, although little information is available.

Workers on inundated forest regions all consider nutrients of allochthonous origin to be the single most important, if not the only, input into the system. Geisler, for example, has in preliminary experiments found that up to 56 individual pieces of organic material fell on to a $0.25\,m^2$ glue board in the course of one day (Geisler *et al.*, 1973). The extent of leaf fall is indicated by the 6 t or more per hm^2 which drop from many forest trees during the course of one year. Even in savanna floodplains the presence of gallery forest and floodable scrub vegetation provides a substrate from which materials fall into the water.

Vertebrates other than fish

Amphibia
Both larval and adult stages of various species of frogs and toads are plentiful on floodplains. Most fringing areas of the plain and all permanent and temporary swamps are colonized, and in the most deoxygenated areas tadpoles are often the only form of vertebrate life. Similarly, amphibians rapidly appear in the most isolated of temporary pools. Little work appears to have been done on the ecology and dynamics of amphibian populations of tropical and subtropical rivers. They undoubtedly form an important component of the fauna of the floodplain, and probably contribute to the rapid recycling of detritus and mud by converting it into flesh which is usable by predatory species of fish, reptiles and birds. In some regions amphibians have been considered as a suitable basis for a fishery, specifically as frog-legs for export.

Reptiles
Several families of reptiles have remained associated closely with water, and of these, four groups (crocodiles, monitors, iguanas and turtles) are regularly found in and around rivers and the permanent and temporary standing waters of their floodplains. Various forms of crocodile are distributed around the tropical world, and have been widely associated with flood rivers in the past. They have, however, been subject to widespread slaughter and are now virtually absent from many parts of their former range. The economic importance of the crocodile as a consumer of fish has been discussed, principally by Cott (1961). Although crocodiles eat a large quantity of fish, they also prey on other organisms which themselves are predators of fish. Their status as major competitors of man for fish is therefore somewhat obscure. A second function of crocodilia in the ecology of some types of tropical water has been suggested by Fittkau (1970 and 1973). In the nutrient-poor rainforests the larger elements of the community serve as nutrient sinks, which slowly accumulate the few minerals available (Fittkau and Klinge, 1973). Such a system depends much on the abundance of its species which are able to maximize the storage and recycling of nutrients of allochthonous origin. A similar process is thought to occur on the equally nutrient-poor blackwaters of the rainforest zones. In such aquatic systems the low level of nutrients does not permit much primary production, and the food chain originates mostly in the rain of allochthonous material. Fish moving into the mouth lakes are allochthonous to that particular ecosystem and are fed upon by a variety of large predators, of which caymans are perhaps the most significant. A medium-sized cayman can eat between 0·6 and 0·8 per cent of its body weight per day and excrete about 0·20 to 0·27 per cent of its body weight of nitrogen, phosphorus, calcium, magnesium, sodium and potassium ions per day. Their contribution to the nutrient balance of such

environments has been estimated by Fittkau to be locally superior and complementary to the nutrients derived from rainwater, itself the major source of nutrients in the system as a whole. In places where crocodiles have been eliminated, declines in fish production have been noted, possibly because of a drop in the primary production based on the excreted nutrients.

Birds

Birds are a very conspicuous feature of the floodplain ecosystem. As with most wetlands various kinds of waterfowl are extremely common, but it is doubtful whether most of these react directly with fish populations. However, piscivorous predators are also abundant and represent possibly the greatest source of pressure from outside the aquatic system. Reizer (1974) for instance listed 37 species of ichthyopredator in the Senegal river and 19 species are listed by Shepherd (1976) from the Shire river. Birds are capable of taking a wide range of species of all sizes, and the piscivorous bird community appears to be specialized towards the taking of particular sizes and types of prey.

In general, the life cycle of water birds is closely linked to the floods. Avian breeding seasons coincide with those of the fish, and the fledgelings are being reared at just that time when small fish suitable for their feeding are most abundant. There is a particularly heavy predation during the period of receding water when many fish are stranded in temporary pools (Lowe-McConnell, 1964; Bonetto, 1975).

The impact of birds on the fish population is potentially very large, and studies from Africa indicate that the amount of fish taken by them can surpass the amount taken by the fishery. In the Senegal river, for instance, Reizer (1974) presented figures by Morel of between 100 000 and 200 000 herons and cormorants and 2 000 pelicans in the delta alone. Fish consumption was estimated at between 500 and 1 000 g day^{-1} for the darter *Anhinga rufa* and for a heron, 1 000–2 000 g day^{-1} for a pelican and 250 g for the kingfisher *Ceryle rudis*. On the basis of this, birds take about 70 000 t yr^{-1} of fish as compared to a fish catch of about 50 000 t yr^{-1}.

Bowmaker (1963) gave a lower estimate for daily ration of the cormorant *Phalacrocorax africanus* of 78 g day^{-1} leading to a consumption of 286 t yr^{-1} from Lake Bangweulu. Bowmaker concluded that this species is not harmful to the fishery, but could in fact be beneficial by its use of non-commercial species, and by its excreta which fertilize the water. The question of the positive or negative impact of birds on the fish community, therefore, remains open, although there is no reason to doubt the conclusion of University of Idaho *et al.* (1971) that water birds are important to the ecology of the fish, especially at the shallow flooded margins of the plain.

Mammals

Several aquatic or semi-aquatic mammals figure in the ecology of tropical rivers, although their role is by no means clear. Otters are widespread and undoubtedly prey heavily on fish. In some areas they have a bad reputation with fishermen for their habit of robbing traps. Hippopotami in African rivers contribute a large amount of fertilizer to the aquatic system by cropping terrestrial vegetation and excreting it into the waters, but are disappearing throughout the continent.

Members of the family Sirenidae inhabit many tropical coastal rivers and even penetrate a considerable distance inland. The dugong (*Dugong dugon*) is distributed throughout the Indo-Pacific region (Husar, 1975). Manatees are found on both sides of the Atlantic: *Trichechus senegalensis* in West Africa, *T. manatus* in the West Indies and northern South America and *T. inunguis* in the Amazon. Manatees are vegetarian and their introduction into several systems has been proposed for acquatic weed control.

Many large tropical river systems have a species of dolphin, most of which feed on fish and crustaceans. Species of *Platanista* are found in the Ganges, Brahmaputra and Indus rivers where they enter very shallow waters. *Inia geoffrensis* of the Amazon and Orinoco also leaves the main channel and penetrates the flooded forests. Another Amazonian dolphin is *Sotalia fluviatilis*. *Stenodelphis* sp. migrates from fresh water into the coastal waters during winter in the Rio de la Plata. The *Sousa olousa* dolphin enters some east and west coast African rivers, particularly the Zambezi, and is also found in the Mekong and in southern Asia.

The floodplain is also used during the dry phase by a number of wild and domestic animals, but these will be considered separately in Section 5.2.

2.8 Summary

Seasonal increases in the volume of water carried by tropical and subtropical river channels result in lateral overspill, which inundates low-lying ground flanking the river course. Fringing floodplains are a normal feature of rivers in their mature or potamon reaches, but in some areas particularly large and complex systems have arisen by geographic accident. During the floods, water is distributed more or less uniformly over the plain, but during the dry season only the main channels and isolated depressions remain filled, the rest of the system becoming desiccated. Most rivers have unimodal floods, although higher-order streams, particularly those that are densely forested, may have polymodal regimes.

The chemistry of the water in the system is strongly influenced by the flood cycle. During low water, conductivity and temperature rise slightly in the main channel and increase to a much greater degree in the standing waters of the floodplain. Dissolved oxygen tensions tend to be low and anoxic conditions may pertain in floodplain pools and under vegetation mats. Here, pH tends to acid conditions on most plains, but reaches exceptionally low values in the blackwater rivers of the rain forest areas. During the floods, conductivity and temperature are normally lower and pH and dissolved oxygen concentrations are higher than during the dry season. When water is spreading over the floodplain in the earlier stages of flooding, locally increased conductivities are found where salts are entering solution from the newly submerged soil. Dissolved oxygen and pH tend to drop where stagnant waters are flushed out of swamps and pools.

Primary production is mainly concentrated in the higher vegetation, which grows rapidly during the floods to form extensive floating or rooted meadows over the inundated areas. Phytoplankton is sparse on the floodplains, although the low relative numbers may be due to dilution, and the total number of cells present in the system may in fact be increased at high water. Phytoplankton may form blooms in the standing waters during the dry season and quite high densities may occur. Epiphytic algae also contribute a significant amount to the primary production.

Zooplankton is sparse in open waters, although locally dense populations are to be found at the interface between floating or emergent vegetation and the open water. Relative numbers drop during the floods, although there may be an overall increase in number over the plain as a whole. The benthic fauna of floodplain and river channels is limited in species composition and number, although quite dense populations are to be encountered. The area available for colonization increases during the floods. Rich and varied animal communities are to be found in the root masses of floating aquatic vegetation which extends its range during the wet phase.

A considerable amount of nutrients come from outside the aquatic system. In flooded forests the rain of organic detritus, insects, seeds, etc. is often the only source of food.

In general, the increase in the area of water during the floods releases nutrients from the terrestrial into the aquatic components of the system. This results in a surge of production centred primarily on the growth of higher plants, which in turn support both epiphytic organisms and dense colonies of creatures in their root masses.

Chapter 3

The fish

3.1 Fish fauna of flood rivers

Components of the fish fauna

Freshwater species

The majority of fish inhabiting tropical rivers pass their lives in the freshwater parts of the system. In the estuarine zone of the coastal deltas the stenohaline species retreat before the saline water which penetrates upriver during periods of low flow. Certain species are more resistant to saline water and remain in the brackish-water zone, where they contribute to the characteristic fauna of such areas. Some of the most commonly occurring genera of commercial importance from three tropical continental land masses are shown in Fig. 3.1.

The larger species of fish in floodplain systems can be divided into two fairly distinct groups on the basis of their behaviour in response to the peculiar conditions of flood rivers.

1. The first group of fishes avoid severe conditions on the floodplain by migration to the main river channel and frequently by more extensive movements in the river beyond the floodplain area. Members of this group are recognized as 'Piracema' or 'Subienda' species in Latin America and in the Mekong system are termed 'whitefish'. Species of Cyprinidae in Asia and Africa and Characoidei in Africa and South America are conspicuously members of this group, sometimes undertaking very spectacular migrations. Some siluroids and mormyrids are also migratory in behaviour. A few species are confined to the river channel at all times and never penetrate the plain.
2. The second group of fish consists of species which have considerable resistence to deoxygenated conditions and which are termed 'blackfish' in Southeast Asia. Their movements are therefore more limited than those of the 'whitefish'. They frequently remain in the standing waters of the floodplain during the dry period, and if they move to the river they remain within the vegetated fringes or in the pools of the river bed as it dries. Most siluroids belong to this category, together with ophiocephalids (channids), anabantids, osteoglossids, polypterids and lung fishes.

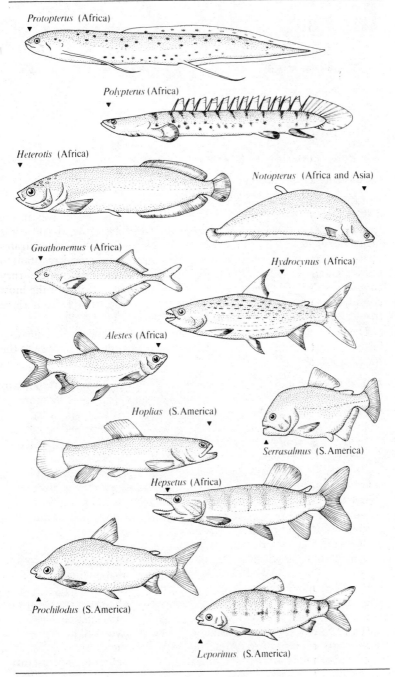

Fig. 3.1 Representative genera of fish from tropical river systems.

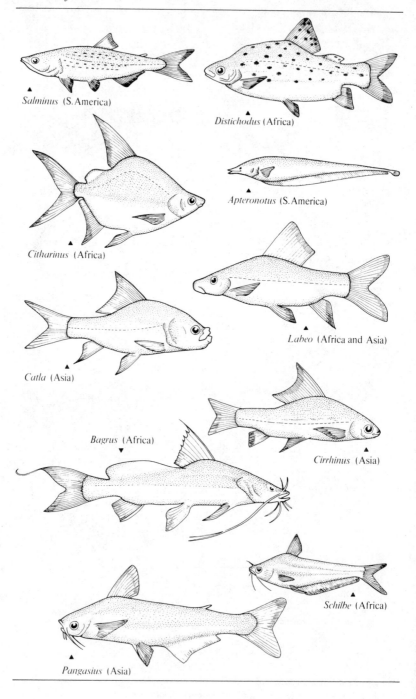

Salminus (S. America)

Distichodus (Africa)

Citharinus (Africa)

Apteronotus (S. America)

Catla (Asia)

Labeo (Africa and Asia)

Bagrus (Africa)

Cirrhinus (Asia)

Schilbe (Africa)

Pangasius (Asia)

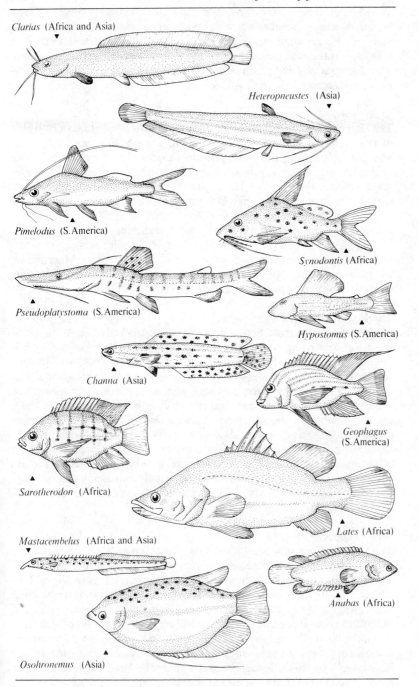

Clarias (Africa and Asia)

Heteropneustes (Asia)

Pimelodus (S. America)

Synodontis (Africa)

Pseudoplatystoma (S. America)

Hypostomus (S. America)

Channa (Asia)

Geophagus (S. America)

Sarotherodon (Africa)

Lates (Africa)

Mastacembelus (Africa and Asia)

Anabas (Africa)

Osohronemus (Asia)

Although it is very rough, the distinction between blackfish and whitefish is very useful as a first-level ecological classification of species and will be retained in this book for this level of discussion.[1] The response of the two groups to varying conditions on the floodplain are very different and have important implications for the management of the ecosystem and the fish stock.

Brackish-water species
The estuarine zone of the coastal floodplain usually contains a complex of channels and lagoons where the salinity varies between fresh water and highly brackish, depending on the flood and tidal conditions. The species living in these areas come from three sources. Freshwater stenohaline species, which enter the zone during the flood, marine stenohaline species, which penetrate inland during the dry season, and a complex of euryhaline species of freshwater or marine origin which inhabit the zone at all times of the year. Euryhaline freshwater families include Cichlidae, Cyprinodontidae and some siluroids. Euryhaline fishes of marine origin include members of the Clupeidae, Atherinidae, Mugilidae, Lutjanidae, Sciaenidae, Ariidae, Pomadasyidae, Gerridae, Carangidae, Centropomidae, Eleotridae and Gobiidae.

Diadromous species
Several species migrate between the river system and the sea, either for breeding or feeding. Anadromous forms, where the breeding cycle is completed in fresh water, include several estuarine species of marine origin, the Eleotrids *Batanga lebretonis* for example, which undertake limited migrations upstream, as well as coastal marine species such as the clupeids which sometimes migrate over large distances in the river. In the temperate flood rivers of southern Europe the sturgeons (Acipenseridae) and salmonids are the main anadromous fishes. Truly catadromous species are somewhat rarer in large tropical rivers, although eels are present in some systems, notably *Anguilla nebulosa* in the Zambezi and its tributaries. Many normally marine species enter the lower reaches of rivers to feed during the dry season and return to the sea during the rains.

Size of species
The species of fish inhabiting floodplain rivers cover a wide range of size as is illustrated by the maximum recorded lengths of the individual species from communities inhabiting three typical rivers in Fig. 3.2, in which the histograms represent the number of species classified according to their total lengths. Sizes normally span three orders of magnitude (i.e. from about 1·5 to 1 500 cm). There tends to be a high proportion of fish of very small adult size (less than 10 cm) on floodplains, even though some of those which are recorded in the histograms are from feeder streams on rocky headwaters and never descend to the potamon reaches of the river. Small size is advantageous

in most floodplains, as pigmy species can mature more rapidly (often within one year) and can seek refuge in the root masses of vegetation and other small crevices. Equally, they can colonize the surface area of the water and more readily exploit the neuston or allochthonous food sources found there. Most river systems have a few species of truly gigantic size. In Latin America the characteristic giant species are *Arapaima gigas, Pseudoplatysoma* spp. and *Brachyplatystoma* spp., in Africa, *Lates niloticus* and in the Mekong *Pangasianodon gigas*, although these by no means are the only fish attaining lengths of 1·5 m or more.

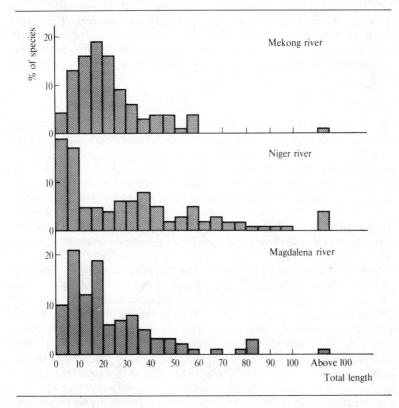

Fig. 3.2 Histograms showing the proportion by number of species of different maximum lengths in three typical tropical river systems.

Abundance of species in river systems

The fish fauna of tropical and subtropical rivers are often very complex consisting of up to or more than 1 000 species. There are considerable differences in the numbers of species inhabiting the various systems. This is largely a function of the size of the river as represented by the area of its basin (Fig. 3.3) or some correlate of basin area, such as the length of the main channel, or stream order. Although not strictly linear on a log-log scale, a relationship of the form $N = fA^b$ (where N = number of species and A = basin area in km²) can be fitted to the dispersion in Fig. 3.3. When all points are included, a regression $N = 0.297\,A^{0.477}$ is obtained. In fact there are differences with latitude which are apparent when individual blocks of data are analysed separately. These give the following relationships:

South America	$N = 0.169A^{0.552}$	($n=11$, $r=0.95$)
Africa	$N = 0.449A^{0.434}$	($n=25$, $r=0.91$)
Europe	$N = 3.359A^{0.236}$	($n=7$, $r=0.73$)

A further block of data from the north-flowing Russian rivers gives: north-flowing rivers $N = 5.607A^{0.151}$ ($n=6$, $r=0.77$). Daget and Economidis (1975) have independently fitted similar log-log regressions to data from Portugal and Greece obtaining:

Greece	$N = 2.319A^{0.24}$	($n=12$, $r=0.94$)
Portugal	$N = 1.786A^{0.19}$	($n=12$, $r=0.92$)

which agree well with the regression established for Europe. These relationships enable us to conclude that while species diversity increases with basin area at all latitudes, it does so faster as one approaches the tropics – as indicated by the larger exponent at lower latitudes. Because a log-log relationship does not completely describe the distribution of points, the intercept, which Daget uses as a relative index of faunal richness, is probably not a reliable predictor for basins of extremely small area. Many reasons have been advanced for the increased diversity at low latitudes, and these are discussed more fully by Lowe-McConnell (1975).

As to the influence of size, the number of ecological niches is probably greater in large river systems than in small ones. Meandering creates a regular series of habitats in the main course of the river and some floodplain lakes are often isolated from the rest of the system for long periods. Furthermore, similar habitats in the subsystems are often separated by considerable distances of inimicable biotope, leading to the formation of distinct groups of species adapted to similar conditions along the length of the river. Roberts (1973) has described the factors bearing on the faunas of the two largest rivers of the world, the Amazon and the Zaïre. Such differences do not occur solely in the larger systems for they have also been noted from small rivers and streams of sixth order or lower by Kuehne (1962); Harrel *et al.* (1967) and Whiteside and McNatt (1972) from the United States, and Bishop (1973) from the Gombak river in Malaysia. The aquatic component of river basins resembles islands in their relative isolation one from another. The mathematical relationship between the size of islands and the number and diversity of species inhabiting them has been examined by McArthur and Wilson (1967), who concluded that the equilibrium between the extinction of species and the colonization with new species

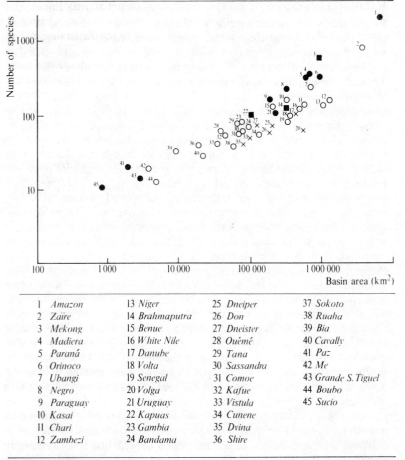

Fig. 3.3 Number of species of fish present in different river systems plotted according to their basin areas. (●) South America; (O) Africa; (■) Europe; (×) Asia.

1	*Amazon*	13	*Niger*	25	*Dneiper*	37	*Sokoto*
2	*Zaïre*	14	*Brahmaputra*	26	*Don*	38	*Ruaha*
3	*Mekong*	15	*Benue*	27	*Dneister*	39	*Bia*
4	*Madiera*	16	*White Nile*	28	*Ouémé*	40	*Cavally*
5	*Paraná*	17	*Danube*	29	*Tana*	41	*Paz*
6	*Orinoco*	18	*Volta*	30	*Sassandra*	42	*Me*
7	*Ubangi*	19	*Senegal*	31	*Comoe*	43	*Grande S. Tiguel*
8	*Negro*	20	*Volga*	32	*Kafue*	44	*Boubo*
9	*Paraguay*	21	*Uruguay*	33	*Vistula*	45	*Sucio*
10	*Kasai*	22	*Kapuas*	34	*Cunene*		
11	*Chari*	23	*Gambia*	35	*Dvina*		
12	*Zambezi*	24	*Bandama*	36	*Shire*		

differs according to the size of system; larger systems favour higher diversity, perhaps because of the type of biogeographical factors mentioned above.

Although total numbers in large systems tend to be high, groups of species are often located in very different portions of the system, thus only a certain percentage concerns the floodplain or its fishery at any one point. Some species also are limited to the turbulent waters of rapids and headwater tributaries and are rarely, if ever, found in the slower-flowing floodplain reaches. Nevertheless, individual fisheries in larger rivers do have many more species available to them than those of smaller streams, and catches consisting of over 50 species in one type of gear are not uncommon in the biggest systems.

Relative abundance of species within one system

In his review of data covering a number of areas and taxa, Preston (1962a and b) found that within a particular taxon and region, the relative abundance of species followed a lognormal distribution (i.e. the logarithms of the species' abundance were normally distributed). These distributions were, of course, truncated at very high and very low levels of abundance, but over the observed range distributions of this type described most of the sets of data well. In theory there are an infinite number of lognormal distributions that could describe the relative abundance of a given number of species, but Preston found a very close empirical relationship between the number of species in an assemblage and the precise form (i.e. the variance) of the observed lognormal distribution of relative abundance. He proposed that distributions obeying this relationship be called 'canonical distributions'. Daget (1966) concluded from two samples from the flooded plain of the Benue river that the distribution of numerical abundance and rarity of fishes in the sample locality did indeed conform to the canonical type. A similar conclusion was reached by Loubens (1970) on the basis of 15 samples from various parts of the Lake Chad–Chari river complex. Here samples were distributed lognormally, both when analysed by number and by weight, although in the latter case the correlations were less exact. With smaller sample areas a simpler exponential relationship between ranked species (R) and number (N) of the form $N = ab^r$ was equally applicable. The extension of this type of analysis to other series of data from other water bodies throughout the world demonstrates the wider application of these principles, both to areas sampled by complete fishing and to samples obtained with individual types of gear. Preston (1969) expanded the idea of relative abundance of taxa in one place at one time to suggest that commonness and rarity are also distributed lognormally in space and in time.

These conclusions are of interest when considering the community dynamics of floodplain ecosystems in so far as they affect the dominance of species especially favoured by the fishery. They also imply that the fish catch will tend to be dominated by only a few species, even in communities of high specific diversity and abundance. For this reason changes in population structure under exploitation deserve further investigation. Particularly interesting is Preston's contention that the distribution of commonness in any sample of a population is a truncated lognormal, having the same modal height and logarithmic distribution as the 'universe' from which it is drawn. The abundance structure of fish isolated within floodplain depressions and lagoons may thus be linked by similar relationships to the abundance structure of the fish community in the river as a whole.

Subpopulations

There is very little information on the fine structure of species distribution within fishes inhabiting floodplain rivers. From the behaviour of freshwater fish elsewhere it might be expected that any one species is far from homogeneous and that subpopulations or stocks might be set up within the system. In rivers such as the Niger, where the floodplain reaches alternate with stretches of rapids, conditions seem particularly suitable for the type of genetic isolation which leads to the setting up of separate breeding populations. In the Mekong, Sao-Leang and Dom Saveun (1955) noted that populations north of the Khone Falls migrate downstream of them, whereas the fish from the southern reaches often move upstream of the falls. Blackfish species, particularly those whose longitudinal migrations are minimal, seem likely candidates for the evolution of subpopulations along the length of the river. The more mobile whitefish, however, have much more opportunity for dispersal and mixing of genetic strains, but even here there are some indications that subpopulations are formed. There are hints that some species have a homing instinct. Bonetto *et al.*, (1971) has found tagged individuals of *Prochilodus platensis* in the same floodplain pool in successive years, as has Holden (1963) with individuals of *Lates niloticus* and *Hydrocynus lineatus*. This, of course, may mean simply that the fish have not moved at all in the intervening flood period, but it does imply a certain degree of territoriality in the species concerned. Furthermore, Godoy (1959 and 1975) removed tagged individuals of *P. scrofa* from one site on the Mogi Guassu to a place several hundred kilometres away and even located on different branches of the same river system. Some fish returned rapidly to the site where they were captured originally, indicating the type of homing ability which is often associated with distinct stocks of migratory species.

The existence of separate subpopulations of species in river systems has also been proposed on other grounds. According to Durand and Loubens (1969), *Alestes baremoze* has two populations, one of which is migratory within the Chari and Logone rivers, the other resident in Lake Chad. A similar separation has been attributed to *Basilichthys bonariensis* on ecological evidence. Here there is an estuarine population in the Rio de la Plata, and a riverine population in the Paraná. The riverine population can also be distinguished by its faster and more consistent growth rate (Cabrera, 1962). From the results of their tagging experiments, Bonetto and Pignalberi (1964) suspected the existence of an upstream and downstream population of *Prochilodus platensis*. This species also has two body forms, 'longilineas and brevilineas' which may depend on the early nutritional history of the individual fish (Vidal, 1967). Studies on a more restricted area of the La Plata estuary have also shown that this species has subpopulations with different growth characteristics (Cabera and Candia, 1964), whereas *Parapimelodus valenciennesi*, a blackfish species from the same region, has only a single homogeneous population (Cabrera *et al.*, 1973b; Candia *et al.*, 1973). Bayley (pers. comm.) has also collected meristic evidence of the existence of several distinct subpopulations of *Prochilodus insignis* in the Amazon.

From the above it appears that subpopulations of any one species may exist in some river systems. Although the present evidence is far from conclusive, there is certainly very good support for this idea from other inland waters (Loftus, 1976). Whether or not the population is dissociated into separate stocks is of great significance to the management and conservation of fisheries for that species. Where separate subpopulations exist, local depletion of the fish fauna by overfishing or by other environmental pressures, is less likely to be compensated for by recolonization from larger populations.

3.2 Habitats of the river floodplain ecosystem

Chapter 2, dealing with the environment, briefly describes the conditions in the various morphological subdivisions of the river floodplain system. A number of areas can be considered distinct habitats from differences in their morphology, chemical and physical conditions in the various morphological subdivisions of the river abundance and type of food. Table 3.1 based on such ecological characteristics lists the major habitats found in river floodplain systems.

Table 3.1 Major habitats of river–floodplain systems

Flood	
River	Floodplain
1. **Main channels:** Rapid and turbulent flow; fairly uniform; floating sudd islands	1. **Flooded Grassland** (A) Floating meadows: these are probably not uniform as there are slight differences in bottom substrate and relief, floral associations are variable.
2. **Tributary Streams** (A) Small rocky torrential streams – descending from unflooded terrace, or upstream of main floodplain area. (B) Small channels – linking floodplain to subsidiary marsh or lake areas above main floodplain level – terra firma lakes of the Amazonas type or type 1 lakes (Svensson, 1933)	(B) Open water (C) Littoral fringe areas at limit of advancing or retreating water, submerged grass; often low DO in sheltered areas; higher DO in turbulent wave-washed areas.
	2. **Lagoons and depressions** (A) Open water (i) *mud bottom* (ii) *sand bottom* (B) Standing vegetation (C) Floating vegetation mats (D) Floating leafed vegetation (E) Submersed vegetation
	3. **Lakes** (as above but with a greater proportion of open water and deeper)

Table 3.1 Major habitats of river–floodplain systems **(contd.)**

Flood	
River	Floodplain
	4. Flooded forest (A) Dense rainforest (B) Gallery or levée woodland (C) Acacia and bush scrub
	5. Flood areas outside main flood area (Terra firma lakes of the Amazonas type or type 1 lakes (Svensson, 1933)

Dry season	
River	Floodplain

1. Semi-permanent channels
(Break up into an alternation of pools and rocky riffles)
(A) Pools (in extreme form pools become isolated and deoxygenated)
    (i) *mud bottom*
    (ii) *sand bottom*
    (iii) *leaf litter*
      (a) *forested*
      (b) *open*
         (α) floating vegetation fringe
         (β) submersed vegetation
         (γ) emergent vegetation
(B) Rock riffles (a variety of habitats under rocks or on surface of rocks)
(C) Tree trunks and other debris
 	
2. Permanent channels
(Meanders produce a regular succession of habitats of varying depth and bottom type)
(A) Shallows
    (i) *mud bottom* ⎫ with no current or
    (ii) *sand bottom* ⎬ with slight
    (iii) *leaf litter* ⎭ current
(B) Deeps with slow or faster current
    (a) shaded by forest
    (b) open
      (α) floating vegetation
      (β) emergent vegetation
	1. Floodplain pools
	(A) Pools which dry out completely
	(B) Marshy pools (heavily vegetated with little dissolved oxygen)
	    (i) *surface film*
	    (ii) *deeper water*
	(C) Shaded pools (in forested or wooded areas)
	    (i) *clear*
	    (ii) *with tree trunks and other debris*
	
	2. Lagoons
	(A) Deeper open waters
	    (i) *mud bottom*
	    (ii) *sand bottom*
	(B) Vegetated fringes
	
	    (α) floating mats
	    (β) submersed vegetation
	    (γ) emergent vegetation
	
	3. Large lakes (subhabitats as for lagoons but more inclined to set up permanent stratification, greater depth, more open water relative to shoreline, often with sheltered and exposed shores)
	
	Backwaters connected to main channel
	Lentic water regions, open to main channel but with many of the characteristics of lagoons or lakes above, may be:
	(A) Shaded
	    (a) *clear*
	    (b) *with tree trunks and debris*

Table 3.1 Major habitats of river–floodplain systems (contd)

Dry season	
River	Floodplain
	(B) Open with
	(a) deep water (i) *mud bottom*
	(ii) *sand bottom*
	(b) shallow water with
	(α) floating vegetation mats
	(β) submersed vegetation
	(γ) standing vegetation
	(δ) floating leafed vegetation
	(c) shallow littoral usually vegetated
	Downstream larger water bodies
	Lakes, sea or larger river system

During the floods the main river channel is filled with rapidly flowing water, but at its margin the floating vegetation fringe merges with the flooded banks of the plain itself. Large masses of vegetation become detached and are swept downstream as floating islands. The main river channel is usually comparatively sparsely populated at this time, although some species, for instance *Petrocephalus bane* or *Hydrocynus forskahlii*, never move out of the river on to the plain (Daget, 1954). In Latin American rivers, the upstream migration, 'Piracema' or 'Subienda', of the major characins during low water and the beginning of the flood also ensures that some species are present in the channel during at least the earlier phases of rising water. The fringing vegetation and floating sudd islands shelter juvenile fish or small characteristically vegetation-dwelling species, which may become distributed throughout the system in this way.

Most species of fish move to the main channel during the dry season and settle in different habitats along its length. Some dry-season habitats can lie a considerable distance away from the main floodplain, and may even be located in entirely different aquatic systems such as the sea or major freshwater lakes.

Semi-permanent channels, which are more characteristic of low-order streams, frequently become broken up into a series of pools and rocky riffles. In the pools, species may segregate according to the type of bottom, vegetation cover or dissolved oxygen concentrations, which may often be severely low. Very great densities of fish may be found in such pools which essentially represent the sump into which most of the population drains. Lowe-McConnell (1964), for instance, found 870 fish belonging to 36 species in a pool of 19 m^3. This she attributed to a three-dimensional use of space within the pool, together with an alternation of activity between two very different nocturnal and diurnal fish faunas. The species composition of main river pools is rarely the same as that of floodplain pools, and within the pools segregation appears to occur by bottom type. Lowe-McConnell recorded 44 species of fish in the pools of the Rupununi river, of which 37 (84 per cent) were found over only one type of substrate.

Rocky riffles are often inhabited by rheophilous species, many of which do not form part of the floodplain community. Nevertheless, some species are found in both habitats, necessitating adaptations to both deoxygenated conditions and swift current.

In the deeper permanent channels, fish separate by depth, type of bottom and vegetation cover. Many smaller species inhabit the root masses of the floating vegetation at the edge of the river, finding there both abundant food and shelter. Several species have specific adaptations to this habitat. The 'upside-down' swimming position of some *Synodontis* species enables them to browse on the root fauna, and the serpentine shape of *Mastacembelus* or *Calamoichthys* enables them to weave among the entangled stems of the plants. Deeper areas of the main channel attract the larger fish species. *Pangasius sutchi*, for example, migrates to the deepest reaches of the Mekong river between Sambor and Stung-Treng during the dry season (Sao-Leang and Dom Saveun, 1955). The larger individuals of *Lates niloticus* are reputed to frequent the deeper parts of the African rivers within its range. Similarly, Carey (1967b) noted that individuals of several species were much larger in the Kafue river than in the adjacent lagoons.

Several species pursue a pelagic existence within the main channel, and also in the larger permanent water bodies. In African rivers, small groups of *Alestes macrolepidotus* are to be seen cruising at the surface under overhanging vegetation, and small clupeids, characins or cyprinids occur in the surface waters of all three continents. The surface film presents a specialized habitat occupied by small cyprinodonts which are found in all quiet stretches of river and floodplain alike.

Three other special habitats have been noted by Lowe-McConnell (1964, 1967) and Mago-Leccia (1970). Some fishes burrow into sand bottoms. *Gymnorhamphichthys hypostomus* of the Rupununi and Venezuelan savanna rivers has an elongated snout which facilitates respiration while buried. *Potamotrygon hystrix* and *Xenogoniatus* have also been recorded from the bottom of Venezuelan streams. A somewhat similar habit has been noted by Daget (1954) for *Cromeria nilotica* which burrows in sandy bottoms of the Niger river when alarmed.

Leaf litter on the bottom of forested streams and pools also yields a rich harvest of small species, some of which do not occur elsewhere in the system. Lowe-McConnell listed *Agmus lyriformis* and *Farlowella* sp. to which Mago-Leccia added *Aequidens, Apistogramma, Orinocodoras, Corydoras, Agamyxis, Homodiaetus* and *Hyphessobrycon*. The crevices and hollows of the mass of decaying branches, which also accumulate in such creeks, are inhabited by several small types of fish. Lowe-McConnell reported having collected 17 species and over 200 individuals in two hours from split logs and branches. In the Rupununi these were mostly catfish, such as *Platydoras, Trachycorystes,*

Pseudopimelodus, Hoplosternum or *Ancistrus*. In the Apure river some gymnotids also have been recorded from the crevice-dwelling habitat, including *Electrophorus electricus, Sternopygus macrurus* and *Apteronotus albifrons*, although catfishes such as *Panaque nigrolineatus* also occur there. Both Lowe-McConnell and Mago-Leccia maintained that crevice dwelling is associated with nocturnal habits. Specialized habitats of this type have only been studied in Latin America, but it seems probable that they also exist in both African and Asian inland waters.

The blind arms and backwaters of the main channel remain in communication with the main river at one end, but are otherwise lentic, having many of the characteristics of floodplain lagoons. They are usually especially rich localities, as silt accumulates in them, giving rise to plankton blooms and increased primary production. They are sheltered, so many fishes enter them as a refuge from the current of the main stream. Backwaters are of particular importance as major concentrators of ichthyomass, and in rivers such as the Danube are the main surviving features of the flood system.

When inundated the plain has a rich mosaic of habitats, although there is little information on the distribution of fishes among them. A basic difference exists between forested and savanna plains, although originally many plains that are now exposed supported greater tree cover. This means that much of the present-day fauna on the now denuded plains has become modified in recent times as human activities have worked upon the environment. Flooded rainforests themselves appear to be variable habitats. Observations on the fish faunas of flooded forests are limited, but indications from Grand Lac of the Mekong (Bardach, 1959), the Zaïre river (Matthes, 1964) and the Amazon (Roberts, 1973) attest to the variety of species in such fish communities.

On floodplains with more restricted gallery forest or bush scrub, the submerged branches and roots provide a feeding substratum and concealment for many species. Mago-Leccia (1970) lists several fishes from the Orinoco river which occur among flooded scrub. These include nocturnal armoured catfishes such as *Hypostomus* and *Pterygoplichthys* and the gymnotids, *Sternopygus macrurus, Rhamphichthys rostratus, Adontosternarchus sachsi* and *Eigenmannia*. Diurnal forms such as the cichlid *Astronotus ocellatus* and a multitude of characids including *Triportheus, Cynopotamus, Astyanax, Moenkhausia* and *Thoracocharax* were also found. The flooded scrub habitat is common on most tropical plains and, as observed above, probably more nearly approximates to the original condition of most of them. Thus, fish communities of this type are presumably widespread, although they have not been specifically described from other systems.

The floating meadows which now seasonally cover many of the world's savanna floodplains, appear at first sight to contain little variation. Closer examination reveals a fine texture allied to contour. There are deeper places around lakes and depressions which are often free of vegetation or have a flora more typical of permanently wet areas, and shallower places over the levées and terraces. Local differences in vegetation and bottom type are associated with these features and it may be assumed that fish segregate accordingly. There is no doubt that certain areas do have particular attraction for characteristic species. The most important factors controlling such distribution are probably dissolved oxygen concentration, depth, substrate and vegetation cover.

The littoral zone of the plain, that area of interface between land and water, is usually colonized by young fish. In Africa these are almost entirely cichlids of the genera *Tilapia* and *Sarotherodon* and cyprinodonts, which have specific tolerance to the elevated temperatures found there.

On some of the most extensive plains, where sheet flooding is common, there is an intermediate zone where the areas flooded by rainwater meet those inundated by the rising river level. This zone marks the boundary between two types of water of different productivity and may limit the distribution of fish on the plain. Blanc *et al.* (1955) distinguished two zones on the Niger river floodplain: (1) a zone corresponding to the major bed of the river which was rich in fish; and (2) a peripheral flood area which was less densely colonized. A similar distribution pattern has been reported from the Arauca–Apure flood system by Matthes (pers. comm.) and from the flooded forests of the Mekong by Le-Van-Dang (1970). Some of the patchiness in fish distribution on other large floodplains, for example, the Sudd (Rzóska, 1974), may be attributable to such differences in water quality.

In the dry season most of the plain is drained, leaving only the network of depression pools, lagoons and swamps, some of which dry out and some of which persist until the next flood. Most fish leave the plain at this time, but a certain section of the community remains in these standing waters. Of the fish remaining a proportion is composed of species which would normally retreat to the river channels, but which have become isolated in various depressions. The majority of these die through desiccation of the water body in which they find themselves, through deoxygenated conditions, or through exposure to excessive temperatures. Some find their way to deeper lakes where they may survive.

An assortment of fish stay on the plain. Daget (1954) and Blanc *et al.* (1955) listed *Marcusenius* (*Gnathonemus*) *senegalensis*, *Pollimyrus* (*Marcusenius*) *isidori*, *Petrocephalus bovei* (mormyrids), *Gymnarchus niloticus*, *Heterotis niloticus*, *Ctenopoma*, *Parophiocephalus*, *Polypterus*, *Synodontis*, *Clarias*, *Hepsetus*, *Auchenoglanis* and *Heterobranchus* as comprising the characteristic fauna of the floodplain pools of the Niger river. These genera recur on floodplains throughout their range in Africa, which is often very widespread. In the Mekong, the blackfish assemblage described by Sao-Leang and Dom Saveun (1955) contains a similar group of fishes, many of which belong to the same families and closely resemble the African species. Major examples such as *Ophicephalus striatus, O. micropeltes, Anabas testudineus* and *Clarias batrachus* remain in depression pools throughout the dry season to spread over the plain during the flood. Species recorded from the lagoons and pools of the Apure river, Venezuela, by Mago-Leccia (1970) included *Hoplias malabaricus, Serrasalmus notatus, Callichthys callichthys, Hoplosternum littorale, Pseudoplatystoma fasciatum, Sorubim lima, Pimelodus, Leporinus* and *Pimelodella*. Similar assemblages, often involving the same species or genera, have been described from the Rupununi by Lowe-McConnell (1964), from the Paraná river by Bonetto *et al.* (1969b) and from the Magdalena by Kapetsky *et al.* (1976).

There are considerable differences in the species composition of fish populations from floodplain pools of the same system, as typified by the data given in Fig. 3.4. Attempts have been made to correlate these with the number of variables. Welcomme (1975a) traced the increased specific diversity of populations with size of pool in the Ouémé system (Table 3.2). That size of pool can influence species composition has also been found by Lowe-McConnell (1964) who found that larger species inhabited the larger bodies of water. Holden (1963) found the same

Table 3.2 Differences in species composition of catches from permanent floodplain lagoons of different areas on the Ouémé floodplain (FAO/UN, 1971a)

| | Species | Percentage of species in lagoons | | |
		Small (up to 500 m²)	Medium (500– 5000 m²)	Large (over 5000 m²)
Normally swamp-dwelling species with auxiliary breathing organs	*Clarias ebriensis*	72·2	20·0	1·3
	C. lazera	5·0	13·6	3·4
Habitually found only on floodplain	*Ctenopoma kingsleyae*	0·9	7·2	P*
	Gymnarchus niloticus		P	2·1
	Heterotis niloticus		26·0	2·6
	Parophiocephalus obscurus	23·8	27·2	1·6
	Polypterus senegalus	P	0·3	0·7
	Protopterus annectens	P	0·8	0·9
	Xenomystus nigri	P	0·2	P
Occasional swamp-dwelling species without auxiliary organs	*Citharinus latus,*		0·1	1·2
	Distichodus rostratus		0·7	8·1
	Hepsetus odoe		2·3	2·6
Found in floodplain or river	*Chromidotilapia guntheri*	P	P	P
	Hemichromis spp.	P	P	P
	Tilapia spp.		1·6	2·2
	Synodontis spp.			15·2
	Small mormyrids			18·4
Species normally found in river	*Hyperopisus bebe*		P	5·4
	Mormyrops deliciosus			18·4
	Labeo senegalensis			P
	Schilbe mystus			6·0
	Lates niloticus			10·1

*P = present at less than 0·1%.

effect on the Sokoto river and noted that individuals of the same species tended to be larger in the bigger pools. The influence of size of pool may depend on the heightened dissolved oxygen concentration arising from lessened vegetation cover and improved aeration by wind. Such

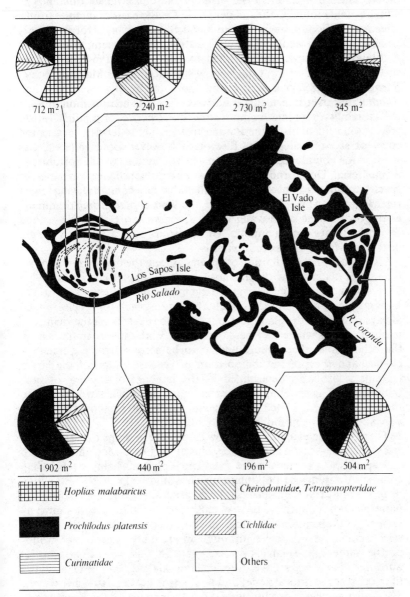

Fig. 3.4 Percentage representation of major fish groups in six floodplain depression lakes of the middle Paraná system. (After Bonetto *et al.*, 1969b.)

relatively favourable conditions allow many more species to survive, including some which would normally return to the river channel in the dry season. Greater area also leads to a greater diversity of habitat, with more varied bottom types, submersed, floating and emergent vegetation, and open water in the place of the densely packed stands of aquatic plants found in the smaller pools. On the basis of samples from a selection of floodplain pools from the Sokoto river, Holden (1963) concluded that several species were distributed according to substrate. Although no species was confined to any one bottom type, certain species, such as *Alestes dentex*, were more common over sand. *Sarotherodon galilaeus* was found more frequently over mud, and *Tilapia zillii* over intermediate bottoms. There is little explanation for the variability in species composition found by Bonetto *et al.* (1969b) (Fig. 3.4) in the pools of the Paraná river, either in terms of vegetation cover or size of water body. Elsewhere, however, Bonetto (1975) has stressed the abundance of mud-eating fish in lagoons whose bottom is of this material. Depth and exposure may also influence the distribution of species composition of the shallow sheltered bay habitat of Magdalena river lagoons, where *Potamotrygon* and *Pseudoplatystoma* dominate, as opposed to the open water where *Hemiancistrus*, *Triportheus* and *Prochilodus* are more common. Other species such as *Plagioscion* are distributed more or less indifferently.

How much the distribution of species among the dry-season habitats is a matter of chance, with only those specially adapted species surviving adverse conditions, and how much is a matter of deliberate selection of habitats is not clear. It seems likely that those blackfish species, which always remain on the plain, seek out or maybe never leave the vicinity of the depressions where they pass their lives. With migratory species, on the other hand, there would appear to be a considerable element of chance and the precise composition of the fish fauna of the larger lagoons is probably determined by the haphazard trapping of such individuals. The shoaling habit of many of these fishes would lead to them being either isolated in large quantities, or not present at all, giving very skewed distributions of abundance.

There is some evidence from the Rupununi swamps that species do select their dry-season habitats very closely. In Lowe-McConnell's list of 129 species, 79 per cent were found in only one habitat (excluding channels draining the floodplain which would be likely to have a high proportion of transient species). More generally, however, distribution patterns do not appear to be so exclusive and preferences are shown by greater concentrations in one locality rather than another. Such selection may be by species, although different life stages or age groups of the same species may also segregate in this way. For instance, *Sarotherodon* species have different habitats for feeding of juveniles (nurseries in the littoral zone) and adults (the bottom in deeper water). They also segregate for breeding, with the mature males being found over distinct nesting sites on the bottom, non-breeding adults, both male and female, staying in mid-water adjacent to the breeding sites, and brooding females carrying eggs in their mouths being located in sheltered brooding sites near the nurseries. Not all fishes show such complex distribution patterns, but in many, some phase of the life cycle (usually, but not always the immature stage) is passed in a habitat other than that frequented by the other age groups of the species.

3.3 Adaptations to extreme environmental conditions

Many of the habitats within the floodplain ecosystem described above have extreme physical or chemical conditions which call for special adaptations on the part of the fish inhabiting them. Many of the adaptations are behavioural, involving migrations or local movements whereby the adverse conditions are avoided. However, a certain section of the fish fauna has specific anatomical or physiological adaptations which permit the species concerned to survive low dissolved oxygen concentrations or even complete deoxygenation, high temperature and desiccation.

Low dissolved oxygen concentrations

Some species which inhabit the lentic waters of the floodplain are strangely sensitive to low dissolved oxygen levels. *Serrasalmus nattereri* and *S. rhombeus*, for instance, show the first symptoms of asphyxia when the oxygen falls below only 20 per cent saturation. Such species are especially sensitive to sudden drops in dissolved oxygen and are among the first to suffer catastrophic mortalities. There are two sources from which fish may obtain supplementary oxygen in poorly aerated waters. These are: (1) the air above the water, and (2) the thin, but well-oxygenated surface layer which is often only a few millimetres deep. Many of the blackfish species inhabiting swamps have modifications which allow them to benefit from one or other of these sources. For example, Carter and Beadle (1931) found that 8 out of 20 species occurring in the Paraguayan Chaco had anatomical respiratory modifications for air breathing, whereas the rest used the surface layer as a source of oxygenated water.

The development of specialized organs which enable fish to breathe air has occurred independently in many taxa and in all zoogeographic regions. Respiratory modifications have been centred around three main anatomical systems, the mouth and digestive tract, the gills and branchial chamber, and the lung or swim bladder. These are discussed in detail by Carter (in Brown, 1957), Norman (1975) and various contributions in Hughes (1976), particularly that of Dehadrai and Tripathi. Adaptations to air breathing are sometimes so highly developed as to allow the fish to migrate for considerable distances over dry land. Several species have become so dependent on air that they die if prevented from reaching the surface. Thus, the lung fishes are obliged to breathe at frequent intervals, and the paiche (*Arapaima gigas*) needs air every 10–15 minutes when adult and more frequently when young (Sanchez Romero, 1961).

Dehadrai and Tripathi (in Hughes, 1976) mention the energy cost of this type of adaptation. Young *Ophicephalus punctatus* kept in 40 cm of water, surfaced 1 879 times per day at a cost of 161 cal day^{-1}. In 2·5 cm of water the same species surfaced 482 times per day at a cost of 92 cal day^{-1}. Fish living in deeper water consume about 1·5 times as much food as those from the shallower waters, presumably to compensate for the additional energy required.

Modifications of the digestive tract for air breathing is made possible by the stopping of feeding during the dry season (Lowe-McConnell, 1967), at just those times when deoxygenation is most extreme. Most parts of the alimentary canal have been modified in one family or another. The mouth cavity and pharynx are highly papillated and well supplied with blood in *Electrophorus electricus* which surfaces to gulp air. Air bubbles are passed backwards to lodge inside the heavily vascularized stomach of *Ancistrus* and *Plecostomus* spp., the intestine of *Hoplosternum* or the rectum of *Misgurnus fossilis*.

The branchial or pharyngeal cavity has become modified by simple vascularization in *Hypopomus* and *Monopterus*. *Mastacembelus* spp. secrete a protective slime over the unmodified gills which permits a

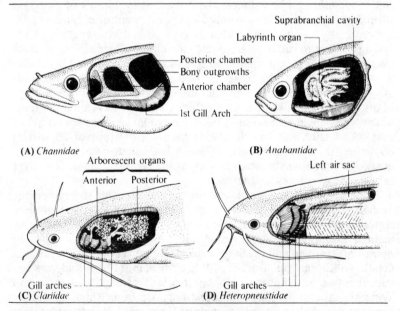

Fig. 3.5 Adaptations for air-breathing in: (A) Channidae, *Channa*; (B) Anabantidae, *Ctenopoma*; (C) Claridae, *Clarias*; (D) Heteropneustidae, *Heteropneustes*.

limited amount of aerial respiration. Three different families have developed diverticula of the branchial cavity (Fig. 3.5). These are least developed in the Channidae whose supra-branchial chambers are simply lined with a richly vascularized epithelium. The Anabantidae have labyrinth organs elaborated from the first gill arch. In the Clariidae the II and IV gill arches have become modified into arborescent organs in many genera, and in *Heteropneustes (Saccobranchus) fossilis* the branchial chamber is extended backwards along the body.

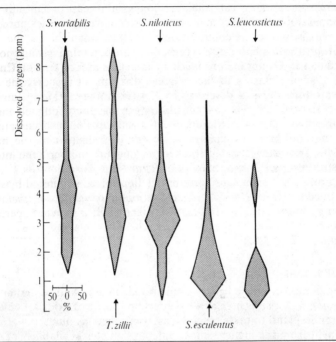

Fig. 3.6 Comparison of percentage representation of five species of *Tilapia (Sarotherodon)* in different concentrations of dissolved oxygen on beaches in the Lake Victoria and adjacent floodplain swamps. (After Welcomme, 1964.)

Only the lung fishes (Dipnoi) and bichirs (Polypteroidea) have true lungs, but several physostomous families have modified swim bladders which act in an almost identical manner. These include Osteoglossidae (*Arapaima gigas*), Lepisosteidae (*Lepisosteus* sp.); Gymnarchus and several species of Mormyridae, Erythrinidae (*Erythrinus* and *Hoploerythrinus*), Notopteridae, and Umbridae (*Umbra*). Young forms of Lepidosirenidae, Polypteridae, Osteoglossidae and Gymnarchidae have external gills which are resorbed during development when the lungs or swim bladder take over the main respiratory function.

Anatomical modifications which enable certain small species of fish to use the oxygenated surface film of the water have been described by Lewis (1970). These adaptations include the small dorsally oriented mouth and dorso-ventrally flattened head found in most cyprinodonts. Lewis carried out experiments to show that in deoxygenated conditions *Fundulus, Poecilia* and *Gambusia* all adopted a characteristic posture at the water surface where they can survive indefinitely, provided a critical population density is not exceeded.

Physiological mechanisms in some species allow the fish to withstand low dissolved oxygen concentrations, although not necessarily to survive under complete anoxia. For instance Blažka (1958) found that *Carassius carassius* can tolerate anoxia for at least two months at low temperature. At higher temperatures, tolerance time is lessened. Much of this is due to the composition of the blood which in some species, notably those inhabiting oxygen-poor waters, is relatively unaffected by changes in O_2 uptake produced by increases in CO_2 tension (Lagler *et al.*, 1977). There is in fact a great diversity of response by fish to respiratory stress as described by Fry (in Brown, 1957).

Dissolved oxygen concentrations are probably one of the most influential factors determining the distribution of individual species. An example of how this may occur in one genus is given by Welcomme (1964) who investigated the environmental factors regulating the distribution of five species of *Tilapia* (and *Sarotherodon*) in Lake Victoria and on an adjacent small floodplain. There was a clearly defined preference for different conditions of oxygenation, some species being found mainly in well-aerated areas, such as exposed beaches and the main channel of the river, and others in the standing water of the swamps (Fig. 3.6).

High temperatures

Temperatures at the fringes of the flooded plain, and in shallow water bodies, may rise as high as 40°C. Certain species of fish, particularly the juveniles, tend to prefer such areas, using them as nurseries. Here they benefit from the higher temperature and greater availability of food to grow faster, and also as a partial refuge from predation (Welcomme, 1964). There is experimental evidence that species inhabiting these warmer-water areas have a much greater physiological resistance to the effects of high temperatures than most other species. For example, Fig. 3.7 illustrates the difference between the survival of *Tilapia zillii* and *Haplochromis* spp. under experimental high temperatures. *Tilapia zillii* survive indefinitely at 38°C, a temperature at which half of the sample of *Haplochromis* would die within two minutes.

There are indications that such thermal tolerance may be cyclic, at least in some species. Johnson (1976) has shown that there is a daily rhythm of thermal tolerance in *Gambusia affinis* which rises some 3°C between morning and midday and falls away again towards evening.

Desiccation

Very few species are adapted to survive desiccation, and annual losses of

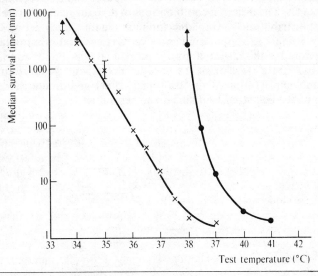

Fig. 3.7 Survival of *Haplochromis* spp. and *Tilapia zillii* in high temperatures when acclimatized to 27°C. (After Welcomme, 1964.)

fish trapped in temporary water bodies is enormous. Some species, however, survive the dry period by cocooning. The African lung fishes *Protopterus annectens* and *P. aethiopicus* burrow into the bed of a drying pool and secrete a cocoon of hardened slime in which they rest coiled so that the mouth is upwards and connected to an air passage. Fish have been recorded as having survived over a year of aestivation. Some murrels (Ophicephalidae) are reputed to survive short periods of drought in a similar manner. Dehadrai and Tripathi (in Hughes, 1976) also report that *Clarias* and *Heteropneustes* take refuge in soft mud in drying pools; however, these species are probably unable to withstand complete desiccation.

Several species of cyprinodont can maintain permanent populations in temporary aquatic habitats. These are annual fishes which complete their life cycles in as little time as a few weeks. The lowering of the water level in their environment, and possibly the associated physical and chemical changes in water quality, appear to act as the stimulus for reproduction. The eggs are shed on the bottom where they settle or are pushed into the mud by the parent fish which die shortly afterwards. The eggs and growing embryos may stop their development for variable periods, and such arrests (diapauses) may occur at three stages, described by Wourms (1972) as Diapause I (dispersed cell phase), Diapause II (long somite embryo) and Diapause III (pre-hatching). In some species the arrest is facultative at Diapause I and II, but obligate at Diapause III. The different combinations of diapause can generate eight different distributions of total development time as shown in Fig. 3.8. In this way a single egg population can give rise to several subpopulations which allow for the repeated loss of individual eggs under conditions which can start development, but do not allow maturation and successful reproduction. This 'multiplier' effect guarantees that some portion of the egg stock will survive to reproduce.

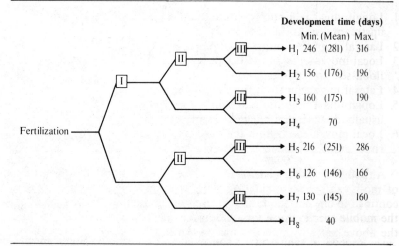

Fig. 3.8 'Multiplier' effect of various combinations of diapause on the egg stock of annual fish. (After Wourms, 1972.)

3.4 Migration and movements

Types of migration and movements

Because most species have two distinct centres of concentration, fish have to travel, sometimes over long distances, to reach their respective wet- and dry-season habitats. Two components of such movements have been recognized by Daget (1960a) for tropical African species. His categories of longitudinal and lateral migration are of general application to flood rivers everywhere. Longitudinal migrations are those which take place within the main river channel, and lateral migrations are those whereby fish leave the main channel and distribute themselves over the floodplain. Originally it was suggested that only the longitudinal component of the migration was active, being directed by physiological stimuli, and that lateral migration was more of a passive affair with fish being swept by the rising floods on to the plain. It has since become apparent from the orderly succession of the migrations, and from the way in which fish often swim against the current to gain access to the plain, that this is not generally the case. In fact it would appear from the available but rather circumstantial evidence that most movements of healthy adult fish are directed rather than passive. Passive drifts do occur, nevertheless, where the eggs and larval forms of several species profit by the current for transport from the spawning site.

Four phases of fish movement have been identified separately by Blache (1964) and Williams (1971) from the Chari and Kafue rivers respectively. Combining their two classifications, six main phases in the distribution of fish emerge:

1. Longitudinal migrations within main channels: these are usually upstream, but not always so.
2. Lateral migration on to the floodplain.
3. Local movements on the floodplain and distribution among flood-season habitats.
4. Lateral migration from the floodplain towards the main channel.
5. Longitudinal migrations within the main channel: these are usually downstream but not always so.
6. Local movements within the dry-season habitat: this may be the river, adjacent lake or in some cases the sea.

Although these are broadly applicable to the majority of individuals of most fish species inhabiting flood river systems, some species are confined to one habitat only. It is also not certain that all individuals of the mobile species do in fact undertake migrations every year. Within the above pattern three distinct groups of freshwater species can be distinguished:

(a) The 'blackfish' species, whose migrations between dry-and wet-season habitats are restricted and which, at the most, undertake lateral migrations to the fringes of the main channel. These species are more normally confined to the plain spreading over it during the floods from the residual pools and lagoons which are the dry-season habitat.

(b) Those species which undertake moderate movements within the river, but which spawn on the floodplain. The major migrations are for dispersal to dry-season habitats such as those of the African *Alestes leuciscus* described by Daget (1952) or *Crossocheilus reba* (Tongsanga and Kessunchai, 1966), and other Mekong species (Bardach, 1959). Migrations to the favoured breeding places on the floodplain may be either upstream or downstream and rarely involve the formation of large shoals. Migrations of this type appear to be mainly for the avoidance of unfavourable conditions on the plain.

(c) The 'whitefish' species which undertake an upstream migration during the dry season or early in the wet season, and some of which spawn upstream. Where upstream spawning occurs the adults usually return to the downstream floodplain habitats soon after spawning, whereas the eggs and young may return somewhat later. In South America such migrations are characteristic of the characins and certain siluroids and are known as 'Piracema' or 'Subienda'. They have been recorded from the Paraná by Bonetto and Pignalberi (1964), the Mogi Guassu by Godoy (1975), the Magdalena (Dahl, 1971) and the Amazon (Ihering, 1930; Geisler *et al.*, 1973), also Lowe-McConnell (1964) described the upstream migration of *Boulengerella cuvieri, Hydrolycus scomberoides,* and *Myleus pacu* in the Rupununi river. In Africa a slightly different pattern of migration is shown where there are upriver floodplains adjacent to major lakes. In this continent, too, characins and some siluroids are conspicuous among the migratory species, but cyprinids also show this type of behaviour. Potamodramous migrations, whereby adult fish leave lakes and ascend rivers during the floods to spawn in the upstream swamps, have been described by Blache (1964) for the Lake Chad–Yaérés system, where numerous species are involved, Whitehead (1959a) for the 18 migratory species of the Lake Victoria–Nzoia river system, and De Kimpe (1964) for some mormyrids, characins and cyprinids including *Labeo altivelis* of the Lake Mweru–Luapula river system. Similar spawning migrations have been described from a tributary of the Mekong by Sritingsook and Yoovetwatana (1976). Here *Probarbus jullieni* migrate up the Mekong river to spawning places having shallow water, moderate current and sandy bottoms. Day (1958) notes that there is a section of the fish population of Indian rivers which move long distances to the spawning sites in the hill tributaries of the major rivers. One such migrant *Tor* sp. is famous for its ascent of Himalayan tributaries. In European rivers several species undertake migrations similar to those of the 'Piracema' species. Zambriborsch and Nguen Tan Chin (1973), for instance, cited examples of semi-anadromous migrations by *Aspius aspius, Blicca bjoerkna* and *Abramis brama* from the Kiliya arm of the Danube, and Belyy (1972) attributed similar behaviour to *Lucioperca lucioperca* from the Dnieper. Several cyprinid species migrate during the early part of the spring flood in the Tigris–Euphrates system. Notable among these are *Barbus xanthopterus, B. grypus* and *Aspius vorax* whose adults spawn on upstream gravel beds, and whose young later drift downstream to occupy the floodlands in the lower reaches of the river complex. Other cyprinid species remain downstream to spawn in the river channel or in the swamps, for example *Barbus sharpeyi* or *B. luteus*. Most of the Mesopotamic fishes also move out of the marshes and floodplain lakes at low water (FAO/UN, 1954).

Potamodromous migrations would appear to have several advantages for the fish species undertaking them. In the 'Piracema'-type migrations of Latin America there is the lengthening of exposure to the flood. By placing the young nearer the headwaters, their journey downstream coincides with that of the flood wave over several hundred kilometres and this is likely to take several weeks. Furthermore, there must be considerable dispersal of the population which may ensure mixing of stocks over such long river systems as the Paraná. There has been much discussion of the role of the potamodromous habit in African species, Jackson (1961a) maintaining that it is principally a device to protect the young from predation, whereas Fryer (1965) saw it mainly as a mechanism to secure dispersal over the whole river course. As in so many such arguments both participants are probably partly correct and there is no doubt that the use of upstream swamps and spawning habitats does have the double advantage of presenting the young fish with a rich habitat in which to start life, while at the same time giving considerable shelter from the predation to which they would be exposed in the adult lacustrine habitat.

Return movements by the younger stages are often by a passive drift with the current, at least initially. Thus Godoy (1959) noted that the eggs of *Prochilodus scrofa* are semi-pelagic and are carried downstream by the current from the spawning sites which are in mid-channel. The eggs, however, develop rapidly and the fry soon take refuge in flooded oxbows only to be washed out later by falling water. They then swim downstream to the major feeding grounds. In the Pilcomayo river, lateral floodplains are absent in the upper courses and Bayley (1973) supposed that the eggs and fry of *P. platensis* are swept directly downstream, as are the young stages of *Hilsa ilisha* in the Indus (Islam and Talbot, 1968). This behaviour contrasts with that of fry spawned in the mountain headstreams of Indian rivers, which according to Day (1958) take their time migrating downstream and are often trapped for one or more dry seasons in the residual pools of the main river channel. The larvae of some species which lay their eggs in floodplain lagoons congregate on the bottom and show the peculiar behaviour of frequently ascending to the surface and then sinking back down again. Daget (1957a) noted this behaviour in *Heterotis niloticus* and interpreted it as a respiratory adaptation. However, similar behaviour in *Labeo niloticus* (Fryer and Whitehead, 1959) and *Lucioperca lucioperca* (Belyy, 1972) is thought to be to catch currents for transport to the river and eventually downstream. In fact, Belyy found that fry were moved for considerable distances in this manner and it could be that the same behavioural pattern serves the two functions equally.

In estuarine deltas where sea water penetrates upstream in the dry season, freshwater species also undergo local movements to avoid the saline conditions. Reizer (1974) has noted that the more sensitive species move as a wave in front of the saline tongue. In the Senegal river these are *Hyperopisus bebe*, *Mormyrus rume*, *Mormyrops deliciosus*,

Marcusenius senegalensis, Alestes dentex, Citharinus citharus, Labeo senegalensis and *Schilbe mystus*. Similar migrations undoubtedly occur in all rivers having a long zone of interaction between sea and fresh waters.

Marine and brackish-water species also show a variety of migration patterns. Entry into the lower reaches of the river with the saline waters during the dry season may be regarded as an extension of the estuarine environment. However, penetration into the fresh waters further upstream is also a common feature which has been described from many systems. Fish of marine origin regularly move many hundreds of kilometres up such rivers as the Niger in Africa (Reed *et al.*, 1967), the Mekong in Asia (Shiraishi, 1970) or the Magdalena in South America (Dahl, 1971). These penetrations of the freshwater habitat may be for feeding or for breeding. Some notable anadromous migrations also occur, for instance that of *Hilsa ilisha*, which moves up many Indian and Southeast Asian rivers to spawn (Pillay and Rosa, 1963) or the golden perch which migrates up to 800 km up the Murray river in Australia (Butcher, 1967). Other, less spectacular, breeding migrations are those of the eleotrids, such as *Batanga`lebretonis* or *Dormitator latifrons*, which enter rivers to spawn on the flooded vegetation fringes of the lower reaches.

Distance and speed of movements

The main long-distance migrations of tropical freshwater fish are those undertaken by the South American 'Piracema' species. Tagging experiments on various characin species of the Paraná system have yielded considerable information on the complexity and extent of such migrations (Fig. 3.9). Bonetto and Pignalberi (1964) tagged 40 000 fishes of which 70 per cent were *Prochilodus platensis*. Fish released upstream in Paso de la Patria ((1) in Fig. 3.9) in August and Puerto Gaboto (2) in July and September, moved downstream. Fish released near the middle of the river at Paso de la Patria in September moved both upstream and downstream. Those released at Bella Vista (3) in May and at La Plata (4) in April and November migrated upriver. These movements were interpreted as reproductive migrations upriver in spring and autumn and trophic migrations downstream after spawning. The patterns are complicated by the nature of the flood regimes and by the assumed existence of separate upriver and downriver populations. In this series of experiments the maximum distance travelled downstream by *P. platensis* was 650 km at 3·3 km day^{-1}, although the mean migration speed was 7 km day^{-1}. In 1962 the maximum distance covered downstream was 500 km at a mean speed of 5·8 km day^{-1}. However, a considerable proportion of the fish did not migrate but stayed near the site of release. *Salminus maxillosus* tagged in the same series of experiments travelled further, 1 000 km in 60 days (16·7 km day^{-1}).

A second series of taggings described by Bonetto *et al.* (1971) gave more details of migration distances. Fish were tagged at Sauce Vieja (5)

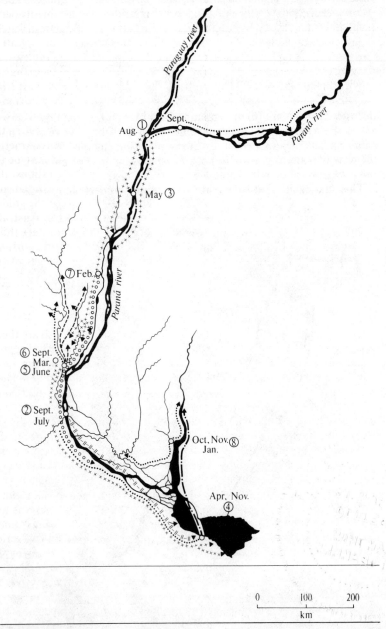

Fig. 3.9 Migration patterns of *Prochilodus platensis* within the Paraná river system (adapted from Bonetto and Pignalberi, 1964 and Bonetto *et al.*, 1971); the different symbols distinguish between the various batches of fish marked on the results shown in the figure. Encircled figures referred to in text.

Table 3.3 Upstream and downstream migration rates in km day⁻¹ of *Prochilodus platensis* and *Salminus maxillosus* from Argentinian waters of the river Paraná (from data in Bonetto *et al.*, 1971)

	Upstream			Downstream		
	Min.	Mean	Max.	Min.	Mean	Max.
P. platensis	0·5	(3·2)	8·7	0·3	(2·8)	7·0
S. maxillosus	0·9	(9·3)	21·5	0·4	(3·9)	2·5

in June, Monte Vera (6) in September and March, Laguna Los Jacintos (7) in February and Gualeguaychu (8) in October, November and January. The mean speed of upstream migration emerged as faster than the downstream migration in both *Prochilodus platensis* and *Salminus maxillosus* as shown in Table 3.3.

This indicates that upstream migrations undertaken under the

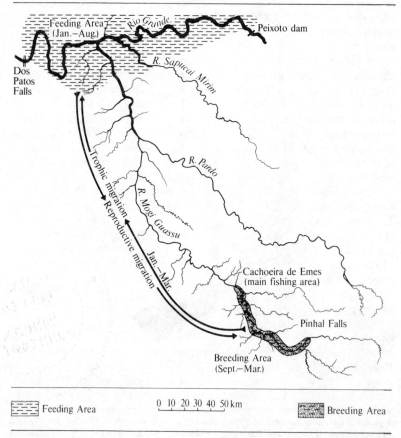

Fig. 3.10 Migration of 'Piracema' species within the Mogi–Pardo–Grande river ecosystem. (After Godoy, 1975.)

powerful physiological stimuli associated with breeding are likely to be generally faster than the more leisurely return, with deviations for feeding and resting on the way.

A similar conclusion was reached by Godoy (1975) in his work on the Mogi Guassu and Rio Grande subsystem of the Paraná (Fig. 3.10). Here, 17 species of characins migrate every year over a total distance of 1 228 km to and from the upriver spawning sites. Recorded speeds upriver ranged from 5 to 8 km day^{-1} for *Prochilodus scrofa*, 2·5–10·0 km day^{-1} for *Salminus maxillosus* and 3 km day^{-1} for *Leporinus copelandii*. After spawning, fish moved downstream at between 3 and 5 km day^{-1}.

Bayley (1973) also recorded migrations of *Prochilodus platensis* in the Pilcomayo tributary of the Paraná. Here he assumed the fish to travel at least 450 km from the downstream floodplains to the upriver spawning site. Migrations of the same type were described by INDERENA (1973) from the Magdalena river, Colombia, where the 'Subienda' migration of *Brycon moorei, Pimelodus clarias, Prochilodus reticulatus* and *Pseudoplatystoma fasciatum*, among other species, from the cienagas of the floodplain to the breeding grounds in small Andean tributary streams is about 500 km.

In Africa the dry-season migrations are associated mainly with dispersal of fish in the river system. In the Niger river, for instance, Daget (1952) studied *Alestes leuciscus* which travelled at 1–1·5 km hr^{-1} up to a maximum of about 9 km day^{-1}. Total distances traversed were as great as 400 km before the construction of the Markala dam. Many migratory species including *A. baremoze* and *A. dentex* are indicated by Blache and Miton (1962) as undertaking potamodromous movements of up to 650 km between Lake Chad and the upstream swamps. Other recorded African breeding migrations are of shorter, but still impressive lengths. The ascent of species from Lake Victoria up the Nzoia river in Kenya during the flood were classed by Whitehead (1959a) as long duration (80 km or more), *Barbus altianalis*; medium duration (15–25 km), *Labeo victorianus* and *Schilbe mystus* and short duration (up to 8 km), *Alestes nurse*. Another *Labeo, L. altivelis* migrated up to 150 km up the Luapula river from Lake Mweru at the beginning of the floods. Williams (1971) tagged several species of fish as they left the Kafue river plains and found that most undertook movements of up to 60 km upstream and 120 km downstream.

Among Asiatic species the Indian major carps appear to move only locally and mainly laterally on to the floodplains within the Ganges and other river systems (Jhingran, 1968, for *Catla catla*, and Khan and Jhingran, 1975, for *Labeo rohita*). In the Mekong, however, several species have been recorded as covering large distances. Shiraishi (1970) quoted migration distances of up to 1 000 km between the delta and Vientiane during the wet season. However, there appears to be little evidence to support this and more reasonable estimates were given by Bardach (1959) for the movement of *Pangasius sutchi* from the Grand Lac to the Khone Falls, a distance of some 300–400 km. Pantulu (1970) did mention that *Pangasianodon gigas* is suspected of spectacularly long migrations, although other species in the Mekong, including *Pangasius pangasius, P. sanitwongsei, Cirrhinus auratus, Probarbus jullieni* and *Thynnichthys thynnoides* only undertake medium to long-range migrations.

Timing of migrations

The timing of the initiation of longitudinal migration varies considerably according to various groups of species.

Movements of fish in the Mekong river recorded from the commercial fishery at Khone Falls (Chanthepha, 1972) showed two separate groups. The first, consisting of cyprinids, passed upstream in November to February and probably represented dispersal migrations after leaving the floodplain. The second group, mainly of siluroids, passed up through the falls from mid-April to July and were possible pre-spawning migrations. The 'Piracema' species of the Mogi Guassu river (Godoy, 1975) and the 'Subienda' species of the Magdalena (INDERENA, 1973) migrate upstream at low water and so time their movement as to arrive in the upstream spawning sites as the flood begins to rise there. The same pattern also appears in the Lake Chad basin, where *Alestes dentex* and *A. baremoze* move up the Chari and Logone rivers at low water, arriving at the entrance to the Yaérés floodplains at the beginning of the flood (Stauch, pers. comm.). This recurrence of pattern in two continents gives the impression that extensive dry-season breeding migrations tend to be a characin characteristic, although some siluroids also participate in the 'Subienda'. This impression is supported by the movements of *A. leuciscus* and *A. nurse* within the Central Delta of the Niger, although in these species the migration is for dispersal rather than spawning (Daget, 1952). The timing of the 'Piracema' in Latin America gives the impression that it is a continuation of the dispersal migrations from the floodplain at drawdown. This could similarly apply to movements of *Alestes* in the Central Delta and riverine stocks of *Alestes* in the Chari and Logone rivers of the Lake Chad basin. Migration of *Alestes* out of Lake Chad itself at this time is less easily explicable on these grounds, unless it is interpreted as a relict behaviour pattern of these primarily riverine species.

Other families of migratory fish, particularly the mormyrids in Africa and some siluroids and most cyprinids in Africa and Asia, normally initiate their riverine spawning migrations as the floods appear. In some cases, for example, *Labeo victorianus* and other small cyprinids in Lake Victoria, riverine migration may be preceded by a preparatory movement to the river mouth in the lake itself (Cadwalladr, 1965a). However, the arrival of the first freshets of the floods in the river seems to trigger longitudinal migratory behaviour in the majority of species. This migratory urge appears to be transformed into a general impulse for lateral movements as the bankfull stage is reached and floods spill on to the floodplain. The observations of several workers that many fish migrate actively against the current up channels where water is flowing out of the plain, rather than to enter passively on inflowing currents, points to the physiological orientation of such movements.

Migration on to the floodplain seems to develop as an ordered sequence of species. Sao-Leang and Dom Saveun (1955) described the movements of fish in the Mekong as a series of waves with siluroids entering early in the sequence and whitefish later. In the Niger (FAO/UN, 1970), swamp-tolerant species which often stay in the larger lagoons over the dry season, tended to enter first from the river. Earlier entries included species of *Clarias, Distichodus, Citharinus* and *Labeo*, while *Alestes, Tilapia,* mormyrids, *Schilbe* and *Synodontis* entered second. In the Kafue flats, Williams (1971) has observed a different sequence that to a certain extent contradicts that observed above. Here, *Clarias, Schilbe, Barbus* and *Tilapia* migrated on to the plain while the water is still quite low and *Serranochromis* and *Haplochromis* only moved on to the plain later. The early movement of *Tilapia* and the clariids is confirmed by the University of Idaho *et al.* (1971) for the same area. Because of the lack of information, which is difficult to collect, the situation with regard to movement during rising water is far from clear, although the concept of phased migration of species on to the plain is probably sufficiently well established.

Movements off the plain are more easily studied and these, too, show that fish leave in a distinct sequence. This appears to be roughly the reverse of the sequence in which fish enter the plain. In the Mekong, studies by Blache and Goosens (1954) and by Sao-Leang and Dom Saveun (1955) from trap catches of over 100 species showed that movement at the level of Quatre Bras occurs between October and February. Here the sequence of migration was apparently conditioned primarily by the size of the fish, the larger fish and larger species leaving first. Lunar phase also influenced the timing of the migration of whitefish which takes place only during the second quarter to full moon each month. Thus, there were monthly waves of migration in which a few of the largest fish moved in October and November. In December to January mixed groups of large fish including *Cirrhinus auratus, Osteochilus hasselti, Pangasius sutchi, P. larnaudi, Belodontichthys* and *Cyclocheilichthys* were caught. In February smaller species such as *Thynnichthys thynnoides, Cirrhinus jullieni* and *Botia modesta* dominated in the catch.

Studies by Durand (1970 and 1971) on the succession of species passing through the El Beid river which drains the Yaérés, also pointed to there being a definite sequence of species which correspond to different water masses. The first group, which moved at high water and had a very clear peak in November and December, consisted of *Marcusenius cyprinoides, Hyperopisus bebe, Alestes dentex* and *Labeo senegalensis*, preceded by a group of accompanying species, *Alestes baremoze, Polypterus bichir, Hydrocynus brevis* and *Lates niloticus* and followed by *Distichodus rostratus, Sarotherodon aureus,*

Pollimyrus isidori and *Distichodus brevipinnis*. A second well-defined group consisting of *Sarotherodon galilaeus, Brienomyrus niger, Barbus* and *Clarias* species was very abundant in January and *Ichthyoborus besse, Synodontis auritus, S. schall* and *Schilbe mystus* appeared most strongly in February. The first group corresponded to fish migrating at the end of the Logone floods, the second and third groups move with the water draining off the flooded plain. This example of the migrations from the Yaérés serves to illustrate the probable complexity of migration patterns elsewhere.

That adult fish leave the plain before the young-of-the-year is borne out by many authors. For example Motwani (FAO/UN, 1970a) remarked that older age groups leave the swamps of the Niger and Benue river first. The juveniles remain on the floodplain until the later stages of its emptying. The University of Idaho *et al.* (1971) and Williams (1971) noted the same phenomenon in the Kafue river. In the Yaérés, the breeding fish often do not return through the El Beid river, preferring to re-enter the lake via the main channels of the Chari and Logone rivers. Thus Durand (1970) was able to record that young fish make up 95 per cent of the El Beid catch by number and weight. This phenomenon is mainly caused by the peculiar flow patterns of this system (Fig. 3.11) which only allow the adult fish to fight against the currents entering the plain through the levées and thus to regain the main channel of the river. The young fish are not strong enough to do this and are more strongly influenced by the current which directs them down the El Beid as it drains the plain. More extreme examples of delayed migration are shown by the juveniles of *Prochilodus platensis*, which remain in the floodplain pools of the Paraná river during an entire dry season before entering the river after the next flood (Bonetto, 1975). *Prochilodus* species in the Apure river show similar behaviour (Matthes, pers. comm.). That return migrations by juveniles are more complex than just a passive movement under the influence of the movement of water as it leaves the plain is indicated by the different behaviour of two very similar species of small cyprinid in a stream system flowing into Lake Victoria (Welcomme, 1969) (Fig. 3.12). Here the adults of both species left the upstream swamps towards the end of the flood. The juveniles of one species, *Barbus kerstenii* remained only a short time in the swamps, moving quickly to the drainage channels and the river and migrating shortly after to the lake. *B. apleurogramma,* on the other hand, tended to hold on in the swamps until they are almost dry, moving to the drainage channels and later to the river where it remains throughout the dry season. These movements occurred at quite characteristic sizes. By contrast a third sequence of movement is shown by a small cichlid which inhabited the same system and did not enter the lake.

External factors which might stimulate spawning migrations have been discussed for many years, somewhat inconclusively. In view of the great differences in timing, both of the initiation of movement and of

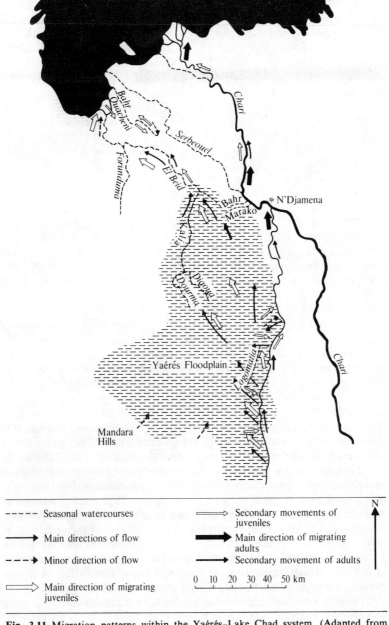

Fig. 3.11 Migration patterns within the Yaérés–Lake Chad system. (Adapted from Durand, 1970.)

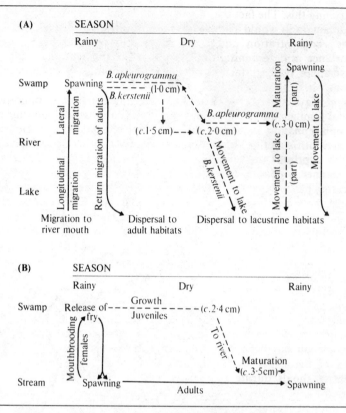

Fig. 3.12 Distribution and sequence of migration of species in a river floodplain system adjacent to Lake Victoria: (A) *Barbus kerstenii* and *B. apleurogramma*; (B) *Hemihaplochromis multicolor*. (After Welcomme, 1969.)

spawning among the many species inhabiting tropical river systems, it is likely that there are a whole range of fine-tuning stimuli which influence the various species in different ways. Because the end of the flood tends to be less predictable than the beginning, and the behaviour of the fish at this time is not apparently subject to a strong physiological impulse such as reproduction, it seems reasonable to suppose that simple mechanical and chemical factors would be sufficient to initiate movement out of the floodplain habitats. It is important to the survival of the species that such signals should anticipate the onset of conditions that would be lethal to the majority of the population. Nevertheless, it does seem that stimuli for return migrations are often less than totally effective in this respect, as huge quantities of fish are stranded and die every year.

The fairly generally noted tendency for both the larger species and the larger individuals of each species to leave the floodplain earlier than the smaller fish is probably indicative that depth is one of the major factors controlling this. The fact that large fish often fail to move out of deeper floodplain pools would also tend to support this supposition. Dissolved oxygen concentration and temperature also seem to be of major importance in determining the distribution of fish within the system, and changes in these factors are liable to provoke fish into leaving regions where conditions are less than optimal.

Light plays a very strong role in regulating the time of migration. Several families move mainly at night. In Asia these include siluroids and ophicephalids, in Africa siluroids, ophicephalids and mormyrids, and in South America siluroids and gymnotiids. Other fishes including cichlids, cyprinids and some characins, tend to move by day. There is, in this manner a possibility for round-the-clock utilization of both the migratory pathways and the slack-water refuges and resting places. That diurnal sequences of migration may be quite complex is evidenced by Lowe-McConnell's (1964) observations on the Rupununi system. Here, the periods for peak migration were more closely defined as follows: dawn and early morning – *Cichla ocellaris, Osteoglossum*; daytime – *Serrasalmus nattereri, Metynnis* sp., *Geophagus jurupari, Cichla ocellaris, Cichlosoma severum, Leporinus friderici*; late afternoon – *Brycon falcatus, Metynnis* sp.; evening (just after dark) – *Prochilodus insignis, Schizodon fasciatum*; night – *Pimelodus* and other catfishes.

The strong influence of lunar phase on the timing of the migration of whitefish in the Mekong has already been mentioned. A similar phenomenon has been described for *Alestes leuciscus* in the Central Delta of the Niger by Daget (1952). This characin species forms extensive shoals during moonlit nights for their upstream dispersal migrations. When there is no moon the shoals dissociate. Migration is also initiated as soon after the draining of the floodplain as is consistent with lunar phase, and because of the topography and drawdown regime of the Central Delta, four different migratory groups are formed according to the successive coincidence of full moon and low water as the flood recedes downriver. Other *Alestes* species, *A. nurse, A. dentex* and *A. baremoze* also migrate upstream, but are not ordered by lunar phase. In fact, upstream movements of *A. nurse* always precede movements of *A. leuciscus* from the same portion of floodplain.

3.5 Feeding

Source of food

The richness and variability of the floodplain habitats provide a wide range of possible food organisms and substrates. These originate either from within the aquatic system itself (autochthonous food sources) or from outside the system (allochthonous food sources), although they are all ultimately dependent on allochthonous materials in the form of alluvial silt, dissolved nutrients or decomposition products on inundated ground. The major sources of food are as follows:

Autochthonous: Plankton community   – phytoplankton
                                        – zooplankton
                  Benthic community   – mud and associated
                                          microorganisms
                                        – insects, worms and
                                          small crustaceans
                                        – molluscs
                                        – larger decapod crustaceans
                  Plants, including filamentous algae and sub-
                  mersed, floating or emergent higher vegetation
                  'Aufwuchs' community – epiphytic or epilithic algae
                                        – associated animals
(This category can include the root fauna and flora of floating
vegetation.)   Neuston, including surface-living insects and
                  larvae at the air/water interface.
                  Fish, including eggs and larval forms.
Allochthonous: Vegetable matter   – leaves, roots, flowers, fruit
                  and seeds of plants growing near water which
                  contribute to the surface drift and to the
                  mud and detritus.
                  Animal matter   – insects, including ants,
                  termites, beatles, flies, together with arachnids,
                  worms, etc. falling into the water.

Feeding habits of individual fish species inhabiting floodplains have
been described by many authors (Daget, 1954 for the Niger; Blache,
1964 for the Chad basin; FAO/UN, 1968b for the Zambezi; Carey, 1968
for the Kafue). These show that, despite considerable anatomical
specialization of dentition, jaw shape, body form and alimentary tract,
there is apparently little corresponding exclusiveness of food selected in
many of the species. Because of this Knöppel (1970), in his study of the
nutrient ecology of 49 species from streams and lakes of the Amazonian
floodplain and terra firma, was forced to conclude that there were no
specialists in these habitats. That fish of the type of forested aquatic
habitat studied by Knöppel concentrate on allochthonous food as the
most abundant food source, is borne out by other workers, but
considerable opportunism has also been found in species from savanna
rivers. For example, Cabrera *et al.* (1973b) found that the diet of
Basilichthys bonariensis in the Plata system could be separated into
three main elements. These were:
1. constant elements – algae, mud and vegetable remains;
2. seasonal elements – cladocerans, copepods, diatoms, gasteropods,
   malacostraca and fish, which appeared mainly during the flood;
3. occasional elements – such as rotifers and ostracods.
   This type of feeding is very common where a basic type is at the same
time flexible enough to take advantage of any other food items as and
when they are available. Even species such as piranhas (*Serrasalmus*
spp.) which are noted for their predatorial ferocity can switch to an

alternative diet of mud and vegetable detritus during the dry season (Mago-Leccia, 1970). Many species select a succession of food types as the flood cycle progresses. Typical of these are the *Alestes* spp. studied by Daget (1952) that changed from a diet of insects and seeds or even higher vegetation during rising waters, to feeding on phytoplankton as the waters begin to contract. There is a tendency for food preferences to change as individuals grow older, and the diet of juvenile fish often differs widely from that of the adults of the same species. Young of *Prochilodus platensis*, for example, feed on planktonic diatoms and crustaceans, whereas the adults are uniquely mud-eaters (Vidal, 1967). Most extreme in this respect are the juveniles of the major piscivorous predators, such as *Lates niloticus* or *Hydrocynus* sp. which eat small crustaceans or even phytoplankton. It may be concluded from this that the majority of floodplain species are very flexible in their feeding habits.

Nevertheless, despite the variety of food taken by any one species, it is generally possible to classify fish into broad categories according to their predominant feeding habits. Matthes (1964) distinguished the following categories in the Zaïre river basin.

Mud-feeders, which eat finely divided silt, together with the microorganisms and organic decay products it contains. In the floodplain pools this niche is filled by *Phractolaemus ansorgei*.

Detritus-feeders, which ingest mainly vegetable debris, leaf litter and the associated animal communities: e.g. *Stomatorhinus humilior, Clarias buthupogon, Clariaballes variabilis, C. brevibarbis, C. melas, Channallabes apus*.

Omnivores, which are widely represented by all families and most genera in the floodplain water bodies by *Stomatorhinus fuliginosus* and *Ctenopoma fasciolatum*.

Herbivores, which can be further separated into:
1. microherbivores which eat algae and diatoms;
2. macroherbivores which eat higher plants.

These were unrepresented in the floodplain pools, but in adjacent floating prairies *Neolebias gracilis, Distichodus affinis* and *Synodontis nummifer* ate this type of food.

Plankton feeders, which are rare owing to the lack of plankton in the riverine environment, but which are nevertheless represented by *Aplocheilichthys myersi* in the floating vegetation.

Carnivores, the most important group which subdivide into:
1. Meso-predators which feed mostly on insects and crustaceans and which are either:
    (a) Feeders on allochthonous matter or neuston, such as *Pantodon buchholzi, Ctenopoma nigropannosum* or *C. ansorgei* in the pools;
    (b) bottom feeders which eat insects and molluscs from the bottom, such as *Polypterus retropinnis, Stomatorhinus polli, Clarias submarginatus, Kribia nana*; or

    (c) carnivorous browsers which inhabit floating vegetation and feed on the small insects and crustaceans found there, for example *Xenomystus nigri, Nannocharax schoutedeni, Hemistichodus mesmaekersi, Heterochromis multidens* or *Ctenopoma kingsleyae*.

2. Macro-predators:

    (a) generalized predators which feed on fish or larger invertebrates such as decapod crustaceans or insect larvae; in floodplain pools *Clarias platycephalus* feeds in this manner;

    (b) piscivorous predators which feed only on fish; although Matthes did not record any such species in the floodplain pools, fish such as *Parophiocephalus obscurus, Hydrocynus vittatus* or *Lates niloticus* have been recorded from such habitats elsewhere.

    (c) fin nippers which are representative of specialized predators generally.

Similar tabulations have been presented by other authors, for example Marlier (1967) who investigated the feeding habits of fish in the Lago Redondo of the Amazonian várzea (Table 3.4) and Vaas (1953) who classified the fish fauna of the Kapuas river, West Borneo (Table 3.5).

The trophic relationships of river and floodplain communities can be summarized as a generalized food web of the type shown in Fig. 3.13. Not all elements of this diagram are necessarily present in all environments. As we have seen, the heavy bias towards allochthonous food in the forest environment favours sequences following from this source of nutrition and diminishes the importance of phytoplankton.

When feeding habits are matched with habitats some complex relationships emerge, as is shown by Matthes (1964) for Lake Tumba and the adjacent forested floodplains of the Ikela region. Table 3.6 illustrates this for the lower Ouémé river and floodplain during the dry season. Note in this instance that one of the major primary feeders on detritus are the decapod crustacea *Macrobrachium macrobrachion* and *Caridina* spp. which, because of their size and abundance, are more closely allied to the fish ecologically than they are to the other invertebrate fauna.

Primary production is located more in the proliferation of higher plants than in the phytoplankton. Epiphytic algae are abundant only at the fringes of the vegetation mass. Higher plants are themselves useful for food when young and tender, although fruit and seeds do figure in the diet of some species. The major contribution of higher plants to the nutrient flow is by decay and the consequent enrichment of the detritus. Because accessible primary plant foods are not common on the river–floodplain habitats, purely herbivorous species are relatively rare. Species that do eat higher plants or phytoplankton usually have an alternative source of food. In the case of higher plant browsers such as

Table 3.4 Fish fauna of the Lago Redondo classified according to their feeding habits (after Marlier, 1967)

STENOPHAGES

Carnivores

Unspecialized	Specialized	
Serrasalmus nattereri	Piscivores	*Arapaima gigas*
S. elongatus		*Boulangerella cuvieri*
Eigenmannia virescens		*Ageneiosus ucayalensis*
Pimelodella cristata		*Symbranchus marmoratus*
Plagioscion squamosissimus		*Cichla ocellaris*
Geophagus surinamensis	Insectivores	*Triportheus elongatus*
Apistogramma taeniatum		*Oxydoras niger*
Colomesus psittacus (= *asellus*)	Zooplankton feeders	*Metynnis hypsauchen*
		Astyanax fasciatus
		Hypopthalmus edentatus

Herbivores

Unspecialized	Specialized	
Anodus laticeps	Grass seeds	*Ctenobrycon hauxvellianus*
Cichlasoma bimaculatus	Water grasses	*Metynnis maculatus*
C. festivum		*Leporinus maculatus*
	Fruit	*Colossoma bidens*
	Algae and 'Aufwuchs'	*Poecilobrycon trifasciatus*
		P. unifasciatus

Mud-eaters

Curimatus spp.
Prochilodus sp.
Pterygoplichthys multiradiatus
Potamorhina pristigaster

EURYPHAGES

Predominantly carnivores

Osteoglossum bicirrhosum
Serrasalmus rhombeus

Predominantly herbivores

Phytoplankton, zooplankton	*Anchoviella brevirostris*
Grass leaves and seeds, insects	*Pyrrhulina brevis*
	Hyphessobrycon rosaceus
	H. callistus
Benthic and epiphytic diatoms and Cladocera	*Hyphessobrycon* sp.
	Cheirodon piaba
Algae, grass and Cladocera	*Metynnis lippincottianus*
'Aufwuchs'	*Corydoras* sp.
Seeds, molluscs	*Acarichthys heckeli*
Littoral zooplankton and higher plants	*Pterophyllum scalare*

Table 3.5 Fish fauna of the Kapuas river and adjacent lakes and river arms, classified according to their feeding habits (after Vaas, 1953) (main food = xx, additional food = x)

Plankton feeders	*Helostoma temmincki*
	Thynnichthys thynnoides
	T. polylepis
	Dangila ocellata
	D. festiva
Periphyton and vegetable feeders	*Amblyrynchichthys truncatus*
	Osteochilus melanopleura
	O. brevicaudata
	O. waandersi
	O. vittatus
Vegetable feeders on submerged higher plants, inundated land plants, fruits and seeds	*Puntius waandersi*
	P. nini
	P. bulu
	P. schwanefeldi
	Leptobarbus hoeveni
	L. melanotaenia
	Pristolepis fasciatus
	Osphronemus gouramy
Omnivores feeding mainly on insects and larvae, zooplankton	*Balantiocheilus melanopterus*
	Cyclochilus repasson
	Luciosoma trinema
	Rasbora argyrotaenia
	R. vaillanti
Eaters of insects at surface	*Chela oxygastroides*
	Toxotes chatareus
Omnivorous bottom feeders	*Barynotus microlepis*
	Pangasius pangasius
	P. polyuranodon
	Mastacembelus armatus favus
	Mastacembelus argus
Omnivorous predators	*Macrones nigriceps*
	M. nemurus
	Hemisilurus chaperi
	H. scleronema
Predators on small fish and small animals, insects, shrimps	*Lycothrissa crocodilus*
	Cryptopterus cryptopterus
	C. schilbeides
	C. limpok
	C. micronema
	Macrochirichthys macrochirus
	Setipinna melanochir
	Datnioides microlepis
	Hampala bimaculata

Phytoplankton	Periphyton	Filamentous algae	Bottom algae	Submerged plants inundated land plants, fruit seeds	Small zooplankton	Cladocera, copepods Rotifera	Insects and their larvae	Allochthonous insects	Shrimps	Insect larvae in the Bottom, worms	Fish, prawns, crabs
XX					X						
XX	XX	X			X						
XX	X	X			X						
XX	X	X			X						
XX	X	X			X						
X	XX		X		X						
X	XX	X	X	XX							
X	XX	X	X	XX							
X	XX	X	X	XX							
		X		XX			X				
X		X	X	XX	X	X	X				
		X		XX			X				
		X		XX			X				
		X		XX							
		X		XX							
		X		XX							
		X	X	XX			X				
X						XX	X				
		X					XX				
X		X			X	XX					
X		X			X	XX					
X		X			X	XX	X	X			
					X	XX	X	X			
					X	X	X	XX	X		
				X			XX		X		
				X			X			XX	
				X			X			XX	
				X			X			XX	
				X			X			XX	
						X	XX		XX		X
						X	XX		XX		X
						X					XX
						X					XX
							X		X		XX
							X		X		XX
							X		X		XX
							X		X		XX
							X		X		XX
							X		XX		XX
							X				XX
									XX		XX
							X		X		XX

(Continued)

Large predators eating fish of all sizes, shrimps, prawns and crabs	*Ophicephalus striatus*
	O. micropeltes
	O. pleurophthalmus
	O. lucius
	Notopterus chitala
	Wallago leeri
	Silurodes hypopthalmus

Tilapia zillii, the fish often have recourse to vegetable detritus for the consumption of which they are equally well adapted. Similarly, the fine gill rakers of microphages, such as *Sarotherodon galilaeus* or *Heterotis niloticus* are as well adapted for the straining of flocculent mud deposits as phytoplankton.

The general absence of primary feeders means that other types of food dominate in the diet of floodplain species. Three categories emerge as of particular importance. These are:

1. allochthonous material;
2. mud and detritus; and
3. other animal elements of the aquatic community.

Allochthonous material
Many workers from all three continents have remarked on the quantity of allochthonous material consumed by fish living on floodplains. Geisler *et al.* (1973) and Roberts (1973) have noted that food from terrestrial sources is important in forested blackwater rivers, both in the Amazon and Zaïre basins. The same phenomenon has been observed in the Mekong basin, especially in the flooded forest surrounding the Grand Lac. In fact, on forested floodplains the rain of animal and vegetable matter from the overhanging vegetation is the only appreciable source of food and all food webs start from it. Most species in these habitats show great flexibility in the type of allochthonous food taken, but some fish such as the fructivorous *Colossoma* have specialized in using particular food items. Other species have become adapted to taking organisms from outside the aquatic system, the most extreme example of this being found in the Archer fish (*Toxotes*) which shoots water droplets at insects which settle on overhanging vegetation so as to knock them into the water. Fittkau (1973) has illustrated the type of simplified nutrient–food–consumer cycles that are found in the

Phytoplankton	Periphyton	Filamentous algae	Bottom algae	Submerged plants, inundated land plants, fruit seeds	Small zooplankton	Cladocera, copepods Rotifera	Insects and their larvae	Allochthonous insects	Shrimps	Insect larvae in the bottom, worms	Fish, prawns, crabs
									X		XX
									X		XX
									X		XX
									X		XX
									X		XX
									X		XX
									X		XX

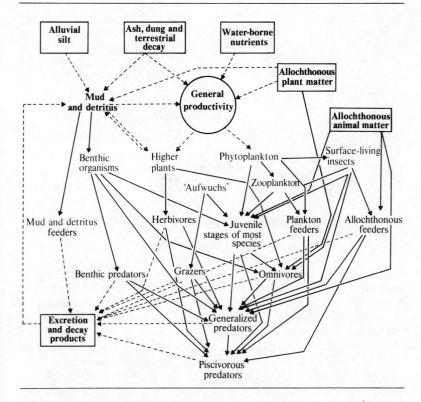

Fig. 3.13 Diagram of trophic relationships in a river–floodplain community. Broken line = influence; solid line = feeding interaction.

Table 3.6 Food sources and principal dry-season habitats of Ouémé fishes

	Main river channels		
	Open water	Bottom	Vegetated areas
Mud feeders		*Heterotis niloticus* *Citharinus latus* *Labeo ogunensis*	
Detritus feeders		*Physailia pellucida* *Eutropiellus buffei* *Synodontis schall*	*Synodontis schall*
Omnivorous	*Alestes nurse*	*Marcusenius brucii* *Brienomyrus niger* *Auchenoglanis* *occidentalis*	*Alestes macrolepidotus* *Neolebias unifasciatus*
Herbivorous: micro		*Labeo senegalensis*	*Tilapia mariae*
macro			*Distichodus rostratus* *Tilapia guineensis*
Plankton feeders	*Ethmalosa fimbriata** *Pellonulla afzeliusii*		
Carnivorous: **Bottom feeders**		*Hyperopisus* *occidentalis* † *Mormyrus rume* † *Synodontis sorex* *Synodontis* *melanopterus* † *Petrocephalus bane* ‡ *Cyphomyrus pictus* ‡	*Hemichromis* *bimaculatus* *Synodontis* *melanopterus*
Allochtonous **+neuston feeders**	*Alestes chaperi*		*Ctenopoma kingsleyae*
'Aufwuchs' browsers		*Brienomyrus* *brachyistius* *Chromidotilapia* *guntheri*	
Generalized **predators**	*Schilbe mystus* *Eutropius niloticus*	*Chrysichthys* *auratus* *C. nigrodigitatus* *Eleotris senegalensis*	*Parophiocephalus* *africanus*
Piscivorous **predators**	*Hydrocynus* *forskahlii* *H. vittatus*	*Bagrus docmac* *Lates niloticus*	*Hemichromis fasciatus* *Polypterus senegalus* *Hepsetus odoe*

* Marine origin.
† Mud bottom.
‡ Sand bottom.

Floodplain pools and lagoons

Open water	Bottom	Vegetated areas
	Heterotis niloticus *Citharinus latus* *Clarias dahomeyensis*	*Clarias dahomeyensis*
	Heterobranchus longifilis	*Phractolaemus ansorgii*
	Protopterus annectens *Synodontis nigrita*	*Clarias lazera*
	Tilapia mariae	
		Distichodus rostratus *Tilapia guineensis*
Sarotherodon galilaeus		
	Pollimyrus adspersus	*Chromidotilapia guntheri*
	Synodontis melanopterus	*Thysia ansorgii*
		Ctenopoma kingsleyae *Epiplatys sexfasciatus*
		Xenomystus nigri Juvenile Synodontis and Cichlidae
	Malapterurus electricus	*Calamoichthys calabaricus*
		Parophiocephalus africanus
Hepsetus odoe	*Parophiocephalus obscurus*	*Polypterus senegalus* *Gymnarchus niloticus*

mouth lakes of the Amazonian tributaries (Fig. 3.14). The role of food coming from outside the aquatic system is not confined to forested rivers, as some species inhabiting savanna plains also rely heavily on this source (Kelley in FAO/UN, 1968b). Adaptations to this are such that *Alestes nurse* has been recorded as deliberately jumping against the stems of rice plants to bring down seeds for consumption (Matthes, 1977a).

Mud and detritus

Bottom deposits really represent two rather different kinds of food. The detritus feeders rely on coarser decomposing plant material, together with associated microorganisms and animal communities. These comprise a high proportion of species, particularly in forested habitats or close to floating vegetation where leaf litter is abundant.

Mud itself contains amino acid and other organic products of decay which can be used by fish in combination with the saprophytic bacterial and protozoan microorganisms. Bakare (1970) has analysed this element of the diet of *Citharinus* and *Labeo* in the Niger river. The finer the particle the greater its alimentary value and the preferred particle size was between 0·10 and 0·05 mm, although grains as large as 0·18 mm were taken. The finer fractions contained relatively larger amounts of carbon and nitrogen than did the larger particles. The size of particle

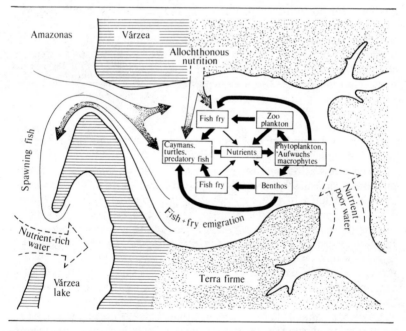

Fig. 3.14 The nutrient cycle in the mouthlake of an Amazonian tributary. (After Fittkau, 1973.)

and the food content of the deposit, which the fish seemed able to detect, appeared to be the major factors limiting the distribution of these species. At the time of sampling about 70 per cent of the bottom deposits were suitable for food. Bakare noted that bottom deposits became progressively depleted of carbon and nitrogen during the flood when *C. citharus* was actively feeding. Periodic drying of the mud may recharge the organic content through the incorporation of dung and other decaying animal and vegetable matter. Both Bakare and Sandon and Tayib (1953) found a high proportion of mud-feeders in the fish populations of the Niger and Nile rivers. In the Niger 10 per cent of the species feed exclusively on this source of food and 10 per cent more include it as a major element of the diet. The number of species, however, is little guide to the true abundance of mud-eating fish. In the La Plata system, for instance, 60 per cent of the ichthyomass of the floodplain pools is located in the main mud-eating (iliophagus) species *Prochilodus platensis* (Bonetto *et al.*, 1969b). Fish of the genus *Prochilodus* are widespread mud-eaters in Latin America and are met in equal abundance in other systems such as the Mogi Guassu (Godoy, 1975) and the Magdalena (Kapetsky *et al.* 1976).

Predation

The population structure of fish in tropical and subtropical rivers usually contains a very high proportion of predatory species. There is a tendency for bottom-feeding forms to dominate by weight on savanna floodplains, but there are usually only a few species at this trophic level. In some systems, too, the decapod crustaceans perform the primary scavenging role and fish are confined to the higher links of the food chain. Piscivorous predators are generally very common and their relative abundance tends to increase during the dry season, giving the very high predator–forage fish ratios recorded by some observers. Mago-Leccia (1970) noted that up to 75 per cent of the population of some floodplain pools consisted of fish-eaters such as *Hoplias malabaricus*. Lowe-McConnell (1964) and Bonetto *et al.* (1969a) equally commented on the abundance of piscivores and the absence of small fish in flood pools at the end of the dry period. I have observed the same phenomenon in the Ouémé river and a number of other workers have commented on it in passing with reference to other African systems. Strangely, prolonged and stabilized high water in the normally fluctuating Everglade marshes also produced an increase in predatory species according to Kushlan (1976). This change was due to the migration into the marsh of large predatory species which are normally intolerant of the extreme swamp conditions. Similar shifts may be anticipated where floodplains are impounded to increase the inundation time.

Lowe-McConnell (1975) concluded that there is a linear succession of dominant food sources in streams and rivers. Fishes in headwater streams depend mostly on allochthonous foods. As the stream enlarges, generalized predators feeding on benthic invertebrates become more important. Finally, in the lower reaches, the accumulation of detritus and soft mud supports a number of mud-eating species. Nikolsky (1937) described this same succession from the Amu Darya and Syr Darya and correlated with it the increase in length and complexity of the guts of fish as one proceeds downstream in these rivers. Floodplains are usually located in the lower or potamon reaches, and, as would be expected from the above succession, trophic chains in savanna rivers are founded on mud-eating forms. However, in forested equatorial rivers, allochthonous material is still of major importance. Food chains of the form:

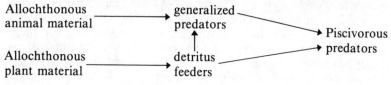

are therefore inclined to be dominant.

Seasonality of feeding

Chevey and Le Poulain (1940) remarked on the fact that fish did not feed in the Mekong system during the dry season. Since then it has become generally accepted that feeding by fish in floodplain rivers is highly seasonal all over the world. The feeding cycle is clearly linked to two factors, firstly the food supply and secondly the population density. During the flood the rapid increase in food organisms, together with the wide dispersal of fish over an extensive biotope, favours intensive feeding. At low water, when the aquatic environment is contracted the fish are concentrated in a few permanent reserves of water and food sources are limited or exhausted, fasting therefore ensues. In the tropics this contrasts with the more or less continuous feeding of fish in lakes; although in some species inhabiting rivers closely allied to lakes such as the Lake Chad–Yaérés system the fish cease feeding at low water despite the adequate supply of food which would enable them to continue feeding at all times of year. In reaches of Indian rivers having little or no floodplain the seasonality of feeding may be reversed. Bhatnagar and Karamchandani (1970) attributed this to the food being washed away by the high current during the flood in the case of *Labeo fimbriatus*. *Tor tor* showed a similar pattern to *L. fimbriatus*, although in this case Desai (1970) correlated the lessened feeding with breeding. It would seem that feeding stops just before and during breeding in floodplain and non-floodplain rivers alike. There are, nevertheless, seasonal differences in the availability of food which depend on the morphology of the river.

The intensive feeding by fish on the floodplain permits them to build up large stores of fat which are sufficient not only to tide the animals through the barren dry season but to elaborate gonadial tissue in preparation for breeding before the floods. Starvation during the dry season causes fish to lose condition and Daget (1956) has traced this for *Tilapia zillii* in the Niger. Figure 3.15 shows the variation in weight over the dry season using condition factor *K*, where

$$K = \frac{weight\ in\ g \times 10^5}{total\ length\ in\ mm^3},$$

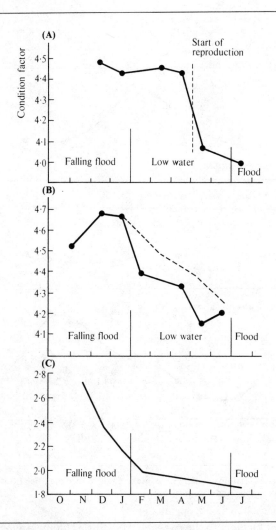

Fig. 3.15 Changes in condition factor between October and July for adult *Tilapia zillii* in (A) the Niger river, and (B) two floodplain pools (after Daget, 1956). Also shown are (C) changes in the condition factor of *Alestes leuciscus* (after Daget, 1957b).

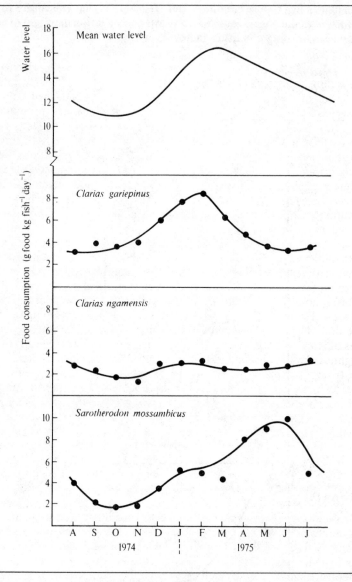

Fig. 3.16 Seasonal variations in daily food intake by three species of fish from the Shire river. (After Willoughby and Tweddle, 1977.)

as an index of change. In the river relatively little change occurred over the dry season until the start of reproduction when there was a sudden reduction in weight corresponding to about 10·7 per cent for the whole period. In a floodplain pool fish ended the flood in better condition, but lost weight more evenly through the dry season: in October and November – fish were fat and full of food ($K = 4·52$); in December – feeding was reduced ($K = 4·68$); January – stomachs empty ($K = 4·67$); February – very little food ($K = 4·39$); March – even less food ($K = 4·48$); April – only mud ($K = 4·34$); May ($K = 4·16$); June ($K = 4·2$). The net loss in weight over five months was 11 per cent. In a second, somewhat richer, pool the loss in weight was less rapid (Fig. 3.15, dashed line). Daget (1952) had previously noted similar seasonal changes in weight with *Alestes*.

The pattern of abundant feeding during the flood and fasting during low water is, perhaps, not as simple as it appears. Observations by Willoughby and Tweddle (1977) indicated that peak feeding takes place at different times in different species (Fig. 3.16). The food consumption of *Clarias gariepinus* in the Shire river system, for instance, reached its maximum just before the flood peak, whereas *Sarotherodon mossambicus* fed more intensively as the floodplains were draining. A third species, *Clarias ngamensis*, fed at a fairly constant rate for most of the year. In all three species food intake was minimal at low water. There are also indications that certain categories of feeders continue to feed throughout the dry season. Microvores such as *Heterotis niloticus* may feed throughout the year, although only at maintenance level during the dry season (Daget, 1957b). Surface feeders also have a continuing food source and *Alestes macrolepidotus* continues to feed long after other species of *Alestes* in the Niger. The change in predator–forage fish ratio throughout the dry season, and the gradual disappearance of smaller fishes from floodplain pools, has been noted by Lowe-McConnell (1964). Nevertheless, predators must stop feeding in other systems and Mago-Leccia (1970), in noting that piranhas turn to mud as a feeding substrate in the dry season, also remarked that small fish are not eaten by predators at low water. Such continued feeding does appear to be somewhat exceptional and most observers confirm the dry-season fast.

3.6 Growth

Fish from most river systems have well-defined rings or annuli on their scales, bones or otoliths, a fact which has been noted from tropical and subtropical systems, as well as from temperate ones. The feature is shown by fish from several families as a representative cross-section of the literature shows. Chevey and Le Poulain (1940) noted rings on the scales of cyprinid species in the Mekong, and rings have been described from other cyprinids such as *Alburnus alburnus* in the Danube (Chitravadivelu, 1974), *Labeo* spp. in both the Gambia (Johnels, 1954) and Indian rivers (Khan and Jhingran, 1975) and *Catla catla* from the Ganges (Natarajan and Jhingran, 1963). Numerous characin species have been studied: *Prochilodus scrofa* (Godoy, 1975) and *P. platensis* (Cabrera and Candia, 1964; Vidal, 1967) in South America, and *Alestes leuciscus* (Daget, 1952) and *A. baremoze* (Durand and Loubens, 1969) in Africa. Cichlids from both African (*Sarotherodon* spp. Dudley, 1972) and Latin American rivers (*Cichlasoma bimaculatus*) (Lowe-McConnell, 1964) have been recorded with annuli on their scales. Johnels (1954) also mentions rings on the scales of *Notopterus* sp. and mormyrids. Other hard parts of the fish also show growth rings. Opercular bones were used by Cordiviola (1971) for ageing *Prochilodus platensis*. In the scaleless siluroids (Candia *et al.*, 1973) have shown clear rings in the otoliths and pectoral spines of *Parapimelodus valenciennesi* and Fenerich *et al.* (1975) have demonstrated their existence in the otoliths of *Pimelodus maculatus*. Pectoral spines and vertebrae were used to age *Clarias* spp. from the Kafue flats by the University of Idaho *et al.* (1971)

The marks or rings have been correlated with the partial or complete cessation of growth during one or more periods of the year. However, in many cases more rings have been recorded than would be expected if ring formation depended solely on a regular seasonal event. Care, therefore, has to be taken in interpreting rings in scales or other hard structures as indicators of age or time series. Nevertheless, at low water feeding either stops completely or is seriously reduced in most species. The fish live on their fat reserves, sometimes losing condition to the point where resorption occurs at the margin of the scales. Durand and Loubens (1969) made a useful distinction between growth in weight and growth in length. The latter is a good indicator of long-term change, but as it depends mainly on skeletal structures it is not so liable to modification during the growth arrest. Growth in weight is as much through the addition of soft tissues including fat. These fat stores are liable to be rapidly modified under adverse conditions, as has been shown for *Tilapia zillii* and *Alestes leuciscus* (Fig. 3.15), and as Durand and Loubens (1970a) showed for male *A. baremoze*, where the condition factor (K) falls from 1·30 in April to 1·00 in September. Of course, care has to be taken in the interpretation of changes in weight and condition factor, as the development of gonadial tissue and discharge of eggs or milt is also reflected in these parameters. However, changes in K are more often slow over the whole dry period than abrupt at the time of breeding, as would be the case if the discharge of reproductive products were the sole cause.

Three main reasons have been advanced for the arrest of growth during several months of the year:

1. temperature;
2. effects associated with drawdown; and
3. reproduction.

In several river systems the growth arrest coincides with a drop in temperature. In the Lake Chad basin, winter temperatures drop at least 8° C below the summer maxima (Durand and Loubens, 1969). Similarly, in the Senegal, Reizer (1974) considered the slower growth from December to February to be correlated with lower temperatures, and in both the lower La Plata system and on the Kafue flats, the minimum rate of growth occurs at the same time as similar drops in temperatures. However, in most of these rivers, low water coincides with the winter and it is difficult to distinguish the effects of the two factors. In the southern Okavango swamps the floods arrive during the colder part of the year (Fox, 1976) which leads to very low growth rates of the fish living there. It is not yet clear when the growth arrest occurs in these waters, although current work may shed some light on this.

In equatorial rivers growth checks occur regularly where there are only minimal changes in temperature. In such circumstances Lowe-McConnell (1964) has suggested that crowding and lessened availability of food brought about by drawdown conditions are responsible. That this, too, cannot be the whole answer is shown by the Lake Chad fishes which stop growing in the lake, even though there is abundant food. In the Niger river Daget (1957b) reported that growth arrests can be distinguished on the scales of carnivores, herbivores, limnivores, insectivores and plankton-eating species, despite the fact that the predators and limnivores at least have sufficient food. Furthermore, some fish such as the young of *Sarotherodon* and *Tilapia* in the Kafue, resume feeding before the onset of the floods, at a time when conditions are at their most cramped (Dudley, 1974).

The effects of population density on growth rate are somewhat problematic. In the Danube, Chitravadivelu (1974) was unable to detect changes in the growth rate of *Alburnus alburnus* and *Rutilus rutilus*, despite great differences in biomass and population density from one year to another. However, Frank (1959) did record increase in growth in *R. rutilus* and *Abramis brama* when the population decreased from $69\,124i$ hm^{-2} to $19\,394i$ hm^{-2} in an Elbe oxbow. This he traced to the greater availability of planktonic food following the decline in competition for this food source. Such conflicting results indicate a need for further investigations of the question of the relationship of food supply to population density, as this, too, influences the amount of fish available to the fishery.

The elaboration of gonadial products during the fasting period probably accelerates the depletion of fat reserves and exaggerates the low physical condition which is reflected as an annulus. It is, however, doubtful whether this is the prime reason for growth checks, as maturation is frequently preceded by a long period of negligible feeding in many species. Furthermore, rings are laid down by immature fish as well as adults. That there may be deep physiological rhythms which dictate the seasonal cessation of growth is suggested by an isolated experiment quoted by Johnels (1954). Here some *Barbus gambiensis*, which had been transported to Sweden and were being maintained in the even conditions of an aquarium, still stopped growing and laid down scale rings at precisely those times when their congeners did so in the Gambia river.

Models of growth

Annuli on scales and other hard parts have been used to calculate growth in many species. Supplementary information and independent estimates of growth have also been made from the analysis of length–frequency distributions for the progression of individual age groups and also from the growth of tagged fish. Comparisons between the various methods of age determination show that they give good agreement, at least in some species (Rao and Rao, 1972; Gupta and Jhingran, 1973). Several workers have used the Von Bertalanffy model of growth:

$$L_t = L_{t\,\infty} \left\{ 1 - \exp[-k(t-t_0)] \right\}$$

in which length at time $t+1$ (L_{t+1}) is a function of length at time t (L_t) according to the Ford–Walford equation:

$$L_{t+} = e^{-k}L_t + L_\infty(1 - e^{-g})$$

where k is the coefficient of growth and L_∞ the theoretical asymptotic length achievable by the species if it grows for an infinite period of time. Most species seem to conform well to this model in respect of growth in length, or when subject to an appropriate conversion factor, in respect of growth in weight, as is shown by examples in Table 3.7

Table 3.7 Representative Von Bertalanffy relationships for growth in length of fish from some tropical river systems

Species	Sex	Growth equation	Authority
Alestes baremoze	M	$L_t = 237.8 \; \{1 - \exp[-0.816(t-0.57)]\}$	Durand and Loubens (1969)
	F	$L_t = 267 \; \{1 - \exp[-0.717(t-0.52)]\}$	Durand and Loubens (1969)
Catla catla	M+F	$L_t = 1275 \; \{1 - \exp[-0.28(t-0.11)]\}$	Natarajan and Jhingran (1975)
Labeo rohita	M+F	$L_t = 1015 \; \{1 - \exp[-0.276(t-0.333)]\}$	Khan and Jhingran (1975)
L. calbasu			
(Ganga river)	M+F	$L_t = 1028 \; \{1 - \exp[-0.15(t-0.19)]\}$	Gupta and Jhingran (1973)
(Godavari river)	M+F	$L_t = 944 \; \{1 - \exp[-0.14(t+0.86)]\}$	Rao and Rao (1972)
Parapimelodus valenciennesi	M+F	$L_t = 333 \; \{1 - \exp[-0.14(t-2.4)]\}$	Candia *et al.* (1973)
Pimelodus maculatus	M	$L_t = 45.4 \; \{1 - \exp[-0.2104(t+0.61)]\}$	Fenerich *et al.* (1975)
	F	$L_t = 56.5 \; \{1 - \exp[-0.1938(t+0.36)]\}$	Fenerich *et al.* (1975)
Prochilodus reticulatus	M+F	$L_t = 41.0 \; \{1 - \exp[-0.20(t-0.35)]\}$	Espinosa and Gimenez (1974)

From the table it may be seen that male and female fish of the same species frequently have different rates of growth and also maximum sizes as indicated by L_∞. Growth curves of some representative species from an African river (Niger) and the Latin American La Plata system show part of the range of interspecific variation (Fig. 3.17). Most species grow very rapidly in their first season, which Lowe-McConnell (1967) regarded as adaptive. Predation is intense in floodplain rivers, so rapid growth to get to a size too large to be swallowed before the shelter of the floating vegetation on the floodplain disappears, is a great advantage. Fish probably also need to attain an adequate size to migrate by the time the floods recede.

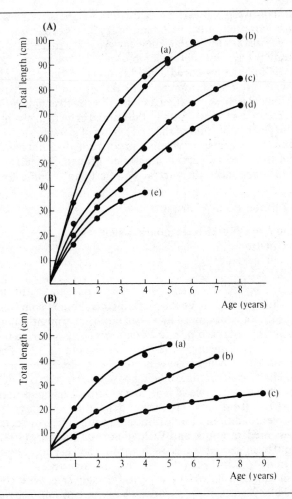

Fig. 3.17 Growth in length of representative fishes from floodplain rivers. (A) Niger river: (a) *Heterotis niloticus*, (b) *Lates niloticus*, (c) *Mormyrops deliciosus*, (d) *Citharinus citharus*, (e) *Eutropius niloticus* (after FAO/UN, 1970a). (B) La Plata system: (a) *Prochilodus platensis* (after Cordiviola de Yuan, 1971), (b) *Pimelodus maculatus* (after Fenerich, *et al.*, 1975), (c) *Parapimelodus valenciennesi* (after Cabrera *et al.*, 1973a).

Whereas the Von Bertalanffy growth curve adequately describes year-to-year progression in length, growth in any one year does not conform to the model. The long period in which growth either ceases completely or is considerably restricted, means that most of the year's increase in length occurs during a comparatively short period. Dudley (1972), for instance, recorded that 75 per cent of the expected first year's growth of *Sarotherodon andersoni* and *S. macrochir* took place within six weeks of peak floods in the Kafue river. Growth in weight is even more subject to seasonal variation, often with temporary losses occurring during the dry season. Because the within-the-year growth pattern has important implications for the estimation of biological production, Daget and Ecoutin (1976) have produced a modified growth model applicable to species with prolonged annual growth arrests. This requires the introduction of two new parameters into the growth equation. These are q, which represents the duration of the annual growth arrest in months, and t, which is the duration of the first period of growth, also in months. The parameter t is necessary where reproduction does not coincide with the end of the parent's period of arrested growth. When the growing period is $12 - q$ months, the normal Von Bertalanffy curve is expressed as:

$$L_t = L_\infty \ \left\{ 1 - \exp[-g'(t - t_0)] \right\}$$

where t and t_0 are expressed in months and $g' = g/(12 - q)$; t_0 is obtained from the equation

$$t_0 = t_1 + \frac{\log(L - L_t) - \log L}{g' \log e}$$

The arc of the growth curve thus obtained is thereby compressed into $12 - q$ months and is followed by a horizontal line q months long. Daget and Ecoutin applied this model to *Polypterus senegalus* from the middle Niger, obtaining the mean growth curve shown in Fig. 3.18. This model describes situations where growth stops completely during the dry season and has the advantage of being based on current growth models, but is somewhat inflexible if it is to be applied to conditions where growth varies from year to year depending on favourable or unfavourable conditions. Such a model requires a growth trajectory which is less predetermined and Welcomme and Hagborg (1977) had to adopt a different model for growth within the year to allow for this. Their formula $L_{t+t'} = L_t + G(e^{t'})$ has the characteristics of fast initial increase in length followed by a period of slower growth (but not a complete halt). Values of L_t for successive years can conform to the Von Bertalanffy relationship, although the form of the curve within one year calculated for successive weeks does not. The advantage of this relationship in modelling the growth of fish living on floodplains, is that the terminal value of the year's growth can change according to the intensity of flooding by the operation of an appropriate coefficient on G.

In his studies on fish production in the Kafue river, Kapetsky (1974a and 1974b) was presented with a similar problem of modelling within-year growth patterns. From his own observations as well as those of Dudley (1972) it was obvious that growth in weight of *Sarotherodon* sp. on the Kafue flats does not stop completely in the dry season, although it is considerably slowed. Kapetsky, therefore, proposed to rotate the relationship $W_t = W_0 e^{gt}$ on its diagonal and then reverse it. This gives an equation of the form:

$$W_t = W_0 + W_1(1-e^{-gt})$$

where $W_1 = W_0 e^{g(12)}$. Here W_1 = the weight at the end of a year's growth, whereas individual segments of t and the growth coefficient g are in months.

Year-to-year variations in growth

From the studies of growth of fish species inhabiting floodplain rivers it has become obvious that there are considerable year-to-year variations in growth within the same species. The most detailed examination of the possible causes of such variations has been carried out for some cichlid species in the Kafue river. Here, Dudley (1972 and 1974) and Kapetsky (1974a) found significant correlations between some physical variables and the mean growth increment. In particular, the intensity and duration of flooding could have accounted for much of the year-to-year variation in the growth of year class I and II, *Tilapia rendalli, Sarotherodon andersoni* and *S. macrochir*. Low temperature in the dry season also appeared to influence some year classes and gave good partial correlations when entered into the equation after some measure of flood intensity. Typical relationships are shown in Table 3.8, where TI is an index of temperature, FI is an index of flooding drawn from the area under the flood curve, (Dudley 1972) and HI2 and HI3 are indices summarizing the degree of drawdown in the dry season (Kapetsky, 1974a; see also Appendix).

Table 3.8 Parameter estimates for simple and multiple linear regressions of first- and second-year growth increments on temperature and hydrological indices

Species	Year of growth	Sex	Model	r
Sarotherodon andersoni	1	M	Growth (cm) = $0.02 FI + 12.87$*	0.92
	1	M	TL (mm) = $146.51 - 0.11(HI2)$†	0.94
	1	F	Growth (cm) = $0.014 FI + 13.4$*	0.78
	2	M	TL (mm) = $-29.47 + 1.98(TI)$†	0.90
	2	F	TL (mm) = $38.24 - 0.30(HI3) + 0.83(TI)$†	0.93
Sarotherodon macrochir	1	M	Growth (cm) = $0.2 FI + 11.02$*	0.9
	1	M	TL (mm) = $130.39 - 0.13(HI2)$†	0.92
	1	F	TL (mm) = $130.13 - 0.32(HI2)$†	0.85
	2	M	TL (mm) = $74.72 - 0.10(HI3)$†	0.58
	2	F	TL (mm) = $14.69 - 0.18(HI3)$†	0.95
Tilapia rendalli	1	M	Growth (cm) = $0.029 FI + 12.8$*	0.80

*Dudley (1972) (see Appendix).
†Kapetsky (1974) (see Appendix).

Kapetsky's regression equations were successfully used to predict growth increments for certain year classes, but the consistency of the results is not uniform, possibly due to the short time series upon which the calculations were based. They are sufficient, however, to indicate the importance of external physical factors in determining the growth of fish in such systems.

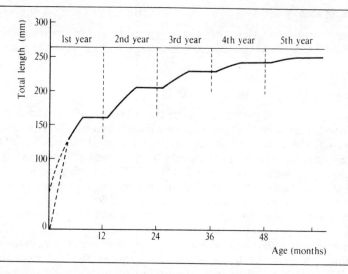

Fig. 3.18 Mean linear growth of *Polypterus senegalus* for the first five years of life, supposing an annual growth arrest of six months and a first-year growth period of seven months ($T_0 = -3$). (After Daget and Ecoutin, 1976.)

This work on the Kafue is not isolated. As early as 1934 Wimpenny (quoted in Holden, 1963) found that the yield of fish from Lake Manzala in the Nile delta was correlated with flood level, high floods being followed by better-than-average yields which were due in part to higher growth rates of first-year fish. Similarly, conditions for feeding, and hence growth, of non-anadromous fishes in the Amur river are considerably improved in years when there is plenty of water (Krykhtin, 1972, quoted by Krykhtin, 1975). The exceptionally poor flood years during the last Sahelian drought provided an opportunity to assess the effects of this on the growth of fish species in the Senegal and Niger rivers. In the Senegal, Reizer (1974) discerned great differences in growth of *Citharinus citharus* between 1968, a year of particularly poor flood, and other years (Fig. 3.19). The first-year class was missing totally for that year. The second-year growth increment for the 1967-year class in the 1968 flood was 3·91 cm, whereas the 1966-year class grew 7·99 cm during the 1967 flood. The third year's growth showed similar differences; an increment of 2·32 cm for the 1966-year class (1968 flood) and 8·37 cm for the 1967-year class (1969 flood). Differences in growth were also noted from the Niger where the floods of 1971 and 1972 were particularly bad. Here Dansoko *et al.* (1976) studied two species of *Hydrocynus, H. brevis* and *H. forskahlii*, and found that growth, particularly of the young of the year in both species, was poor during these two years (Table 3.9).

Hydrocynus forskahlii, which only inhabits the river, showed this effect less than *H. brevis*, which depends much on the floodplain for

Table 3.9 Linear growth increments for five-year classes of *H. brevis* and *H. forskahlii* from the Niger river (data from Dansoko *et al.*, 1976)

Year of growth	Age			
	I	II	III	IV
Hydrocynus brevis				
1970	19·9			
1971	12·8	11·0		
1972	17·6	4·3	10·4	
1973	21·9	10·4	7·9	2·0
1974	27·0	10·7	12·1	
Hydrocynus forskahlii				
1970	17·3			
1971	10·9	6·4		
1972	12·4	5·8	6·1	
1973	15·6	11·2	9·3	8·2
1974	24·1	10·6	6·1	8·7

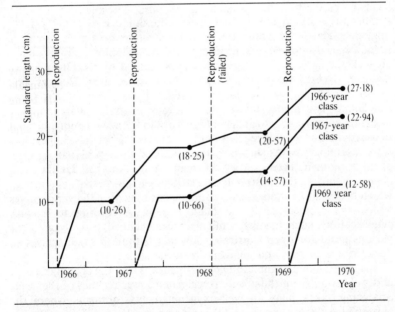

Fig. 3.19 Growth of *Citharinus citharus* in the Senegal river: 1966; 1967; 1969-year classes. Numbers in parentheses = total length at growth arrest in centimetres. (After Reizer, 1974.)

feeding, but none the less the differences were still marked. It is also of interest that year classes with poor first-year growth appear to continue to grow badly despite better conditions in later years. Likewise, year classes with good initial growth do not suffer so badly in a poor year.

3.7 Reproduction

Spawning sites and reproductive adaptations

Fish inhabiting floodplain rivers show a diversity of reproductive habit which adapts them to the particular difficulties inherent in breeding in systems with rapidly fluctuating water levels and often extreme physical and chemical conditions. It seems that physical and behavioural specializations are more varied for reproduction than they are for feeding in these ecosystems. The range of adaptation is indicated by the fact that nearly all of Balon's reproductive guilds (Balon, 1975) are represented in most systems. These guilds, which form a useful ecological classification of breeding behaviour, localities and substrates are listed in Table 3.10, together with some representative taxa.

Several broad reproductive strategies have evolved which are summarized in Table 3.11. As has been shown in the chapter on migration, many characin, cyprinid and siluroid species undertake long reproductive movements upstream away from the feeding habitats. This often means that the eggs are laid outside the floodplain area in headwater streams that are sometimes torrential. The migration of other species takes them from downstream floodplains to those further upstream, *Prochilodus platensis* in the Paraná river or *Alestes baremoze* in the Chari–Logone rivers for instance. That upstream migrants do not all seek the same type of headwater is illustrated by the observations made by INDERENA (1973) on the Magdalena river. Here *Brycon moorei* moved into small, short side arms off the main river, whereas *Prochilodus reticulatus* stayed within the main channel, *Salminus affinis* swam up side-streams to areas of high flow and *Brycon henni* ascended to the highest accessible reaches of the main river. That these migrations were reproductive was shown by the advanced state of sexual maturity of the fish during their journey upstream. In the Amazon, Geisler *et al.* (1973) recorded the upstream migrations of many characin species which breed in the mouth-lakes of the tributaries or in the várzea lakes which are connected to the main stream. According to Balon's classification, such upstream migrants are inclined to belong to the various guilds of open substrate spawners, although some species of *Leporinus* construct and guard nests in the rocks.

The upstream migrant habit generally means that the eggs and fry are laid well away from the poorly oxygenated lower reaches of the river. Spawning takes place in well-oxygenated environments where the current also cleans the eggs and there is also less danger of predation on the young fish.

The migratory blackfishes show a wide range of behaviour. Some are open-stratum phyto-lithophils or phytophils which attach or scatter their eggs among vegetation or over open bottoms on the floodplain. Often the localities chosen for breeding are in the channels conducting water on to the plain, or at the very edge of the flooded area where oxygenation is relatively high. Species migrating on to the floodplains of

Table 3.10 Reproductive guilds of fishes (after Balon, 1975) with representative taxa from floodplain systems

Subsection	Guild	Definition	Typical representative
Open substratum spawners	*Pelagophils*	Floating eggs	*Ctenopoma muriei, Lates niloticus*
	Litho-pelagophils	Eggs laid on bottom, but later become buoyant	*Prochilodus* spp.
	Lithophils	Eggs deposited on rocks or gravel	Many cyprinid and characin species, e.g. *Barbus, Labeo*
	Phyto-lithophils	Unspecific – eggs deposited on plants or other substrates	Many cyprinid species, e.g. *Rutilus rutilus*
	Phytophils	Scatter eggs which adhere to submerged plants	Many cyprinid, characin and siluroid species, e.g. *Puntius gonionotus*
	Psammophils	Deposit eggs on sandy bottoms	Many migratory cyprinid and characin species
Brood hiders	*Lithophils*	Hide eggs in gravel	Many salmonid species
	Speleophils	Restricted to cave-dwelling species	No known examples from floodplains
	Ostracophils	Hide eggs in mussels or crabs	*Rhodeus sericeus*
	Aero-psammophils	Restricted to marine species in tidal zone	No known examples from floodplains
	Xerophils	Annual fishes with dormant eggs	Many annual cyprinodonts, e.g. *Nothobranchius*
Guarders Substratum choosers	*Lithophils*	Attach eggs to rocks, males sit on eggs	*Loricaria parva, L. macrops,* some small cichlids
	Phytophils	Attach eggs to submerged plants and guard and fan them	*Polypterus* spp.
	Aerophils	Attach eggs to leaves overhanging water and splash them	*Copeina arnoldi*
	Pelagophils	Floating eggs guarded by parents	Some *Ophicephalus* and *Anabas* spp.
Nest spawners	*Lithophils*	Eggs attached to prepared areas of rock or gravel	*Aequidens* and many other cichlids, some characins, e.g. *Leporinus*
	Phytophils	Construct nest of vegetation	*Clarias batrachus, Gymnarchus niloticus*
	Psammophils	Shallow nests in sand	Some cichlids, e.g. *Tilapia zillii*

Table 3.10 (contd)

Subsection	Guild	Definition	Typical representative
	Aphrophils	Floating bubble or froth nests	*Hepsetus odoe, Hoplosternum*, some anabantids
	Speleophils	Deposit eggs in cleaned holes or or crevices in rock	Several cichlids
	Polyphils	Build nests with anything, anywhere	*Notopterus chitala, Hoplias malabaricus*
	Ariadnophils	Build nests out of viscous secretions	*Gasterosteus aculeatus*
	Actinariophils	Nest in sea anemones	No representatives in floodplains
Bearers			
External bearers	*Transfer brooders*	Fish which carry their eggs before depositing them	*Callichthys, Corydoras*
	Forehead breeders	Eggs stuck on to special skin on forehead	No known representatives, but some *Loricaria* carry eggs on a special prolongation of lower lip of males
	Mouthbrooders	Carry eggs in mouth	Many cichlids, *Osteoglossum*
	Gill chamber brooders	Carry eggs in gill chamber	No known examples on floodplains
	Skin brooders	Eggs carried on special skin on ventral surface	*Loricaria, Bunocephalus* and some other S. American catfish
	Pouchbrooders	Skin structures modified to form a pouch	*Loricaria vetula* and *L. anus*
Internal bearers	*Ovi ovoviviparous*	Internal fertilization, eggs expelled immediately afterwards	*Pantodon buchholzi*
	Ovoviviparous	Eggs incubate in body cavity: nutrition by yolk	*Potamotrygon*
	Viviparous	Eggs incubate in body cavity: nutrition by absorptive organs	Poeciliidae

the Ayuthaya province of Thailand (Chao-Phrya river system) illustrate the selection of substrates for spawning (Tongsanga and Kessunchai, 1966). *Crossocheilus reba* spawns in the inundated rice-fields as does *Wallago attu*. Another catfish, *Pangasius sutchi* spawns among submerged weeds and bushes in the shallow inundated margins of the klongs or canals. The spiny eel, *Macrognathus aculeatus* spawns both in flooded rice-fields and in the channels on clean bottoms or among weeds. Some species, such as *Puntius gonionotus* spawn in the

Table 3.11 Examples of main types of reproductive behaviour in fishes from floodplain rivers (adapted from Lowe-McConnell, 1975)

Type of fecundity	Seasonality	Examples	Movement and parental care
Big bang	Once in a lifetime	*Anguilla*	Very long catadromous migrations, no parental care
Total spawners (very high fecundity)	Highly seasonal concentrated on annual or biannual floods	Characins: e.g. *Prochilodus, Salminus, Alestes* Cyprinids: e.g. *Labeo, Barbus, Cirrhinus* Siluroids: e.g. *Schilbe*	Long-distance migrants, open substratum spawners
		Heteropneustes, Catla catla, Labeo rohita Mormyrids	Local lateral migrants, open substratum spawners
Partial spawners	Throughout flood season(s)	Some cyprinids, characins and siluroids: e.g. *Clarias, Micralestes acutidens*	Mainly lateral migrants, open substratum spawners
Grades into		*Protopterus, Arapaima, Serrasalmus, Hoplias, Heterotis*	Bottom nest constructors and guarders
		Ophicephalus, Gymnarchus	Floating nest builders
		Hepsetus, Hoplosternum, Anabantids	Bubble nest builders
Small brood spawners (low fecundity)	High water, but may start during low water or may continue throughout the year	*Tilapia, Hypostomus*	Nest constructors with various behavioural patterns
		Aspredo, Loricaria sp.	Egg carriers
		Osteoglossum, Sarotherodon spp.	Mouthbrooders
		Potamotrygon, Poeciliids	Live bearers
	End of rains	Some cyprinodonts	Annual species with resting eggs

middle of channels, and do not seem preoccupied as to where the fertilized benthic eggs lodge.

Many blackfish species have some form of parental care, and in some genera a variety of behavioural patterns are found. This is typified by the genus *Loricaria*, where *L. parva* and *L. macrops* sit on eggs which are attached to cleared areas of rock. The eggs are cleaned and fanned by the parents from time to time. Female *L. piracicalae* develop a special spongy skin on their ventral surface. The fish roll on the fertilized eggs which adhere to this region. *Loricaria vetula* and *L. anus* have a pouch formed by the enlargement of the lower lip of the males into which the eggs are lodged, and in *Loricaria* sp. (near *microdon*: Lowe-McConnell, 1964) the lower lip is extended into a special elongation from which the young are suspended.

Nest building is very common among floodplain species. *Arapaima gigas* scoops out hollows in the bottom of the flooded savanna and both parents guard the eggs that are deposited (Sánchez Romero, 1961). Various species of cichlid make nests. Some of these are simply cleared areas of rock, others holes under rocks or vegetation, and in yet others excavated pits, sometimes of complex design. *Heterotis niloticus* construct nests in the middle of masses of vegetation at the shallow margins of the plain, whereas *Gymnarchus niloticus* make floating flask- or raft-shaped masses of aquatic weeds in which they lay their eggs (Svensson, 1933). The different architecture of nest of *Protopterus* has been described by Johnels and Svensson (1954) for *P. annectens* and Greenwood (1958) for *P. aethiopicus*. These range from simple sunken areas in a sandy substrate to complex domed structures of papyrus roots. The characin *Hoplias malabaricus* constructs a simple nest on the bottom with whatever material is readily available, and some species of *Serrasalmus* are also reputed to guard egg masses laid on tree roots, and aquarium observations have shown them to excavate nests in plant masses (Braker, 1963).

Floating nests are found in some species. Primitive types are made by some ophicephalids. *Ophicephalus micropeltes* allows its pelagic eggs to float to the surface in a cluster, and then surrounds them with a ring of pieces bitten off surrounding vegetation (Tongsanga and Kessunchai, 1965). The floating mass is guarded by the male. *Hepsetus odoe* is unique among the characins in constructing a nest of foam which is lodged between the stems of weeds or grasses at the margins of the plain. Froth or foam nests made of mucus secretions from one or both parents are common in other families. Among the siluroids *Callichthys callichthys* and *Hoplosternum littorale* both make a raft constructed of bubbles and aquatic plants. Floating nests are made by many anabantids including *Ctenopoma damasi* in Africa (Berns and Peters, 1969) and *Colisa, Betta* and *Trichogaster* in Asia. The building of nests enables the eggs and newly hatched fry to be concentrated in a protected locality that is easily defended by one or both parents. Floating nests also bring the eggs and young fish into contact with the better-oxygenated upper layers of the water column, a very necessary feature as most species making this type of nest inhabit highly deoxygenated waters. Juveniles of species which build their nests on the bottom often have gill filaments to improve their oxygen uptake, and the parent fish fan the nest to ensure a flow of aerated water. Furthermore, nests are usually placed at the limits of the advancing water where the dissolved oxygen levels are still moderately high. Such constructions are, however, vulnerable to sudden changes in water level which can either leave the nest stranded, or submerge it in too great a depth of anoxic water, and to avoid this happening some cichlids move their eggs up and down by mouth to follow the advancing or receding flood.

Parental care reaches its most extreme among those species which bear their young throughout their development. Many of the African and some South American cichlids and other species such as *Osteoglossum bicirrhosum* incubate their eggs in their mouths, and continue to shelter their fry until they become independent. The mouthbrooding habit enables spawning to take place before the floods. The young can be conserved in a well-oxygenated environment (the parent's mouth) throughout their development, and they can be deposited on the nursery grounds at the fringes of the plain which are far distant from the breeding sites. Most mouthbrooding species also construct nests which serve both as territorial markers for their breeding rituals and as clean places upon which the eggs are deposited prior to being picked up by one or other of the parents. Most cyprinodonts and the glandulocaudine characins have progressed even further and have developed internal fertilization which in many cyprinodonts is coupled with live bearing. Nelson (1964) in his study of the glandulocaudines considered that internal fertilization is an adaptation to the floodplain environment permitting mating to occur when the fish are concentrated in the dry-season habitats. Egg laying, or in the case of the poeciliid cyprinodonts the birth of the young, can thus be delayed until the female can move into the flooded shallows at the margin of the floodplain.

Fecundity and spawning patterns

The fecundity and spawning pattern of fishes is correlated with the types of breeding behaviour described above. Two main categories exist: total spawners, in which all the eggs ripen and are shed within a very short time, and multiple spawners, in which repeated breeding occurs in any one season with only a small proportion of the total stock of eggs becoming ripe at any one spawning.

Long-distance migrant species of whitefish, which are usually open substratum spawners showing no parental care, belong to the first category. Their eggs are usually small and are produced in very large quantities to compensate for the wastage inherent in this type of spawning. Fish such as *Prochilodus platensis* produce between 360 000 and 750 000 eggs for individuals between 40 and 65 cm, respectively

(Vidal, 1967). Egg counts for *P. scrofa* (Ihering, 1930) and *P. argenteus* (Fontenele, 1953) also fall within this range. *Salminus maxillosus* of between 52 and 100 cm were reported by Ringuelet *et al.* (1967) to produce between 1 152 900 and 2 619 000 eggs. The regressions for the fecundity of *Hilsa ilisha*; $F = 0.9550 e^{0.5396}$, formulated by Pillay and Rosa (1963) predicts between 250 000 and 1 600 000 eggs for individuals within the normal size range. The fecundity of *Alestes baremoze* ranges between 32 000 eggs for a female 24·4 cm long (177 g) and 111 000 eggs for a female 31·4 cm long (394 g) and is described by the relationship $F = 0.345 \, wt \, of \, female \, in \, grams - 25$ (Durand and Loubens, 1970b). Really large species such as *Lates niloticus* can produce extraordinary quantities of eggs, over 11 million having been recorded from some individuals by Okedi (1971). Although the above examples indicate the numbers of eggs produced by total spawners, the listing is far from complete and more details are given by Lowe-McConnell (1975).

Partial spawning is usually associated with some degree of parental care. The eggs are larger as is reflected in the lesser numbers per gram wet weight of ovary. A total spawner such as *Eutropius niloticus* has 2 950 eggs g[-1], whereas *Sarotherodon* sp. have about 135 eggs g[-1] (Willoughby and Tweddle, 1977). The number of eggs released at any one spawning is much lower than in total spawners. However, partial spawners may breed several times during any one season and it is, therefore, difficult to estimate the total fecundity of the fish. This is further complicated by the fact that the number of young reared is more often a function of the parent's capacity to care for a brood, than of the ovarian egg production. A typical example of this is the mouthbrooding cichlid, *Sarotherodon leucostictus* whose ovarian egg production increased approximately as a square of the standard length ($F = 1.091L^{2.156}$), but whose brooding capacity only increased linearly ($B = 17.6L - 78.2$) (Welcomme, 1967). The partial spawning habit is highly adapted to floodplains as it allows for the loss of one or more broods due to the unpredictability of the environment. In species such as *Arapaima gigas* only one-third of the available eggs ripen at any one time, the rest being available should earlier broods be lost due to sudden changes in water level.

Timing

Reproduction of most fish in floodplain rivers is highly seasonal and in the majority of species coincides with the earlier phases of the flood. Only a few species have been described as breeding throughout the year. In the Shire river some *Sarotherodon* spp. possibly continue sexual activity outside·the flood season (Willoughby and Tweddle, 1977), and mouthbrooding cichlids generally have been seen to spawn at low water in rivers elsewhere (personal observations) although the frequency of breeding is usually much reduced at this time. Other species have been reported as breeding during the dry season in the Zaïre river (Matthes,

1964); also Roman (1966) noted that *Micralestes acutidens* breeds on the floodplain during the floods, but continues to breed at all times of the year in the main channel of the Volta river, the only one of the dwarf forms studied by him to do so. Nevertheless, the observations of most authors indicate the similarity in breeding periodicity in tropical rivers from Asia, Africa and South America. The synchronization of the reproductive cycle with the flood is sometimes so good that in systems where the flood-wave takes a considerable time to progress down-valley the breeding of downstream populations is delayed, often for up to a month, relative to the fish upstream. This has been noted from the Mekong by Sao-Leang and Dom Saveun (1955) and the Paraná by Bonetto *et al.* (1971). It is also evident from a comparison of Daget's (1954) data for the middle Niger where fish breed mainly in July – August, with that of FAO/UN (1970a) for the Niger in Nigeria, where breeding occurred from August to October.

In some equatorial rivers, such as parts of the Amazon and Zaïre systems there are two rainy seasons which produce bimodal floods. In these areas many species have more than one breeding season per year (Roberts, 1973). In the Zaïre most species breed at the start of the September–October floods. In the April–June high water there is also a period of reproduction, although Matthes (1964) considered this to be less important. Biannual breeding takes place in the rivers leading into Lake Victoria where species ascend the streams during the equinoctial floods to reach the flooded swamps near the headwaters (Welcomme, 1969). INDERENA (1973) record two migrations of fish in the Magdalena river, the main 'Subienda' during the February–April low water, and a second during the summer low water, but it was not clear whether the second movement, known as the 'mitaca', is for breeding or merely for dispersal. More recent observations by Kapetsky *et al.* (1977) on the number of species with ripe gonads and the number of juveniles present each month, indicated that breeding patterns in the Magdalena are rather more diffuse.

On the basis of 18 species studied, Kapetsky was able to distinguish three main groups of fish as distinguished by their spawning behaviour: those species which apparently breed only once per year, those which have two or more reproductive periods and those species which breed almost continuously. More than half of the species studied bred during the February–April low water and in the first stages of the rising flood. There was another peak of breeding activity during the second stage of rising water (October), but few species bred during falling water (December–January).

The factors which initiate maturation and stimulate breeding of floodplain fishes remain largely undetermined. A number of factors have been implicated, including changes in individual physical parameters such as temperature, conductivity or flow, as well as the assemblage of conditions that mark the beginning of the flood. It is probable that each species is affected by the various factors in different ways and that such external releasers are only effective when superimposed on an internal physiological rhythm of the fish. In some species very specific conditions are necessary. For instance, Basile-Martins *et al.* (1975) considered that maturation of *Pimelodus maculatus* in the Jaguari river (Fig. 3.20) started when the temperature reached 22° C and that a temperature of 25° C was needed for breeding to occur. Temperature did not appear to be the only regulatory mechanism in the species as a minimum increase in water level of 1 m over the low-water base also seemed necessary. Changes in the Gonadosomatic Index,

$$\text{GSI} = \frac{wt\ of\ reproductive\ organ}{wt\ of\ fish} \times 100$$

have also been used by Durand and Loubens (1970b) to define the breeding season of *Alestes baremoze* in the Chari delta (Fig. 3.21). The relationship between endocrine activity, spawning, rainfall, temperature and daylength have been presented for the Indian catfish *Heteropneustes fossilis* (Viswanathan and Sunderaraj, 1974). These three examples, together with other observations, show the underlying similarity of timing of maturity and spawning. It is well known that many of the migratory characins and cyprinids will not spawn unless the flood materializes. As Bonetto (1975) has noted, individuals of *Prochilodus platensis* which are isolated in the floodplain lagoons do not mature when do fish in the river channel. Most Indian investigators agree that the major carps will not breed if the flooding associated with the monsoon fails (Parameswaran *et al.*, 1970). Under these conditions, suitable inundated spawning grounds also have to be available for reproduction to be successfully concluded, although one cyprinid, *Cirrhinus reba* differs from this in that it can breed even at low water in the Cauvery and Bhavani rivers, provided sexual readiness is induced by a short initial spate (Rao *et al.*, 1972). According to Sidthimunka (1972) *Probarbus jullieni* shows similar behaviour in the Mekong system, and Krykhtin (1975) reported that while many food fishes from the river Amur bred only on the floodplain with rises in water level, some species (e.g. *Elopichthys bambusa, Erythroculter* sp.) also reproduced when the water level did not rise. Another exceptional breeding pattern was reported by Fox (1976) from the Okavango delta. Here, spawning of most species takes place in the warmer months of the year, September–March, which coincide with the flood in the north basin of the swamp, but in most of the delta the flood occurs in the coldest part of the year and the majority of fish breed during low water. Many cyprinodont fishes spawn towards the end of the flood. This is correlated with their annual habit whereby one year's fish hatch at the beginning of the rains and develop throughout the life of the temporary waters which they populate. As pools desiccate in the dry season the fish lay small batches of their dormant eggs in the bottom.

It may be concluded that in the majority of total spawning migratory

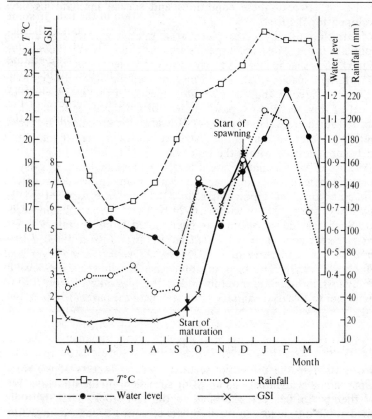

Fig. 3.20 Gonadosomatic Index (GSI) of *Pimelodus maculatus* in the river Jaguari compared with temperature ($T°$C), water level in river (m) and rainfall (mm³) for 1971–73. (After Basile Martins *et al.*, 1975.)

and non-migratory species breeding is so timed that if the floods are delayed or inadequate to trigger migration, reproduction may fail in that year. Partial spawning blackfish such as *Clarias* spp., *Loricaria* spp., appear to be capable of breeding whenever suitable conditions are present. As has been already noted some such species breed throughout the year. Many others have longer and more diffuse breeding seasons, starting to breed in the river channel before the flood arrives and continuing with subsequent broods well into the flood season on the plain. Generally, the reproductive strategies are aimed at securing;

1. safe and protected places for laying and rearing the eggs;
2. maximum feeding and growing time for the young fish; and
3. freedom from predation.

The period when the water is invading the plain is obviously the best for the last two of these conditions and special mechanisms have developed for the first.

Maturation usually takes place at a relatively early age among floodplain fishes. Most small species are ready to spawn by the onset of the next rainy season and have very short life cycles (Lowe-McConnell, 1975). Larger species often do not mature until the third or fourth year of life. The *Tilapia* and *Sarotherodon* species of the Kafue river are typical of this, starting to spawn under normal flood regimes in their third to fourth years (Dudley, 1974). However, in particularly dry years, when little water remains in the system at low water, the fish may stunt and become mature within the first year of life (Dudley, 1976).

Because of the fluctuating water levels, which may leave eggs dry or submerge them in too great a depth of water, many species have evolved rapid embryonic development to reduce the time the eggs are at risk. In some fishes the fry hatch within 16–24 hours of the eggs having been laid. Such fast development has been noted from migratory open-substrate spawners, such as *Hilsa ilisha* (Pillay and Rosa, 1963), *Labeo rohita* (Khan and Jhingran, 1975) or *L. victorianus* (Fryer and Whitehead, 1959). The eggs of some nest-building species develop equally fast, although in mouthbrooders the eggs take a longer time to hatch (four to five days) and fry often stay with the parent for up to two weeks.

The influence of the flood on breeding success

As discussed in the preceding sections, several aspects of the flood regime can have an impact on breeding success or on the survival of fry, and thereby influence recruitment to the fish stock. That there are considerable differences in the numbers of young produced in various years is well known. Holden (1963) noted that some species were only represented by one year class in the Sokoto river. There were also great variations in the relative abundance of species, indicating year-to-year differences in breeding success. Non-migratory species were most abundant in one year (1955) owing to a strong 1954-year class correlated with a good early rise of the river. The same factor obviously did not favour the migratory species. Holden also mentions the observations of Wimpenny (1934) on the Nile delta lakes where heavy floods were followed by good recruitment giving a high density of fish. Lowe-McConnell (1964 and 1967) noted large fluctuations in abundance of different species in different years, which she attributed to differential breeding success, short life cycles and rapid maturation. Here strong year classes of *Serrasalmus nattereri* and *Prochilodus* were found in different years.

In the Amur system, the yield of phytophilous species, which breed on the floodplain of the river, is also directly related to the flood regime. Year classes are usually weak in years of light flooding and strong when floods are heavy (Nikolsky, 1956).

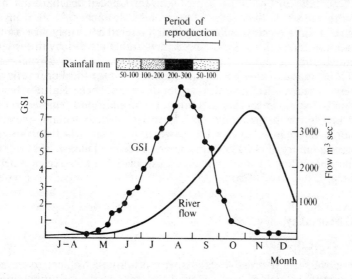

Fig. 3.21 Variations in the Gonadosomatic Index of female *Alestes baremoze* in the Chari river. (Adapted from Durand and Loubens, 1970b.)

From fluctuations in the number of *Sarotherodon andersoni, S. macrochir,* and *Tilapia rendalli,* Dudley (1972) deduced that there were seasonal changes in abundance. Furthermore, from differences in the abundance of *Sarotherodon* juveniles he concluded that breeding success and recruitment to the stock were much better in those years having good floods. Later work on *S. andersoni* and *S. macrochir* indicated that spawning success might have been depressed by high dry-season water levels. The reason advanced for this is that *Sarotherodon* normally stunt under the severer conditions where drawdown is greater. The stunted fish mature and breed earlier than they would in years when the high volume of water retained allows fish to grow to their normal maturation size.

The extreme hydrological conditions of the Sahelian rivers during the 1970–74 period have provided examples of the effects of failed floods on the recruitment of several fish species. In the Central Delta of the Niger, Dansoko *et al.* (1976) compared the biology of *Hydrocynus brevis* and *H. forskahlii.* The two species are of interest as *H. brevis* breeds on the floodplain during the floods, whereas *H. forskahlii* passes the whole of its life in the river and breeds in the main channel during low water. They therefore give a useful contrast in that the effects of variability in flooding should be reflected in one species rather than the other. This was confirmed by poor recruitment in *H. brevis* during the years when the flood failed. A similar instance happened in the Senegal river where recruitment of all freshwater fish was lacking in the poor flood years of

1968 and also in 1971. This can be seen for *Citharinus citharus* in Fig. 3.19. In the Chari river several species have disappeared following the failure of three successive floods which hindered breeding in the Yaérés floodplains, as well as producing unfavourable conditions in the river channel and in Lake Chad. Here the larger species, *Distichodus, Citharinus* and *Labeo* and the migratory *Alestes dentex* and *A. baremoze* have declined drastically in abundance and have been replaced by other species including *Hemisynodontis membranaceus* and *Brachysynodontis batensoda*. In species such as *Alestes* where the majority of the new recruits are spawned by the second- and third-year classes, a failure of two floods in succession can so weaken the stock that it may be difficult for it to recover, especially in the face of a heavy fishery (Quensiere, 1976).

3.8 Mortality

Causes of mortality

There are several possible causes of mortality in tropical rivers, but because of the lack of knowledge of this important topic, much of the following section is speculative. There has been no attempt so far to separate natural and fishing mortalities, and such rare estimates of mortality rate as have been made concern total mortality (Z). However, it is necessary to consider the various components of Z, even on a theoretical basis, as they bear directly on the way fish populations respond to changes in the natural habitat.

Death due to stranding or isolation of fish in temporary water bodies is probably one of the major elements of natural mortality. Bonetto *et al.* (1969b) estimated that some 40 000 t of fish are lost in this way from the Paraná system, basing their estimate on the area of standing water on the plain (2×10^6 hm^2) and the standing stocks of 20 kg hm^{-2} as estimated from a small sample of them. This figure was greatly superior to the 10 000 t which were reported to have been caught by the fishery in 1967. There is no doubt that enormous quantities of fish are lost in this manner in most systems, and this apparent wastefulness has been widely remarked upon in the literature. Mortality through stranding is obviously closely related to the flood regime. It is not particularly prominent during the rising flood, although temporary recessions can leave fish isolated in pools and can destroy young fish in nests at the flood margin. More extensive flooding can raise the total number or biomass of fish in the system through improved reproductive success and growth, making the whole community more sensitive to later contractions in the volume of the aquatic environment. The form of the falling flood would appear to be critical, as a more rapid draining of the plain would seem to give the fish less time to abandon their flood habitats and would increase the chances of their being isolated in unsuitable places. On the other hand there is a possibility that there might also be some favourable effects because of the stronger pattern of currents which may make the fish more responsive to such stimuli. However, the behaviour of fish during the return movement to the main channel has not been studied in any great detail and needs considerable work in the future. The duration of the dry season equally affects the proportion of the standing water that will disappear through evaporation or be rendered unsuitable for habitation by certain species. Presumably the longer and more severe the dry period, the greater the mortality due to this cause. The impact of stranding mortality on the dynamics of the community as a whole is difficult to assess. If all of the fish produced during one wet season were to enter the permanent standing water at the end of the flood, densities far surpassing the carrying capacity of the water might well result. This could give rise to a corresponding increase in density-dependent mortality with a final survival not far different from that resulting when a proportion of the individuals are lost by stranding.

Deaths due to unfavourable hydrological conditions during the floods have been described from several systems. In the Kafue flats (Tait, 1967b) and the Paraná these have been traced to the deoxygenation of the whole water column in lagoons when lowering of the temperature and high winds cause the breakdown of stratification and sudden overturn. Similar cold spells have been the source of recorded mortalities in the Nile and in the Amazon, where they are known as 'friagems' (Brinkmann and Santos, 1973). In the Amur river, winter kill conditions arise in years of poor low-water flow when the main channel separates into a number of pools. These become deoxygenated, causing heavy mortalities of adult fishes (Krykhtin, 1975). Fish kills due to such causes are often spectacular in that large numbers of dead fish appear on the surface, but they generally seem to be highly localized in space and time.

Mortality of small species and of the juveniles of larger species owing to predation by fish is probably maximal during the draining of the floodplain after the flood peak has passed. Evidence presented in the section on feeding indicates that in many tropical rivers, predators do not feed extensively during the dry season. Unfortunately, there are no data on the intensity of predation during the rising floods. At this time cover for prey is maximal and the fish are probably dispersed widely over the plain. Nevertheless, the condition of the predators improves throughout this period, indicating that they are feeding to a certain extent. The juveniles of most predatory species use alternative food resources during the earlier stages of the flood, but are already turning to a piscivorous habit as the flood nears its end. During the run-off phase the stomachs of most predators are full, and personal observations on the Ouémé and Niger showed them to be typically packed with the juveniles of a wide range of species. Prey may include the young of the predators themselves whose non-specific feeding habits may lead them to cannibalism. However, selection by length of prey is much more widespread, and there would appear to be a relatively narrow size range at which different species are vulnerable to predation.

Predation by animals other than fish also appears to be at its highest during the period of the draining of the plain. Williams (1971) and Lowe-McConnell (1964), together with several other workers, have remarked in particular on the number of water birds preying on the fish stranded in floodplain depressions or leaving the area by way of the channels.

Another possible contributor to total natural mortality is disease. This may become extremely important during the phase of high fish concentrations at the end of the dry season. There is little knowledge of the epidemiology of tropical fishes in their natural habitats, although Khalil (1971) recorded 215 genera of helminths and Awachie *et al.* (1977) listed a range of bacteria, protozoa and crustacea, all of which are parasitic on fish in African inland waters. According to Awachie *et al.* (1977) the lotic conditions in rivers are not favourable to heavy infestations with parasites. That reservoirs of infection are present among natural populations in rivers is, however, indicated by the rapidity with which a variety of diseases appear and spread through populations of ornamental fish after their capture. Much would appear to depend on the concentration of fish in the habitat and the swiftness of the current. In sheltered lentic environments the abundance of parasitic organisms increases. Such conditions are present in floodplain pools where the lack of current, warm temperatures and high population densities of fish favour the spread of infection. Likewise, parasitic infestations are readily discernible on nursery beaches where young *Sarotherodon* and *Tilapia* congregate. Under crowded conditions, too, there is a build-up of toxic excretory products, mainly NH_3 and NO_2, in the water. These lead to gill or skin damage, which in conjunction with heavy parasite infestations can cause death.

Reduced survival of the young of upstream spawners (e.g. piracema species) can be anticipated in years of exceptionally heavy flooding. In such an eventuality the semi-pelagic eggs and juveniles could be swept downstream past the most favourable sites for their development. Similarly, fish may be lost to the community by the downstream drift of sudd islands in which they have taken refuge. These islands may eventually reach saline or other unsuitable waters where the fish die. In estuarine systems, too, mortalities of freshwater fish have been observed when they have been carried out to sea by excessive currents.

Many of the species of fish inhabiting rivers are of small size and have life spans of one or at the most two years. Death in such fishes is possibly associated with stresses arising from spawning or from senescence. However the mechanisms defining the life span of any species are not well understood and many fish live for considerably longer periods in captivity than they would seem to do in their natural habitats.

Detailed descriptions of fishing will be given in Section 4.5; however, fisheries are constrained by the flood cycle. There is little fishing activity during the flood phase on most floodplains, but effort intensifies during the period of run-off and continues throughout the dry season when the fish are most accessible. Fishing therefore follows the same pattern as most other causes of mortality.

Seasonality of mortality

The various factors contributing to total mortality tend to follow a similar pattern. Apart from deaths due to unfavourable conditions during rising floods, and also the sweeping away of juvenile or small fish during this time, most causes of death intensify as the flood cycle passes from wet to dry phase. Owing to the fluctuating volume of the aquatic component of the river there is a range of ichthyomass that can be supported by it. Available evidence suggests that the maximum amount of fish is present during the flood and the minimum just before the onset of the next flood. This means that there is an overproduction of ichthyomass during the flood which persists throughout the period of falling water and which must be lost through total mortality during the dry season. It also implies that the amount of water remaining in the system during the dry season relative to the amount of water present during the wet, is one of the major factors determining mortality. Because there is an overproduction of ichthyomass during the wet season the biotic system can respond to differences in the amount of water during the dry season so as to assure maximum survival into the next year. What proportion of total mortality can be taken as fishing mortality without affecting this flexibility of response is one of the key questions in the dynamics of river fish communities and in the management of their stocks for fisheries.

Models of mortality

Models of mortality must take into account this effect of the flood regime on both the natural and the fishery components of total mortality. Simple exponential models of the form $N_t = N_0 e^{-zT}$, which have been widely used under the more stable conditions of tropical lakes, do not suffice to describe mortality in rivers within any one year. Where t_0 is equivalent to the time of recruitment, Kapetsky (1974a) suggested that the form of the mortality curve might conveniently be represented by rotating the curve for exponential decrease in number around its diagonal axis. This gives a curve of the form:

$$N_t = N_0 - N_0 e^{-zT}(e^{zt} - 1)$$

where z is a weekly mortality coefficient, t time in weeks and $T = 52$ weeks. Such a curve gives a mortality rate which increases steadily throughout the year (Fig. 3.22). This is not a wholly satisfactory model of the mortality of fish in the type of fluctuating environment with which we are dealing, although it is a useful generalization for broader

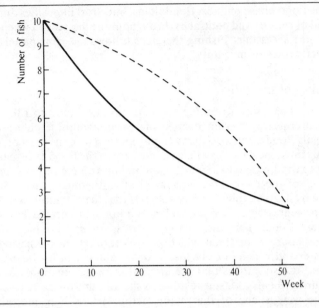

Fig. 3.22 Changes in the number of fish in one age group over 52 weeks as predicted by a simple exponential model (————) and Kapetsky's (1974a) 'floodplain' model (— — — —) : $Z = 1.5$.

productivity models. The seasonal patterns of mortality described above indicate very little mortality during the wet season and increased mortality as the year progresses. The majority of causes of death: predation, fishing, disease, hostile environments, etc., would seem to be density linked, and for this reason Welcomme and Hagborg (1977) reduced the number of fish in a simulated floodplain population by inserting a density-dependent mortality parameter in the simple exponential model:

$$N_{t+1} = N_t e^{-zM}$$

In this simulation z was obtained from a mortality coefficient characteristic of selected floodplain fish species; M was calculated from a formula of the form $M = aB^x$, where B is the weight per unit volume of the fish in the system. Here, M was adjusted to unity at a preselected biomass typical of a floodplain system, producing slower mortality rates when densities fell below the biomass and increased mortality rates at greater densities. The results of such a simulation are shown in Fig. 3.23.

Estimates of mortality rate

Total mortality rates (Z) are derived from the formula

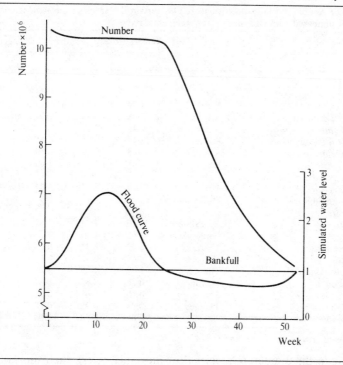

Fig. 3.23 Changes in the number of fish in one age group over 52 weeks, assuming recruitment at the start of week 1 when generated by the simulation of Welcomme and Hagborg (1977). Also shown are the water levels used in the simulation.

$$Z = \log_e \frac{number\ t_1}{number\ t_0}$$

and represent loss from a habitat or component of the ecosystem by death from all sources including fishing, and the difference between immigration into and emigration from the area under study. Obviously, the larger the area sampled to establish N_t and N_{t_0} relative to the size of the whole system, the more errors arising from immigration and emigration are liable to be reduced and the more Z tends to represent death rate. Only very few estimates have been made for species of fish inhabiting tropical rivers and these are given in Table 3.12. Values of Z are generally quite high in the early years of life ($Z \geqslant 4$), but tend to drop during the later years ($Z \leqslant 1$). This may be because the fish become less susceptible to predation as their size increases, although heavy fishing pressure continues on most species throughout their lives. In the extreme case of fishes whose life spans are very short, for instance the one to two years of many species of *Barbus*, cyprinodont or small mormyrid, values of Z can be very high. Comparison with mortality rates of fish from temperate rivers shows that, although survival is better

Table 3.12 Annual mortality coefficients (*Z*) for certain fish species from some tropical rivers as compared with fish species from temperate rivers

Species	River	Year		
		1	2	3
Tropical				
Polypterus senegalus	Chari		0·54	0·53
Alestes leuciscus	Niger	1·20		
Hydrocynus brevis	Niger	3·08	0·98	
H. forskahlii	Niger	2·49	2·67	
Sarotherodon andersoni	Kafue	2·47	0·65	0·65
S. macrochir	Kafue	3·98	0·70	0·70
Tilapia rendalli	Kafue	4·61	1·40	1·40
Serranochromis angusticeps	Kafue	3·12	2·20	
Hepsetus odoe	Kafue	2·74	1·84	1·84
Total community*	Bandama			
Temperate				
Salmo trutta	Bere stream	2·10	1·34	1·81
Cottus gobio	Bere stream	1·66	1·33	
Rutilus rutilus	Thames	0·42	0·42	0·68
R. rutilus	Danube	0·69	0·98	0·65
Alburnus alburnus	Thames	1·29	1·29	1·29
A. alburnus	Danube	0·88	0·86	0·82
Leuciscus leuciscus	Thames	0·60	0·60	0·60
Perca fluviatilis	Thames	0·98	0·98	0·98
Gobio gobio	Thames	0·88	0·88	0·88

*Dominant species *Labeo coubie* and *Alestes rutilus*

initially in the temperate species (low mortality rates), their mortality rates tend to increase with age.

An accurate knowledge of mortality rates is essential to the calculation of production in animal communities, the lack of precise knowledge on this parameter for tropical riverine fish is a severe handicap in understanding the dynamics of such populations.

3.9 Estimates of standing stock and production

Standing stock

Estimates of ichthyomass or standing stock are available from several tropical rivers and can be contrasted with similar estimates from temperate waters. Standing stock estimates are usually made by one or more of three basic techniques: multiple fishing to the exhaustion of the stock, mark and recapture experiments, and poisoning a sample area with piscicides. These are described in more detail in the Appendix. The assessment of the total fish population by these methods is not wholly reliable owing to sampling errors of various kinds, but the combination of several methods and the taking of large sample areas improves the reliability of the estimate.

The density of the population present in any body of water in a river–floodplain system also depends much on the amount of water

Year						Authority
4	5	6	7	8	9	
						Daget and Ecoutin (1976)
						Daget and Ecoutin (1976)
						Dansoko (1975)
						Dansoko (1975)
0·65	0·65	1·70	0·58	0·58		Kapetsky (1974a)
0·70	0·70	0·70				Kapetsky (1974a)
1·40	1·40					Kapetsky (1974a)
						Kapetsky (1974a)
1·84						Kapetsky (1974a)
2·67						Daget *et al.* (1973)
						Mann (1971)
						Mann (1971)
0·70	0·92	1·00	1·26	1·86		Mann (1971)
0·70	0·56	0·61	0·68	0·75		Chitravadivelu (1974)
3·90	4·80	4·10				Mann (1971)
0·84	0·73	0·63				Chitravadivelu (1974)
0·60	0·56	1·15	1·28	1·46		Mann (1971)
1·61	1·49	1·39	1·45	1·47		Mann (1971)
0·88	2·52	4·24				Mann (1971)

present at the time of sampling. Population densities (ichthyomass per unit area) are generally higher during low water when the fish are concentrated together than at high water when they are dispersed, even though the total weight of fish in the system may be larger during the floods. Furthermore, the degree of exploitation affects the standing stock with probable reduction in mean ichthyomass as fishing pressure increases. As many tropical water courses are very heavily fished, the values of ichthyomass might be expected to be lower than they would be in a virgin or unexploited stock. Comparison between different systems is therefore difficult and can only legitimately be made on the basis of samples taken during the same phase of the flood cycle and taking into account the state of exploitation of the stock.

Main river channel
In most rivers, flows are too swift for accurate samples to be taken during the floods in the main channel. Consequently, most estimates have to be made during low water. It was assumed by University of Michigan *et al.* (1971) that during the floods the ichthyomass in the Kafue river would not differ significantly from that of the open-water areas of the floodplain. On the basis of repeated fishing with seine-nets and on rotenone samples in the open waters, an ichthyomass of 337 kg hm^{-2} was established. Samples taken in the channel at low water showed the standing stock to be less, 204 kg hm^{-2}. In the light of work by

Kapetsky (1974a) this dry-season estimate may be somewhat low. Kapetsky found the standing stock of the five main commercial species to be very different for three separate reaches of the Kafue river, being $106 \cdot 5 \pm 29 \cdot 2$; $576 \cdot 7 \pm 129 \cdot 2$ and $386 \cdot 6 \pm 63 \cdot 9$ kg hm^{-2}, respectively. The differences in standing stocks were attributed to differences in fishing intensity in the various reaches. The discrepancy between the mean $348 \cdot 2 \pm 59 \cdot 5$ kg hm^{-2} and the 204 kg hm^{-2} found by the University of Michigan could be explained in part by the reduction in water volume by a factor of $0 \cdot 7$ between the two sets of samples, but because the University estimate is based on all fish species, the actual difference between the two estimates is most probably greater than it appears.

In the Chari river, Loubens (1969) carried out an estimate of standing stock in a 360 m pool left in the main channel at low water, obtaining 15 138 fish hm^{-2} weighing 861 kg hm^{-2}. More comprehensive results were quoted by Daget *et al.* (1973) whose rotenone sampling at two sites in the Bandama river enabled the evaluation of changes occuring in the dry season. These were reduced into the following formulae:

$$\log d_j = 1 \cdot 632\,92 - 0 \cdot 003\,202_j$$

and

$$\log d_j = 1 \cdot 672\,86 - 0 \cdot 003\,166_j$$

for the reduction in number (d_j) with time in days (j). At one site, numbers were reduced from 3 417 hm^{-2} on 31 January to 1 411 hm^{-2} on 30 May, and biomass fell from 125 to 50 kg hm^{-2} in the same period. At the other site, 2 271 fish hm^{-2} on 31 January decreased to 996 fish hm^{-2} on 2 August, a loss of biomass of 144 kg hm^{-2}, from 257 to 113 kg hm^{-2}. Much lower estimates of standing stock were obtained from the Mekong by Sidthimunka (1970) who poisoned an area enclosed with a 100 m seine-net. The very low values obtained, $5 \cdot 92$ and $11 \cdot 79$ kg hm^{-2} may be because the reaches sampled lay upstream of the main flood zone. However, Bishop (1973) found the much higher ichthyomass of 179 kg hm^{-2} in the small Gombak river in Malaysia. Furthermore, recent but yet unpublished fishery studies relating to the lower Mekong basin, prepared under the auspices of the Mekong Committee, present values of 60 kg hm^{-2} for the upstream Mun river tributary to the Mekong, and $91 \cdot 9 \pm 51 \cdot 7$ kg hm^{-2} for 11 other tributaries. The value of 60 kg hm^{-2} for the Mun river is a mean of several estimates which fall from 120 kg hm^{-2} at low water to 5 kg hm^{-2} during the rising flood. The progressive drop of ichthyomass per unit area is attributed to the dispersal of the stock with increasing volume of water. Downstream in the main inundation zone the riverine standing crop was estimated at 135 kg hm^{-2}, but as this and the other values quoted are derived from capture fisheries the authors consider them to be low and they probably exclude the first-year fish which, as has been shown, contribute the major part of the ichthyomass.

The estimates of ichthyomass from the main channel of tropical rivers thus roughly vary from about 100 to 600 kg hm^{-2} and fall within much the same range as samples taken in temperate waters. For example, Mann (1965) found a total ichthyomass of 659 kg hm^{-2} in the river Thames, a value which has proved high for temperate rivers, although Backiel (1971) estimated that total ichthyomass in the Vistula river may be between 200 and 1 100 kg hm^{-2}. In Belgian rivers of various sizes, Timmermans (1961) and Huet and Timmermans (1963) found between 130 and 300 kg of fish hm^{-2} by electrofishing. The Horokiwi stream in New Zealand supported up to 311 kg hm^{-2} (Allen, 1951), and ichthyomass in trout streams in North America may reach 471 kg hm^{-2} (McFadden and Cooper, 1962). Swingle (1954) recorded 143 kg hm^{-2} from deep parts of the Coosa river and 154 kg hm^{-2} for shallow areas. Ichthyomass in deep parts of other large Alabama rivers varied from 51·2 to 1 730 kg hm^{-2}, this latter being attained in the Tenson river which had a particularly wide floodplain.

Backwaters

Secondary channels and blind river arms, which have many of the characteristics of floodplain standing waters but remain connected to the main channel for most of the year, are richer habitats than the main river and also higher in backwaters than in the main channel. As many as 22 350 fish hm^{-2} were found in a secondary arm of the Chari by Loubens (1969), although 98 per cent of these were small fish of less than 10 cm length. By contrast, 96 per cent of the 2 150 kg hm^{-2} were contributed by the few fish larger than this length. The same backwater had 5 616 kg of fish hm^{-2} at the end of one flood, which had fallen to 1 600 kg hm^{-2} two months later. A fourth sample from the same area a year later, yielded only 369 kg hm^{-2}, indicating the year-to-year variability that can be expected in the same body of water. Another backwater of the Chari gave an estimate of 2 166 kg hm^{-2} from an area of 6 000 m^2. In the Bandama, Daget *et al.* (1973) showed that population densities can increase in such backwaters. Contrary to the trends shown in the main channel, the number of fish in a minor river arm increased from 1 408 individuals hm^{-2} in March to 3 311 individuals hm^{-2} in June. This corresponded to an increase in weight from 149 kg hm^{-2} in March to 350 kg hm^{-2} in June. These figures, coupled with those for the main river indicated that there is some movement during the dry season from the open pools of the main river into the more shaded habitats of the backwaters. Sidthimunka's (1970) figure of 219·8 kg hm^{-2} for a backwater to the main stream of the Mekong was also considerably higher than the estimates from the main river itself, although the Mekong Studies figure of 125 kg hm^{-2} for a non-flowing backwater is similar to that in the main river. In the large Alabama Tombigbee river the ichthyomass in a backwater sampled by Swingle (1954) was much higher at 2 084 kg hm^{-2}, than either deep or shallow areas of the main stream with 457 and 570 kg hm^{-2}, respectively.

Perhaps the most detailed studies of fish populations of river backwaters come from the Danube. Bastl *et al.* (1969), Holčik (1972),

Holčik and Bastl (1973 and 1976) and Chitravadivelu (1974) have investigated the Biskupicke and Zöfin branches using mark-recapture and repeated catching methods. Their work led to the generalization that ichthyomass varies between 300 and 500 kg hm^{-2}. About 20 species were present, although species number varied with the area of the arm. Population densities were high in the summer when fish took refuge in the side arm from the current in the main channel. In the autumn the ichthyomass dropped as larger fish disappeared from the shallower waters. Summary values are shown in Table 3.13.

Table 3.13 Abundance of fish and ichthyomass in the Zöfin arm of the Danube in summer and autumn 1969–73 (after Holčik and Bastl, 1976)

	Abundance (no. hm^{-2})			Ichthyomass (kg hm^{-2})		
	Min.	Mean	Max.	Min.	Mean	Max.
Summer	6 438	12 528	18 619	136·5	326·7	516·2
Autumn	614	12 201	23 788	23·0	256·6	489·0

Very low values, often below 100 kg hm^{-2}, were associated with unusually strong flooding which dispersed the population, or with pollution which was especially common in some side arms of the Danube. A similar ichthyomass has been recorded from the Poltruba arm of the Elbe, where Oliva (1960) found a population density of *Rutilus rutilus* and *Alburnus alburnus* of 222·3 kg hm^{-2} using rotenone. As this was obtained from only two species the total ichthyomass was presumably somewhat higher.

Standing waters of the floodplain

Populations of fish in the floodplain lakes of the Danube are of similar densities to those of the backwaters. Balon (1967) in his sample of 13 water bodies, found between 335 and 318 632 fish hm^{-2}. The composition of the population varied considerably from one sample to another. The ichthyomass also had a wide range of variability: 230·4 ± 277·6 kg hm^{-2}. It was lowest during high water (136 ± 127 kg hm^{-2} in July) and highest during low water (480 ± 334 kg hm^{-2}). In the Russian Nyamunas river the floodplain is inundated by the spring floods which bring large quantities of fish into the oxbows and artifical channels. These are isolated during the summer, and Gaygalas and Blatneve (1971) estimated that about 200 kg hm^{-2} of fish remained in the autumn. As about twice this number were caught by anglers the total spring biomass was probably closer to 500 kg hm^{-2}.

In tropical rivers standing stocks of floodplain pools tend to be somewhat higher, although on some floodplains, such as the Magdalena and Mekong, there is a very considerable movement out of the depressions towards the main river channel which may account for the low values obtained from such systems. Table 3.14 summarizes the dry-season ichthyomass from the standing waters of a sample of tropical rivers. Ichthyomass apparently varies according to a number of factors.

Table 3.14 Estimates of dry-season ichthyomass in pools and lagoons of the floodplains of some tropical rivers

River	Size of sample	Estimated ichthyomass (kg hm^{-2})	Authority
Apure	1	982	Mago-Leccia (1970)
Candaba	–	500–700	Delmendo (1969)
Chari	2	701–2 166	Loubens, 1969
Kafue	8	444	Univ. of Michigan *et al.* (1971)
Magdalena	28	122	Kapetsky *et al.* (1977)
Mekong	1	63	Sidthimunka (1970)
		390	Mekong Fish. Studies (pers. comm.)
Okavango	2	200–700	Fox (1976)
Ouémé	68	1 835±825	FAO/UN (1971a)
Mogi Guassu	1	313	Gomez and Montiero (1955)
Paraná	8	1 264±2 216	Bonetto *et al.* (1969b)
Sabaki	1	786	Whitehead (1960)
Senegal	8	110±144	Reizer (1974)
Sokoto	25	661±557	Holden (1963)

As with other parts of the aquatic system, population densities are normally greater during the dry season. Thus, when Kapetsky *et al.* (1976) estimated a minimum biomass of between 0·23 and 251 kg hm^{-2} (mean 55·7 kg hm^{-2}) as being present in the open water and between 20 and 232 kg hm^{-2} (mean 79·8 kg hm^{-2}) in the bay areas of the cienagas of the Magdalena floodplain, he also found a good negative correlation between the population density and the water level in the cienagas. Strangely enough, while the University of Michigan *et al.* (1971) also found population densities to be higher in the open waters of the lagoons of the Kafue river during the dry season (426 kg hm^{-2}) than during the floods (337 kg hm^{-2}), vegetated areas showed the opposite tendency, and very high concentrations of fish (up to 2 682 kg hm^{-2}) were present in such areas at high water. However, high densities of fish under floating vegetation seem to be comparably rare, and permanent swamps, particularly those under papyrus, are notorious for the poverty of their fish communities. This situation may change temporarily during the flood when currents can oxygenate the water column under the plants. The University of Michigan study also indicated the loss of ichthyomass during the dry season when in one pool an initial standing stock of 2 693 kg hm^{-2} diminished by 75 per cent to 684 kg hm^{-2} in three months. In a second pool a similar decline from 3 306 to 501 kg hm^{-2} occurred in 10 weeks, although in this case the pool was connected to the river for part of the time and emigration might have occurred.

The form of the lagoon and the nature of the bottom may also influence ichthyomass. In the Senegal river, long narrow pools formed from isolated drainage channels supported a much higher standing stock than round depression pools, 205 ± 155 kg hm^{-2} as against 13 ± 6 kg hm^{-2} (Reizer, 1974). In the Sokoto, Holden's (1963) analysis shows that a greater proportion of fish preferred intermediate sand/mud bottoms (1 012 kg hm^{-2}) as opposed to sand (785 kg hm^{-2}) or mud (233 kg hm^{-2}).

Differences in standing stock have been related to the degree of organic fertilization of the water body by Fox (1976). His estimates for small unenriched pools in the southern Okavango delta showed between 100 and 200 kg hm^{-2} to be usual, whereas a highly enriched peripheral lagoon had the highest estimate of 700 kg hm^{-2}. While this evidence is far from conclusive, owing to the small sample size, it would appear reasonable that eutrophicated waters should support higher densities of fish relative to those less rich in nutrients.

Total system

The only study covering the total system is that of the University of Michigan *et al.* (1971) who extrapolated rather widely from a limited number of samples of four different habitats of the Kafue river and floodplain. Their results are shown in Table 3.15

Table 3.15 Summary of high-water and low-water estimates of ichthyomass from the Kafue river and floodplain system

	Area (hm^2)	Ichthyomass (kg hm^{-2})	Total ichthyomass (tonnes)
High water			
Open-water lagoon	126 000	337	42 462
Vegetated lagoon	16 000	2 682	42 912
Grass marsh	136 000	64	8 704
River channel	5 300	337	1 786
Total	283 300		95 864
Low water			
River channel	4 800	204	959
Open-water lagoon	113 000	426	48 138
Vegetated lagoon	14 000	592	8 288
Total	131 800		57 405

The dry-season estimate for total ichthyomass in the system was 57 405 t, representing about 60 per cent of the wet season estimate of 95 864 t. However, the ichthyomass per unit area was lower in the wet season (338·4 kg hm^{-2}) than in the dry (435·6 kg hm^{-2}).

Production

Production can be defined as the total elaboration of fish tissues during any specified period of time, including gonadial products and material formed by individuals which do not survive to the end of the period (Ivlev, 1966). In many temperate waters the production by individual species does not exceed 200 kg hm^{-2} yr^{-1} (data in Chapman, 1967). However, work on the Thames by Mann (1965) and the Horokiwi stream by Allen (1951) showed that higher productions were being achieved in some rivers. In the Horokiwi, the production of brown trout was estimated at 533 kg hm^{-2} yr^{-1}. This was relative to a mean ichthyomass of 311 kg hm^{-2}, giving a production/biomass ratio (P/B) of 1·7, and was achieved mostly in the first year of life. In the Thames a composite population of five species was estimated to produce 426 kg hm^{-2} ($P/B = 0·64$), although in a later publication Mann (1972) quoted a higher value of 2 000 kg hm^{-2} yr^{-1} after including the first-year fish in the calculation. This age group accounted for about 70 per cent of the total production. Production/biomass ratios, which are useful indicators of the rapidity of turnover of biomass, were 1·12 for *Rutilus rutilus* and 1·92 for *Alburnus alburnus* when the young fish were taken into account. Chitravadivelu (1974) also worked on these two species on the Zöfin backwater of the Danube. His results showed considerable year-to-year variation. In the case of *R. rutilus* the production was 14·49, 9·00 and 47·99 kg hm^{-2} yr^{-1} in 1969, 1970 and 1971, respectively; in *A. alburnus* the production was 90·98 (1969), 5·25 (1970) and 11·75 (1971) kg hm^{-2} yr^{-1}. These variations were correlated to some extent with a very strong 1970 flood which lowered total biomass in that year and contributed to better production in 1971. This did not entireely explain the full variability which was also associated with differences in relative species abundance. That the changes in production were mainly linked to changes in biomass is shown by the relative constancy of the P/B ratio: 0·41 (1969), 0·48 (1970), 0·61 (1971) for *R. rutilus*, and 0·53 (1969); 0·48 (1970), 0·68 (1971) for *A. alburnus*.

The only tropical river fish for which production has been studied in detail are three cichlids from the Kafue floodplain. Here Kapetsky (1974b) found that *Tilapia rendalli* produced 198·00 kg hm^{-2} yr^{-1} with about 53 per cent coming from fish in their first year of life and 91 per cent from fish in their first two years. Early production is also high in *Sarotherodon andersoni* where 64 per cent of the yearly total of 118·56 kg hm^{-2} was produced by fish in their first two years, and *S. macrochir* where 74 per cent of the total of 144·94 kg hm^{-2} was produced by the first two age groups. Production/biomass ratios varied from 1·63 for *T. rendalli* to 0·75 for *S. andersoni*. As these three species comprised between 53 and 73 per cent of the standing stock, total annual production of all species from the Kafue system might be expected to be about 630–870 kg hm^{-2}. Thus, although it has been generally assumed that productivity is higher in tropical than in temperate waters it would seem that there are insufficient studies on rivers at the present time for any definite conclusions to be drawn. The Kafue shows much higher productions than does the Danube, but ranks in the same order as the Thames or the Horokiwi.

These limited results indicate the great contribution made by the youngest age groups to the total production. Unfortunately, it is precisely this group – fish within the first 6–12 months of life – for which reliable numerical, growth and mortality data are hardest to acquire. For this reason several workers have resorted to modelling to give some indication of the processes involved in the earlier part of the life cycle.

Models of dynamics of floodplain fish populations

As has been pointed out in the sections on mortality and growth, simple exponential models of these parameters are inconsistent with what is known of the biology of floodplain fishes, and are thus inadequate to derive within-the-year changes of biomass and production. Because the catch that can be expected from floodplain rivers is most probably linked to the excess of ichthyomass produced in the flood over that which can be supported in the dry season, a more detailed knowledge of within-the-year changes in these parameters is necessary for the management of both the fish stock and the hydrological regime. Alternative models, based on the assumption of rapid growth and low mortality during the flood, and low growth and high mortality during the dry season, have been proposed. Kapetsky (1974a) contrasted the production derived from standard models of growth and mortality, with linear and 'floodplain' models of these parameters, and found that production estimates for age group III fish onwards gave very different results according to which model was used. The 'floodplain' model, combines number

$$N_t = N_0 - N_0 e^{-zT}(e^{zt}-1)$$

and mean weight

$$W_t = W_0 + W_1 e^{gT} - (1 - e^{gt})$$

in the form $B_t = N_t\ W_t$. It gives estimates for production of up to 4·4 times that of the simple exponential model and twice that of the linear model. The reason for this is shown in the differences between the theoretical biomass—time curves for age group 0 fish which are plotted in Fig. 3.24, from the simple exponential (a) and 'floodplain' (b) models for two values of Z and a growth rate ($G = 5\cdot3$).

Daget and Ecoutin (1976) have also derived a model of biomass and production based on their growth equation for fish undergoing an annual growth arrest. Biomass is calculated from $B_t = N_t\ W_t$, where $W_t = 0\cdot68\ 10^{-5}L_t^{\,3}$, L_t is derived from the formulae discussed in the section on growth (see Section 3.6, p. 135) and N_t is derived from the simple exponential mortality equation $W_t = N_0 e^{-zt}$. The model was applied to *Polypterus senegalus*, giving good comparability with observed results. Estimates of production ranged from 528·54 kg ($P/B = 0\cdot559$) to 281·65 kg ($P/B = 1\cdot123$) for mortality coefficients $Z=0\cdot04$ and $Z=0\cdot10$, respectively. This illustrates the importance of mortality rate in deriving production and biomass values. However, the application of a constant mortality factor in this model is possibly somewhat limiting, and the abrupt termination of growth produces a rather sharply peaked annual biomass curve (Fig. 3.25), which may or may not approach the natural situation.

A more detailed simulation of the dynamics of a floodplain fish community has been proposed by Welcomme and Hagborg (1977). Basically, this represents the combination of their growth and mortality

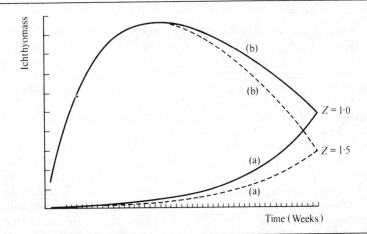

Fig. 3.24 Theoretical biomass–time curves for age group 0 fish during one year when calculated from (a) simple exponential expressions for growth and mortality, and (b) 'floodplain' expressions.

models (see Sections 3.6 and 3.8.). By introducing density-dependent mortality rates and growth rates and recruitment which were dependent on the intensity of the simulated flood, the model enabled the exploration of the effects of changes in both high- and low-water components of the flood regime on a theoretical fish community. The simulation gave a series of curves for total ichthyomass which were derived from hydrological regimes in which either the flood intensity or the amount of water remaining in the system at low water could be varied independently of one another (Fig. 3.26). These indicated that differences in high-water or flood regimes produce great differences in within-the-year ichthyomass, but that the magnitude of the population passing through to the following year is largely dependent on the amount of water remaining in the system at low water. They also indicated that the more water that remains in the system at low water the more differences induced by the high-water regime are transmitted to the next year. The curves in Fig. 3.26 were combined into a three-dimensional plot of mean ichthyomass for different high- and low-water regimes (Fig. 3.27). Values for fish production per mean flooded area derived from this simulation agree well with the general findings presented above. They range from 241 to 564 kg hm^{-2} yr^{-1}, depending on flood regime with P/B values of between 1·35 and 1·77. Production and biomass are maximal in higher floods but the P/B ratio increases as the maximum area flooded decreases.

These three models indicate a similar evolution of biomass throughout the year with a convex ichthyomass–time curve. According to this, there is an initial rapid increase in ichthyomass which attains a maximum at about bankfull on the declining flood and which would

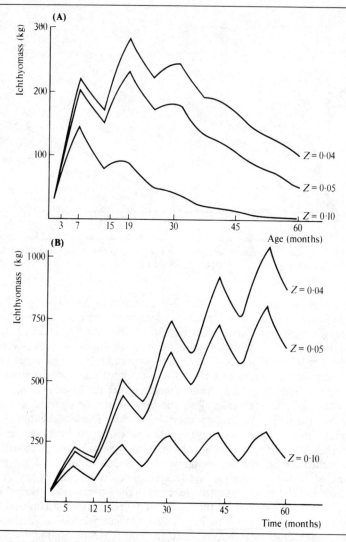

Fig. 3.25 (A) Variations in ichthyomass of one cohort as a function of age for three different mortality coefficients; (B) ichthyomass of a population for three different mortality coefficients, assuming the same recruitment each year and the accumulation of cohorts. (After Daget and Ecoutin, 1976.)

seem to represent the natural state fairly accurately. The models equally emphasise the great importance of age group 0 fish which contribute up to 80 per cent of the total ichthyomass, depending on mortality rate. Both the shape of the biomass–time curve and the great preponderance of juvenile fish have important consequences for the management of

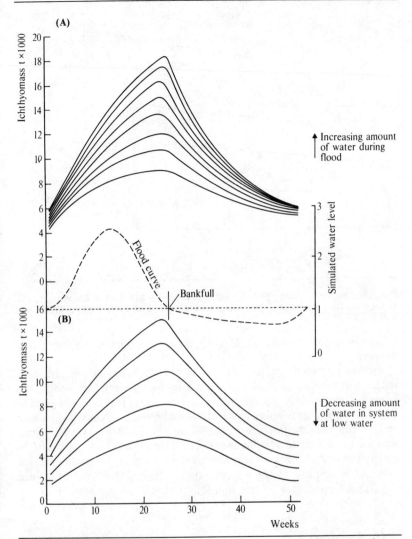

Fig. 3.26 Computer-generated curves showing changes in total ichthyomass with time for different flood regimes where (A) the low-water regime is constant and the high-water regime varies; and (B) where the high-water regime is constant but the low-water regime varies. Also shown is a typical water regime (–––––). (After Welcomme and Hagborg, 1977.)

floodplain fish populations for fisheries. The variations in production and ichthyomass corresponding to differences in flood regime predicted by the simulation suggest that equivalent year-to-year variations occur in the fish populations themselves. From records in many systems it is well known that the catch does indeed fluctuate in this manner, and so

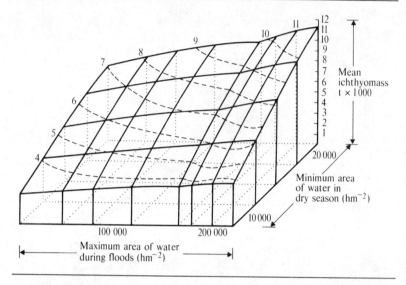

Fig. 3.27 Three-dimensional plot of mean annual ichthyomass as related to water regime. Dashed lines join points of equal ichthyomass on the derived surface. (After Welcomme and Hagborg, 1977.)

presumably do production and ichthyomass (see Section 4.5 for further details).

Curves plotted from the simulation for ichthyomass per unit area indicate that the population is very dispersed during the floods, but concentrates rapidly as the water drains from the floodplain until bankfull (Fig. 3.28). This phase is followed by a steady attrition which reflects the real situation observed by Daget *et al.* (1973) in the Bandama and the University of Michigan *et al.* (1971) in the Kafue. Changes in the ichthyomass per unit area are also evident from the seasonality of the fisheries which are at their most intense during those periods when the fish are concentrated, i.e. late falling flood and dry season.

3.10 Summary

Tropical river basins are inhabited by a great variety of species whose number is a function of the size of the system, larger systems having relatively more species. The relative abundance of species within a basin or sub-basin tends to conform to a lognormal distribution. Freshwater, brackish-water and occasionally marine species, are all represented in floodplain rivers. Specializations are shown by the various fishes and are mainly adaptations to the fluctuating hydrological regime.

For fisheries purposes species may be roughly separated into two major ethological groups, 'whitefish' which avoid unfavourable

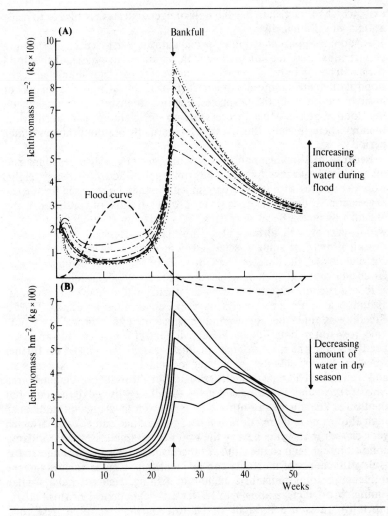

Fig. 3.28 Computer-generated curves showing changes in population density (kg hm^{-2}) with time for different flood regimes where (A) the low-water regime is constant but the high water regime varies; and (B) the high-water regime is constant but the low water regime varies. Also shown is a typical water regime (– – – – –). (After Welcomme and Hagborg, 1977.)

conditions during low water by migration into and within the main channel of the river, and 'blackfish' which are specialized to resist the conditions on the plain. Migrations in whitefishes may take place over large distances. Anatomical specializations to resist extreme environmental conditions usually take the form of accessory respiratory organs which enable the fish to use atmospheric oxygen, but adaptations also exist which allow fish to use the well-oxygenated surface film or to resist anoxia physiologically.

Although apparent trophic specializations exist, feeding habits are very flexible and are apt to vary with the different phases of the flood cycle. Broad trophic groups are, however, distinguishable and the floodplain fish community is characterized by a high proportion of piscivorous and detritivore species. Feeding intensity is maximal during the flooded phase. Most species store up sufficient body fat at this time to carry them through the fast which persists throughout the low-water period.

Because of the seasonality of feeding, growth is also seasonal and increase in length takes place mainly during the flood. Growth in weight, which coincides with the increase in length, may be reversed during the dry season, and many species suffer progressive loss of condition as the season advances. Because of this, Von Bertalanffy models do not fit within-year growth, although they have been successfully applied to the overall growth of some species. Growth in any one year is positively correlated with the duration and intensity of the flood during that year. Good and poor growth-year classes are thereby generated.

Reproduction usually takes place just prior to or early in the flood, although a number of species have more extended breeding seasons. Breeding adaptations correspond to those for avoidance of unfavourable low-water conditions. Whitefish tend to migrate towards the headwaters of the river to breed just before or at the start of the floods, whereas blackfish show a variety of behavioural and anatomical adaptations such as nest construction, mouthbrooding or viviparity for care of the young. Breeding success is also closely linked to the nature of the flood. Years with smooth increase in water level and with floods of high amplitude and long duration tend to produce numerically stronger year classes than years having the opposite characteristics. Poor flood conditions can lead to the failure of recruitment from one or more years.

Several causes of mortality can be identified, but the various factors influencing total mortality, including fishing, tend to have similar timing. Most factors appear to be density-dependent. For this reason, mortality rates are thought to be low during the flood, rise to a maximum as the water leaves the plain and continue to be high during the rest of the low-water season. Standard simple exponential models of mortality are inappropriate for within-year mortality rates and alternative exponential relationships have been proposed to describe them.

Estimates of standing crop have been made in several parts of the world, giving variable results. Some very high values have been obtained in dry-season pools and, in general, it would seem that the population density is closely related to flood state.

The parameters for mortality and growth have been combined into models which describe the theoretical behaviour of fish populations or communities under regimes in which the water level fluctuates seasonally. These agree in that they predict a variation in total biomass which corresponds to the flood cycle. Total biomass increases throughout the wet season to a maximum towards the end of the flood phase. It then declines as the dry season progresses.

The production and biomass of fish in any river therefore fluctuate according to the flood regime. Good floods inundate larger areas, making available greater quantities of food, and improving conditions for reproduction and shelter. Recruitment, growth and survival are as a consequence better in years when discharges are high, subject to their timeliness, and the population is correspondingly greater. The natural year-to-year variation in flood intensity thereby produces a similar variation in the magnitude of the fish stock.

Note

1. The classification of fish into 'black' and 'white' categories adopted here is not precisely the same as that used in the Mekong area where it originated. In the Mekong 'blackfishes' are all species of fish having a slippery body, many without scales or with small scales, whereas the whitefish comprises all species of fish having light or silvery-white scales. The differences in behaviour of these two categories are fundamental and only in certain siluroids do fish normally classifiable as 'whitefish' show blackfish features. In this book the terms are used for all systems and more generally refer to: (a) 'whitefish', those species undertaking long migrations within the river with high fecundity and egg-scattering habit and low tolerance to deoxygenated conditions; (b) 'blackfish' those species which inhabit the floodplain and its residual waters, which usually exhibit some degree of parental care and have high tolerance to deoxygenated conditions. For fisheries purposes these two blocks are very distinct and have to be managed in different ways.

Chapter 4

The fishery

4.1 The fishermen

All fisheries are to a great extent shaped by the nature of the environment and the characteristics of the fish stocks they exploit. The factors influencing fisheries in rivers are very different from those shaping lacustrine and marine fisheries. Three factors in particular give river fisheries their character; diffuseness in space, seasonality and diversity. Because these are common to the great majority of tropical river systems, there is a remarkable parallelism in the general form of riverine fisheries and the communities which exploit them.

Rivers are lineaform and of limited width so the total area of water that can be reached from any point on the bank is limited by the ability to travel upstream or downstream. In most tropical waters, movement is by hand-propelled canoes, although outboard motors are also used. These have a very restricted radius of action and it is rare for there to be an expanse of water accessible to any one landing which is sufficiently large to support a capture and marketing operation of any great size. The problems posed by the linear form of rivers are aggravated by the swampy and changeable nature of the terrain, which, together with their periodic submergence, hinders the installation and maintenance of permanent roads and other forms of communication, rendering the heart of the floodplain inaccessible to most types of transport. Spatial dispersion and inaccessibility have so far combined to make river fisheries labour-intensive, artisanal operations which are located in a series of small settlements along the channels or spread on islands of higher elevation over the floodplain. There are some obvious exceptions to this general principle in estuarine waters, large floodplains or floodplain lakes, where the available area of water is greater.

As has been described, the flood regime of rivers causes a seasonal expansion and contraction of water area which can separate settlements from the main course of the river by many kilometres in the dry season, even though they are at the water's edge during the flood. Coupled to this hydrological cycle are the migrations of fish within the system which cause them to undergo changes in abundance, density and location. In response to the fluctuations in the ecosystem fishermen either have to alternate fishing with other occupations or they themselves have to migrate. Because of this it is very difficult to define accurately who is, or is not, a fisherman. In some systems the situation is fairly clear, as fishing is the task of one particular ethnic group or tribe, and practically the whole of the active population of such a group may be interpreted as being involved in the fishery in some way. In such cases the fishing group often does not own land and coexists with other groups equally specialized in agriculture or pastoralism. In other rivers, the riparian population remains relatively unspecialized as a whole, although subgroups may concentrate on one or more of the specialized activities, including fishing. Within the fishing community there is usually a well-defined division of labour. The men fish, construct and maintain the gear and build the boats, while the women collect, treat and market the produce. In such populations most able-bodied male, and sometimes female, individuals fish at some time or other. Furthermore, the role of small pre-adolescent boys in many artisanal fisheries should not be underestimated as they act as fisheries aids. In this capacity they paddle canoes, bait and control long lines, lift traps and generally keep the fishery going when the adult members of the community may be occupied elsewhere.

For the purposes of convenience fishermen may be classified into three categories on the basis of the time they spend fishing (FAO/UN, 1962). These are:

1. occasional fishermen;
2. part-time fishermen;
3. full-time fishermen.

Occasional fishermen
In contrast to lakes where a boat is usually essential to reach fishing grounds and to operate gear, many floodplain waters can be reached on foot during the dry season and fished by simple apparatus from the bank or by wading. This relative ease of access for the inhabitants of the floodplain, coupled with a certain amount of free time between the sowing and the harvest of floodplain crops, means that casual fishing for subsistence is popular in floodplain communities. Furthermore, in many areas of Africa and Asia, certain depression lakes or sectors of the river and floodplain are traditionally reserved for the inhabitants of particular villages. These are fished during festivals or fish drives which take on all the aspects of a holiday and in which all members of the community participate. Most of the fish caught enters directly into the diet of the fishing community. The individual time spent is low and for the most part the gear used is simple and relatively unproductive. On the other hand the numbers participating are often very high. It is therefore difficult to assess the contribution of such efforts to the total catch of any particular system.

Part-time fishermen
Many sedentary peoples living on floodplains fish during part of the

year. This is an activity that is co-equal to or inferior to the alternative activities of such populations. The flood cycle, the biological cycle of the fish, and the seasonal needs of agriculture impose a cyclicity on such communities. During the floods there is very little activity in either domain, but as the waters drain from the plain, fishing increases. As the floodplain dries, the preparation of the soil and sowing of the seeds take priority, to be followed with a second burst of fishing at low water. Harvesting of the crops follows, and the cycle repeats itself year by year. It is perhaps not surprising that, while part-time fishermen use most of the types of gear used by professional fishermen, they also have a tendency to practice various types of extensive aquaculture techniques. For example, the development of drain-in fish ponds, which will be discussed in Section 4.2, is associated with a certain agricultural type of land and water tenure in countries as widely separated as Cambodia (Chevey and Le Poulain, 1940) and Benin (Hurault, 1965). Similarly, the association of drain-in ponds with paddy-fields is a feature of many rice-growing communities (Tang Cheng Eng *et al.*, 1973).

Professional fishermen
In most aquatic systems there are groups of individuals that live entirely by fishing. The need for year-round employment and the movements of the fish stocks often force such groups to be nomadic. Migratory fishermen have been noted from many systems and are a particular feature of river fisheries. For example, Bhuiyan (1959) described the migrations of the *Hilsa* fishermen of the Indus who followed the movements of that species up and down the river. The fishermen of the Kafue similarly move around, depending on the water level and abundance of the fish stocks (Everett, 1974). In the Magdalena fishery the fishermen move from the cienagas where they fish in the dry season, to intercept the 'Subienda' migration in the river (Bazigos *et al.*, 1977). Some of these migrations by fishermen can be of very large proportions. The upstream movements of the Haoussa in the Niger river (Daget, in FAO/UN, 1962), might reasonably be compared to the operations of factory trawlers in oceanic fisheries when the size of the investment relative to the per-capita income of the community is taken into account. This movement, which may be taken as fairly typical, involved whole families of 20–30 persons who moved upstream in September and October to fish the northerly portions of the Central Delta on the falling flood. The distance moved was in excess of 1 000 km. The main vessels, which were often up to 15 m long and were equipped to support whole families on the journey, were accompanied by a flotilla of small craft which were used in the actual fishing. On the return journey, which was made on the next flood, the main vessels were loaded with many tons of fish for sale in the Nigerian markets. These northern parts of the Central Delta are far from the main centres of population, and have been exploited by wandering fishermen for many centuries. Therefore, the incidence of nomadism increases from the southern parts of the basin,

where only 2 per cent of the population are mobile, to 52 per cent in the heart of the lake district (Raimondo, 1975).

Not all nomadic fishermen undertake such long journeys, but most have to leave their native villages during at least part of the annual cycle. Many fishermen construct temporary fishing camps on high ground within the floodplains which they occupy during the fishing season and which they move following changes in the river level. To encourage this, it has been proposed that artificial islands be constructed on some floodplains, especially the Kafue and the Sudan Sudd, to enable the fishermen to exploit areas that have so far remained undeveloped for lack of suitable living space. In some flooded areas, such as the Mesopotamic area of the Tigris–Euphrates system or the Ganges delta in Bangladesh, the rural community, including fishermen and their families, already live on islands made of soil and domestic refuse accumulated over the years. As an alternative many fishing communities have developed houses on stilts which remain above all but the highest floods. These are typical of the lowland rivers of the West African coast (Fig. 4.1) and of Asia. In Asia, too, some fishermen live, at least temporarily, on boats or rafts which are associated with traps, stow-nets or lift-nets in the river channel (see Fig. 4.13).

Fig. 4.1 Stilt houses on the banks of the So river of the Ouémé delta. Note circular brush park in foreground.

Professional fishermen use a vast range of fishing gear, but in recent years have tended to concentrate on one or two of the more sophisticated modern fishing methods such as seine-nets, gill-nets or cast-nets. Such fishermen, too, use powered craft to a great extent, if not for fishing then for the transport of fish from the fishing grounds to the markets.

In recent years long-distance nomadism has been discouraged in many parts of the world as this practice has involved the movements of the nationals of one country into the waters of another. With increasing awareness of the potentialities of their inland fisheries most countries have felt the need to retain these benefits for their own nations and have trained local people accordingly. Many of the traditional movements, such as that described for the Niger, have therefore broken down and in their place shorter local migrations have intensified.

4.2 Fishing and fishing gear

Seasonality

Fish are vulnerable to the fishery for only part of the year, and their accessibility depends much on the ichthyomass per unit area, as represented in Fig. 3.28, or on temporary concentrations of migrating fish. During high water they are dispersed over the floodplain and concealed by thick mats of vegetation. The bulk of the population are juveniles, often too small to be captured by any practical gear. Physical conditions are also not favourable, as strong currents sweep down the main channel and over the plain, carrying with them logs and floating masses of vegetation that carry away any fixed engines. As a consequence there is a slackening or complete absence of fishing during the flood season in most river fisheries, although some gears, such as the 'atalla' lift-net of the lower Niger, are operated at this time to catch small species which have taken refuge in vegetation fringing the main channel or juvenile fish which are concentrated in the shallow marginal waters of lagoons (Awachie and Walson, 1977). Fishermen may also continue to be active in some of the larger floodplain lakes where conditions are more stable. In older and more tradition-bound fisheries this cessation of activity is often reinforced by laws and taboos which close the fishery to some or all gears. Many such traditional bans seem to have arisen as a result of the recognition of the flood season as a period of breeding essential to the continued existence of the fish stock.

Fish become more available for capture as they congregate in the channels and pools of the floodplain and the water begins draining into the main channel. At this time there is a very heavy and concentrated fishery. Intensive fishing is continued throughout the dry season in the standing waters of the floodplain and in the main river channel. Later, as the water begins to rise once more, fairly specialized fisheries concentrate on the adult fish migrating to their breeding sites. The various types of fishery carried out through the season need a variety of methods which succeed one another in a regular pattern. A typical example of this is the Mekong fishery (Fig. 4.2) where there is little or no activity on the rising flood (July–September). The greatest concentration of gears is present on the falling flood (October–January), and a different set of methods takes over at low water (February–May). As has been observed in the section on migration, there is strong lunar rhythm in the movements of fish in this system, accounting for the peaks in fishing intensity of certain gears which are operational as fish leave the plain.

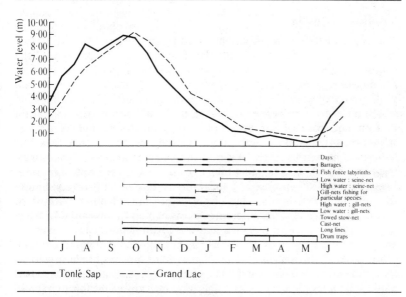

——— Tonlé Sap   – – – – – Grand Lac

Fig. 4.2 Fishing timetable for the Mekong fishery. Thin line = fishing possible; thick line = peak effort with method. Subsistence methods are not included in this tabulation. (Adapted from Fily and d'Aubenton, 1966.)

Boats

A detailed description of the various kinds of fishing craft is not appropriate here, but the availability of suitable means of water transport is crucial in a fishery which depends much on the mobility of the fishermen. Furthermore, as the plain is inundated for several months of the year, the communities inhabiting them are forced to adopt a semi-aquatic way of life. During the floods water-borne transport is the only means of communication, and even the markets are conducted from canoes. As a simplification, there are two main types of boat used in river fisheries. The first are the fishing craft themselves which are usually dugout canoes or planked craft between 4 and 6 m long. Motorization of the smaller fishing boats is comparatively rare, especially among part-time fishermen, and is in many cases of no great advantage. The second class of boats are longer, often up to 10 m long, and are used for transport of fish from the landing to the market. These are more frequently motorized. In the main equatorial rivers, the construction of boats presents few problems as wood is plentiful and dugouts are easily made. However, in the savanna rivers the lack of good wood is limiting and canoes are often scarce and expensive as they have to be imported from elsewhere. The development of suitable substitutes for traditional types of craft, which are cheap enough for the fishermen, is one of the main preoccupations of fisheries administrators in such areas.

Capture methods

The types of fishing methods in use in rivers are conditioned by two factors; firstly, the nature of the fish stock, and secondly, the characteristics of the raw materials from which the gear is constructed. As has been described, the fish communities of tropical rivers are particularly diverse. They contain a large number of species, most of which differ to some degree in their selection of habitat, diet, migration pattern and ease of capture. They are also represented by an age structure which is more than usually biased towards juvenile fish. The fishermen have, therefore, to establish priorities for their fishery with respect to which species and which age classes they attempt to capture. Preference is often imposed by local food taboos or customs, although there are a few fisheries which have been founded on the export of species which are not locally accepted items of diet. In some fisheries a few species may be selected from the many as forming the basis for capture, and in these the range of gear in use is quite limited. However, in many other systems the fishery exploits all species that are catchable, and to do so a great number of fishing methods have evolved. Until recently, when cotton and later nylon twine and nets were introduced into tropical river fisheries, gear was constructed uniquely from local materials. Roots, vines, plant fibres, leaves, stems, etc. have been – and still are – used for much of the gear encountered in river and floodplain systems. The similarity of the comportment of the different elements of the fish community and the raw materials from which the gear is made, have led to a considerable parallelism in most methods, even though they have in all probability been developed independently. There are of course a number of local variations, and these are described in the many catalogues of fishing methods in various countries such as Chevey and Le Poulain (1940) for the Mekong, Ahmad (1956) for the waters of Bangladesh or Blache and Miton (1962) for the Chari–Lake Chad basin. A detailed description of all gear used in river fisheries is clearly inappropriate here so this chapter will examine the general principles of the capture methods used in as far as they are relevant to the broad ecology of these systems. Clearer descriptions of artisanal and other fishing gears, classified by type are available elsewhere, for instance in Andreev's (1966) *Handbook of Fishing Gear and Its Rigging* or in Brandt's (1972) book, *Fish Catching Methods of the World*.

Certain types of fishing gear relying on modern industrially manufactured twines are in widespread use. These are the seine-net, the gill-net and the cast-net. In many systems these methods are replacing much of the traditional gear, and they are especially favoured by professional (full-time) fishermen as their individual catching power is superior. Their care and maintenance requires an expertise often lacking among the more casual elements of the fishing community. The cast-net is in fact one of the mainstays of these fisheries. Conditions in flood rivers, especially in the floodplain lakes and the main stream at low water, are well suited to its use. The water is fairly shallow, the bottom unencumbered and the fish are sufficiently concentrated to give a good chance of capture. The mesh size can be varied according to the species and size of fish sought. Fishermen using cast-nets may fish either individually or in combination with others whose manoeuvres serve to concentrate the fish still further. The seine-net requires relatively large teams to operate it and is very expensive. It is, therefore, the gear of the professional *par excellence*. Its use is limited by current, and especially by the availability of bottoms which are sufficiently free of obstructions which would otherwise cause the net to snag. The tenure of suitable seining beaches is often hotly disputed in the fishing community. As a gear it has several precursors among traditional methods and communal fish drives often have a seine-like approach with lines of fishermen wielding baskets or clap-nets. Alternatively, a barrage fence, which is one of the basic items of equipment for the floodplain fisherman, is set in a large semicircle and moved inshore in the same way as the seine. The gill-net is also common, although it is sensitive to floating vegetation and will not operate in strong flows. On the other hand, it does come into its own in the larger floodplain lagoons and lakes where the depth, the large stretches of open water and lack of current make it one of the most effective gears.

Table 4.1 Typical values for catch from seine, gill and cast nets in some tropical rivers

	Seine-net (kg net^{-1} day^{-1})	Gill-net (kg 100 m net^{-1} day^{-1})	Cast-net (kg net^{-1} day^{-1})	
Barotse		6·2		FAO/UN (1969)
Chao-Phrya	1 149–3 006*			Tongsanga and Kessunchai (1966)
Kafue	461	10		Everett (1974)
Magdalena	110–125*	13·2		Granados (1975)
Mekong	150–500*	24	15	Fily and D'Aubenton (1966)
Niger		9·3	7·9	FAO/UN (1971a)
Ouémé (1958)		10·4	2·7–5·6	FAO/UN (1971a)
Pendjari		4·5		FAO/UN (1971a)
Shire		12·2	14·8	Willoughby and Walker (1977)

* Depending on size of net.

These gears either singly or together dominate certain fisheries. In the Magdalena river the cast-net is the main method, although seines, gill-nets, traps and spears are also used to some extent (Kapetsky *et al.*, 1977). In recent years the seine-net has become the principal gear in the Senegal river, to the exclusion of many traditional methods which are still current in the neighbouring Niger river (Reizer, 1974). The Kafue river fishery also relies almost entirely on the combination of gill-net and seine-net (Everett, 1974).

Catches by these methods vary very considerably according to the construction of the gear, the habits of the fishermen and the time of year. It is perhaps useful nevertheless, to have some idea of the general order of magnitude of catch to be expected and typical values are given in Table 4.1.

Fishing during the rising and receding floods
As the floods start to rise there is a burst of activity by the fish as the adults move preparatory to breeding. Locally high concentrations are present, giving rise to very heavy but localized fisheries. When the floods recede from the plain the water becomes confined increasingly into depressions and channels. The fish follow these flow patterns to reach either the main channel or what will become the standing waters of the plain itself. Fishing methods take advantage of these movements and are mainly aimed at either directing the fish into places where they are more easily captured, or to retaining the fish in floodplain depressions from which they may be more easily removed later. Such gear may be based on bamboo or palm-frond fish fences which are installed across the plain or the channels through which the water enters or leaves. They can reach a considerable length and can be arranged in complex forms, giving a labyrinth-like effect. Capture is either in trap-shaped chambers (Fig. 4.3), or in special cylindrical traps or nets which are placed in openings in the barrage. Durand (1970), for instance, has described a cross-river barrage from El Beid river which drains the Yaérés floodplains of the Logone river. Here the fences are arranged in a series of vees at the apexes of which are held large hand-nets. Both upstream and downstream migrants may be caught in the same type of trap. Thus, in the Nzoia river the 'kek' type of barrier trap (Fig. 4.4) intercepts breeding fish moving upstream, as well as adult fish returning from the spawning grounds (Whitehead, 1959b). Such fences can contribute a large proportion of the total annual catch in some systems. In the Lubuk Lampam (Indonesia) guide fences accounted for about 50 per cent of the fish caught in 1975 (Arifin and Arifin, 1976) and on the African Barotse plain the 'maalelo' fishery produced about 25 per cent (631 t) of the total in 1969. The 'maalelo' of the Barotse floodplain is perhaps typical of the more open-plain type of barrier fishery. Here the fish guides are usually earth bunds some 75 cm high and between 3 and 40 m long, which deflect fish into traps placed at intervals along their length, although reed, wire-mesh or brushwood fences may also be used. Alternatively, the bunds may join two areas of high ground so as to retain a pool behind them. When eventually the dam thus formed is breached, the fish are caught in

traps and baskets at the outflow, giving a yield equivalent to about 33·6 kg hm^{-2} of area impounded (Bell-Cross, 1971). A few 'maalelo' are fished during the rising flood. Weiss (FAO/UN, 1970b), estimated that there were some 10 000 of these weirs operating each year on the Barotse plain.

Complete blocking of small channels leading water out of depressions is common in other systems; it has been noted from the Gambia river by Svensson (1933) and by Chevey and Le Poulain (1940) from the Mekong. The pool thus created is fished, often considerably later in the dry season, either by breaching the dam and catching the fish in traps, baskets or nets or by bailing the water out until the enclosed section is dry. This principle has been suggested as a means for improving the fishery productivity of floodplains, and experiments with more permanent dams have been carried out by Reed (FAO/UN, 1969b), in the Niger, and Reizer (1974) in the Senegal, and are continuing on several floodplains. Reed's work showed that the area of standing water on the plain was increased by such installations (Fig. 4.5), and Reizer has shown how the level and area of such pools differ before and after damming (Fig. 4.6). Harvests from such ponds are quite respectable – about 185 kg hm^{-2} in the case of the Niger dams – and systematic development of the method will probably be rewarding. On the other hand the slower growth of tropical river fish during the dry season, even when abundant food is present, may prevent possible harvests from being as high as anticipated.

In large channels which are not easily blocked with dams, stow-nets and wing-traps form an alternative to the barrage trap. The stow-net is a conical fixed gear which operates rather as a static trawl, the water passing through the net rather than vice versa. In the Ouémé such nets

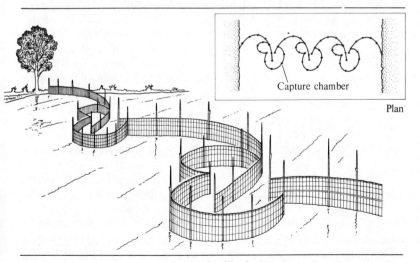

Capture chamber

Plan

Fig. 4.3 Barrage trap from coastal floodplain of Benin. Note heart-shaped trap chamber.

are slung from poles securely stuck into the bottom, but in the Tonle Sap, which drains the Grand Lac into the Mekong, they reach complex proportions in the form of the 'day' (Fig. 4.7). Such gears give very high

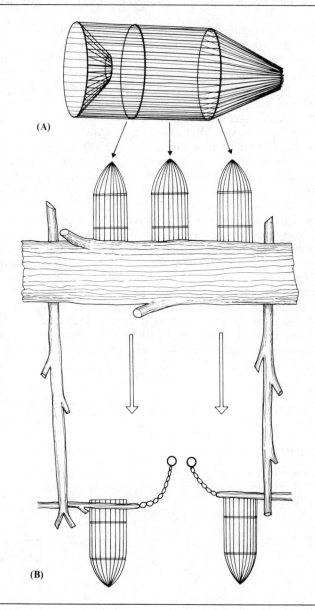

(A)

(B)

Fig. 4.4 Fishing basket used in Kenya (A), and arrangement in a Kek barrage trap (B). Fish enter through the vertical funnel. (After Whitehead, 1958.)

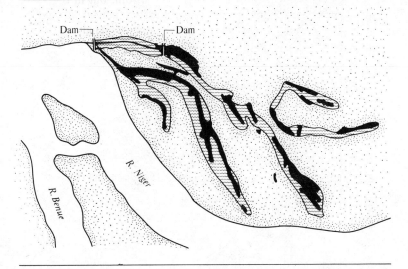

Fig. 4.5 Tracing from aerial photograph of the Niger floodwater retention dams, showing the original water area and the area flooded after the placing of the dams. (After FAO/UN, 1969b.)

yields during the main migrations into and out of the major flood depressions and in the main channel. Fily and D'Aubenton (1966) recorded a mean catch of 33 t per unit for two lunar catching periods for 11 installations in 1962–63. Earlier results by Chevey and Le Poulain (1940) for 1938–39 gave about twice this figure (64·5 t). In the rivers and canals of the Chao-Phrya and Mekong deltas, stationary wing-traps of the type illustrated in Fig. 4.8 also take large quantities of migrating fish as they move up and down the channels during the dry season. According to Tongsanga and Kessunchai (1966) catch rates ranged between 1·2 and 3·8 t day^{-1} in various canals.

Low water
During the low-water period the majority of fish tend to remain relatively static. The riverine migrant species, which ascend the main course of the river and its tributaries at this time, are an exception to the more general behaviour pattern and form the basis of such fisheries as those of the 'Subienda' and 'Piracema' in Latin America, the *Alestes* fishery of the Chari river, and the Khone Falls fishery as described by Chanthepha (1972). Fishing methods tend to be rather more active than the static gear favoured at times of high flow. Some static gear is used during low water, although this is often baited for, despite the general lowering of feeding intensity, fish are still attracted to baited gear. At this time the use of gill-nets, seine-nets and cast-nets is maximal both in the river and in the lakes and lagoons, but these gears on their own

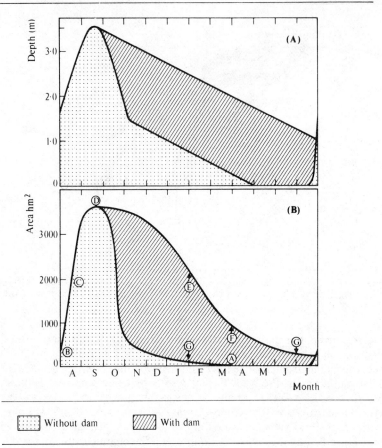

Fig. 4.6 Differences in changes of (A) depth, and (B) area of a floodplain pool before and after damming of the main access channel. Encircled letters refer to individual illustrations in Fig. 2.3. (After Reizer, 1974.)

cannot reach all habitats or catch all species, consequently many other fishing methods are in use.

Hook lines of various types are common in the main river channels. Long lines, baited with starch paste, offal, small fish, etc. are stretched across the river and catch mainly the larger predatory species which are often not vulnerable to other gears. Unbaited snagging and entangling lines are laid in the deeper portions of channels where big fish are accustomed to rest, and small boys are usually to be seen in most places with a rod or leger line, with which they capture a seemingly endless succession of small fish.

Barrages are common throughout floodplain systems, sometimes taking complex labyrinth-like forms, but more often simply dividing the

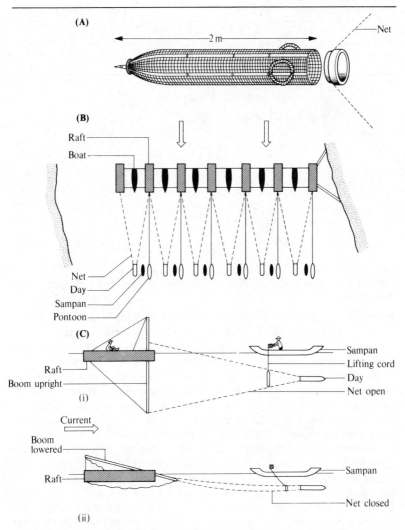

Fig. 4.7 Construction of a 'day' stow-net from the Tonle Sap: (A) cylinder trap (day); (B) disposition of individual day traps in stow-nets mounted in a barrage; (C) method of use – (i) with gear lowered, (ii) with gear raised. (After Chevey and Le Poulain, 1940.)

main river channel or the smaller drainage canals into sections which limit fish movement and facilitate their capture by other means. Many types of trap (Fig. 4.9) are associated with the barrages where they capture the fish that are milling about trying to pass the barrier. Traps are also set by themselves among vegetation where they attract fish seeking refuge there. The traps may be unbaited, but they may also be

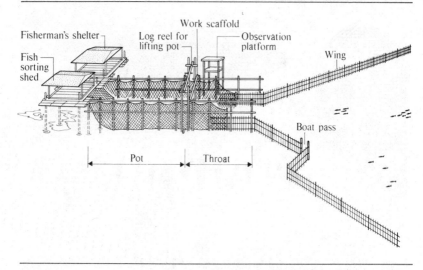

Fig. 4.8 Stationary wing-trap from the Chao-Phrya delta. (After Tongsanga and Kessunchai, 1966.)

baited to select for certain species. In West African rivers, for instance, the same type of cylindric trap catches greater proportions of *Clarias* when baited with oil-palm fruits, *Tilapia* when baited with maize meal and *Macrobrachium* when rotting meat is used.

The problem of extracting fish from under the vegetation which fringes lagoons and river channels is tackled in a number of ways. Special robust hand-nets, which may be made out of netting or basketwork (see Fig. 4.12), are scraped along the under-surface of the vegetation, or the vegetation mass might be surrounded by a fish fence. In the latter case the plants are cut out piece by piece and the fence advanced inwards so as to enclose the fish within a small space from which they can be captured by hand-nets or baskets. In the Ouémé river such vegetation masses may be planted deliberately at the end of the flood, either attached to the bank (Fig. 4.10) or recessed into it at the mouth of the channels which drain the plain (see also Fig. 5.4). They are left to collect fish for about two months, after which they are fished and replaced to be emptied again towards the end of the dry season. Harvests from such 'refuge traps' or 'fish parks' can be quite high, and in the Ouémé river 15 installations of this type of mean area 440 m^2 gave a mean harvest equivalent to 1·88 t hm^{-2} (of park) per fishing or 3·88 t hm^{-2} yr^{-1} between 1958 and 1968.

The practice of deliberately planting vegetation or branches on the water to attract fish is in fact very widespread, having been recorded by Chevey and Le Poulain (1940) from the Mekong, Stauch (1966) and Reed *et al.* (1967) from the Niger and Benue systems and Meschkat (1972) for Ecuador. Welcomme (1972b) carried out an evaluation of this

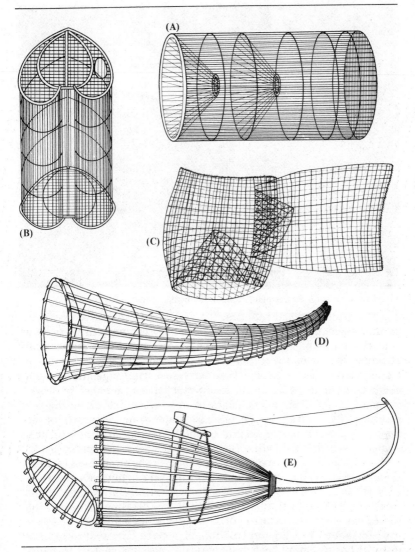

Fig. 4.9 Various types of fish trap from tropical rivers: (A) cylindrical drum trap (worldwide distribution); (B) vertical slit trap (Asia, Bangladesh and Mekong river); (C) folded woven trap (Niger river); (D) funnel trap (widespread); (E) spring trap (Africa – Niger, Chari and Zaïre rivers).

method of fishing as it is practised in the lagoons associated with the delta of the Ouémé river. The refuge traps in this river and its associated lakes and lagoons are of two types in addition to the masses of floating vegetation described above. There are small circular types about 22 m² in area (see Fig. 4.1) which give up to 2·8 t hm⁻² for each harvest. As they

Fig. 4.10 Vegetation masses planted along the banks of the Ouémé river.

are harvested up to 10 times during the seven-month dry season an annual yield as high as 28 t hm^{-2} can be obtained without apparently affecting the catch by other fishing methods in the area. Larger rectangular parks or 'acadjas' are harvested less frequently, but also achieve very high yields. In the freshwater zone, a variety of species are attracted to the Ouémé fish parks from which up to 32 species were recorded. By contrast in the brackish-water zone, only two species, *Sarotherodon melanotheron* and *Chrysichthys nigrodigitatus* made up 95 per cent of the individuals present. These breed actively in the fish park throughout the year and as a consequence the population builds up rapidly (Fig. 4.11), thus accounting for the very high yields of up to 8 t hm^{-2} yr^{-1} in 1957–59. More recent investigations have shown that the fish stock increased in a similar manner in 1969–70, although yields were somewhat lower as a result of changes in the lagoon environment brought about by the construction of a port. The only other such installations that have been systematically investigated are the 'Samra' parks of the Grand Lac which, according to Chevey and Le Poulain (1940), would appear to have given comparable yields to the Benin type of installation. Brush park fisheries are regarded by many as a somewhat mixed blessing. There is little doubt that they put up the overall productivity of the body of water in which they are used, but they also may shorten its life through accelerated silting.

A variety of gears have been developed to fish the main channel, especially the deeper portions where the larger fish come to rest. Many of these are drawn or propelled by boats. A fairly widespread device is

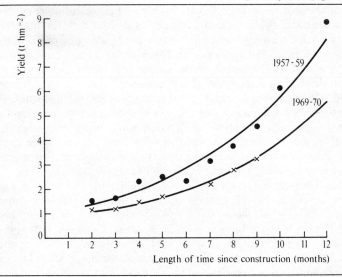

Fig. 4.11 Relation between yield and length of time of installation of fish parks in the Ouémé delta: (●) means for 1957–59, (×) means for 1969–70. (After Welcomme, 1972b.)

the frame-trawl drawn by one or two boats, but the most popular is probably the vee-shaped net (Fig. 4.12) which can be mounted in a variety of ways and has great operational flexibility. Armed with small-mesh netting, it can, for instance, skim the surface to catch the small pelagic clupeid, cyprinid and characin species found there, or be scraped along the bottom to capture many small bottom-living species. With larger mesh it can also be plunged near the bottom where it drags for bigger bottom-living siluroids. Nets similar to this may also be mounted on the bank where they take migrating fish as they follow the shoreline or move inshore away from the current (Fig. 4.13). In Asian rivers lift-nets perform a similar function. They may be mounted on the bank, but are sometimes operated from rafts on which the fishermen live with their family. Such an apparatus is the 'sadung' of the middle Mekong, whose operation was described by Fraser (1972).

The standing waters of the floodplain are often the property of a particular village or group which exploits them communally, using clap-nets or plunge baskets to virtually empty the water of any living thing. But many waters are exploited by individuals. Larger lakes, of course, are fished in much the same manner as the main channel with a full variety of gear. However, smaller floodplain lakes are usually either poisoned or fished out with fences in much the same manner as the brush parks. There are many plant toxins which are used to capture fish, both in the lagoons and in pools of the main river channel. Table 4.2 gives some indication of the number of bio-active plants in the Benue river system alone, although many of the shrubs listed are also found in other parts of the world. In recent years even more powerful poisons have become available in the form of insecticides such as dieldrin or endrin, which are used with apparent abandon. Fishing with poisons is one of the main methods used by occasional fishermen and has the unfortunate side-effect that it selects against the young fish which are particularly susceptible to these substances. Its effect on the fish stock is of course minimal where temporary pools are fished – for there the fish would die anyway before they could rejoin the stock – but in permanent standing waters the annihilation of the population is more serious, as here the fish take refuge during the dry season to form a reconstituted stock in the floods. Poisons are also used to eradicate unwanted species, for example the piranhas (*Serrasalmus sp.*) in Brazil (Braga Adhemar, 1976).

As has been shown in the section on standing stocks, many lagoons contain a very high ichthyomass, most of which is removed during intensive fishing of these waters. This fact has apparently been recognized and, as we have seen in some areas, fishermen attempt to retain the maximum volume of water in the depressions by damming the outlet channel. In more developed floodplains the shape of the lagoons

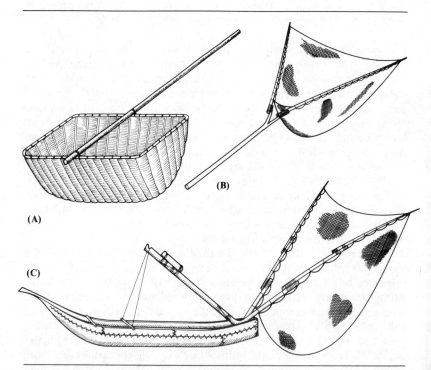

Fig. 4.12 (A) Basket dip-net (Ouémé); (B) 'vee'-shaped dip-net (worldwide distribution); (C) 'vee'-shaped net mounted on canoe (Chari river). (Adapted from Blache and Miton, 1962.)

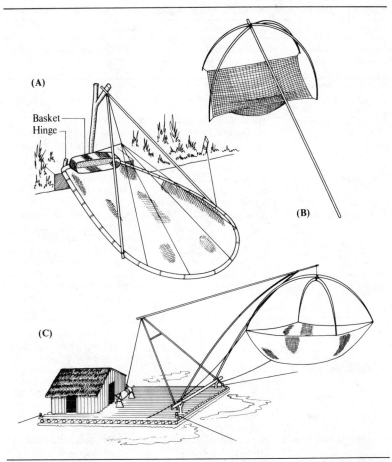

(A)

Basket
Hinge

(B)

(C)

Fig. 4.13 (A) Bank-mounted lift-net (widespread in different forms, example shown from Niger river); (B) hand-held lift-net (widespread, example shown from Bangladesh); (C) Raft-mounted lift net 'Sadung' (middle Mekong).

may be regularized, and eventually drain-in fish ponds may be dug into the surface of the plain. Three river systems in particular have benefited from this form of management. In the Ouémé, about 3 per cent of the 1 000 km^2 surface area is occupied by drain-in ponds, some of which are kilometres long (Fig. 4.14, see also Fig. 5.4). Width and depth are more or less standard at 3–4 m and 1·5 m, respectively. Similar constructions on the Mekong floodplain ranged between 20 and 100 m in length and 2 and 3 m in depth. In Bangladesh some 30 000 ponds are formed from the borrow-pits which are excavated during the construction of the artificial islands upon which much of the rural population lives. Drain-in ponds are usually fished by blocking a portion with a bamboo barrier, removing the vegetation contained therein, and advancing the barrier

Table 4.2 Ichthyotoxic plants used in fishing in Benue river (after Stauch, 1966)

Plant	Active Part	Effect
Balanites aegyptica	Bark which is crushed	Kills fish within a few hours
Tephrosia vogelii	Leaves and young shoots crushed	Fish appear on surface very quickly and die soon after
Momordica charantia	Dried leaves and fruits: usually mixed with *Balanites*	Effect very slow
Unidentified plant (local name: horesoungsoungko)	Whole plant used after crushing in a mortar. The shallow lagoon to be fished is stirred up and the poison mixes with the mud	Especially effective for catching bottom-living mud-eating species such as *Clarias*
Crinum sp.	Bulbs crushed in a mortar and put in a sack which is drawn through the water	Very effective, kills all fish in a short time
Indigofera pilosa	Ripe seeds	Useful in waters of little volume but is more often mixed with other products
Parkia filicoidea	Pre-ripe seeds pulped	Slow in action and ineffective against siluroids
Syzygium guineense	Bark which is crushed	Rapid effect against all species
Euphorbia kamerunica	Latex	Renders fish inedible in large quantities: small amounts are used to intensify the effect of other poisons
Prosopis africana	Seed pods dried and crushed	Very slow (three days to produce death), but intensifies effect of other poisons
Sarcocephalus esculentis	Bark which is rubbed between two stones	Irritant which fish avoid by taking refuge in traps which are placed in the pool to be fished
Adenium obaesum	Fresh wood cut in discs and sun dried for two days	Kills fish within three hours
Moringa pterygosperma	Bark crushed between two stones	Kills fish within three hours
Acacia ataxacantha	Flowers dried in the sun	Never used alone, but acts as an intensifier to *Balanites* or *Momordica*
Ximenia americana	Bark which is pounded in water	Particularly effective against cyprinids and characins which appear belly up on the surface within an hour. Frequently mixed with *Balanites*
Ziziphus mucronata	Flowers which are pounded in a mortar	Kills all fish within two hours, even siluroids

until the fish are enclosed in a small space from which they are easily captured. Figure 4.15 shows two stages in such a fishery. Drain-in ponds are also widely used in conjunction with rice-fields where, as the water is drained prior to harvesting, the fish may retreat into ditches or ponds prepared for this purpose. Yields from drain-in ponds may be high. In 1955–58, 34 ponds from the Ouémé produced a mean of $2 \cdot 1$ t hm^{-2}, and even though the catch had dropped 10 years later the same installations were still producing over 1·5 t hm^{-2}. In the Mekong, however, this type of pond was suppressed following the recommendations of Chevey and Le Poulain (1940), who felt that the stagnant waters retained at the end of the dry season damaged the crops as they spread out over the plain at the beginning of the next flood.

4.3 Species caught

Because of the large number of species involved in tropical river fisheries, detailed species lists serve little purpose. Analysis of catch data from most gears shows them to conform to the canonical distribution of species abundance described in Section 3.1. Distributions of this type predict that only a few species will be dominant in the catch of any gear, and a knowledge of these is essential, both for the management of the stocks and for establishing priorities for research.

The river fisheries of Latin America have concentrated mainly on the low water 'Piracema' or 'Subienda' migrations. The fisheries are still

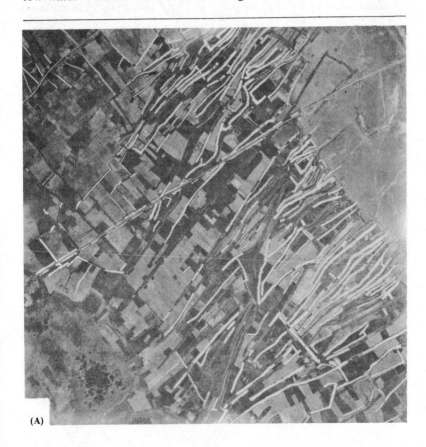

(A)

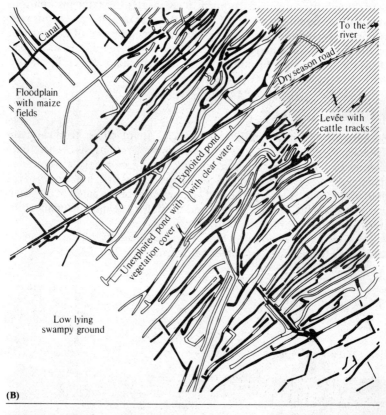

(B)

Fig. 4.14 Portion of the Ouémé floodplain showing the distribution of the drain-in floodplain pools ('whedos'). (A) Air-photograph (by courtesy of IGN, Paris); (B) interpretation: black areas are ponds that have already been fished; white parallel lines indicate vegetation-covered unfished ponds.

relatively undeveloped and have selected for species of large size and consumer appeal. Consequently, catches are composed of the larger characins or siluroids. In the Magdalena river well over half the catch consists of *Prochilodus reticulatus* (Granados, 1975), although *Pseudo-platystoma fasciatum*, *Pimelodus clarias*, *P. grosskopfii*, *Brycon moorei*, *Sorubim lima*, *Plagioscion surinamensis* and *Ageneiosus caucanus* also contribute significantly. The preoccupation with the 'Subienda' species in Colombia has led to a neglect of other potential food fishes and Bazigos *et al.* (1977) estimated that there is a presently (December 1977) unexploited stock of *Hemiancistrus* and *Pteri-goplichthys* in the cienagas which could almost double the yield from this system. Fish of the genus *Prochilodus* are the mainstay of other South American fisheries. *Prochilodus reticulatus* forms the basis of a

Fig. 4.15 Views of a typical drain-in pond: (A) before fishing; (B) after fishing.

heavy fishery in the southwestern portion of Lake Maracaibo and the inflowing floodplain river Catatumbo (Espinosa and Gimenez, 1974). In the Apure and Orinoco systems, however, the fishery concentrates on the larger Pimelodidae: *Pseudoplatystoma fasciatum, P. tigrinum, Brachyplatystoma filamentosum* and *B. vaillantii* (Canestri, 1972). In the Paraná, Vidal (1969) listed 18 species in terms of principal commercial value (Table 4.3). Further upriver, in the Mogi Guassu, *Prochilodus scrofa* makes up 50–60 per cent of the catch which also contains 16 other species of characin (Godoy, 1975). Although the Amazon basin contains some 2 000 species, only a small proportion of these are captured by the fishery. Meschkat (1975) listed the major commercial species, based on the catch statistics for Amazonas state (Table 4.4).

Table 4.3 Species of major commercial value in the fishery zone of Rosario, river Paraná (not listed in order of importance) (from data in Vidal, 1969)

Lycengraulis olidus	*Colossoma mitrei*	*Pimelodus albicans*
Brycon orbygnianus	*Ageneiosus brevifilis*	*Zungaro zungaro*
Salminus maxillosus	*A. valenciennesi*	*Luciopimelodus pati*
Prochilodus platensis	*Oxydoras kneri*	*Pseudoplatystoma fasciatum*
Leporinus spp.	*Rhinodoras d'orbignyi*	*P. coruscans*
Hoplias malabaricus	*Pimelodus clarias*	*Basilichthys bonariensis*

Table 4.4 Species of commercial value in the Amazon listed in order of importance (from data in Meschkat, 1975)

1. *Arapaima gigas*	10. *Leporinus* and *Schizodon* spp.
2. *Myletus (Colossoma) bidens*	11. *Brachyplatystoma flavicans*
3. *Prochilodus insignis*	12. *Brycon hilarii*
4. *Plagioscion surinamensis*	13. *Oxydoras kneri*
5. *Plecostomus* spp.	14. *Osteoglossum bicirrhosum*
6. *Brycon nattereri*	15. *Cichla ocellaris*
7. *Colossoma* sp.	16. *Hypophthalmus edentatus*
8. *Rhinosardinia* sp.	17. *Pseudoplatystoma fasciatum*
9. *Prochilodus corimbata*	18. *Astronotus ocellatus*

The heavy and selective fishing pressure on the largest species, *Arapaima gigas* and *Myletus bidens*, have led to a sharp decline in the populations of these fishes (Junk and Honda, 1976).

In Africa, the river fisheries are exploited at a much greater intensity and a very broad spectrum of species are caught, especially in the basins of the western side of the continent. In the Niger river gill-net and cast-net catches can contain over 50 species and it is difficult to identify the major elements of the catch. However, Raimondo (1975) listed the nine most important species (Table 4.5).

Table 4.5 Predominant species in the catch from the Central Delta of the Niger (from data in Raimondo, 1975)

Alestes dentex	*Lates niloticus*
Brachysynodontis batensoda	*Bagrus bayad*
Hydrocynus forskhalii	*Mormyrus rume*
Sarotherodon niloticus	*Citharinus latus*
Labeo senegalensis	

Other species commonly represented are *Auchenoglanis occidentalis*, *Clarias anguillaris* and particularly *Alestes leuciscus* which forms the basis of a specialized fishery for fish-oil production.

Catches from other West African rivers have a similar combination of species. In the Senegal river, Reizer (1974) investigated the number of species captured as a function of mesh in gill-nets (Fig. 4.16) and showed that number of species increased as mesh size decreased. On the basis of these experimental fishings it appeared that the 10 most important species to the fishery were *Schilbe mystus, Lates niloticus, Alestes dentex* and *A. baremoze, Hydrocynus brevis, Labeo senegalensis, Eutropius niloticus, Citharinus citharus, Heterotis niloticus* and *Hepsetus odoe*. In some systems, such is the diversity of gear that it is almost impossible to establish the true weighting of the various species in the total catch. In these instances, studies of the abundance of fish in the markets adjacent to the fishery give some idea. For instance, in the Ouémé system the order of abundance of the various species was as shown in Table 4.6, although as many as 40 species figured in the fishery as a whole. This abundance is, of course, biased by the food preferences of the fishermen themselves as some of the species caught rarely reach the market.

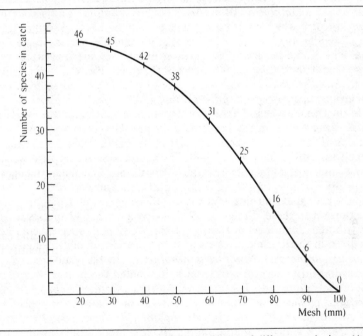

Fig. 4.16 The number of species captured by gill-nets of different mesh sizes. (After Reizer, 1974.)

Table 4.6 Order of abundance of major species appearing in the markets of the Ouémé valley

1. *Clarias ebriensis*	6. *Synodontis melanopterus*
2. *C. lazera*	7. *S. schall*
3. *Parophiocephalus obscurus*	8. *Schilbe mystus*
4. *Heterotis niloticus*	9. *Distichodus rostratus*
5. Mormyrids	10. *Ctenopoma kingsleyae*

In the Chari–Logone system the elements of the catch are very difficult to separate from those produced in the lake. However, Blache and Miton (1962) listed the principal elements of the catch from a number of fishing methods in the Chari and Logone rivers. From these it appeared that the migratory *Alestes dentex* and *A. baremoze* were by far the most important species to the fishery. Several larger species were also of major importance, including *Citharinus citharus* and *C. latus, Distichodus rostratus* and *D. brevipinnis, Labeo senegalensis, Hydrocynus brevis* and *H. forskahlii,* and *Lates niloticus.* Some smaller species were also important, including *Sarotherodon galilaeus* and *S. niloticus, Schilbe mystus, Alestes nurse* and divers *Synodontis* spp. In the swamps *Clarias lazera* and *C. anguillaris* were particularly abundant.

In contrast to the specific richness of West African fisheries, the rivers of East Africa produce only a restricted variety. The Shire river fishery was found to have main species, *Clarias gariepinus, C. ngamensis, Sarotherodon mossambicus, Marcusenius macrolepidotus* and *Eutropius depressirostris* which made up about 90 per cent of the catch (Willoughby and Tweddle, 1977) despite the fact that there are 39 species in the system. The Kafue fishery takes a greater number of species (18), but of these 6 contributed about 90 per cent of the catch (Everett, 1974). These were: *Sarotherodon andersoni, S. macrochir, Tilapia rendalli, Serranochromis angusticeps, Schilbe mystus* and *Clarias gariepinus.*

In the rivers of the Indian subcontinent there is one migratory species, *Hilsa ilisha,* which in the Indus, Ganges and Godavari systems, is the subject of specialized fisheries. Apart from this the fisheries are based largely on a series of large cyprinids known as the major carps, as well as some siluroids, ophicephalids and notopterids. The major Gangetic carps are *Labeo rohita, L. calbasu, Catla catla* and *Cirrhinus mrigala,* and the principal siluroids *Mystus aor, M. seenghala* and *Wallago attu.* In addition to these, Jhingran (1975) listed a further 12 species which contributed significantly to the catch. A similar species complex occurred in the Brahmaputra river, with the addition of *Labeo gonius, Puntius sarana* and *Notopterus notopterus.* In the Cauvery river a somewhat different group of species dominated the fishery: *Acrossocheilus hexagonolepis, Tor putitora, Barbus carnaticus, Labeo kontius, Cirrhinus cirrhosa* and *Osteochilus brevidorsalis* among the cyprinids, *Glyptothorax madraspatanus, Mystus aor, M. Seenghala, Pangasius pangasius, Wallago attu* and *Silonia silondia* among the siluroids, together with *Channa marulius* a murrel and *Notopterus notopterus.*

Hussain (1973) listed the 13 principal species of the lower Indus fishery as shown in Table 4.7, although these were drawn from a pool of 66 species. From the list it will be seen that there are many elements in common with the Indian rivers, although *Sarotherodon mossambicus* has been introduced from Africa.

Fishing in the Chao-Phrya river is largely done by stationary wing-traps which block most of the main channel (Tongsanga and Kessunchai, 1966). Of the 77 species commonly captured, *Crossocheilus reba* made

Table 4.7 Main food fishes of the river Indus (after Husain, 1973)

Hilsa ilisha	*Rita rita*
Notopterus chitala	*Mystus* spp.
Catla catla	*Sarotherodon mossambicus*
Cirrhinus mrigala	*Channa marulius*
Labeo calbasu	*C. striatus*
L. rohita	*C. punctatus*
Wallago attu	

up about 60 per cent of the catch. Other important species were *Wallago attu*, *Macrognathus aculeatus*, *Ophicephalus micropeltes*, *O. striatus*, *Puntius gonionotus*, *Pangasius sutchi* and *Cirrhinus microlepis*.

More than 150 of the total 800 species that inhabit the Mekong make up the bulk of the catch in that system. Of these a few may be singled out as being particularly conspicuous or sought after. These vary with the region of the river fished, and separate authors have identified different dominant components. *Pangasianodon gigas*, in particular, is distinguished by its size, but has diminished in importance owing to overfishing. Adopting the summary of Fily and D'Aubenton (1966) the species listed in Table 4.8 made up over 1 per cent of the catch in Cambodian waters.

As with the Asian rivers, catches in European floodplain rivers are dominated by cyprinids as are in fact the potamon reaches of all European rivers. Liepolt (1972) listed *Cyprinus carpio* and *Abramis brama* as major elements, to which can be added *Rutilus rutilus* and *Alburnus alburnus*. Other fishes regularly found in the floodplain lakes

Table 4.8 Species comprising over 1% of total catch in the Cambodian waters of the Mekong in order of importance (after Fily and d'Aubenton, 1966)

1. *Pseudosciaena soldado*	10. *Ambassis wolffii*
2. *Cirrhinus jullieni*	11. *Puntius orphoides*
3. *C. auratus*	12. *P. altus*
4. *Ophicephalus micropeltes*	13. *Notopterus notopterus*
5. *Thynnichthys thynnoides*	14. *Hampala macrolepidota*
6. *Kryptopterus apogon*	15. *Puntius bramoides*
7. *Macrones nemurus*	16. *Pangasius larnaudi*
8. *Cyclocheilichthys enoplus*	17. *Wallago attu*
9. *Labeo chrysophekadion*	18. *Clupea thibaudeani*

are *Lucioperca lucioperca*, *Esox lucius*, *Perca fluviatilis* and *Silurus glanis*. In the lower Danube and delta, migratory fishes make up a great proportion of the catch. Prevailing anadromous species are *Huso huso*, *Acipenser ruthenus*, *A. stellatus*, *A. guldenstaedtii* and *Alosa pontica*.

4.4 Preservation of fish

Types of products

A certain amount of the fish caught in river systems is consumed fresh by the fishermen themselves and by communities within a limited radius of the fish landings, but in the more important fisheries a surplus to local requirements is produced which is sold for transport elsewhere. To improve the quality of their product, fishermen from as far apart as the Mekong river and the Magdalena river keep their catch in live chambers and even transport it in special boats with wet holds. Some species survive and keep better than others in the fresh state after landing, and air-breathing fish in particular are sought after because of the time they can be kept alive after capture. In India and part of Africa, murrels, catfish and some anabantids are transported for considerable distances in baskets lined with damp weeds or moss. However, because of the dispersion and inaccessibility of fishing sites in the river–floodplain system, and the rapidity with which fish deteriorate under tropical conditions, most fish has to be preserved by one means or another for it to arrive in the markets in an acceptable condition. Furthermore, the seasonal nature of the fishery means that a period of excess fish production is followed by one of scarcity. Preservation techniques are thus needed to prevent fish that are in excess of demand being lost and to even the supply over the year. Several types of treatment are used, depending on local conditions and preferences

Iced fish

The preservation of fish by icing or freezing is a comparative innovation to the river fisheries. Even now its use is limited to areas where sufficient fish is caught to justify the expense of ice-making plants, and where communications are sufficiently easy for the fish to be collected, iced and removed rapidly. This method of keeping fish has grown up on major fisheries located in the main river channel such as that for *Hilsa ilisha* in the Indus (Husain, 1973) where the fish are collected at certain landings for icing prior to transport by rail to the major towns. Icing is especially popular in Latin America, where the comparatively recent development of the river fisheries has left little time for traditional methods of preservation to have arisen. On the Magdalena river and the Amazon, for instance, fish traders come to the fishing sites in motorized boats equipped with ice to preserve the fish. In recent years, preservation in ice has tended to replace other methods of treatment. In the Mekong, Fraser (1972) recorded the addition of ice-preserved fish to the customary range of products, and in the Kafue, Williams (1960) commented on the growing proportion of fish which is carried in this form.

Dried fish

Simple drying of fish is not practical in many of the world's river systems because of the high atmospheric humidity. But in desertic or Sahelian savanna rivers the practice is common, especially for smaller species. In the Senegal basin, for example, simple drying is the usual form of treating the fish after they have been eviscerated, scaled and, in the case of larger species, cut into strips. On the Niger, only the smaller species, such as *Alestes* are sun-dried, and in the Chad basin one of the traditional fish products, 'salanga', consists of *Alestes dentex* and *A. baremoze* which are split open ventrally and laid on mats to dry in the sun. In the Mekong, and other Asian rivers, sun-drying is also common, although this is sometimes combined with salting.

There is a noticeable loss of weight as fish dry. This varies much with the species of fish, for instance, *Clarias* with their massive head bones tend to lose less than do characins or cyprinids. As a rule of thumb it is generally agreed that the ratio of wet fish to dry fish is about 3·1.

Salting

Preserving fish with salt is not common in inland waters, largely because of the high cost of the salt, and secondly because in the more humid areas the deliquescence of the salt shortens the life of the product rather than increasing it. In the Indus valley, salting is used only when there is a very heavy catch of *Hilsa* which exceeds the capacity of the ice plants (Husain, 1973). Certain species are prepared in this way in the Paraná river (Vidal, 1969), where *Lycengraulis olidus* and more recently *Hoplias malabaricus* and *Pseudoplatystoma* spp. are treated with salt prior to sun-drying.

Smoking

Smoke-drying is perhaps the most widespread way of preserving fish in Africa, and is practised in nearly all river systems. Techniques vary somewhat and the type of oven used changes from place to place. In Malawi, fish are smoked in a special thatched smoke-house, whereas in other regions ovens constructed of clay are open to the air (Fig. 4.17). Small fish are usually smoked whole. Medium-sized fish are scaled, eviscerated and sometimes split open or slashed down the sides. The largest fish are cut into pieces before treatment. As they are smoked fish lose weight in about the same proportion (3 kg fresh fish = 1 kg wet fish) as when they are dried. One treatment is rarely sufficient, especially in more humid areas, consequently the fish have to be re-treated at intervals of between a week and 10 days to keep them in acceptable condition. The smoke-dried product is often stockpiled over a considerable period of time, especially in those temporary camps furthest from major centres of communication.

In some areas the lack of wood for smoking is causing problems for the fishery. In the Sahel, for instance, the non-availability of domestic firewood is becoming one of the factors limiting human occupation. Studies carried out in Mali by Operation Pêche, indicate that about 1 kg of wood is necessary to produce 1 kg of smoked fish, using traditional ovens. An improved oven is being introduced in the Central Delta of the Niger, which will reduce the demand to 0·5 kg of wood for every kilogram of smoked fish produced (Operation Pêche, 1976). A similar type of oven is being used in the development of the Elephant Marsh fishery in Malawi where it is also intended to plant copses of trees to

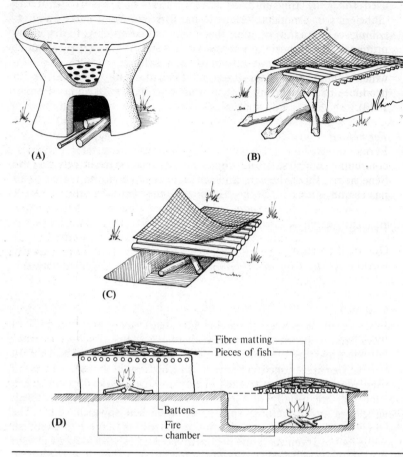

Fig. 4.17 Different types of smoking oven: (A) circular oven (Haussa); (B) rectangular oven made of baked earth; (C) pit oven; (D) sections of rectangular and pit ovens. (Adapted from Blache and Miton, 1962.)

supply them with wood; a copse of about 1 hm² is thought adequate to serve one oven (Tweddle *et al.*, 1977).

Fish meal
The only river fishery whose catch is used for making fish meal is the *Prochilodus* fishery of the Paraná. According to Vidal (1967) these 'Sabelerias' accounted for nearly 70 per cent of the total inland catch of Argentina, although these have declined considerably from about 1965 onwards.

Fish oil
Several species of fish are particularly rich in fats and are traditionally

used for extracting oil. Oil is, for instance, a by-product of the 'Sabelerias' fish-meal factories. *Alestes leuciscus* is exploited early in the fishing season in the Niger for its oil, and several species of the Mekong, principally *Cirrhinus* and *Dangila* are taken for the same purpose. The extraction process involves boiling for a certain time to release the oil which floats to the surface and may be skimmed off. *Dangila* sp. can produce up to 15 per cent of their weight in oil (Chevey and Le Poulain, 1940).

Fermented products
Fermentation of the cleaned and gutted fish in water for 12 h is a common preliminary to salting in the Mekong, or to sun-drying in the Senegal river. In Asia a number of fermented products, including fish pastes and sauces with a high salt content, are also produced.

Protection against insect infestation

One of the major curses of the fishing industry in many parts of the world is the infection of the treated fish with insects. In the case of West Africa it is the *Dermestes* beetle which lays its eggs on smoked and dried fish. The larvae develop there and eat the flesh, causing enormous losses of protein that is potentially consumable by the human population. Early attempts to control this included scorching, whereby during the hot-smoking process the outer skin of the flesh was blackened and hardened to lessen the successful penetration of the flesh by the beetle. Other techniques have included packing the fish in bales wrapped with matting as soon as it is smoked, but such attempts have largely failed. Recently, Operation Pêche in Mali has claimed a certain success by treating the fish with natural insecticides (Bioresmetrine) after drying or smoking, but improved hygiene and heat treatment using a polyethylene tent and solar energy and simply keeping fish off the ground probably provide more satisfactory alternatives.

4.5 Catch

Analysis of catch in different rivers

Catch statistics from rivers are often of low quality because of the difficulties inherent in collecting data from fisheries which operate from many landings dispersed along a system that may traverse several countries. As in most fields of fisheries, there is a need to improve the quality and quantity of the catch statistics and the collection of biological and other data as a prerequisite for the proper management of the riverine stocks. However, because of the lack of concise information on many of the individual systems, attempts have been made to extrapolate general principles from the small group of water bodies about which something is known. Despite the inadequacies of the data, an analysis of fish-yield patterns from African rivers has given a fairly coherent picture of the factors involved in determining the catch that can be expected from any particular system (Welcomme, 1976). In the rivers used in this analysis, all of which were moderately to heavily fished, there was a good correlation between the drainage basin area of the river system in square kilometres (A) and the catch in tons obtained from it (C). Rivers without exceptionally large flooded areas, i.e. those with 'normal' development of fringing floodplains, conformed to the relationship $C = 0.12A^{0.85}$. Because the basin area and the total length of the longest channel of the river are also simply related (main channel length = 5.24 *basin area*$^{0.45}$, in African rivers), this equation transformed into a relationship for yield in tonnes as a function of the main channel length in km: $C = 0.0033L^{1.95}$, or approximately one three-hundredth of the square of the length of the stream ($L^2/300$).

The catch of any reach of river of length x km at distance y from its source can be calculated from $_xC_y = C_{y+x} - C_y$, where values of C_y can be obtained from the preceding equation. In its most extreme form, where $x = 1$ km, this yields a theoretical equation for the catch that might be expected for any kilometre of river at different distances from the source

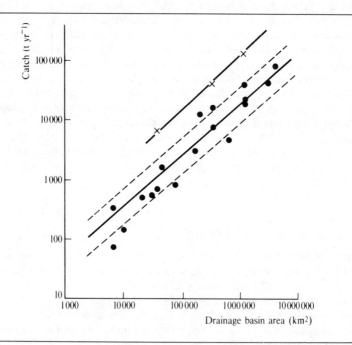

Fig. 4.18 Catch relative to drainage basin areas in African rivers (●—●—●) rivers with 'normal' floodplain development. Calculated line $C = 0.1326A^{0.8533}$, also plotted are the limit lines at $S_{y \cdot x} = 0.2961$ (-----); (×—×—×) rivers with extensive floodplain systems, calculated line $C = 0.4434A^{0.9024}$. (After Welcomme, 1976.)

(i.e. *Catch at* $km_y = 0.0064y^{0.95}$). Values predicted by this relationship are of course averages over a number of systems from which actual values from individual rivers deviate quite widely. Such deviations were traced to two main natural sources. Firstly, edaphic factors, represented by the conductivity of the water as a measure of its general richness (see Table 2.10), accounted for about 60 per cent of the observed variation between rivers, or streams of the same system, in the African waters analysed. Secondly, morphological factors, in this case differences in floodplain area, explained over 70 per cent of the difference between the actual catch and the expected catch in different reaches of rivers of the same system. Reaches with a greater area of floodplain not unexpectedly produce more fish. Unfortunately, it has not been possible to compare the influence of morphological factors directly between river systems, but returning to the original analysis of catch/drainage area two distinct sets emerged, each with its own regression line (Fig. 4.18). There was firstly a group of rivers with extensive floodplain systems, whose flooded areas cover between 2·5 and 3·8 per cent of their river basin area. Secondly, there were those rivers with the 'normal' development already referred to, whose floodplain areas are rarely measured but where less than 1·5 per cent of the total basin seems to be liable to flooding (where figures are available for the calculation). Such an analysis is perforce crude owing to the nature of the various inputs, but hopefully further studies will refine understanding of this aspect of river productivity. When other systems are compared with these relationships they conform well. The Mekong, Danube and Magdalena rivers, with floodplain areas of between 3 and 8 per cent of their respective basins, are distributed around the extensive floodplain regression line, whereas rivers such as the Mogi Guassu or Indus, with no extraordinary development of their floodplain fit the 'normal' relationship almost exactly.

Table 4.9 Number of fishermen, catch and maximum flooded area of some tropical rivers

River	Number of fishermen (f)	Catch in tons (c)	Area in km² (a)	f/a	c/f	c/a (kg hm⁻²)	Authority
Shire (1970)	2 445	9 545	665	3·68	3·90	143·5	Tweddle (pers. comm.).
(1975)	3 324	7 890	665	5·00	2·37	118·6	Tweddle (pers. comm.).
Kafue (1963)	1 112	8 554	4 340	0·26	7·69	19·7	Zambia (1965)
(1970)	670	6 747	4 340	0·15	10·06	15·5	Zambia (1971)
Senegal Central Delta,	10 400	36 000	12 970	0·80	3·46	27·8	Reizer (1974)
Niger	54 112	90 000	20 000	2·71	1·66	45·0	Konare (1977)
Pendjari	65	140	40	1·65	2·15	35·0	FAO/UN (1971a)
Ouémé (1957)	25 000	10 400	1 000	25·00	0·42	104·0	CTFT (1957)
(1968/69)	29 852	6 500	1 000	29·85	0·22	65·0	FAO/UN (1971a)
Niger, Niger	1 314	4 700	907	1·45	3·58	51·8	FAO/UN (1971b)
Niger, Nigeria	4 600	14 350	4 800	0·96	3·12	29·9	FAO/UN (1969b, 1970a)
Benue, Nigeria	5 140	9 570	3 100	1·66	1·86	30·9	FAO/UN (1969b, 1970a)
Barotse	912	3 500	5 120	0·18	3·84	6·8	Zambia (1974)
Magdalena	30 000	65 000	20 000	1·50	2·17	32·5	Bazigos et al. (1977)

The floodplains examined were selected because of their active fisheries, but many other floodplains are less intensively exploited. The effects on the catch of the number of fishermen operating in a body of water has already been investigated in some African lakes (Henderson and Welcomme, 1974) and some data are available for a similar analysis for rivers, although such information is unfortunately limited to only a few systems. Table 4.9 shows the number of fishermen, catch and total flooded area of these, from which two indices are derived, number of fishermen per square kilometre and catch per fisherman. The indices are plotted in Fig. 4.19 which shows that catch per fisherman declines with increasing numbers of fishermen in much the same manner as in other fisheries. The best-fit regression line for these points is derived from the relationship:

$$\text{catch per fisherman} = 3 \cdot 87 \, (0 \cdot 91^{\, \text{number of fishermen km}^{-2}})$$

which tends to a mean catch per fisherman of $3 \cdot 87 \, \text{t yr}^{-1}$ at very low fisherman densities. Obviously, deviations from this will occur in different systems and catch rates as high as $10 \, \text{t yr}^{-1}$ have been recorded from the Kafue. This relationship can be used to generate a curve for total catch per unit area of floodplain as a function of the density of fishermen (Fig. 4.20). According to this catches on a floodplain should increase until there are about 10 fishermen km^{-2}, after which the total yield declines. From this rather scanty preliminary analysis, it would seem that floodplains may reach their theoretical maximum level of yield with considerably more fishermen per unit area than do tropical lakes, which appear to reach their optimum at between 1 and 2 fishermen km^{-2}. Two reasons may contribute to this. Firstly there are high proportions of part-time and occasional fishermen on the plains whose numbers are likely to increase as the plain becomes more densely occupied. The number of fishermen cannot, therefore, be taken as directly proportional to effort. Secondly, in heavily exploited fisheries

Table 4.10 Catch and maximum flooded area of some tropical river

River	Area (km$_2$)	Catch (tonnes)	Catch unit area kg hm^{-2}	Reference
Mahaweli (Sri Lanka)	121	413	34:1	Indrasena (1970)
Ganges–Brahmaputra (Bangladesh)	93 000	727 000	78·2	FAO (1976)
Lubuk Lampan	12	29	24·2	Arifin and Arifin (1976)
Lower Mekong	54 000	220 000	40·7	Mekong Fish Studies (pers. comm.)
Yaérés	7 000	17 500	25·0	Stauch (pers. comm.)
Massilli	150	475	31·7	Barry (pers. comm.)
Niger, Dahomey	274	1 200	43·7	FAO/UN (1971a)
Okavango	16 000	800	0·5	Cross (pers. comm.)
Kamulondo	6 639	7 355	11·1	Poll and Renson (1948)
Danube	26 450	49 400	18·7	Liepolt (1967)

there is a tendency for forms of fish husbandry to be developed which probably allow the productivity of the unaltered environment to be exceeded to a certain degree. It is, however, by no means certain that floodplains can sustain their yield under conditions of such intense exploitation, and as few have been fished at these levels for any length

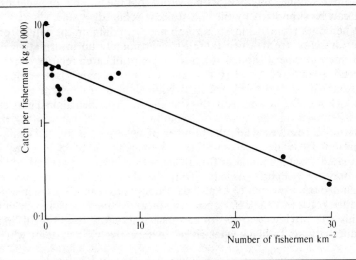

Fig. 4.19 Catch per fisherman as a function of number of fishermen per square kilometre with calculated regression line $C = 3 \cdot 955(0 \cdot 910^{N})$.

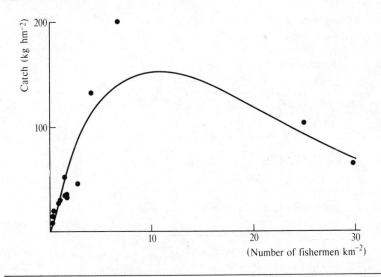

Fig. 4.20 Theoretical relationship between number of fishermen and catch for tropical rivers; also plotted are actual values from Table 4.19.

of time the ultimate fate of their fisheries is difficult to predict.

The relationships derived in Figs. 4.19 and 4.20 depend much on the apparent similarity in performance of artisanal fishermen from a number of river systems. Should more efficient methods of capturing fish be successfully introduced, then the catching power of any one fisherman will be increased, with a result that the number of fishermen that can be supported by the fish stock is reduced.

When data from Table 4.9 is combined with data on the catch from other systems, from which there is unfortunately no information on fishermen number (Table 4.10), a scatter plot of catch relative to total flooded areas is obtained (Fig. 4.21). The points conform to a linear relationship, $C = 3.83\ A$, which is equivalent to a constant yield of 38.3 kg hm^{-2}. Deviations from this line can be explained almost entirely by differences in the degree of exploitation and 92 per cent of the variation is resolved when the number of fishermen is plotted against deviations from the expected values. The mean yield of 38.3 kg hm^{-2} is calculated from a sample of floodplains which includes several which are only very lightly fished. From the data available, it may be concluded that normally exploited floodplains can be expected to produce between 40 and 60 kg hm^{-2} yr^{-1} on a sustained basis. Exceptions to this will obviously arise, for instance where low fertility will limit productivity, as in blackwater rivers. Alternatively, in systems where

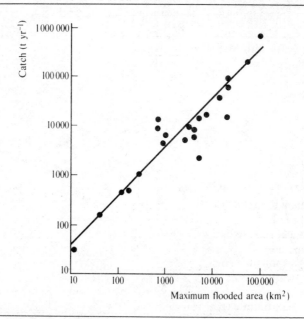

Fig. 4.21 Catch per maximum flooded area of various floodplain rivers. Calculated regression line $C = 3.83A$ (plotted on a log-log scale for maximum dispersion of points).

the amount of water remaining in the dry season is unusually extensive, higher yields will result. In the Shire river, for instance, the permanently flooded area is some 48 per cent of the total, accounting for the very high mean values for catch from this system. Much of the catch comes from large permanent lagoons, such as the Bangula lagoon studied by Shepherd (1976). Here yields fluctuated around a mean of 333 kg hm^{-2} and reached values as high as 538 kg hm^{-2}. Year-to-year variations were strongly correlated with differences in the depth and extent of flooding in previous years.

Fluctuations in catch between years

As has been discussed in the section on standing stock, the amount of fish in the river changes from year to year, depending on the history of the intensity of flooding over several previous years. When the catches from typical floodplain systems are followed over a number of years, it is apparent that these, too, fluctuate in a manner that is in some way dependent on changes in the flood cycle. Such changes in yield were remarked on early in the studies of river fisheries, for Antipa (1910) concluded that fisheries production of the Danube was directly proportional to the extent and duration of the floods, a sentiment echoed by subsequent workers on that river (Botnariuc, 1968; Holčik and Bastl, 1976, 1977). That a similar state of affairs existed in tropical rivers was suspected by Wimpenny (1934) (in Holden, 1963) and many other workers on tropical fisheries. The response of the Sahelian river systems to the drought of 1970–74 is a confirmation of this fluctuation. In both the Niger and Senegal, catches declined considerably over the drought years, although they recovered reasonably rapidly once normal flood regimes were re-established (Table 4.11).

Table 4.11 Trends in catch in Senegal river and the Central Delta of the Niger (data from Senegal, Direction des Eaux, Forêts et Chasses, 1976 and Konare, 1977)

River	Catch tonnes $\times$ 1 000								
	1967	1968	1969	1970	1971	1972	1973	1974	1975
Senegal	30	25	20	18	18	15	12	21	25
Niger*	9·5	10·8	11·1	11·2	8·8	7·8	4·2	3·6	7·6

*Smoked fish at Mopti landing only.

Sufficient data are available from the Kafue, the Shire and the Central Delta of the Niger for an assessment of the effects of differences in the hydrological regime upon fish catch. Unfortunately, none of these sets of data include reliable estimates of changes in fishing effort, which may itself be responsible for year-to-year variations in catch.

In the Kafue river, water level and catch records are available from 1954 until the time of writing. However, the fishery is not judged to have reached maximum expansion until 1958 (Muncy, 1977), and the flood regime has been altered by the construction of a downstream dam in 1972. Calculations have therefore been based largely on the years

1958–71, although they have also been carried out less successfully over a longer period. The University of Michigan *et al.* (1971) found a correlation ($r = 0.77$) for catch as a function of the amount of water retained in the system during the preceding dry season, with the relationship $C_{n'} = -6630 + 1830 \log_e DDF_{n-1'}$ where *DDF* is a drawdown factor[1]. The University of Idaho *et al.* (1971) found similar relationships using flood index (FI) as a representation of the intensity of flooding. Here correlations were $T = 0.72$ on the preceding year's flood and 0.71 on the flood two years previously. Muncy (1973 and 1977) has presented a complete analysis of these factors. In summary, he found a very weak negative correlation ($R = -0.171$) for catch of any one year as related to the water stage derived from September–December water levels in that year. This he attributed to the lessened efficiency of fishing during the more intense floods. He also presented good positive correlations for catch and flood intensity of the preceding years ($y-1$ and $y-2$).

Sets of data for water level and catch are also available for the Shire river (1969–73) and the Central Delta of the Niger (1966–74) and have been analysed by Welcomme (1975a). As a measure of flood intensity this analysis used a simple sum of all weekly mean water levels which exceeded the level at which overspill on to the floodplain occurred (bankfull stage). The results of preliminary simple regressions showed that a highly significant correlation existed between catch and flood regime in the previous year ($y-1$) in all three systems. Correlations of catch with flooding in the same year were not so successful. Because the fishery of most rivers is based mainly on fish that are one and two years old, it might be expected that the flood regime in both preceding years ($y-1$ and $y-2$) might exert an effect on the catch of fish in year *y*. When regressions of combined and weighted hydrological indices from the preceding years were used, some improvements in the correlations were noted, and it was finally concluded that catch in year *y* is better explained by a combination of flood history from the two preceding years than by either year on its own. In this way the best-fit linear regression lines, which are plotted in Fig. 4.22 were calculated as:

Kafue: $C_y = 2962 + 70.54(0.7HI_{y-1} + 0.3HI_{y-2})$
Shire: $C_y = 5857 + 38.11(0.9HI_{y-1} + 0.1HI_{y-2})$
Niger: $C_y = 3239 + 32.10(0.5HI_{y-1} + 0.5HI_{y-2})$

Differences in hydrological index accounted for 57 per cent of the variation in catch between years in the Kafue river, 82 per cent in the Shire and 92 in the Niger. These results, while still being rather imprecise, indicated clearly that there was a relationship between the hydrological regime and the catch, as would be expected from the biology of the fish in floodplain rivers.

One question that has been posed by several authors in the analysis of such data is whether the factor responsible for the fluctuation in catch is the intensity of flooding or the severity of the drawdown period. The

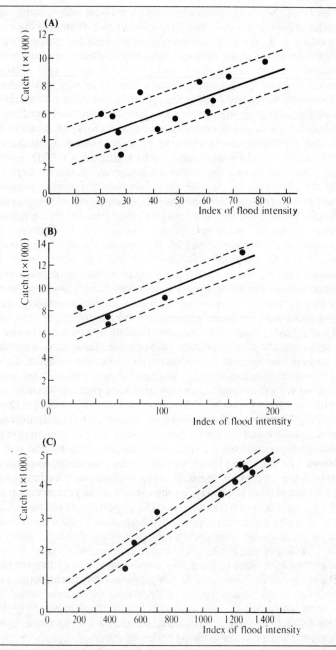

Fig. 4.22 Best-fit regression lines for the relationship between catch and flood regime for: (A) the Kafue flats fishery; (B) the Shire river fishery; (C) the Central Delta of the Niger at Mopti.

similarity of the correlations obtained from these two possible sources of variation in the Kafue is hardly surprising as in that river the intensity of flooding was inversely correlated with the severity of drawdown ($r = -0.78$). The correlation between intensity of flooding and severity of drawdown in the Shire was much lower ($r' = -0.45$), as was the correlation between drawdown and catch. However, this cannot be taken to imply that the high-water regime is the most influential of the two phases of the aquatic cycle in all systems, because the differences in response to low-water levels in the Kafue and the Shire could also have been due to differences in the area of water remaining in the system relative to the area at peak floods. In the Kafue, about 27 per cent of the water remained during the dry season, whereas in the Shire there was some 48 per cent. It may be surmised that the more stringent the drawdown, as reflected by the lessened percentage of water remaining in the system during the dry season, the greater the influence of fluctuations in the low-water regime on the catch in the next year. This is to a certain extent borne out by the simulation of a floodplain fish population and its fishery (Welcomme and Hagborg, 1977), which predicted that the more water remaining in the system at low water, the more differences in ichthyomass induced by the high-water regime are transmitted to the next cycle. In this model, catch was directly related to ichthyomass and therefore responded accordingly.

An analysis of catch related to the flooding in a river has been carried out independently by Krykhtin (1975) on the Amur river who reached similar conclusions as to the effects of flood intensity on catch. He found that the best correlation was obtained when catch in any year was compared with the flood regime three to four years previously. Ivanov (quoted by Chitravadivelu, 1974) also noted a similar effect in the Zofin arm of the Danube, but with a lag time of one year. The lag between the year of flooding and the time when its effects are reflected in the catch is probably dependent on the time taken for fish to enter the size range captured by the fishery. In Africa this is extremely short, less than a year in some cases, because of the small size and rapid growth of some species, and also because of the heavy fishing for fish of the year as they leave the plain. Ivanov also remarks on the high proportion of young age classes in the Danube fishery one year after high floods and a corresponding drop in catch a year after particularly poor flow. In some rivers, where growth is slower and the larger species are favoured by the fishery, they take at least two years to reach the length that is susceptible to the gear. In the Amur river fishery, Krykhtin proposed that the effect on catch is only felt after the incorporation of 20–30 per cent of the new year classes into the fishery.

The fishing-up process, with its tendency to force the community structure towards faster-growing forms which enter the fishery earlier in their lives, will tend to shorten the lag between the time of a flood and the time when its effects are reflected in the catch. Where there is heavy fishing over a number of years, such internal changes in the composition of the stock may make the analysis of possible relationships between hydrological factors and fish catch more complex.

On the basis of the obvious correlation between flood height and catch it is tempting to try to predict catches in future years from the flood of the year, using regression formulae similar to the above. It may be assumed that, if one can indeed predict the catch of any one year from its flood or the flood of a preceding year, the accuracy of the prediction for any one river would improve as an increasing number of years of data are added to the regression. When the data for the Kafue, Shire and Niger rivers were treated individually in this way there was no improvement in the accuracy of an estimate of future catch. From which it has been concluded that, at our present state of knowledge, it is not possible validly to predict catches in river systems in coming years from regression analyses of the past performance of the fishery with a useful degree of accuracy. Holčik and Bastl (1977), on the other hand, found correlations between water levels in year y and fish catch in years y and $y+1$ in the Czechoslovak reaches of the Danube, and concluded that the prediction of catch from hydrological data in that river may be possible from the relationships they obtained. Because of the importance of such predictions for the management of fisheries in river basins, further work on this topic is desirable.

4.6 Management of river fisheries

Purpose of exploitation

The fish stocks of rivers and their floodplains are of interest to man for three main purposes. They provide a source of animal protein as a component of his diet, they form the basis for sport fisheries, and they supply a variety of attractive or curious species for ornament. The total annual world catch from inland waters has been estimated at some 10 million t for 1974 (*FAO Yearbook of Fishery Statistics*, 1975). While it is difficult to separate the production obtained from rivers from that of lakes and intensive aquaculture in ponds, it seems fair to assume that about half of this comes from running waters, their floodplains and from aquaculture associated with lands inundated for rice culture or other purposes. Certainly in Africa just under half of the catch of 1·4 million t is estimated as coming from these sources (Welcomme, 1976) and in Latin America, most of the production of 180 000 t is from rivers, as there are very few lakes in that continent. But by far the greatest proportion of inland fish catch is derived from Asia, and in particular from China, where various types of extensive aquaculture are common but river fisheries are also pursued. Fish rearing in floodplain rice paddies is widespread throughout Southeast Asia and the production of major rivers such as the Ganges, Brahmaputra, Mekong and Indus alone combine to give some 1·25 million t.

The use of fish resources for sport on a large scale is comparatively new, and has been confined by and large to the more industrialized countries. In the larger flood rivers of Eastern Europe this use probably has a significant impact on the management policy. In the rivers of North America, too, there has been a trend away from food fisheries towards sports fisheries which more or less coincides with the bringing under control of the flood regime of these waters. Sports and commercial fisheries often compete for the same resource, as the large and lively species beloved by sports fishermen all too often form the basis of the commercial fishery as well.

Most of the freshwater ornamental fish species are exported from tropical rivers, especially those of the great forest areas. They are generally small fish of no value for food, although the juveniles of some food fishes are also popular. Fairly large numbers are caught to make up for wastage through disease and transport mortalities. Colombia, for instance, exported some 10 million fish in 1974, Peru 15 million, Brazil 3·5 million, Venezuela 10 million – all from the Amazon and Orinoco basins (Conroy, 1975). As mortalities between capture and export range between 50 and 70 per cent, this represents a catch of at least 70 million fish, most of which are withdrawn from such restricted environments as floodplain pools or small feeder streams to the main rivers. Local disappearances of species due to overexploitation have already been reported from some countries and may be expected to expand if adequate precautions are not taken.

Within these categories of use objectives can be made more precise. For instance, food fisheries can be managed for a few preferred species only or for maximum production of fish flesh irrespective of its type. Only rarely can a community be managed for some mix of these. Similarly, while it is often assumed that a more or less even annual withdrawal of fish from the stock is desirable, circumstances may arise where exceptionally heavy fishing is necessary in one year, to compensate for a shortfall in other food sources, for example, and lower catches taken in other years. Fisheries are also managed for socio-economic objectives, among which that of employment has long been a subject of ambiguity. The desire has frequently been expressed that the maximum number of fishermen be employed, and yet that at the same time the fishermen individually derive the maximum benefit from the fishery. In fact such objectives generally resolve themselves into quality versus quantity alternatives that seem mutually exclusive, although compromises almost always have to be reached. Scrutiny of a catch per fisherman curve such as Fig. 4.19 suffices to show that such disparate objectives can only be achieved by sacrificing a little of the pure spirit of both alternatives.

Yield concepts

One of the commonest concepts for the regulation of fisheries is that of maximum sustainable yield (MSY), which predicts that any fish stock has a constant surplus production which may be removed by a fishery each year. A considerable amount of attention has been paid to methodologies for deriving MSY, but the concept is applicable mainly to single stocks whose abundance is relatively unaffected by changes in the environment. As few fisheries are typical of this situation, and because the concept also introduces severe economic weaknesses in that it is heavily biased towards the long-term situation, MSY has been somewhat discredited in recent years. However, the hunt for a successor concept has proved unrewarding, and MSY is still loosely cited as representing the general productivity of a body of water or a fish stock. The concept is particularly inappropriate to river fisheries as they are based on multispecies communities whose abundance is largely determined by an environmental variable, the flood intensity. Unfortunately, in rivers, as elsewhere, it is very difficult to find a simple replacement whereby to manage the fishery. In its place we can offer only such generalizations that the yield of a floodplain river is about 40–60 kg hm^{-2} at maximum flood, or to select somewhat arbitrary management measures based on a knowledge of the fishery itself and other fisheries, and subsequently to monitor their effects in order periodically to revise management policy. This approach is possibly very common and has the advantage of flexibility in altering strategies to bring them in line with changing objectives of the fishery, but sometimes fails where damaging practices are tolerated for too long a period.

Fisheries for juveniles

The very heavy exploitation of juvenile fish, in the form of fish of the year moving to the dry-season habitats at the end of the flood, is a particular feature of floodplain fisheries. In the Ouémé, as in many African and Asian fisheries, small-mesh nets of various types are used intensively in the canals draining the plain. Cross-channel dams and barrages, such as those of the El Beid or the Barotse plain, are also designed for the capture of young fish. Durand (1970) estimated that up to 90 per cent of the catch by number and weight of the El Beid river was made up of juvenile fish moving from the Yaérés floodplain towards Lake Chad. The 'maalelo' fishery of the Barotse removed about 3·7 per cent of the juveniles of the 15 most important species each year (Bell-Cross, 1971). Many millions of fingerlings and fry of the major carps are withdrawn annually from Indian rivers to stock reservoirs in their basins, and the capture of fry is common throughout Asia for the stocking of floodplain depressions, rice paddies and culture ponds.

It is common prejudice that the removal of large quantities of juvenile fish will prove harmful to the stock. The persistence of many of the fisheries themselves, indicates that there is little danger so long as the practice is kept within reasonable limits. Both Reed *et al.* (1967) in his defence of the 'atalla' fishery for juveniles on the Niger river, and Bell-Cross (1971) in his analysis of the 'maalelo' fishery, made the point that, with the high mortality rates current among river fishes, the loss of a proportion of year–class I fish is hardly liable to affect the final population at all. A theoretical analysis of such a fishery (Welcomme and Hagborg, 1977) indicated that a high proportion of the juveniles can be removed during the period of drain-off without damaging the fishery, and in simulated fisheries, where juveniles were exploited at the same time as adults, the combined catch exceeded the maximum catch of either juvenile or adult fisheries on their own. However, careful control of these fisheries is essential and further studies are needed on actual situations where the juveniles are heavily exploited.

Changes in exploited fish populations

It is unfortunate that systematic monitoring is still not carried out on most river fisheries. As a consequence, judgements on the impact of the fisheries on the riverine fish stock are still somewhat speculative. The problem is further complicated by the fact that environmental effects produced by other, non-fisheries, activities can affect the fish stock in ways which often resemble those resulting from fishing pressure (see Sections 5.4 and 5.5). This means that a consideration of the management of the fishery in isolation from other uses of the water is a somewhat sterile exercise. Experience has shown that, in lakes at least, an evolution of the fishery, which has come to be termed the 'fishing-up process', occurs as fishing pressure is applied (Regier and Loftus, 1972). Initially, fishing tends to reduce the average age of the stocks fished, increasing the efficiency of utilization of their food. In river fisheries, where as we have seen a very high proportion of the population is in any case in the first one- or two-year classes, the 'slack' within which this may occur is rather limited, and although new fisheries inevitably have an accrued number of older fish to draw upon these are quickly exhausted. There is often a rapid drop in the catch as the accumulated larger individuals are removed from the stock, but this is generally followed by a more stable period as the fishery concentrates on the younger year classes. Acceleration in growth rate, and a reduction in the size of maturation of the exploited species is also common. Subsequently, as fishing is further intensified, the larger, slower-growing, longer-lived species are apt to be replaced by smaller species of higher turn-over rate (see for example Christie, 1968, for the North American Great Lakes, and Turner, 1977, for Lake Malawi). In other words there is a tendency for 'K' selected communities to become substituted by r selected communities (Lowe-McConnell, 1977). These latter have higher P/B ratios and raise productivity somewhat through the more rapid recycling of nutrients. Furthermore, as more predators are removed relative to the planktonic and benthic feeders, the overall food-chain efficiency may be expected to improve, but this does not in fact happen as much as is often assumed owing to the trophic intolerance of the modified community (Regier and Henderson, 1973; Dickie, 1976). In river communities, in particular, the paucity of species at lower trophic levels, as shown by the high predator/forage fish ratios, limits the capacity of the system to benefit by such changes. In the case of the nutrient-poor blackwaters, where the nutrients locked up in the fish represent a significant proportion of the total nutrient pool, removal of larger predators, whether fish or crocodiles, has even been held accountable for the decline in long-term productivity of the environment (Fittkau, 1973). In such systems rapid declines in catch may follow the onset of exploitation, as happened in the Kamulondo depression where the catch fell from 9 063 to 4 810 t in the space of four years after the introduction of an intensive fishery based on nylon gill-nets (Poll and Renson, 1948). Eventually the nutrients normally channelled through the fish community will find their way to other parts of the system as the limits of the adaptation of fishes to high removal rates are reached. At this point the production of the fish community will drop rather rapidly. In floodplain river communities, much of the adaptation is to compensate for high natural removal rates, and perhaps because of this they appear to be more resistant to heavy fishing than the equivalent populations in lakes.

During the period when biological fish production changes rather little with increasing exploitation, the ichthyomass will tend to remain relatively constant or decrease as the species composition shifts to species with higher turnover rates. With decreasing biomass and higher turnover, higher exploitation rates can maintain catches, even allowing increases if the biomass does not decline too rapidly. The tendency for ichthyomass to remain constant may be reinforced in rivers where only a certain proportion of it is able to survive through the dry season anyway. It is arguably better for the stock that this consists of more numerous younger fish than fewer older specimens.

The number of species which make up the catch will initially increase, although in some regions market preferences may be very restricted so that only a few stocks may be fished. When these are reduced, it may take some time before the markets can be reoriented to replacement species. Until this happens catches may fall and fishing initially may be reduced, as has happened on the Paraná river, with the decline of the 'Sabalo' *Prochilodus platensis* fisheries. Where the market demand is highly diverse, as it is in most African and Asian countries, the number of species in the catch will first rise rapidly, and then diminish as the more susceptible forms succumb to fishing and other pressures.

These changes are summarized graphically in Fig. 4.23. They are particularly noticeable in fisheries using modern mesh-selective gears, such as the gill-net, cast-net or seine-net, where changes in the size and species composition of the stock are accompanied by a classic pattern of successive replacement of large-mesh gear by smaller and smaller mesh sizes. Such changes are more difficult to detect in the traditional fishery, which from the outset exploits a broad spectrum of sizes and species, with a variety of gears. But the available evidence from fisheries such as the Ouémé is that the use of gears designed to capture larger species and individuals progressively declines as the fishery becomes heavily exploited.

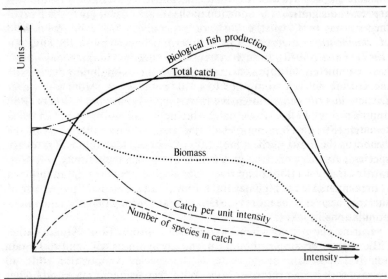

Fig. 4.23 Diagram of theoretical changes in a multispecies fishery brought about by increasing intensities of fishing. (After Welcomme and Henderson, 1976.)

Status of fisheries

Actual experience in a number of river systems tends to confirm that the fishing-up process as deduced from lake fisheries, also applies to rivers, although with secondary complications arising from the nature of the hydrological regime. During the drought in the Senegal and Niger rivers fish populations gave every symptom of overfishing, with the disappearance of larger species, and smaller species and individuals appearing in declining numbers in the catch. Fishing pressure was high, as most of the fishermen were obliged to concentrate on a very much reduced area of water, and their dependence on the fishery was heightened by the failure of both agriculture and animal husbandry throughout the Sahelian zone. Nevertheless, the fish stock recovered and returned to previous catch levels shortly after the re-establishment of more normal flood conditions, which indicates that these systems are not excessively exploited during their normal regimes. In the Chari, on the other hand, the fishery also declined in a similar manner during the same period but has not yet recovered. Catches in standard experimental nets during the last four months of each year fell from 916 kg in 1971 to 70 kg in 1973, and were accompanied by the virtual disappearance of *Alestes dentex* and *A. baremoze*, the previously principal components of the fishery, together with many of the larger species (Quensière, 1976).

This state of affairs, which has persisted up until the time of writing, demonstrates that the combination of irregular flood regimes with a level of fishing that was not apparently excessive previously, can lead to the collapse of a fishery. Both *Arapaima gigas* and *Colossoma bidens* are now considered rare in the Amazon, whereas previously they were the mainstay of the fishery. In the Rio de la Plata the coastal population of *Basilichthys bonariensis* was considered overfished by Cabrera (1962). *Lates niloticus, Heterobranchus longifilis* and *Bagrus docmac*, have completely disappeared from the heavily fished lower reaches of the Ouémé river, and other large species such as *Citharinus latus*, *Distichodus rostratus, Labeo senegalensis* and *Heterotis niloticus* have diminished much in abundance. Sritingsook and Yoovetwatana (1976) remarked on the disappearance of large migratory species such as *Probarbus jullieni* from the Mekong river and its tributaries. Migratory species generally seem especially vulnerable to overfishing, possibly because they are attacked principally at the time when the ripe adults are congregated in their breeding migrations. An example of the collapse of such a fishery is shown by *Labeo victorianus* which has virtually disappeared from the rivers leading into Lake Victoria. In the Kagera river the decline was shown by the drop in catch per gill-net from 1935 to 1939 when 10 kg net $^{-1}$ were caught, until 1963 when the catch was 0·5 kg net $^{-1}$ (Caldwalladr, 1965b). A parallel decline was noted in the nets and weirs of the Nzoia river which was attributed to the heavy gill-net fishery at the mouth of the rivers which prevented a sufficient number of fish reaching their upriver breeding grounds. *Labeo altivelis* pursued a similar history. In 1945 it used to contribute about 40 per cent of the total catch of the Luapula river–Lake Mweru fishery. In 1958, it only contributed 2 per cent (Soulsby, 1959), and in later years has been considered virtually extinct (Jackson, 1961b).

While stocks of individual species may be overfished, well-documented examples of overfishing at the community level in rivers are rare and when recorded are often traceable to environmental variables, as is the case in the Chari river, or to other human interventions, as in the case of the decline of the Mekong Grand Lac fishery from 70 000 t in 1940 to 35 000 t in 1967 (Committee for the Coordination of Investigations of the Lower Mekong Basin 1970). In both cases, however, it is likely that heavy fishing hastened the decline by making the fish stock less resistant to changes arising from other sources. Perhaps the best example of overfishing is shown by the Ouémé and it is useful to examine this in detail. Fishing is again perhaps not the only factor leading to the decline of the stock, as there has also been a change in the nature of the estuarine area by the construction of a port near the outfall of the major lagoon systems. This has allowed a channel to remain open throughout the year, letting more saline water penetrate the lower reaches of the river. There is no doubt that this has caused a fall in the productivity of the lagoon associated with the river system, but any detrimental effects on the river itself are somewhat more open to question. The total catch of the Ouémé floodplain was estimated at 10 400 t in 1955–57 (CTFT, 1957). By 1968–69 this had fallen to an estimated 6 484 t (FAO/UN, 1971a). The fall was accompanied not only by the loss or decline of larger species as noted above, but by a fall in catch per unit of effort (CPUE) in most gears as summarized in Table 4.12. Although there was some increase in total effort during the period (about 19 per cent) this was unlikely to have accounted completely for the drop in CPUE.

Table 4.12 Changes in catch per unit effort in gear from the Ouémé river between 1955–57 and 1968–69

Type of gear	Catch per unit effort		Percentage changes
	1955–57	1968–69	
Cast-nets: large-mesh	1 186 g h^{-1}	249·8 g h^{-1}	−79
medium-mesh	694·1 g h^{-1}	372 g h^{-1}	−46
small-mesh	589·5 g h^{-1}	322·6 g h^{-1}	−45
Long line	286·0 g h^{-1}	193·0 g h^{-1}	−33
Traps: *Clarias* trap	74·0 g day^{-1}	43·2 g day^{-1}	−42
Macrobrachium trap	115·0 g day^{-1}	309·0 g day^{-1}	+269

The mean weight of species caught also dropped in several of the gears. For example, the medium-mesh cast-net caught fish of 124·9 g in 1955–57, but the mean weight had dropped to only 26·5 g in 1968–69. Similarly the small-mesh net caught fish of 25·2 g in 1955–57, but only 9·8 g in 1968–69.

The only gear which showed an increase was the trap for *Macrobrachium*, a detritus-eating freshwater prawn that was previously heavily preyed upon by the fishes.

From this it may be concluded that the ability of fish communities in rivers to support heavy fishing is very good and that most systems are still exploited at a reasonable level despite a considerable range in the effort expended on them. However, certain individual stocks are vulnerable and may easily disappear. Furthermore, environmental pressures, when added to fishing pressures, may cause a collapse in the fishery. Fisheries of river systems will also decline below their optimum productivity if subjected to excessive fishing, even though environmental variables remain relatively unchanged.

Techniques for management

Introduction of new species

In their unmodified condition, most rivers support fish communities that are sufficiently diverse to fill most of the available trophic and spatial niches. But as systems are modified there is a tendency for certain indigenous species to disappear and for others to take their place. This is most noticeable in the case of impoundments where many of the migratory riverine species are lost soon after the stabilization of flow. In many rivers species which are adequately adapted to the new conditions are absent from the original fish fauna, and to overcome this additional species may have to be introduced from other river basins. In some cases introductions have been performed uncritically, and such species as the carp (*Cyprinus carpio*) or *Sarotherodon mossambicus* have been blamed for degradation of the environment or fish community structure on their own account. Furthermore, fishes such as these, which are among the major elements for intensive aquaculture, find their way into natural waters by accidental release from farm ponds. Introduction of new species into the fish fauna of a river basin therefore needs very careful study. However, while widespread or impetuous introduction of new species is to be decried, the great success of these same species in other circumstances, for instance *Sarotherodon* in Asian reservoirs (Fernando, 1976) or the carp in some highly eutrophicated rivers, points to the potential role of properly considered introductions. A further witness to this is the greatly increased catch from the Amu Darya river and irrigation system following the successful implantation of the macrophyte-eating grass carp (*Ctenopharyngodon idella*), together with the plankton-eating *Mylopharyngodon piceus, Hypophthalmichthys molitrix, Aristichthys nobilis* and *Parabramis pekinensis* (Aliyev, 1976). These species have formed breeding populations within the rivers, from which they colonize the adjoining 900 km long Kara Kum canal. In this, the weed-eating habit of the grass carp contributes to the clearing of macrophytes, whereas the other species profit by the planktonic blooms arising from the increased nutrients that become available, giving a high catch to the fishery. They apparently do not interfere with the other elements of the fish fauna. These conclusions are important as these species are under consideration in many tropical and subtropical countries as candidates for introduction. Furthermore, eaters of higher plants are usually rare in river fish communities and the macrophyte-eating niche is often one of the few that is unoccupied.

Closed seasons

By the nature of its biology, the floodplain river fishery has a built-in closed season. From just after bankfull on the rising flood to peak floods the fish population is too dispersed and individual fish are too small in size for them to be readily available to the majority of methods of capture. This generally discourages fishing throughout the period as yields are low, effort needed to capture fish high, and there are additional dangers of loss of gear in the currents and floating vegetation masses. This effective closed season makes biological sense in that it allows the fish to reproduce relatively undisturbed and for the young to grow to a reasonable size before they are exposed to the fishery. Closed seasons outside this time are of limited value, although restrictions on the overly heavy fishing of migrating adult fish to the spawning grounds may be necessary in some places, as experiences with *Labeo* in Africa have shown.

Reserved waters

As fishing of the floodplain and river channel in the dry season becomes more intensive, there is a risk of local overexploitation of the stock. For this reason, traditional fisheries have long been based on the designation of certain floodplain depression lakes and reaches of the river as reserves which remained unfished. In larger systems, there are usually inaccessible areas which form reserves as they are infrequently exploited, and it is probably from such areas that the Niger and Senegal rivers were recolonized after the Sahelian drought. As a management measure the conservation of certain areas is probably a wise move and gains force when other pressures are being applied to the system.

Mesh regulations

The use of mesh-selective gear almost always entails a consideration of the mesh sizes to be adopted. The mesh size, and indeed the desirability of introducing regulations at all, depends largely on the objectives for which the fishery is to be managed. As has been described, the fishing-up process almost always involves a drift downwards in mesh size which needs considerable enforcement of legislation to stop. Any lower limit on mesh size, therefore, has to be imposed in the face of a natural trend to disregard it. It also poses the classic dilemma of how to manage multispecies stocks consisting of species with a range of sizes. If the objective of the fishery is to exploit only the large species of the community, the imposition of mesh limits which protect the immature fish is probably the only way to do it effectively. However, one almost certainly neglects a considerable proportion of the potential ichthyomass in this type of fishery as is shown by the number of species caught by progressively lower mesh sizes (see Fig. 4.16). If the mesh size is lowered to take advantage of the smaller species, then almost automatically the larger ones will disappear. One possible solution to the dilemma is the limitation of mesh size in major gears such as seine-nets, gill-nets, etc. coupled with a use of a variety of minor gears which are aimed at particular smaller elements of the stock. In other words, in a fish community which is highly diverse it is as well to maintain an equally diversified fishery.

Banning of certain gears

The restriction or complete outlawing of more destructive fishing practices is most important. However, even such methods may be appropriate to some circumstances. Poisoning of watercourses is of course liable to damage the stocks of fish when carried out in the main channel of the river, whereas its use for removing fish from temporary floodplain pools or for eradicating undesirable species may be quite permissible. Unfortunately, were the use of poisons allowed in one habitat it would rapidly extend to others. Gear is often prohibited for reasons other than those bearing directly on the fish stock. Long lines, for instance, are regarded with disfavour by users of cast-nets which may become entangled in the hooks. Barriers which completely block the river channel, thus stopping fish migrations, are as likely to be removed for reasons of navigation as for fisheries.

Restriction on numbers of fishermen

As shown in Fig. 4.20, the total catch is related to the number of fishermen in rivers. Furthermore, the individual artisanal fisherman seems to have a limited fishing power in that he is physically capable of removing only a certain quantity of fish from the system in any one year. Because of this, the solution that seems most appealing in this type of fishery, is a simple restriction on the number of fishermen operating in a certain region.

However, on floodplains this presents certain practical problems because the number of part-time fishermen and their rather flexible contribution to the fishery makes them difficult to control. In many rivers, especially in Asia, such control is achieved by dividing the river and the plain into lots, for which individuals or groups of fishermen compete at auction each year. The job of policing the lot rented then devolves upon the fishermen groups.

The renting of stretches of river to fishermen for restricted periods has been criticized on the grounds that any group with only temporary tenure of a fishery will attempt to gain the maximum profit within the time available. This leads to ruinous fishing practices where the stock is exploited to the point of exhaustion. On the other hand, where areas are held by tradition or contract for a number of years as in many parts of Africa, the fishermen are freer to husband the resource and develop the fishery.

Increasing the efficiency of the fisherman

Improvements in the efficiency of the fishermen can be brought about in several ways. Introduction of new types of gear, or the amelioration of existing gear enables the individual to capture larger numbers of fish of a greater range of species. Better materials mean that the gear is less liable to damage, consequently less time has to be spent in its maintenance and more on the fishing grounds. Proper boat design and motorization of craft can get the fishermen to and from the fishing grounds faster. Historically, these processes have already occurred in many rivers, firstly with the introduction of perfected gill-nets, seines and cast-nets; secondly by the introduction of nylon twine and netting; and thirdly by the adoption of the outboard motor. In some fisheries too, traditional methods, especially those centred around cross-river barrier traps which capture migrating fish, are as efficient as the more modern techniques that seek to replace them. The effectiveness of the fishery may also be conditioned by geographical accessibility or by the lack of adequate facilities for treatment which limit the amount of fish that can be handled. Because of this some fisheries do operate below their full capacity. However, the efficiency of much of the traditional and improved modern gear is such that individual stocks have collapsed in some river systems and in others whole communities are near maximum exploitation, if not actually overfished. Therefore, improving the efficiency of the individual fisherman does not appear to be appropriate in many cases and should be regarded more as a means of fine tuning the fishery as development of other sectors occurs. In other words, in areas where there is a great demand for rural employment it is probably advisable to restrain the introduction of more efficient methods and to concentrate on better marketing and other support facilities. In such circumstances, where better gear is introduced, the improved performance is either dissipated in a diminished catch per unit effort as the stock declines, or the less prosperous and efficient fishermen, who cannot use or adapt to the new gear, are forced out of the fishery. On the other hand, as the general economy of a country increases there is a tendency for labour to be withdrawn from the rural sector, including fishing. In such cases fisheries have declined owing to fishermen leaving their trade, which in any case becomes less and less profitable. Here a rapid increase in the individual efficiency of a few fishermen can to a certain extent halt the decline and preserve a reasonable way of life for those that chose to remain in their previous profession.

Husbandry

The simple exploitation of fish stocks in floodplain rivers by capture fisheries does not realize the full potential productivity of the system. The fish stock can benefit much from careful husbandry, and intensive management techniques are used in several parts of the world. The clearing and regularizing of floodplain depressions, the implantation of drain-in ponds, the cutting of appropriate canals for inflow of water and the construction of dams to control the run-off from lagoons can all have an impact, which cumulatively can raise the productivity above that of the uncontrolled system. Many such methods are still in a crude stage in their evolution and need rationalization, but as the floodplains of the world are in increasing demand for purposes other than the fisheries, the development of such appropriate technology for the artificial conservation of fish stocks is extremely important.

Accessibility

One of the main factors determining the degree to which the fisheries of the major floodplains are exploited is their accessibility and proximity to major centres of population. Some of the greatest floodplains are still relatively little utilized by reason of their distance from suitable markets and lack of living space for the fishermen – the Okavango delta, the Nile Sudd and the Gran Pantanal of the Paraguay river are typical examples. Development of such areas can only follow after the provision of suitable access routes and main centres for the marketing of catch as well as artificial mounds or other appropriate locations for the fishermen to settle near the fishing grounds during the flood.

4.7 Summary

The nature of the fishery is very much determined by the seasonality of the flood regime and changes in the distribution and accessibility of the fish. Three categories of fishermen may be distinguished: occasional fishermen whose involvement in the fishery may be limited to the exploitation of certain floodplain lakes; part-time fishermen, who alternate fishing with other activities such as agriculture; and professional fishermen who are obliged to follow the concentrations of fish to secure year-round employment.

A rich assortment of traditional fishing gears is used by floodplain fishermen. Passive gears, such as barrages, traps or stow-nets capture fish as they are migrating on to or away from the floodplain. Active gears, like frame-trawls or scrape-nets are used mainly during the dry season when the fish are not moving extensively themselves. Poisoning is common in residual pools in the dry season, both on the plain and in river channels. Certain types of fish-husbandry methods using branches or vegetation placed in the water, drain-in ponds dug in the floodplain, or lakes produced by damming the outflows of depressions, are also used. In some rivers the traditional methods are being replaced by gill-nets, cast-nets or seines made of manufactured twines. The fishery follows a seasonal pattern according to the accessibility of the fish. Effort is minimal during the floods, rises to a maximum as the water drains from the plain and continues to be high throughout the dry season. Because of the diversity of tropical river fish populations, many species are captured by the fisheries, but as their abundance is distributed lognormally only a few species predominate.

Once caught, fish may be sold fresh by the fishermen to merchants who ice them for transport to the markets. In Africa, fresh fish is less common and the majority of the catch is smoke-dried, although in arid areas sun-drying is also used. In some Asian rivers these products are supplemented by a variety of pastes and sauces which are mostly secondary products of the industry.

The catch of individual fishermen drops with increases in fisherman density. Total catch, however, seems to increase with increasing numbers of fishermen up to a density of about 10 fishermen km^{-2} and thereafter declines with further intensification of exploitation. In systems supporting large numbers of fishermen it seems likely that over-exploitation is a real possibility. The catches of various floodplains are a function of area according to a scatter around a regression line representing $38 \cdot 3 \, kg \, hm^{-2}$. As this includes many systems that are less than fully exploited, it is estimated that real potentials lie between 40 and 60 $kg \, hm^{-2}$ in most systems.

Year-to-year variations in catch occur within the same system. These have been shown to follow the history of flooding in previous years. The extent to which floods one or two years previous to the one under examination influence the catch probably depends on the lapse of time before fish enter the fishery. In many tropical systems this is one to two years, whereas in some temperate systems a lag of three to four years has been recorded.

The fish communities of floodplain rivers are exploited for several purposes including recreation and ornament, but by far the most important is the production of food. Rivers and the flood areas associated with them possibly account for about half of the present world inland catch of 10 million t. The stocks often have to be managed according to objectives imposed by considerations of need and consumer preference that are external to the fishery. A number of techniques are available for the control of the fishery, but lack of adequate statistics and information make it very difficult to evaluate the effects of such measures. Nevertheless, at present, there are few examples of fisheries which are in decline solely because of overfishing. True, certain of the larger species have disappeared, but this is probably more a symptom of a normal fishing-up process than of over-exploitation at the community level.

Note

1. See Appendix for details of the various indices used to estimate flood variables.

Chapter 5

Impacts of other uses of floodplains on fisheries

5.1 Introduction

The aquatic environment, which has formed the subject of the first three chapters of this work, is only part of the total system. On the floodplain itself there is a dry-season component which in its wild state has an ecology that to some extent mirrors that of its aquatic counterpart. Because of the fertility of their alluvial soils, and the proximity to watercourses for irrigation and transport, floodplains are also much in demand for a whole range of human activities. They are commonly regarded as of high development potential, and efforts to 'reclaim' them by flood control are widespread. The floodplain system is not only influenced by interventions within its own vicinity, but actions over the whole river basin upstream and occasionally downstream may affect both the wet and dry ecosystems. Many of these interventions, such as the construction of flood-control dams, are with the express purpose of modifying the floodplain with a view to making it more suitable for some purpose or other. However, other activities upstream can also unintentionally change the nature of the river and its floodplain, and the fish community inhabiting them. In short, the total floodplain ecosystem may be represented as a process in which dry and wet components alternate and which is maintained in equilibrium by certain inputs. Changes occurring in the system throughout one annual cycle are summarized in Fig. 5.1, which shows in cyclic form the nutrient/energy flow within the system. It is known that in stable floodplains the rate of alluvial deposition equals the removal of alluvial matter by erosion over a period of years (Leopold *et al.*, 1964). It may be assumed that, in the wild state, a similar dynamic equilibrium occurs with respect to the nutrients and biomass. However, in the developed state, various outputs in the form of food are removed from the plain (A, B, C and D in Fig. 5.1). In the early stages of exploitation it is doubtful whether the quantity of nutrients extracted in this manner are significant, but if such an equilibrium exists then the productivity of one component could eventually be affected by the bad management or overexploitation of one of the others, and by other interventions which change the essential characteristics of the system. For example, crops grown on newly reclaimed floodlands often give good yields for the first two or three years after the drainage of the land, but thereafter need heavy inputs of fertilizer to compensate for the lack of nutrients deposited during the former floods. Similarly, in blackwater rivers, the removal of portions of the ichthyomass results in a long-term depletion of the nutrient balance with a lowered productivity of the remaining members of the community.

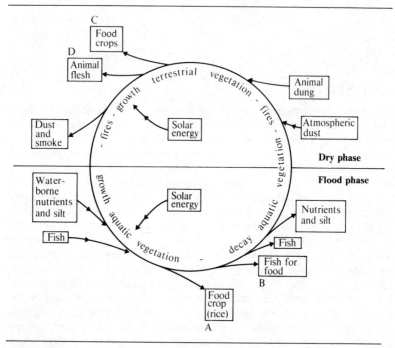

Fig. 5.1 Diagram of nutrient and energy cycles on the floodplain.

5.2 Terrestrial animals

Wildlife

Many species of game animals move on to the floodplain during the dry season in search of the rich grazing to be found there. Certain species are more specialized to this habit than are others, and some are virtually limited to the floodplains for their distribution. Such species as the lechwe (*Kobus leche kafuensis*) migrate from the centre of the plain towards its periphery as the flood rises, and return in the wake of the falling water (Fig. 5.2). Their distribution is, therefore, a mirror image of that of the fish and their dynamics are somewhat similar with a maximum in lambing as the water leaves the plain exposing new pasture (Sayer and Van Lavieren, 1975). Before the construction of the new dams on the Kafue river there was a stable lechwe population of about 94 000 individuals, but changes in the regime following the closing of the

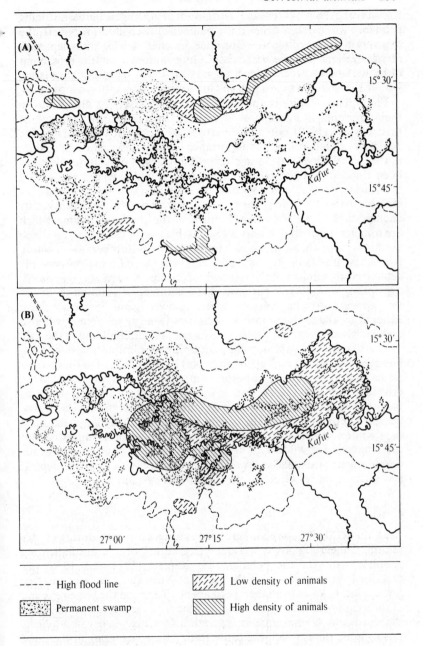

Fig. 5.2 Distribution of Kafue lechwe: (A) at maximum flood, April 1971; (B) at low water, 2–14 September 1971. (After Sayer and Van Lavieren, 1975.)

Kafue Gorge dam has reduced the amount of grazing available and most probably will cause a drop in the number of individuals supported by this plain. According to Gonzalez-Jimenez (1977) the capybara (*Hydrochoerus hyrochaeris*) exists in huge numbers on the floodplains of Latin America where it feeds on grasses, and also eats aquatic plants. Unlike the lechwe it swims well and inhabits permanently swampy areas.

Floodplain wildlife is apt to be affected adversely by alterations to their environment in the same way as the fish. As a further example of this, Attwell (1970) noted some effects of the Kariba dam. Here the Mana floodplain is of great importance for the conservation of wildlife in the valley. Since the closure of the dam a lesser area of the plain has been flooded and the remaining portion is under severe pressure of utilization by the larger species of mammals which has produced changes in the vegetation. The impact of overpopulation is reinforced by changes in the type of grasses favoured by the new flood regime, which are tougher. Growth of plants is also less lush as the rich alluvium which used to fertilize the plain is now removed from the Zambezi water before it reaches the plain. By stabilizing the flow the dam has reduced the ecological dynamism of the river whose discharges are wrongly timed, disrupting reproductive patterns of the mammals. A similar theory to this appears in many systems where mammals and waterfowl have suffered by the drying up of the wetlands (Smart, 1976) and will also emerge when we examine the consequences of dam building to the fish.

The presence of wild ungulates and hippopotami on the floodplain has been considered by Kapetsky (1974a) to be beneficial to the fish and we have already seen the importance attached by Fittkau (1973) to the crocodile populations of Amazonian rivers for the maintenance of balanced communities. In fact, the amount of nutrients recycled by the terrestrial components of the system are probably very large and must have some effect on its overall productivity. It has been suggested that the tendency for wildlife to disappear in favour of cattle early in the development of the plains lowers this productivity as the cattle deposit less of their wastes directly into the aquatic system.

Cattle

Most unmodified floodplains are used as ranges for cattle during the dry season. In certain areas seasonal migrations of the cattle-herding peoples dominate the demography. Rzóska (1974 and 1976) has described the way in which the pastoral Nuer and Dinka of the Nile Sudd migrate away from their permanent villages on the higher ground of the swamps following the receding water. As they progress they burn the dead and drying aquatic vegetation (see Fig. A.4) to obtain the fresh shoots upon which the cattle feed. At the beginning of the flood they return to their island villages after migrating distances of up to 80 km. Similar movements have been noted from the Central Delta of the Niger (Gallais, 1967; Fig. 5.3) and the Okavango swamps (Stannard, pers. comm.), and are a prominent feature of all African wet lands. Patterns do differ in some plains, for instance, the Ouémé, where the characteristic 'lagunair' cattle are confined to the levées which are ditched or fenced off from the back swamp depressions. During the flood the cattle are corralled on artificial islands and fed with aquatic vegetation cut from the floating mats on the plain. Extensive cattle ranching is also a feature of Latin America, and at present the vast 'llanos' of Venezuela and Colombia, which are drained by the Apure, Arauca and Meta rivers, are used mainly for this purpose. Because the llanos are either submerged by sheet flooding or extremely arid, the Venezuelan ranchers are erecting large crescent-shaped dykes called

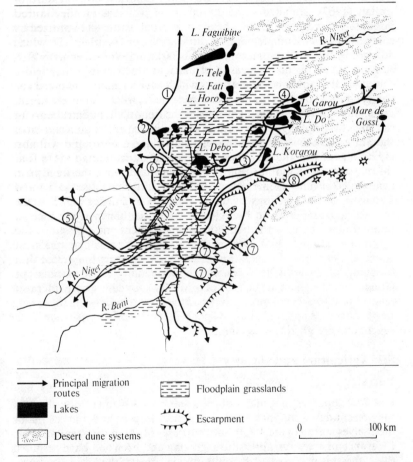

Fig. 5.3 The seasonal migrations of the pastoral peoples of the Central Delta of the Niger: (1) Touareg Kel Antensan. (2) Touareg Tengueriguif; (3) Touareg Irréguénaten; (4) Foulankiabé; (5) Warbé; (6) Sonhabé and Nassadinkobé; (7) Senokobé; (8) Peuhl of Dalla and Bonni. (Adapted from Gallais, 1967.)

'modulos' across the plain. These trap and retain the water as it retreats towards the main river channels and by evaporation and filtration they slowly dry out leaving a well-watered fringe of vegetation available for the cattle. The 'modulos' also tend to trap and retain fish, although their potential as fish-collecting and rearing devices needs to be explored (Matthes, 1977b).

Large numbers of cattle are present on the plains. Rzóska (1974) recorded some 625 000 head as being present in the Sudd. On the Barotse plain there were 310 000 head (FAO/UN, 1969) on the Kafue 250 000 cattle grazed the plain from May to October (FAO/UN, 1968a), on the Shire floodplains 148 000 head are present in the Elephant and Ndinde marshes, and in West Africa on the Central Delta of the Niger Gallais (1967) estimated some 200 000 head, whereas on the Gambia floodplain there were 300 000 head. In general, cattle and fisheries are compatible, even complementary, utilizations of the plain. The dung dropped by the cattle, estimated at about 500 kg hm^{-2}yr^{-1} (Shepherd, 1976) converts much of the dry-season primary production into readily dissolved organic and mineral nutrients which have an important impact on the chemistry of the floodwaters. Several workers have noted the enrichment of some standing waters of the floodplain by cattle who use the lakes for drinking. The exceptional fertility of the Bangula lagoon on the Shire has been attributed to this cause, and according to Gilmore (1976) lagoons of the Okavango frequented by cattle had more than three times the standing crop of more normal pools, 700 kg hm^{-2} as against 200 kg hm^{-2}. Some adverse effects of cattle have also been noted. Extensive use of portions of the Ouémé floodplain for pasture have resulted in trampling and breaking down of the banks of the drain-in ponds found there, with their later abandonment and filling through siltation (Hurault, 1965). On the flooded banks of small channels and streams, clearance of vegetation for intensive grazing may result in a lessening of cover with a consequent reduction of fish population. Gunderson (1968) cited the case of a Montana stream where ungrazed reaches had 76 per cent more cover and the brown trout living there were more numerous and had about 44 per cent more ichthyomass than in the reaches where grazing was common.

5.3 Agriculture and forestry

Forestry

It is now apparent that many of the great open savanna floodplains of the present day were once lined with gallery forests, and that the plains themselves were covered with scrub forests of the bush savanna type. Clearance of trees for agriculture, grazing and firewood have denuded these and this process is still continuing in some of the Latin American plains. As the process of denudation is historically slow it is difficult to assess the impact of these changes on the fish populations, although these have undoubtedly occurred. It seems probable that the rivers have

become less stable with more frequent changes of channel. The flood
regimes would also have changed as extensively forested plains tend to
retain the floodwaters longer. There would be a reduction, too, in the
amount of allochthonous food available to the fish. Nevertheless, most
studies seem to indicate that the savanna plains are more productive
than those that are forested, possibly because they are at a younger stage
of their succession. Clearing the forests allows more sunlight to fall on
the aquatic system, and the recycling of nutrients through the repeated
growth and death of the floodplain grasses is more rapid than on those
plains where they are locked up for long periods in the trees. Perhaps the
best-documented case of deforestation in recent years has taken place in
the surrounds of the Grand Lac of the Mekong. Here the forest has been
cleared for agriculture and for firewood, and has been accompanied by a
decline of the fish catch by about half over 25 years. Sao-Leang and
Dom Saveun (1955) have attributed this to erosion and siltation in the
basin and the lessened availability of allochthonous food arising from
the reduced area of forests. The silting has led to increased turbidity in
the lake through resuspension of particles by wave action in the
increasingly shallow water body. This has in turn led to a drop in
primary productivity which may be reflected in a lowering of the fish
population.

Deforestation in areas far removed from the actual floodplain can
also have a profound effect on the ecosystem. Much of the increased
silting noted in tropical rivers in recent years has been traced to the
denudation of land in the upper reaches of their basins. Here the steeper
slope of the land encourages erosion and the topsoil is rapidly lost,
especially where marginal agriculture is practised (Eckholm, 1976). The
increased silt loads have far-reaching consequences for the morphology
of the river channels as they adjust to the new conditions (Blench, 1972).
Channels lay down natural levées and then raise themselves far above
the surrounding plain until an extreme flood breaches the wall and the
river course changes, sometimes by many kilometres. The Indus river is
particularly noted for this type of erratic behaviour and the eastward
drift of the Ganges–Brahmaputra delta is also attributable to the rapid
silting of the old channels. In addition, individual floodplain features
are obscured more rapidly, with channels and depressions being filled in
the space of a few years. However, at the same time the floodplain grows
apace, especially at the seaward end of coastal deltas where new land
appears all the time.

Deforestation of the catchment area of rivers also leads to changes in
the flood characteristics and in the chemistry of the waters. Flood peaks
tend to become higher and shorter as run-off is decanted straight into
the channels. In forested slopes much water is retained by the vegetation
and also in the topsoil. As the topsoil disappears there is nothing to
delay the water in its move down-slope. The faster rise and fall and the
more unpredictable spiky flood regimes are detrimental to many species
of fish which require a smoother transition from one water phase to

another. The lack of topsoil and the exposure of the bedrock also tends to lower the amount of nutrients entering solution. The conductivity of the water drops, leading eventually to impoverished conditions in the river.

Dry agriculture

The new deposition of alluvial silt on the plains during the floods each year maintains their fertility, making these areas some of the richest of agricultural lands. For this reason, they have attracted man's attention from early in his history as a farmer and some of the earliest civilizations apparently arose in response to the need for communal control of the flooding of the Nile, the Mesopotamian rivers or the rivers of the great plains of China. Where human population density is low, simple culture is common, where small plots are cleared of the moribund aquatic vegetation as the floods subside. Cereal crops such as maize, sorghum or millet are usually sown and, aided by the high water table, grow to be harvested before the next flood. At this level of exploitation little

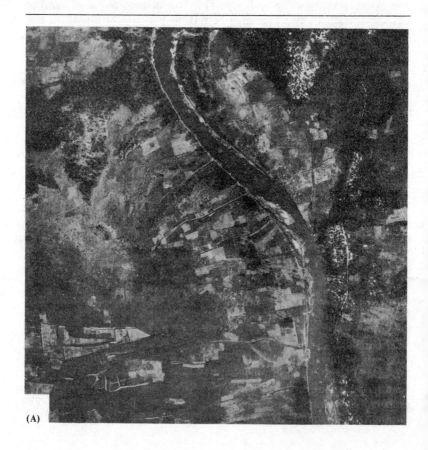

(A)

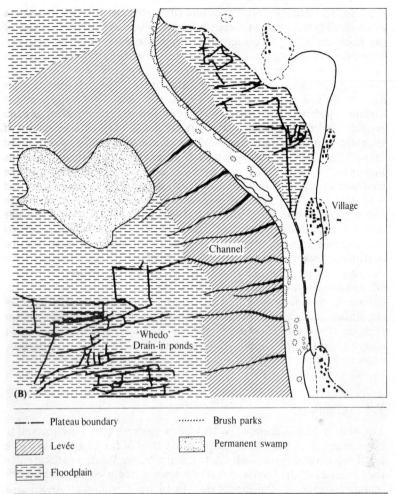

Fig. 5.4 Portion of the Ouémé floodplain showing the distribution of different activities: (A) air-photograph (by courtesy of IGN, Paris); (B) interpretation, for explanation see text.

modification of the plain is needed and the cultivated areas are dispersed among wooded plains. As pressure on the land increases, the floodplain woodland is progressively cleared and the environment further modified by drainage or irrigation. The needs of intensive dry-season agriculture lead to the filling in of many floodplain depressions and reclamation of permanent swamps. To assist in this, drainage canals are dug which dry out permanently wet areas, but these also hasten the run-off from the plain so as to lengthen the growing season.

Irrigation systems often have to be installed in floodplain areas deficient in water or to compensate for water lost through improved drainage. There is thus an increasing tendency to control the flooding of the plain either by poldering, which keeps the water out of some areas, or artificial levée construction which keeps the river channel within its banks and stops the annual flood. To complete the control upstream flood-control dams and reservoirs are also built. In its simple state agriculture does not conflict with fisheries, and on such rivers as the Ouémé a pattern of intensive use has evolved where both activities are pursued together. On the floodplain the maize fields are interspersed with drain-in ponds, the banks of which are used for various types of market culture, tomatoes, peppers or green vegetables. In addition, the higher levées which follow the river are used for grazing cattle, giving a balanced economy which supports a dense population. Figures 5.4 and 4.14 illustrate the typical arrangement of these activities according to Hurault (1965) who described the land-use patterns of this area in some detail. Unfortunately, as agriculture is intensified beyond this level and pursued as a sole objective, the effects of the flood-control works that become necessary on the aquatic system are far-reaching. One result, for instance, is that when the floods are controlled depositions of alluvial silt no longer fertilize the soil which can quickly become exhausted. One finds a decrease in productions such as that experienced downstream of the Kainji dam, where within 10 years of its closure 50 per cent of the land was no longer suitable for agriculture (Adeniji, 1975). To compensate for this, applications of fertilizer are needed, putting up costs and raising the risk of eutrophication and eventually pollution of the watercourses.

Wet agriculture

The hydrological regime of a floodplain environment is well suited to rice culture. This may be at the primitive level of floating rice such as is practised in the Central Delta of the Niger, but in Asia the adaptation of the lowlands of the river systems to intensive rice-growing is one of the major features of the landscape. Intensive rice culture requires a complete control over the hydrological regime. Flood-control dams, polders and networks of irrigation and drainage ditches are therefore installed for this purpose.

Because rice-growing and fisheries use the same phase of the hydrological cycle there are sometimes considerable conflicts between them. Fish are frequently accused of destroying rice and Matthes (1977a) investigated the ways in which the fishes of the Niger river interact with this type of culture. He found that many species were present in the rice-fields, most of which were juveniles. Certain species were, however, present as adults and these could be classed in three groups:

1. Fish feeding predominantly on rice, of which four emerged as the most destructive, *Alestes dentex*, *A. baremoze*, *Distichodus brevipinnis* and *Tilapia zillii* of which the last two nibble through

the stalks at mid-height thus cutting down the whole plant.

2. Fish feeding occasionally on rice, particularly *Alestes nurse* which bites at the leaves of young plants, and *Sarotherodon niloticus* which nibbles epiphytic algae from the stems of the rice plants, but also tears away at the stalk.

3. Species causing occasional damage through other activities such as *Heterotis* and *Gymnarchus* which construct nests of the stems, or *Clarias, Heterobranchus* and *Protopterus* which uproot small plants when probing the mud in search of their benthic food.

Some species probably benefit the rice by seeking out and eating the stem borer and other insect pests or by cleaning the stems of epiphytic vegetation. In the Central Delta of the Niger, fishermen construct low dykes, 50 cm high, which protect the young rice during the early part of the rising flood when it is most vulnerable to attack; these work reasonably well, as by the time fish can penetrate the field the rice is past its most tender stage. For complete protection, permanent dams with screens are needed to exclude fish from the field entirely, but these all too often succeed only in sealing fish in rather than out.

Rice culture may affect fisheries adversely in two ways. Firstly, the need to control insect pests has encouraged the use of insecticides, leading to possible pollution of the water in the rice-field and downstream of it. Secondly, the modifications of the environment associated with intensive rice culture are detrimental to the fish.

The fact that rice and fish are not necessarily mutually exclusive is shown by the widespread practice of fish culture in rice-fields. This may be considered an almost ideal method of land use which produces both a carbohydrate and protein crop from the same piece of land. It has reached very high standards in Asia and Madagascar, but is still in the experimental stage in Africa and Latin America. Coche (1967) has dealt comprehensively with the situation up to 10 years ago. Two main types of exploitation can be distinguished:

1. capture systems where the fish that gain access through natural channels may be trapped;
2. culture systems where the field is deliberately stocked with fry.

The fish may be taken as a single annual crop with a single rice crop, an intermediate crop between one rice harvest and the next planting or during the growing season of the rice. Frequently fish are trapped casually during the growing season, and are then drained into specially constructed sump ponds or canals as the fields are dried. Yields from trapping during the growing period have been measured at about 132 km hm^{-2} by Tang Cheng Eng *et al.* (1973). If the rice is cropped only once per year, the sump ponds yield about 162·8–262·9 kg hm^{-2} (mean 200 kg hm^{-2}), but if the field is double-cropped fish yields drop to 68·2–143·0 (mean 95·7) kg hm^{-2}. At the same time between 2 277 and 2 975 kg hm^{-2} of rice were produced. Fish represents between 12 and 50 per cent of the total income in a single-cropping and 6–27 per cent in a double-cropping system. There has been a long-term decline in catch in the area studied, partly due to the increasing adoption of the double-cropping system and partly due to the more intensive use of insecticides. Similar yields have been recorded in Thailand in the Mekong basin where 433 hm^2 of paddy-fields were sampled giving fish harvests ranging between 50 and 1 710 kg hm^{-2} (mean 433 kg hm^{-2}) (Thailand, Department of Fisheries, 1974). The effects of pesticide treatment of rice for the control of stem-boring insects has caused concern, and such workers as Kok (1972) have attempted to define the toxic and sublethal effects of the common pesticides used (which include endrin, methyl parathion, dieldrin, diazinon and BHC). While no definite conclusions can yet be drawn as to the precise effects of such environmental contaminants, it is evident that the use of less toxic products can result in improved yields of rice while safeguarding the supply of fish. The production of a plant and a protein crop from the same area of floodable land is undoubtedly of great value in maintaining a nutritionally balanced yield pattern, although one that is not necessarily maximal in terms of absolute tonnage. Consequently, projects have been suggested for the extension of this type of culture. For instance, Delmendo (1969) has proposed a rice or melon-cum-fish culture system for the management of the 32 000 hm^2 Candaba swamp. This plain is flooded by the Pampanga and Angat rivers and is one of a similar series of floodplains in the Philippines. The plain has been enclosed in a series of dykes which include a gate for the harvesting of fish. The fields are at present used for growing water melon or rice during the dry season when the fish remain in the canals. Fish yields based solely on natural productivity range from 300 to 500 kg hm^{-2} in seven months. The melon crop produces 5 000 kg hm^{-2}. Delmendo suggested ways in which this area could be improved with the inclusion of fish canals at the foot of the main dykes and an intensification of fish culture by stocking and manuring the ponds.

5.4 Urbanization

With increasing demand for land brought about by population growth, there are much greater pressures than ever before for physical occupation of floodplains. In some parts of the world early settlements, conditioned by their need for access to a transport artery and to a domestic water supply, settled on floodplains and with increasing investment in property have been obliged to stay despite the risk. Such habitation breeds the need for flood control which in turn encourages further occupancy of the floodplain. This may proceed to the point where about 16 per cent of the urban areas of the United States are located on the 100 year floodplain, and of this over 50 per cent is developed for industry or human habitation (Sabol, 1974); small wonder therefore at a certain preoccupation with flooding in these areas, as flood losses mount annually despite the best efforts to contain them. An analysis of the world occupancy of floodplains (UN, 1969) summed up as follows: in Western Europe new flood losses are mounting slowly as a result of the intensified use of areas in major cities which are subject to large but infrequent overflows; in Eastern Europe there is also an increase in flood losses though somewhat slower than in North America; in South and Southeast Asia the intense use of long settled land and the development of new floodplains has more than offset the effects of major river-control works; in South America, there is widespread encroachment of urban growth on floodplains. The situation in Africa is similar for, although the older cities have been sited away from the main flood zones, new cities are expanding into these areas. The result of this gradual invasion is a growing tendency to control the floods.

The construction of cities tends to produce local disturbances in discharge as the existence of large areas of impermeable surface accelerate run-off in the vicinity of the city, but such effects are still slight in the basin as a whole. Some changes to floodplain morphology also follow from the communication systems which support the city and its surrounds. Navigation by commercial craft on the river often requires some measure of regularization of flow, including the installation of weirs and locks, and the canalization of exceptionally tortuous stretches to make passage easier. Wash from boats erodes banks and accelerates siltation and the destruction of marginal habitats. Roads and railways cut across the floodplains, usually on raised embankments which act as polders or dams to seal off large areas of the plain, restricting the movements of fish and, even more important, containing the flood-waters within a smaller area. Urbanization has two additional effects which also bear on the aquatic environment. One of these, the growing need for power, has similar results to the flood-control measures in that it is associated with upstream dam and reservoir construction. The second, loading of the waters with organic and inorganic substances, produces pollution and eutrophication in the waters at the level of the city and downstream of it. Enrichment of the water can have beneficial effects on the fish population for, as we have seen, many of the river systems in the tropics are initially impoverished.

The succession of physical and chemical conditions in rivers from the headwaters to the mouth is in any case a natural eutrophication process. Many potamon reaches are normally enriched and further loading with nitrogen, phosphorus and organic compounds appears acceptable up to a point, but when the capacity of the ecosystem to satisfy the biological oxygen demand (BOD) is exceeded, conditions can deteriorate rapidly. The fish communities inhabiting potamon reaches of rivers are usually adapted to eutrophicated conditions and can support a measure of deoxygenation, although some of the more active species can disappear. Godoy (1975) for instance, traces the disappearance of *Triurobrycon lundii* from the Mogi Guassu river to deoxygenated conditions produced by such eutrophication. Pollution with toxic substances has not so far been widely reported from tropical systems, although the situation in the rivers of India described by Patil (1976) leaves little room for complacency. Here several rivers are suffering from severe contamination with industrial effluents which have adversely affected their fish stocks. In temperate rivers the situation has been more serious, but although Leibman and Reichenbach-Klinke (1967) recorded bad conditions in certain reaches of the Danube caused by domestic and industrial pollution, the self-purifying capacity of this large and swift-flowing river has been sufficient to keep the main stream at an acceptable quality. Studies on the floodplain, however, indicated that conditions in some standing waters can deteriorate to a point where they damage the fish stock, although in others moderate eutrophication by sewage can raise the productivity.

The effects of pollution on the aquatic life of the system may be summarized as follows:

1. Lethal toxicity which kills fish at some stage of its life history. In the case of floodplain rivers this may be indirectly in that the reduction of dissolved oxygen in standing waters of the floodplain and river channel may make them unsuitable for fish that normally live there.
2. Sublethal effects which are usually difficult to detect or prove, but which alter the fish's behaviour in such a manner as to prevent it completing its normal life cycle, or simply to reduce its growth or increase its susceptibility to disease.
3. Cumulative effects which can render fish either unsafe or unpalatable for consumption.

Most pollution effects tend to be very broad, affecting many different species. Whatever their immediate effects, the response at the community level is a reduction in diversity and a shift in species composition towards relatively smaller, shorter-lived forms. In other words they tend to mimic the changes expected from heavy fishing and are therefore apt to reduce the amount of fish available to the fishery.

Moderate enrichment with organic substances, on the other hand, can increase the amount of fish (ichthyomass) supported by the system.

5.5 Hydraulic engineering

Control of the flood in rivers is thought necessary for many of the foregoing uses, and is increasingly pursued as a major objective in the development of river basins. Three main types of structure are used either separately or together:

1. dams and impoundments;
2. levées;
3. canals.

Dams and impoundments

The storing of water behind a dam so that it may be released more slowly throughout the year is probably the most popular of flood-control devices. It has the additional advantage that the water can do work for the generation of power and that it can be used for irrigation or cattle watering. Furthermore, fish can be grown in the sometimes extensive water bodies that are retained. In size, the reservoir can range from vast lakes such as that backed up behind the Akosombo dam on the Volta river, which has a total flooded area of 8 500 km², to small dams which desiccate completely in the dry season. Some major flood rivers such as the Volga, the Missouri and the Columbia have already been converted into a chain of reservoirs, and others such as the Danube, the Indus or the Mekong seem destined for that fate in the near future. The durability of such barrages is questionable, as silting is proceeding at a considerable rate in many rivers and the smaller dams have a predicted useful life of only a few years before their ability to control floods diminishes progressively. Eventually the reservoir will fail in its purpose, whether it be water storage or flood control. Larger reservoirs, of course, may take much longer to silt up, and may last for over a century, but the process is progressing faster than predicted in many areas. As major sites are something of a non-renewable resource the success of a policy of hydraulic control through the use of dams seems somewhat dubious in the long term. Meanwhile, dams produce their changes on the floodplain and the fish. These are brought about by alterations in the flood regime and by changes in silt loading, which in turn alter the dynamics determining the channel shape. This in turn affects the distribution and persistence of vegetation in the downstream stretches of river. For example, below the Volta dam the more stable hydrological conditions and lack of scouring during the flood favoured the rapid development of extensive stands of submersed vegetation such as *Potamogeton octandrus* and *Vallisneria aethiopica* (Hall and Pople, 1968).

The flood regime may be suppressed completely, or at least altered in magnitude so that it does not flood such extensive areas. Very large amounts of floodplain have been lost in this manner as a few documented examples will show. In the Missouri, the amount of floodable wetlands over a 145 km sample reach of river dropped from 15 167 hm² in 1879 to 7 414 hm² in 1967 – a loss of 67 per cent of the area (Whitley, 1974). The Illinois river, too, lost about half of its floodplain as 80 939 hm² of the original 161 874 hm² were drained between 1903 and 1920. Subsequently, 3 238 hm² have been restored as lakes. Following the closure of a dam on the Peace river, the 2 560 km² of the Peace–Athabaska delta were transformed from a thriving floodplain environment into a series of isolated mud-flats (Blench, 1972). Although drainage is not so advanced in other parts of the world the intentions are there. Liepolt (1972) stated that all of the 26 450 km² floodplain of the Danube will eventually be drained for irrigated agriculture and the original floodable area of the river is already much restricted. In the

Mekong the intention is to eliminate flooding from the 49 560 km² delta area and 1 480 km² have already been lost below the Pa Mong dam site. Similarly, in the Senegal river most of the 5 000 km² valley floodplain will become dry after the dams which are at present being planned in the headwaters are built. This presumably is going to be the fate of most of the world's great rivers, at least temporarily. Many smaller watercourses are being modified in a similar manner, and although this is happening with less attention being drawn to individual cases, the effects of the accumulation of environmental modifications brought about by many small dams may well be impressive. A typical example of such an intervention is the Strydom dam on the Pongolo river in South Africa, which has resulted in the disappearance of a 100 km² floodplain and its associated lakes, although in this case there has been an attempt to keep the wetlands intact through controlled discharges (Coke, 1970). In the case of the Mogi Guassu–Rio Grande system in Brazil, described by Godoy (1975) there has been a progressive loss of feeding areas on the floodplains of the Rio Grande by the construction of a series of dams for industrial use.

The loss of floodplain area for feeding and breeding has serious effects on the fish populations, and the reaction of the fish communities of the Chari, Niger and Senegal rivers to flood failures provoked by natural climatic variations such as the Sahelian drought (1970–74) also confirm the highly detrimental effects of suppressing the flood. In the Missouri river, Whitley (1974) traced the steady decline of catch from 680 t in 1894 to 122 t in 1963 mainly to the loss in fish habitats following the construction of the reservoirs. On this river, too, there have been modifications of the main channel by dykes on side channels, and backwaters have been blocked. The river has been trained by revetted banks into a series of bends. Prior to 1900 *Ictalurus punctatus* and *Ichthyobus* spp. made up the major part of the catch, but since then the introduced common carp *Cyprinus carpio* has become dominant. Dam construction on the Colorado river has also caused widespread changes in fish population (Holden and Stalnaker, 1975); endemic fish species have in many cases virtually disappeared, to be replaced by introduced species which are better adapted to the changed hydrological conditions. The same phenomena have been described from Russian rivers. In the Volga, in particular, Chikova (1974) has noted the changes in species composition below the V.I. Lenin Volga hydroelectric station (Kuibyshev reservoir) where the phytophilous fishes, *Abramis brama*, *A. ballerus* and *Rutilus rutilus* are decreasing in number, whereas *Stizostedion* (= *Lucioperca*) *lucioperca* and 'Sichel' (*Pelecus cultratus?*) have increased. Eliseev and Chikova (1974) concluded that the decline of the phytophilous species is due to the failure and unpredictability of the flood, which when it does inundate the plain, does so in a sporadic manner which arbitrarily strands young fish and spawn in isolated pools. Main-stream spawners such as the various sturgeons, *Stizostedion* and 'Sichel' are not so affected. Furthermore, the flood peak of the new regime is now somewhat retarded, favouring the later spawning species which generally belong to the second group. According to Lelek and El Zarka (1973) and Adeniji (1975) the changes in the fish fauna of the Niger river below the Kainji dam are also traceable to the unpredictable nature of the flood. Catch in the reach between the tail of the dam and Lokoja fell by about 50 per cent in three years (1967–69). This was accompanied by changes in species composition whereby the Characidae, Mormyridae and Clariidae declined, but predatory species such as *Lates* and Bagridae increased in abundance (Sagua, 1977).

A localized increase in the abundance of fish, particularly of predatory species, immediately below dams has been noted from many rivers. In the Nile below the Owen Falls dam populations of *Barbus altianalis* and the recently introduced *Lates niloticus* were particularly abundant. In the Niger, as we have seen, *Lates* also appeared in quantity, especially in the reach immediately below the Kainji dam; Chikova also commented on the maximum accumulation of fish in the Volga as occurring in the same regions downstream of the dams. Whitley (1974) explained this locally increased production in terms of the enriched water from the reservoir which, in passing through the sluices, carries with it zooplankton, insects and fish. However, this enrichment does not persist for any great distance and in the Missouri was only detectable for about 2 km downstream. Such concentrations are probably associated primarily with feeding, but fish also accumulate below dams, where they are interrupted in their migrations, and from the basis of rich tailrace fisheries such as that described by Otobo (1977) for the Kainji dam.

A history of diminishing catches in the Columbia river from a peak production of 22 440 t in 1911 to only 6 800 t at present, is mainly due to the blocking of passage to migrating fish and changes in the flow characteristics of the river, rather than to the loss of floodplain area (Trefethen, 1972). In the Murray river, Australia, the 800 km migrations of the golden perch (*Plectroplites ambiguus*) have also been stopped by a combination of water-management practices, including flood-control weirs, which have left few of the original characteristics of the uncontrolled river system unchanged (Butcher, 1967). The Sakkur dam of the Indus did not affect populations of the migratory *Hilsa ilisha*, but the construction of the Gulam Mahommed dam further downstream deprived the fish of 60 per cent of their previous spawning areas. Further upstream in the same river, the Tarbela dam poses a threat to *Tor putitora*, a large cyprinid which migrates from the floodplain to the foothills of the Himalayas to breed. *Hilsa* stocks have become depleted in several other rivers of the Indian subcontinent. In the Godavari river a combination of upstream dams and silting through erosion are restricting the species increasingly to the estuarine delta (Nagaraja Rao and Rajalakshmi, 1976); in the Cauvery *H. ilisha* has ceased to ascend the river following the regulation of flow by the Stanley reservoir (Sreenivasan, 1976). Following the construction of the reservoir *Puntius dubius* has disappeared from the Cauvery and *Tor khudree* is now much more restricted in its distribution. Species have also declined in abundance in Brazilian rivers where dam construction has been intensive in recent years. Many of the 'Piracema' species have largely disappeared from the Rio Grande and its affluents in the Saõ Paulo state, and *Pseudoplatystoma coruscans* was eliminated from the Tiete river soon after the closure of a series of barrages there.

One of the remedies commonly proposed for such blockages to migrations is the construction of fish ladders similar to those which work so satisfactorily for the salmons in north temperate rivers. In some cases fish passes have been successfully installed in the tropics. One such, at Cachoeira de Emas on the Mogi Guassu river, has been functioning since 1936 with little apparent detrimental effect on the stock. Here many characin species leap up a series of shallow steps. The siluroids, which do not jump, migrate past the barrage through special tunnels. The several fishways at dams on the Tigris and Euphrates rivers have also been used successfully by many of the migratory cyprinid species in these rivers (FAO/UN, 1956). Most attempts at using fish ladders with tropical species have been less successful. Bonetto *et al.* (1971) claimed that the efficiency of the fish ladders which bypass a series of dams on the Carcaraña tributary of the Paraná was very low and that *Salminus maxillosus*, one of the major migratory species of the basin, was unable to negotiate them. The fish ladders installed at the Markala barrage on the Niger also did not fulfil their intended function satisfactorily. Here enormous quantities of fish were blocked during their upstream migration at low water, although some fish did get through. The fisheries above the dam declined considerably after it was closed as these reaches depended on a replenishment of their stocks from fish moving out of the Central Delta. The failure of the ladder was attributed by Daget (1960b) to insufficient capacity in view of the very large numbers of fish wanting to pass over it. Furthermore, the migration of the species concerned was a simple dispersal movement rather than a breeding migration, and the stimulus to surmount obstacles was possibly relatively low as a consequence. The failure of conventional salmonid ladders in many tropical rivers is hardly surprising in view of the complex behavioural factors which contribute to the functioning of such structures. For example it has been shown that the form of the standing wave downstream of weirs is essential for salmon to be able to generate enough speed to clear the crest of the weir. Presumably other species have very different requirements which need to be studied before the installation of effective fish passes can be contemplated. In any case the provision of a fish pass or ladder for upstream movement of fish would only be justified where the migration is absolutely essential for the maintenance of the fish stocks.

Reservoirs themselves support populations of fish whose fisheries have formed the subject of numerous studies which are best summarized in the symposia edited by Lowe-McConnell (1965), Obeng (1969) and

Table 5.1 Catch, area and catch per unit area in some African and Asian reservoirs

Reservoir	Catch (tonnes)	Area (km^2)	kg hm^{-2}	Authority
Africa				
Ayame	1 000	135·0	74·1	Henderson and Welcomme (1974)
Kainji	7 200	1 720·0	56·7	Henderson and Welcomme (1974)
Kariba	4 080	5 364·0	7·6	Henderson and Welcomme (1974)
Mwadingusha	5 000	393·0	127·2	Henderson and Welcomme (1974)
Nasser/Nubia	7 000	3 330·0	21·0	Henderson and Welcomme (1974)
Nzilo	2 800	280·0	100·0	Henderson and Welcomme (1974)
Volta	40 000	8 482·0	47·2	Henderson and Welcomme (1974)
India				
Ghandi sagar	479	660·0	7·3	Dubey and Chatterjee (1976)
Stanley	317	146·9	37·3	Sreenivasan (1976)
Bhavanisagar	127	78·8	33·8	Sreenivasan (1976)
Sathanur	110	12·6	162·3	Sreenivasan (1976)
Amaravathy	88	9·2	187·7	Sreenivasan (1976)
Nagaryunasagar	84	184·3	4·5	Natarajan (1976)
Rihand	216	301·5	7·2	Natarajan (1976)
Konar	3	15·4	2·1	Natarajan (1976)
Thailand				
Ubolratana	2 477	410·0	60·4	Bhukaswan and Pholprasith (1976)
Lam takong	98	44·3	22·1	Chukajorn and Pawapootonan (1976)
Lam praploung	252	18·6	135·6	Chukajorn and Pawapootonan (1976)
Lam pao	2 419	230·0	105·2	Chukajorn and Pawapootonan (1976)
Nam pung	131	21·0	62·4	Chukajorn and Pawapootonan (1976)
Nam oon	145	86·1	16·8	Chukajorn and Pawapootonan (1976)
Sirinthorn	3 313	292·0	113·5	Chukajorn and Pawapootonan (1976)
Chulaporn	39	12·0	32·5	Chukajorn and Pawapootonan (1976)
Indonesia				
Jaitiluhur	180	83·0	21·7	Sarnita (1976)
Pening	709	22·0	322·5	Sarnita (1976)
Dorma	111	4·0	277·5	Sarnita (1976)
Jombor	38	1·9	202·1	Sarnita (1976)
Pacal	138	3·9	356·6	Sarnita (1976)
Prijetan	11	2·3	49·1	Sarnita (1976)
Sentir	3	0·7	49·1	Sarnita (1976)
Kalen	2	0·5	39·1	Sarnita (1976)

Ackermann *et al.* (1973). Table 5.1 presents information on areas, catch and catch per unit area from a variety of tropical man-made lakes, many of which are situated on floodplain rivers. There is a great range of yield per unit area, and much of this can be traced to the physical characteristics of the reservoir. As an approximation the yield to be expected from a given lake can be described by an index, the Morpho-Edaphic Index (MEI) which takes the mean depth of the lake and its conductivity as summarizing the form of the basin and the richness of its water (Ryder *et al.*, 1974). In practice, Henderson and Welcomme (1974) found that the differences in yield of African lakes and reservoirs correlated well with the index:

$$\text{MEI} = \frac{mean\ depth}{conductivity\ \mu mhos}$$

This index predicts quantitatively what is in any case well known qualitatively – that shallow lakes or nutrient-rich lakes are more productive than lakes that are either deep or poor in nutrients. Thus, shallow bodies of water such as the Rawa Pening in Indonesia have very high productions. On the other hand, the exceptionally low catch from some of the Indian reservoirs is probably due to the particular management practices which concentrate on a few species of cyprinids which are poorly adapted to lakes, rather than to any lack of production potential (Fernando, 1976). Generally, catches from reservoirs are comparable to or slightly higher than the catches that are obtained from floodplains. In any system where a reservoir replaces a floodplain, either by submerging it, or by stopping its flooding, the benefit or loss to the fishery has to be fairly carefully weighed. In the case of the upper Mekong, many of the impounded tributary rivers had little floodplain, either in the submerged reaches or downstream of the dams (Sidthimunka, 1972). However, according to the Mekong studies the mainstream Pa Mong reservoir will eliminate flooding for some 700 km downstream of the dam, resulting in a loss of catch of about 2 150 t from the river, whereas the reservoir is expected to produce only about the same amount of fish. Similarly, the amount of fish lost below the Kainji reservoir in Africa is probably about the same as the production from the reservoir. In many other reservoirs the amount of fish lost downstream of the dam surpasses the potential of the dam itself. Such considerations are perhaps secondary where power generation or irrigated agriculture are also entered into the account.

The fish community that establishes itself in the reservoir is based entirely on that pre-existing in the river basin, unless exotic species are introduced. There are usually considerable modifications in community structure as many species are unable to adapt to the new environment. Earliest to disappear from the body of the reservoir are the migratory whitefishes although they might survive in the upper portion of the lake from which they can readily move upstream to breed. Blackfishes tend to adapt better, and the main body of the lake is often colonized by species that were relatively insignificant elements of the pre-impoundment fauna. In some rivers, for example those of the Indian subcontinent, Fernando (1976) suggested that few suitable blackfish occur. Consequently, lacustrine fish communities are not readily established with the species native to the system, and, failing the introduction of exotic species, populations have to be maintained by continual stocking.

Levées

The man-made levée is a type of linear dam which heightens the natural levée upwards to prevent water spreading laterally on to the plain. The main impact of this is of course to deny fish access to the feeding and breeding grounds that are necessary for their survival. Catch and specific diversity drop in much the same way as they do for dams. As the water can no longer spread over such large areas, sediment and pollution are concentrated into the river and such standing waters as remain, much as described for the Illinois river by Starret (1972) (Fig. 5.5). Here the lack of spawning grounds caused species such as pike (*Esox lucius*), large-mouth bass (*Micropterus salmoides*) and yellow perch (*Perca flavescens*) to diminish in abundance compared to new species such as *Cyprinus carpio* which were introduced into the system. The commercial catch declined from 2 613 t in 1950 to 182 t in 1973, and angling success showed a similar reduction; effects which were attributed directly to loss of habitat and siltation following the levéeing of the river and the draining of the bottom lands (Sparks and Starret, 1975).

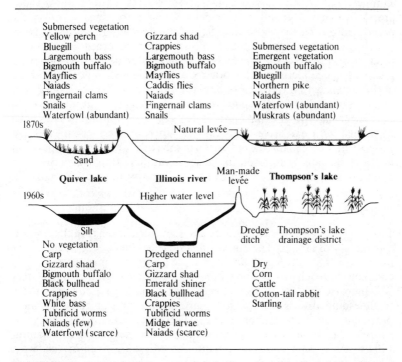

Fig. 5.5 Schematic drawings demonstrating the impact man has had during the past century on the ecology of the Illinois river and two of its adjoining bottom-land lakes near Havana. (After Starret, 1972.)

The flow during the floods is also increased, and as a result fish can be swept out of protected positions into unfavourable environments. The construction of levées in low-lying areas of the Danube delta has increased the rate of descent of the larvae of many of the migratory fishes. Instead of spreading out over the floodplain, to grow in the standing waters, these are ejected into the sea. As a result catches of such species as *Alosa pontica, Aspius aspius, Tinca tinca, Blicca bjoerkna* and *Abramis brama*, are much reduced relative to other arms of the river where no levées have yet been constructed (Zambriborsch and Nguen Tan Chin, 1973). Similar losses are described by Butcher (1967) from the Murray river, and pose a potential source of concern when levées are to be constructed on floodplains supporting 'Subienda' or 'Piracema' types of migrants. Effects comparable to those produced by levées can be anticipated from polders. These essentially enclose areas of floodplain within dykes to prevent them from uncontrolled flooding. In this way many potential breeding areas may be removed from the ecosystem, especially when the poldered area is of any great extent. Gaygalas and Blatneve (1971), for instance, traced the poor recruitment of bream, *Abramis brama* to the poor spawning conditions in the 23 000 hm^2 of summer polders, which were constructed to reclaim the floodplain depressions of the Nyamunas river delta. Summer polders are normally inundated during the winter floods, but are emptied during the spring. Overly rapid drainage does not allow the fish to breed successfully, whereas with correct management, a slight prolongation of the flooded phase improved recruitment in other years, and large fish stocks survived in the canals within the enclosed area. Polders can also be flooded in a controlled manner for rice culture, forms of irrigated agriculture or, as in Venezuela, for grazing reserves for cattle. Such practices can be combined with extensive aquaculture. Where polders occupy a large proportion of the plain, the reduction in area available for the expansion of the floodwaters can result in the acceleration of flow which can alter conditions on the remaining flooded areas in a way unfavourable to fish.

Channelization

The channel is frequently used as a system for simplifying the natural complexity of a river. The banks are smoothed and straightened in the interest of the more rapid and contracted evacuation of water. While channelized reaches of river may protect a particular area their net effect is to increase the energy content of the water, making it potentially more troublesome downstream. Flow patterns are concentrated in time, producing shorter, higher spates. The rivers themselves may be shortened to some degree by the evening-out of meander bends – about 120 km have been subtracted from the Missouri river in this way. Channelization has much the same effects on species composition and abundance of fish and other organisms as other flood-control measures. In the United States workers such as Congdon (1973) and Adkins and Bowman (1976) have found that the channelization of streams considerably reduces both species diversity and biomass when compared with unchannelized stretches of the same river; further references describing the reduction of fish fauna in US rivers due to this type of management were listed by Schneberger and Funk (1971). Channels can also contribute to the diminution of flooded areas by deflecting the flow from one river to another, as in the case of water transfers, or by bypassing major floodplain areas. The greatest projected work of this nature is probably the Jonglei canal, which if completed will lead much of the Nile water past the Sudd to decant it back into the main river downstream of the swamp at Malakal. This will make much more water available for irrigation in the arid Nile basin, but will have as yet undetermined effects on the flora and fauna of the main flood area.

5.6 Floodplain management

Flood control

In countries which have been practising flood control the longest, such as the United States and the USSR, there is a growing awareness of the inadequacies of structural measures for the control of floods. Despite very high investment in public works of this type over several decades, costs of damage caused by flooding are increasing at a greater rate in countries adopting flood-control measures than those where the natural regime is unmodified. In some cases, where the design capacity of the structure is exceeded, floods have been provoked by the very measures designed to prevent them. This has led to the belief that the natural lateral expansion plain of the river is perhaps the best flood-control structure of all, and a series of seminars and symposia (UN, 1969; Economic Commission for Europe, 1971; Sabol, 1974) have advocated floodplain and river-basin management as an alternative to flood control. Writers such as Arnold (1975) consider that floodplain management, which keeps the floodplain free from flood-control structures, is the only method which is effective in the long term. The principle is extended by more extreme views to clearing the plain of housing and industrial installations and reserving such areas for farming, fisheries, recreation, parkland and wildlife. The only exceptions to this are, of course, dams built for power generation and irrigation which are not strictly speaking flood-control structures, although they may also fulfil that role. Such an approach is favourable to fisheries, and it is to be hoped that, where practical, it will be adopted. Unfortunately, there are many areas of the world where population pressure and the need for food will still provoke attempts to encourage higher yields from the environment by such engineering interventions. Whether they can succeed or not in the long term remains to be seen.

Management of floodplains for fisheries

In Section 4.6 we discussed some of the methods that are available to those responsible for the management of fisheries in unmodified floodplains. However, as we have seen, there is an increasing trend at the present time to attempt to master the plain and control its floods so as to make it more productive for agriculture and safer for human occupation. Whatever the long-term benefit and success of these attempts they do modify the aquatic environment in such a manner that the fish stocks are adversely affected. If the floodplains are to continue to produce fish, it must be within an entirely different framework from the capture fishery as practised on the unmodified floodplain. There seem to be two possible approaches to this:

1. preservation of the natural system, but on a reduced scale; and
2. integration of husbandry and culture methods into the general land and water use of the floodplain.

Preservation of the natural system
The biology and ecology of the majority of fishes inhabiting floodplain rivers shows them to be extremely sensitive to any restriction of the floodplain and any modification of the flood cycle. In order to retain something of the natural diversity of the stocks of fish certain areas have to be maintained in their wild state and it is hoped that the setting aside of land for suitable reserves be considered in the planning of land use on the floodplain. As has been discussed, various types of engineering and construction works also interfere with the natural pattern of flooding. Levées, polders and embankments for transport systems prevent the water reaching the floodplain depressions, and the remaining water is restricted in such a way as to modify its flow. An essential part of planning for fisheries is, therefore, to make sure that any lateral expansion zones which are designated as reserve areas should be kept free of such structures. A second important feature is the provision of sufficient water to produce a flood which will have the characteristics needed for the reproduction of fish species. This is a question of both quantity and timing which have to be based on an adequate knowledge of the biology of the fish species concerned. Controlled releases of water have been tried in some systems, and on the Pongola river a series of experimental floods have successfully filled the lagoons and induced breeding in the species inhabiting them (Coke and Pott, 1970; Phelines *et al.*, 1973). Similarly, sufficient water has been released from the Shire river dam to fill the lagoons of the Elephant and Ndinde marshes, with satisfactory results for the fisheries.

The correlations between drawdown factors and catch detected in some floodplain rivers, as well as the theoretical predictions of Welcomme and Hagborg's (1977) simulation (see Fig. 3.27) indicate that standing stock and yield do not depend solely on the flooded area, but also vary according to the amount of water retained in the system during the dry season. Because of this, the shortfall in catch following upon a reduction in flooded area can to a certain extent be compensated for by an increased area of residual water, provided the reduced floods still occur at the appropriate time. Where water-management actions are being planned which will result in the loss of areas of floodplain, the provision of large permanent bodies of water may be considered at an early stage. In all probability fish communities of systems managed in this way will undergo changes in species composition probably in favour of the blackfishes, much as in ordinary reservoirs.

The management of the natural system should not be restricted to the floodplain, but should be extended upstream and downstream as part of the manipulation of the whole basin. As we have seen, activities in the headwaters of the basin can alter the siltation, run-off and flow patterns of the potamon reach, often with far-reaching consequences to the fishery. Equally, pollution or damming downstream can prevent species from moving up to the floodplains to feed or breed.

Husbandry and culture methods
The extensive husbandry methods of drain-in ponds and impounded lagoons in floodplain depressions are particularly appropriate in slightly to extensively modified plains, where sufficient flooding remains for them to be filled. In completely modified plains, however, alternative intensive methods have to be developed. Aquaculture farms, with ponds or pools specially adapted to the rearing of fish, can be associated with the irrigation networks. Such farms can either rear fish to a size where they can be sold directly for consumption, or can raise fry for stocking into such permanent lakes as remain in the plain or, as we have seen in Section 5.3, into fields where fish are reared as a secondary or alternative crop. Developments of this type are perhaps best seen in Thailand, although they are also common in many other parts of Southeast Asia. In the Chao-Phrya river basin for instance, the control of the water regime over much of the floodplain has decreased natural fish production. To compensate for this loss many state and private fish farmers rear various species of cyprinid and siluroid as well as freshwater prawns (*Macrobrachium rosenbergii*). The impervious nature of the alluvial soils, the flat terrain and the ready access to water supplies through irrigation canals makes this type of modified floodplain particularly suitable for aquaculture in ponds. To a lesser degree fish such as *Pangasius sutchii* are reared in cages placed in major canals and permanent water bodies, and raceways may also be incorporated into the canal system for the intensive culture of certain other species.

5.7 Summary

The floodplain ecosystem is composed of two complementary phases, the aquatic phase and the terrestrial phase, which alternate seasonally in dominance. During the terrestrial phase the unmodified plain may be occupied by wildlife or it may be used for grazing cattle, both of which activities benefit the fishery by enriching the aquatic environment during flooding.

As measures for development become greater the floodplain is denuded of trees and is used increasingly intensively for aquaculture.

The growing of crops on the floodplain does not interfere with the aquatic component of the system for as long as the farmer is content to conform to the natural seasonality of the floods. Intensive agriculture, however, demands a control of the flood and the modification of the floodplain by filling in of depressions and the installation of drainage and irrigation networks.

In industralized nations and those agricultural nations where population pressures are highest, there is also a demand for the occupation of the floodplain for housing and industrial purposes. This in turn requires a further control of flooding to make such settlement safe. Urbanization of the plain also poses problems of pollution by the increased quantities of organic and inorganic contaminants which are discharged into the water.

A number of flood-control devices are commonly used in rivers which have similar effects on the river fauna. By restricting the floodplain and by modifying the timing and amplitude of the flood they work together to reduce productivity and species diversity. The changes in fish stocks which are subject to environmental modifications associated with flood control, pollution and other human activities in the river basins, thus tend to resemble those taking place during the fishing-up process (see Fig. 4.23). Reservoirs behind dams have a fish production potential of their own which may be greater than that of the river system they submerge, but often there is a net loss of fish owing to the decline in catch downstream.

Flood-control structures have been found less and less cost effective in industrialized countries. The time for which they can operate is also somewhat restricted. As a result the management of floodplains by allowing them to return to their former natural state is being advocated in some circles. However, the need for increased food and living space is forcing other nations to adopt these methods of control in the hope that they will prove more effective in their cases.

The continuance of fisheries in their traditional form on the completely modified floodplain is difficult and other methods have to be sought whereby such areas can continue to produce fish. To do this, various intensive management techniques including extensive and intensive aquaculture have been proposed, and are indeed successful in many Asian countries.

Chapter 6

Conclusion

Despite the small amount of information on floodplain fish populations and their fisheries the impression that emerges from that which is available is remarkably coherent. Further studies, which are urgently needed to clarify many aspects of the biology and ecology of living organisms of these systems, may well dispel this impression and emphasize differences which until now seemed minor. At present the studies from African, Asian and South American flood rivers are to a large extent complementary, each having approached a slightly different aspect of the problem. At the same time there are sufficient areas of overlap for the comparability between systems from different continents to be checked. Studies from temperate European and North American flood rivers supplement those from the tropical zone with information on systems which have been influenced to a great degree by man's activities. They thus serve as an indicator and perhaps as a warning of the results of management measures now being applied to tropical rivers.

Within the family of flood rivers there are, perhaps, two subgroups whose dynamics are sufficiently different to warrant separate consideration. On the one hand there are blackwater forest rivers which are essentially impoverished environments whose major biomass is concentrated in the longer-lived elements of the biocenose, such as the trees. On the other hand there are the savanna river systems whose turnover of nutrients is much more rapid, and where the major proportion of the biomass is located in annual grasses. These seemingly fundamental differences in the way nutrients and energy pass through the two systems may have important implications for the way they are managed for fisheries, and deserve further study. Aside from possible differences in energy flow, the two types of system behave in a similar manner in terms of the ecology of their fish communities.

There are, of course, other differences in detail, between fish communities from the different continents, such as the widespread dry-season spawning migrations of Latin American fishes which are not nearly so common among African or Asian species. There is, however, no doubt that the flood rivers are complex ecosystems which behave in an essentially similar manner in both the tropical and temperate zone. Even the seasonality of temperate rivers brought about by the climatic winter, has a homologue in the tropics with the growth arrests of fish during the 'physiological winter' of the dry season. On the basis of these similarities, but bearing in mind the differences between forest and savanna rivers, it is probably justifiable to treat flood rivers as a set from which generalizations can be made and applied to other members of the set.

The whole aquatic component of the floodplain system responds to the flood regime in much the same way as temperate ecosystems respond to the march of the seasons. The coming of the flood signals an efflorescence of all forms of life. The nutrients released from the newly inundated soil accelerate the primary production which appears in the form of grasses and higher vegetation and which forms floating mats covering much of the rising water. Epiphytes and animal communities use the root masses of the floating vegetation for support; benthic organisms colonize the newly flooded areas, and the suspension of ash, dung and vegetable debris on the plain mixes with the alluvial silt to form a rich mud which nourishes many detrivore species. The fish reproduce and colonize the plain, benefiting from this mass of food to grow rapidly throughout the flood. As the flood ends and the waters drain from the plain many fish are stranded in temporary pools where they die, but others find their way into the river channel and the permanent water bodies of the floodplain where the majority remain moderately inactive throughout the dry season.

This type of system which Odum (1967) termed 'pulse stable' is held at an early successional stage by the seasonal fluctuation, both in water level and the abundance of the fish stock. Because of this the communities inhabiting it are characterized by great productivity and resilience which enable them to respond quickly to changes in environmental conditions, to benefit from favourable flood years and to survive the years when the flood fails. Communities tend, therefore, to be *r* selected rather than *K* selected, as described by Lowe-McConnell (1977), although many more long-lived and stable elements are also present. This resilience is a feature which makes the community very attractive for fisheries as, because of its surplus production, it can support heavy exploitation with little apparent modification at least until a certain point is reached.

The fishery, not unnaturally, is conditioned by the flood regime which imposes a cyclicity on the activities of the fishermen. The terrestrial component of the system is in some ways a mirror image of the fishery, reaching its maximum productivity during the dry season. Such is the seasonality cycle that both agriculture and fisheries (and pastoralism) are at their height on the plain at the same time during the falling flood and the dry season. This has led to a certain division of labour among the human population of floodplain rivers, for although most individuals do fish at some time of the year part-time fishermen are obliged to schedule their activities according to the agricultural calendar; only professional fishermen are able to pursue their activity full time. During the flood season, fishermen farmers either prepare their gear for the next

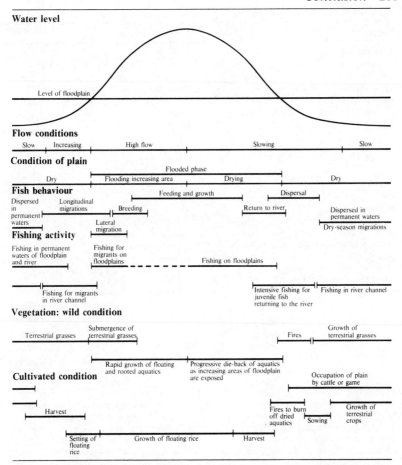

Fig. 6.1 Summary of the major activities on a floodplain throughout the year.

season or cultivate rice as a wet crop. Professional fishermen often migrate, following the fish either in the same river system or in other adjacent water bodies.

The traditional integration of biological and human activities which makes up the ecology of the floodplain river (Fig. 6.1) can only work if there is a community of microorganisms, plants and animals which are adapted to the particular frequency of the environmental event which is fluctuating – in this case the flood. By the same token, human communities and their institutions have to be similarly adapted, and socio-ecological systems have arisen which use the various floodplain resources in an integrated and intensive manner, such as that studied on the Ouémé by Hurault (1965). It would appear that even such systems are insufficiently intensive, and increasing demographic, social and

Table 6.1 Stages in the modification of floodplain rivers

Stage	Floodplain use
Unmodified Floodplain shows most characteristic features, flood regime unhindered by direct human interventions, but indirect effects of activities elsewhere in the river basin may be apparent. Examples: Sepik, Niger, Sudd.	In wild state often forested, Supports game and later used for grazing cattle. Vegetation modified by burning. Seasonal occupation by nomadic fishermen, hunters and pastoralists.
Slightly modified Some drainage channels for more rapid and efficient removal of floodwaters. Smaller floodplain depressions filled or regularized. Flood still largely unaltered in timing and duration. Examples: Senegal, Ouémé.	Floodplain largely cleared of forest, extensive drawdown agriculture, some floating rice in suitable depressions. Some areas reserved for grazing, and zonation of floodplain for different uses often highly developed Settlement on levées and higher ground, or on artificial islands and stilt villages.
Extensively modified Drainage and irrigation common, some flood control through dams and levées which contain main channel. Depressions usually filled or regularized. Flood often modified in timing and duration. Examples: Chao-Phrya, Mekong.	Flood agriculture (usually rice) and intensive dry-season agriculture. Moderately extensive occupation of the dryer areas of the plain for habitation – beginnings of urbanization. Much of plain still subject to flooding.
Completely modified Flood control by large upstream dams and by levées. Main channel sometimes channelized. Floodplain largely dry, although still subject to occasional catastrophic floods. River often reduced to a chain of reservoirs. Example: Mississippi.	Urbanization, intensive use of plain for agriculture, industry and habitation.

Fisheries	Research and management problems
Fish stocks largely in original condition of diversity, but size structure may be modified by fishing. Moderate to heavy fishery in both river channels and standing waters. Area available for fisheries, whole plain.	Exploratory fishing for description of composition of fish stock. Identification of major resources. Studies on biology of individual species and their geographical and seasonal distribution. Studies on local fishing methods and introduction of appropriate additional techniques. Establishment of simple regulatory measures for protection of major stocks. Improve access and marketing network.
Fish stock largely unaltered, although larger species may be becoming rarer and size structure heavily biased towards smaller individuals. Some depressions may be dammed as holding ponds, or for extensive aquaculture, or fish holes may be excavated. Area available for fisheries, whole plain.	Population dynamics of major elements of community to give refined estimates of potential yields. Continue studies on biology to identify possible subpopulations and to describe ecological interactions between species. Monitoring of fishery to detect potential overfishing of major stocks coupled with intensification of regulatory measures to protect fish stock. Investigation of simple forms of extensive aquaculture. Improvement and concentration of fish landings and preservation techniques.
Some modification to fish stock with disappearance of larger species. Wild fisheries often very intense in main river channels, with some new fisheries in reservoirs. Rice fish culture in suitable areas. Drain-in ponds and some intensive fish culture in regularized depressions. River area available for fisheries restricted.	Examination of general dynamics of fish community to judge reaction to various sources of loading. Intensification of monitoring of fisheries with increased control of catching methods by licensing and legislation. Examine impacts of other activities in the river basin on the fishery and endeavour to ensure that suitable conditions are maintained. Investigation of intensive aquaculture methods. Development of reservoir fisheries and seek alternative employment to reduce fishing pressure on main river.
Fish stock changed by loss of some species through pollution and channelization and sometimes by introduction of exotic species. Some sport fisheries in main channels or in few lakes that have been retained on floodplain. Some intensive aquaculture in specially constructed ponds. River area available for fisheries very small, but intensive fisheries may be developed in the reservoirs.	Investigation of pollution and other management impacts to establish criteria for maintenance of fish stock. Regulation of discharge and effluent according to these criteria. Contemplate introduction of new elements to fish community or stocking to support threatened species. Study access problems to fishery to resolve conflicting demands of sport and commercial fishermen. Intensify development of aquaculture and reservoir fisheries.

economic pressures are making demands which cannot apparently be met within the traditional framework of the flood cycle. In response to these demands for increased cereal production and for safe conditions in which to colonize the plain, there is an accelerating tendency to bring the flood under control. Unfortunately, despite its resilience to most forms of exploitation, the floodplain biocenose is fragile in the face of stabilization. When the flood is controlled, adaptations which suit the fish for life in the fluctuating lotic environment select against it in the stable lentic situation. It is not just that the floodplain area is diminished or disappears completely – and it is almost a motto in rivers that 'where there is no floodplain there are few fish' – but that the environmental conditions which trigger breeding are not there either. Many species decline in abundance and may become locally extinct, whereas others hitherto insignificant, may become dominant. Failing this, exotic species have to be introduced to occupy ecological niches which the previous riverine communities are not equipped to fill.

Four main stages can be identified in the modification of the floodplain from the fisheries standpoint (Table 6.1) and three cutting points seem significant, marking the transition of the plain from one developmental stage to the next. The first of these occurs with the introduction of systematic agriculture to the plain, which marks the end of the unmodified stage. Agriculture demands at least some attempt at drainage and regularization of the plain, the population rises and fishing pressure also increases to a point where it produces some noticeable effects on the fish stock. The second cutting point seems to arrive with the installation of flood-control structures which begin to modify the flood and restrict the area of the plain available to the fishery. Exploitation of the wild stock is often very high and its effects, added to the stresses induced by environmental modifications, can bring about rapid changes in species composition and abundance. The last cutting point is reached with the installation of one or more barrages upstream which change the nature of the floodplain completely – from a fluctuating environment with a large aquatic component to a stable one with only a small amount of water. The four stages listed do not necessarily represent an evolutionary sequence. True, most rivers in Europe and North America have passed successively through these steps to reach their present highly controlled state, and similar fates are planned for many tropical rivers, but other rivers will inevitably stay at a slightly or extensively modified stage without ever becoming completely controlled. Nor does the development necessarily proceed at an even pace along the whole length of a river. Indeed in some larger river systems, such as the Mekong or the Danube, different reaches or tributaries may be at different developmental stages.

Only rarely has the planning of the overall development of the floodplain taken into account the living aquatic resources, often because adequate information was lacking when needed. As a result, valuable fisheries have disappeared in the past owing to the modification of the environment. Timely provision of data is necessary to minimize such losses in the future, but it has become increasingly obvious that there are several levels of research and management which are appropriate to the various stages in the transformation of a fishery, a point discussed by Regier (1976). The fourth column of Table 6.1 suggests some of the main priorities for research and management at the various levels of modification of the floodplain. Ideally, this process should be pursued parallel to the evolution of the plain, one step growing out of the knowledge acquired during the previous step. Furthermore, the presence of a developmental stimulus such as an intense fishery, a source of pollution or a particular environmental modification is an integral part of the later stages of study. Unfortunately, in many systems the basic work which permits the more advanced research to be undertaken has not been done. For example, an understanding of the biology of the thousands of individual species inhabiting tropical rivers is very poor, and as a system is entering a phase of rapid modification it is often too late for the base-line observations to be carried out, nor would it be cost effective to do so even were sufficient time available. In these circumstances extrapolation from the behaviour of fish species, populations or communities in other basins is the only solution and, as already noted, this is facilitated by the general similarity of the fisheries ecology of flood-river systems. Fortunately, because of the significant contribution fish make to the dietary and recreational needs of societies living in the vicinity of the world's major rivers, there has recently been a greater tendency to examine the ecological implications of intended actions from all angles. However, it is clear that river basins can only rarely be managed for traditional fisheries of natural stocks on unmodified plains, and new technologies are needed for rearing fish, either in intensive aquaculture units attached to irrigation networks or as an alternative crop in rice and other wet agriculture fields.

Hopefully, the transition from unmodified floodplain to controlled river is a temporary condition designed to solve the grave demographic problems facing us today. The control of the plain demands a considerable price in terms of risk and environmental degradation which future generations may not be willing to pay and already some more developed nations are considering other alternatives. In any case flood-control structures are demonstrably ephemeral in their effects, even though the larger dams may endure for a few hundred years, and it seems more than probable that eventually rivers will once again spread relatively unhindered over the floodplains.

Appendix – Notes on methods for the study of floodplain rivers

Research workers who have investigated floodplain rivers have by and large used standard methods such as those described by Ricker (1971). However, certain methods have since been developed in response to the particular conditions of the floodplains. The standing waters of the plain are relatively easy to sample, but other environments are less easy. The vegetation-grown areas have been studied by methods similar to those used in open waters, and although time consuming, enclosure with fencing and slow removal of the vegetation does give good results. The major problem in any river–floodplain system is the sampling of the main channel, and here a Symposium on Methodology for Sampling Fish Populations in Lakes and Large Rivers (EIFAC, 1974; Welcomme, 1975b) was forced to conclude that there are as yet no reliable methods for sampling these habitats. In fact, in these situations, the researcher has little alternative but to use the commercial catch, especially in areas where large weirs, traps or stow-nets are in operation.

A.1 Population estimates in floodplain lakes

Sampling in lagoons is now fairly well understood and similar methods to those used in small lakes can be employed. The three most popular approaches are:

1. repeated capture;
2. mark recapture; and
3. poisoning.

Repeated capture
Bonetto *et al.* (1969b) used a repeated-capture method to compute the standing stocks of a series of shallow lagoons on the Paraná river. He found that between 9 and 12 hauls were needed before no further fish were caught. The method has advantages in areas where poisoning is not possible, but is unwieldy in that it demands considerable effort on one lagoon and can only be applied to relatively small bodies of water. Bonetto fished his localities to apparent exhaustion, but the process can be shortened, accepting some lowering of precision, by Leslie's method of plotting cumulative catch against catch per unit of effort. The point at

which the line obtained cuts the x-axis indicates the total population of the lagoon (see Ricker, 1975).

Mark recapture

Mark-recapture methods have been described by Holden (1963) working on floodplain pools of the Sokoto river, by Holčik and Bastl (1975) working on the backwaters of the Danube, and by Godoy (1975) to derive population estimates for the Mogi Guassu river fish community *in toto*. Fish were captured with draw seines, and marked by fin-clipping or with tags. Statistical treatment of results was according to methodology described in Ricker (1975).

Poisoning

Many workers have used fish toxicants, usually Rotenone, or more occasionally other commercial products such as Fintrol 15. The University of Michigan *et al.* (1971) used the method on the Kafue floodplain both in open water or under vegetation. Kapetsky (in press) has elaborated the methodology still further for use in the cienagas of the Magdalena river. Here the site to be sampled was surrounded with a 205 m long block net of 2·5 mm stretched mesh, which enclosed a standard area of 2 500 m² . The area was left undisturbed for one hour, during which time the toxicants were prepared. Kapetsky found that in this environment the concentration of 5% Rotenone preparation recommended by the manufacturers (5 ppm) was not sufficient for complete kills and he used a range of concentrations from 0·9 to 6·2 ppm. Fintrol 15 was used as an alternative at between 12·3 and 20·03 ppm. Loubens (1969) sampled backwaters and pools of the Chari river by simple block-netting with a large- and a small-mesh net, and found that the 5 ppm concentrations of Aquatox (Rotenone preparation) recommended were adequate to kill all fish within a few hours. The same concentrations were successfully used by Daget *et al.* (1973) in the quieter protected reaches of the main channel of the Bandama river. Larger lagoons on the Paraná were fished by Bonetto *et al.* (1965) with nets, using Rotenone to clear the residual population. Sampling with toxic substances is probably one of the more reliable means of estimating standing stocks, but is often not practical on legal or sociological grounds. The samples must also take into account fish that fall to the bottom which can represent quite a high proportion of the whole population. There are also grounds for caution in that different species have different tolerances to the toxins. Siluroids, for example, are notably resistant and care should be taken to ensure that concentrations are adequate to give an even kill.

A.2 Remote sensing

One of the main problems in the study of floodplains is obtaining reliable topographic information. Most maps do not give detailed descriptions of floodplain features, and because individual water bodies and river channels are apt to change from one year to the next, such descriptions as are given are frequently out of date. Two of the most important factors in the dynamics of the living aquatic resources of the river–floodplain system are the maximum area flooded and the minimum area of water left at low water. These vary from year to year and are only rarely available from any source. The gathering of this kind of data is nearly impossible at ground level and remote sensing from aircraft and satellites represents the only really viable alternative. Four techniques are currently available, each with its own application.

Aerial photography
Aerial photographs in the visual range are available for many areas of the world, but pre-existing covers suffer from many of the disadvantages of maps in that they are liable to give information which is out of date owing to changes in the topography of the plain. Such past covers are useful, though, for comparison with up-to-date surveys as an indication of the way in which the plain is altering. Aerial photographs are most useful for the detailed high-resolution investigation of certain specific areas of the plain (see Figs. 4.14 and 5.4) with respect to vegetation cover, land-use patterns, particular features such as drain-in ponds, location of villages, etc. which have been identified by a less precise method. They suffer from several disadvantages, not the least of which is cost. A large floodplain needs many hundreds of photographs, requiring a long interpretation time. Furthermore, weather conditions are not always suitable at the time when the imagery is needed, especially in the more humid tropical basins.

Infra-red aerial photography
These difficulties can be surmounted by the newly developed high-altitude infra-red photo cover which can penetrate even thick cloud and has an excellent resolution (better than 2 m). Infra-red distinguishes water-covered areas particularly well, but costs remain relatively high.

Side-looking Airborne Radar (SLAR)
Airborne side-looking radar is particularly valuable for defining the finer details of floodplain structure such as old beds of the channel, main areas of silt deposition or the location of the drainage canals. Flooded areas show up clearly and the images can be taken from high altitude (40 000 ft (12 000 m)) through total cloud cover. The resolution is much lower than that of infra-red photography, but the information given is to a certain extent complementary as SLAR reveals much of the fine relief of the plain.

Satellite imagery
A variety of Landsat products are available for several of the major floodplains, although unfortunately others are partially or completely

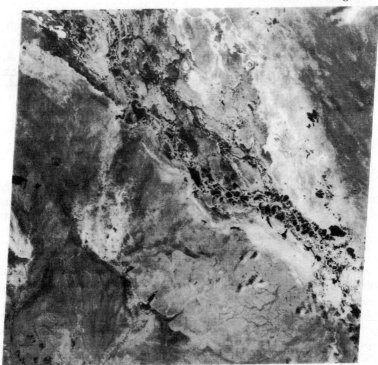

Fig. A.1 Views of a portion of the Sudd swamps of the Nile river in Sudan taken by ERTS E (Landsat) Satellite (Band 7) showing the situation on 7 November 1972 at high flood.

obscured by clouds for at least part of the year. Band 7 near infra-red [0·8–1·1 μm] imagery (Fig. A. 1) gives a great amount of detail on open water, and when combined with other bands (particularly 4 [0·5–0·6 μm] or 5 [0·6–0·7 μm]) in false colour composites gives information on the distribution or type of vegetation cover. A breakdown of floodplain types can be made from the imagery in the photographs (Figs. A.1–A.3), together with some ground-truth data. This analysis is shown in Fig. A.4. The frame shown is part of a survey of the whole Sudd (FAO, 1977). Landsat imagery is particularly useful in that it gives a broad overview of the system which may serve as a basis for stratification of samples, identification of areas for further study either by photo cover or by ground survey, a tracking of seasonal or year-to-year changes in distribution of silt, vegetation and open water and through them monitoring the effects of dams, irrigation schemes and canalizations. However, Landsat imagery can only be used with confidence, when coupled with adequate ground-truth studies which validate its interpretation. The imagery available for the tropical floodplain systems up to 1975 is listed in the *World Bank Landsat Index Atlas of the Developing Countries of the World* (1976, The World Bank, Washington)

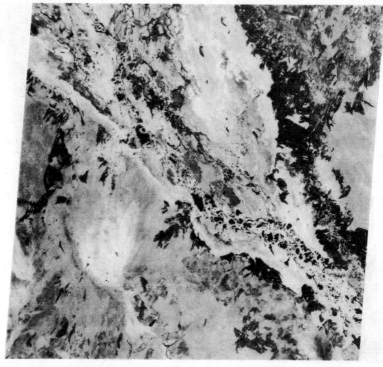

Fig. A.2 The same scene on 13 December 1972 as the flood begins to fall.

and with the launching of Landsat 3 in 1977 new imagery should become available to assist in the studies of floodplains and their fisheries.

A.3 Integrated sampling design

Because rivers with large floodplains are complex aquatic systems which are spatially diffuse, and also have an important seasonal variability in their hydrological and biotic components, sampling programmes are indispensable in order to obtain information on their fisheries and other characters describing the surveyed population. The surveys have to be carefully designed to obtain the maximum amount of reliable data from the modest resources that are usually available for such research. In such multipurpose surveys two aspects have to be considered:

1. the existing fishery; and
2. the biology and ecology of the fish stocks.

The first gives an estimate of the actual catch from the system, its yield–seasonality pattern and centres of concentration of the fishing

Fig. A.3 The same scene on 5 February 1973 at much lower water.

industry over time. The second gives an estimate of the state of exploitation and the potential of the stock. To be of maximum value both activities should be pursued simultaneously and within the same sampling survey system. The first requirement for an efficient sampling design is an understanding of the topography of the system founded on detailed study of maps, supplemented by satellite imagery or aerial photographs and visits to the terrain. On the basis of this the ecosystem can be stratified into zones, using cutting points which correspond, where possible, to changes in morphology brought about by physical features, so that the individual zones are fairly homogeneous in character. In each zone an inventory of the various river channels and standing waters should be made, and from them a group of sampling stations should be selected (sampling in space) and weighted according to the extent and importance of the area. The number of selected stations naturally depends on the resources available, both in finance and manpower. Ideally, sampling sites should be randomized, but on the actual floodplain this is rarely possible as many lagoons are inaccessible, or other conditions, for instance local traditions, may make them impossible to fish. In such a case the randomly selected sites are replaced by others which can be considered as representative units of the surveyed population. For sampling in time, frequency is linked to

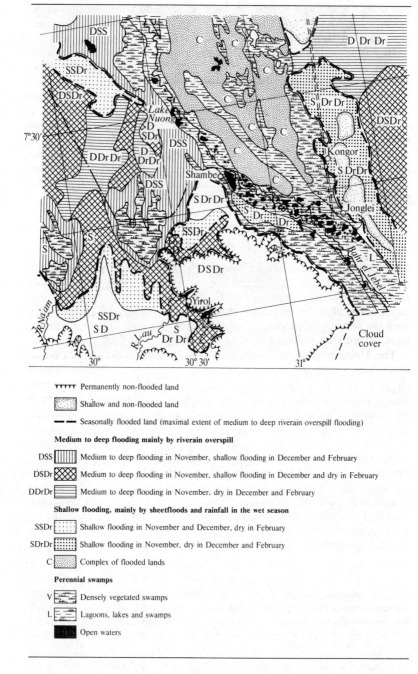

Permanently non-flooded land

Shallow and non-flooded land

Seasonally flooded land (maximal extent of medium to deep riverain overspill flooding)

Medium to deep flooding mainly by riverain overspill

DSS   Medium to deep flooding in November, shallow flooding in December and February

DSDr   Medium to deep flooding in November, shallow flooding in December and dry in February

DDrDr Medium to deep flooding in November, dry in December and February

Shallow flooding, mainly by sheetfloods and rainfall in the wet season

SSDr   Shallow flooding in November and December, dry in February

SDrDr Shallow flooding in November, dry in December and February

C   Complex of flooded lands

Perennial swamps

V   Densely vegetated swamps

L   Lagoons, lakes and swamps

Open waters

Fig. A.4 A detailed breakdown of the main flood conditions for the area shown based on

the hydrological and biological cycle, and should cover the two major seasons (peak flood and low water) at least. Such a procedure has been described by Bazigos *et al.* (1975) for the Magdalena river.

Repeated real-time aerial surveys to count fishing villages or vessels, can be used as a quick method to investigate the mobility pattern of the fishermen in space over time. These should be accompanied by catch assessment surveys at the sample sites which determine the type and characteristics of gear in use and the catch and its composition. If possible the sites should also be sampled for standing stock, and the fish caught by both the commercial and experimental fisheries should be sampled for biological parameters such as reproductive state, condition and feeding state, and scales taken for ageing. The design and interpretation of such surveys has been presented in detail by Bazigos (1974).

A.4 Hydrological indices (Fig. A.5)

One aspect of studies of flood rivers is an adequate measure of the amplitude and duration of various phases of the aquatic cycle. Growth, reproductive success, mortality, and through them standing stock and catch, all appear closely linked either with the intensity of the flood or with the severity of the low-water (drawdown) period. Several workers have formulated indices to describe these aspects of the flood.

The University of Michigan *et al.* (1971) used a drawdown factor (*DDF*) as a measure of the severity of the low-water period. This is roughly the area under the flood storage volume curve during the low-water months calculated, for the Kafue, by summing the volume of water stored on the flats on the first day of each month from September through December. Flood storage volume is, however, a sophisticated measure and is not available for many systems. Because most comparisons are made on the basis of area, the best measure would be the actual area flooded, but this too is difficult to obtain for most systems and a simple correlate of it, such as water level as measured on a gauge, is perhaps the easiest to use without serious loss of precision. Dudley (1972) used a flood index (*FI*) consisting of the area under the water-level curve above an arbitrary water level (in the case of the Kafue 4·88 m). Kapetsky (1974a) to some extent combines these two

---

Figs. A.1–A.3 (after FAO, 1977). This illustrates many of the changes taking place on a typical floodplain during falling water. Note particularly the uniform grey flooded areas at the bottom left of Fig. A.1 (DSS and DSDr here) which change to burnt areas (black) as they become dry. First signs of burning appear on higher ground and levées in Fig. A.2, but cover most of the plain in Fig. A.3. Note also the evolution of the large inland depression which remains wet throughout the three images and the line of permanent water bodies distributed from lower right along the course of the major channel of the Nile. The lighter grey area (bottom centre) which remains relatively unchanged is part of the raised ironstone plateau complex and is not flooded.

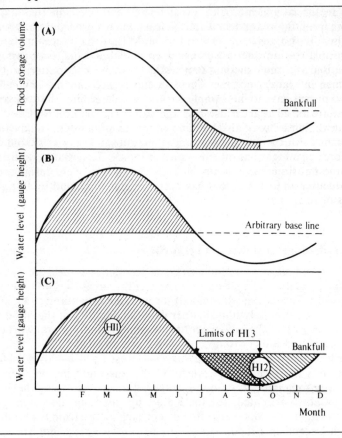

Fig. A.5 Derivation of various flood indices: (A) DDF (University of Michigan, *et al.*, 1971); (B) FI (Dudley, 1972); (C) HI 1, 2 and 3 (Kapetsky, 1974a).

approaches to derive three indices. Hydrological Index 1 (*HI1*) is the area above the water-level curve from the point at which the water starts to overflow on to the plain (bankfull) until it finally becomes dry, and is a measure of the overall magnitude of the flood. Hydrological Index 2 (*HI2*) is the area above the water-level curve from bankfull on the falling flood to bankfull on the rising flood and is a measure of the total amount of water remaining in the system in the dry season. Hydrological Index 3 (*HI3*) is similar to *HI2*, but includes only the area above the curve until minimum water level is reached and is a measure of the contraction of the aquatic environment after the floodplain has dried. Kapetsky used a planimeter for his calculation of areas, but an adequate approximation would be the sum of weekly water levels from one bankfull stage to the next, as used for the analyses presented in Sections 3.6 and 4.5. Failing a knowledge of the bankfull water stage, which in any case varies from one point of the river to the next, and because flood indices are relative measures, an arbitrary base line may be chosen. In some systems such as the Kafue, the three indices are fairly well correlated and one can possibly be substituted for the other for correlation with biological parameters. In other systems, however, the high- and low-water regimes vary more or less independently, and here the two phases have to be treated separately. Hydrological indices such as these are useful as general indicators of the magnitude of the flood or drawdown, but a high-amplitude and short-duration flood can give the same index value as a low-amplitude long-duration one. They do not, therefore, give information on the form of the flood curve and the abruptness of change in level, both of which have biological consequences and have to be taken into account when interpreting the results of such analyses.

References and author index

Page numbers in **bold type** at end of entry indicate reference in text.

* *The Proceedings of the IPFC Symposium on the Development and Utilization of Inland Fishery Resources*, ed. I. Dunn, was published in 1977 by the FAO Regional Office for Asia and the Far East, Bangkok, Thailand as *Proc. IPFC*, **17** (3), 500 pp.

† The Reviews and Experience papers presented at the CIFA Symposium on River and Floodplain Fisheries in Africa, Bujumbura, 21–23 Nov. 1977, ed. R. L. Welcomme, were published in 1978 by FAO, Rome, as *CIFA Tech. Pap.*, **5**, 378 pp.

Academia Republicii Socialiste România (1967) *Limnologia sectorului Românesa al Dunarii*. Bucuresti Studiu Monografic Acadamiei Republicii Socialiste România (Comisia de Hidrologie), 651 pp. **3, 62, 72, 74**

Ackermann, W. C., White, G. F. and Worthington, E. B. (1973) 'Man-made lakes: Their problems and environmental effects', *Geophys. Monog. Ser.*, **17**, 847 pp. **251**

Adams, J. C. (1964) 'Contribution a l'étude de la végétation du lac de Guiers (Sénégal)', *Bull. Inst. Fondam. Afr. Noire (A. Sci. Nat.)*, **26**, 1–72. **59**

Adeniji, E. O. (1975) 'Observations on agriculture and fisheries downstream of the Kainji dam' in *The Ecology of Lake Kainji, the Transition from River to Lake*, ed. A. M. A. Imevbore and O. S. Adegoke. Ile-Ife, Nigeria, University of Ife Press, pp. 181–6. **242, 249**

Adkins, G. and Bowman, P. (1976) 'A study of the fauna in dredged canals of coastal Louisiana', *Tech. Bull. La. Wildl. Fish. Comm.*, **18**. 72 pp. **254**

Ahmad, N. (1956) *Fishing Gear of East Pakistan*. Dacca, Directorate of Fisheries, 33 pp. **184**

Al-Hamed, M. I. (1966) 'Limnological studies on the inland waters of Iraq', *Bull, Iraq Nat. Hist. Mus.*, **3** (5), 1–22. **27**

Aliyev, D. S. (1976) 'The role of phytophagous fishes in the reconstruction of commercial fish fauna and their biological improvement of waters', *J. Ichthyol.*, **16** (2), 216–29. **227**

Allen, K. R. (1951) 'The Horokiwi stream: a study of a trout population', *Fish. Bull.*, *N.Z.*, **10**, 231 pp. **165, 168**

Andreev, N. M. (1966) *Handbook of Fishing Gear and its Rigging*. Jerusalem, Israel Program for Scientific Translations, IPST Cat. No. 1654, 454 pp. **184**

Antipa, G. (1910) *Regiunea inundabilă a Dunării. Starea ei actuală si mijloacele de a o pune in valoare*. Bucharest, Rumania, 318 pp. **3, 215**

Ardizzone, G. D. and Zeisler, R. (1977) *Lista preliminar de las aguas continentales de América Latina (Preliminary List of the Inland Waters of Latin America)*. Rome, FAO (COPESCAL), 144 pp. **41**

Arias, P. A. (1975) 'Contribución al conocimiento limnológico de la Ciénaga de Guarinocito y su relación con el Río Magdalena'. Thesis. Bogotá, Colombia, Fundación Universidad de Bogotá. **44, 50, 52**

Arifin, O. and Arifin, Z. (1976) 'Fisheries in the floodplain area of south Sumatra, a case study of the Lubuk Lampam in 1973'. Paper presented to the IPFC Symposium on the Development and Utilization of Inland Fishery Resources (Abstract), 27 Oct.–5 Nov. 1976. IPFC/76/SYM/10. **186, 212**

Arnold, M. D. (1975) 'Floods as man-made disasters', *Environ. Conserv.*, **2** (4), 257–63. **255**

Attwell, R. I (1970) 'Some effects of Lake Kariba on the ecology of a floodplain of the Mid-Zambezi valley of Rhodesia', *Biol. Conserv.*, **2** (3), 189–96. **236**

Awachie, J. B. E., Ilozumba, P. C. O. and Azugo, W. I. (1977) 'Fish parasites in the ecology, management and productivity of river and floodplain fisheries in Africa'. Paper submitted to FAO/CIFA Symposium on River and Floodplain Fisheries, Burundi, Nov. 1977 (Proceedings in press)†. **158**

Awachie, J. B. E. and Walson, E. C. (1977) 'Atalla fishery of the lower Niger, Nigeria'. Paper submitted to FAO/CIFA Symposium on River and Floodplain Fisheries, Burundi, Nov. 1977 (Proceedings in press)†. **182**

Backiel, T. (1971) 'Production and food consumption of predatory fish in the Vistula river', *J. Fish. Biol.*, **3**, 369–405. **165**

Bakare, O. (1970) 'Bottom deposits as food of inland freshwater fish' in *Kainji Lake Studies*. Vol. 1, *Ecology*, ed. S. A. Visser. Ibadan, Univ. Press, pp. 65–85. **130**

Balon, E. K. (1967) 'Vývos ichtyofauny Dunaja jej súčasný stav a pokus o prosnozu ďalších zmien po výstavbe vodných diel' ('Evolution of the Danube fish fauna: its recent state and an attempt for the prognosis of further changes after the hydro-electric power building'), *Biol. Pr.*, **8** (1), 5–121. **166**

Balon, E. K. (1975) 'Reproductive guilds of fishes: a proposal and definition', *J. Fish. Res. Board Can.*, **32** (6), 821–64. **3, 144, 145**

Bardach, J. (1959) *Report on Fisheries in Cambodia*, Cambodia, USOM, 80 pp. **96, 107, 113**

Basile Martins, M. A. *et al.* (1975) 'Influencia de fatores abioticos sobre a maturacão dos ovarios de *Pimelodus maculatus* Lac. 1803 (Pisces: Siluroidea)', *Bol. Inst. Pesca Santos*, **4** (1), 1–28. **152**

Bastl, I., Holcik, J. and Krupka, I. (1969) 'Abundance and ichthyomass of fish populations in the Biskupicke branch of the Danube river', *Pr. Lab. Rybar.*, **1969** (2), 253–68. **165**

Bayley, P. B. (1973) 'Studies on the migratory characin, *Prochilodus platensis* Holmberg, 1889 (Pisces: Characoidei) in the R. Pilcomayo, South America', *J. Fish. Biol.*, **5**, 25–40. **109, 113**

Bazigos, G. P. (1974) 'The design of fisheries statistical surveys – inland waters', *FAO Fish. Tech. Pap.*, **133**, 122 pp. **273**

Bazigos, G. P., Kapetsky, J. M. and Granados, J. (1975) 'Integrated sampling design for the complex inland fishery of the Magdalena River basin, Colombia', Rome, FAO, FI:DP/COL/72/552, 30 pp. **200, 273**

Bazigos, G. P. *et al.* (1977) 'The present state of the fishery of the Magdalena River basin, Columbia'. Rome, FAO, FAO Working Paper No. 2. FI:DP/COL/72/.552, 30 pp. **180, 211**

Beadle, L. C. (1974) *The Inland Waters of Tropical Africa: An Introduction to Tropical Limnology*. London, Longman, 365 pp. **x, 52**

Beauchamp, R. S. A. (1956) 'The electrical conductivity of the head-waters of the White Nile', *Nature, Lond.*, **198** (4534), 616–9. **48**

Bell-Cross, G. (1971) 'Weir fishing on the central Barotse flood plain in Zambia', *Fish. Res. Bull., Zambia*, **5**, 331–40. **186, 221**

Belyy, N. D. (1972) 'Downstream migrations of the pike perch *Lucioperca lucioperca* (L.) and its food in the early development stages in the lower reaches of the Dnieper', *J. Ichthyol.*, **12**, 465–72. **108, 109**

Berns, S. and Peters, H. M. (1969) 'On the reproductive behaviour of *Ctenopoma muriei* and *Ctenopoma damasi*, *Annu. Rep. EAFFRO*, **1968**, 44–9. **148**

Bhatnagar, G. K. and Karamchandani, B. J. (1970) 'Food and feeding habits of *Labeo fimbriatus* (Bloch) in river Narbada near Hoshangabad (MP)', *J. Inland Fish. Soc., India*, **2**, 30–50. **132**

Bhuiyan, N. I. (1959) 'Hilsa fishing in River Indus', *Agric. Pak.*, **11** (4), 511–9. **180**

Bhukaswan, T. and Pholprasith, S. (1976) 'The fisheries of Ubolratana reservoir in the first ten years of impoundment'. Paper submitted to IPFC Symposium on the Development and Utilization of Inland Fishery Resources, 1976. To be published in *Proc. IPFC*, **17** (in press)*. **251**

Bishop, J. E. (1973) *Limnology of a Small Malayan River Sungai Gombak*. The Hague, W. Junk, 485 pp. **41, 47, 73, 88, 164**

Blache, J. (1964) 'Les poissons du bassin du Tchad et du Bassin adjacent du Mayo Kebbi', *Mém. ORSTOM*, **4**, 483 pp. **18, 107, 108, 120**

Blache, J. and Goosens, J. (1954) 'Monographie piscicole d'une zone de pêche au Cambodge', *Cybium*, **8**, 1–49. **115**

Blache, J. and Miton, F. (1962) 'Première contribution à la connaissance de la pêche dans le bassin hydrographique Logone–Chari Lac Tchad', *Mém. ORSTOM*, **4** (1), 142 pp. **113, 184, 196, 204**

Blanc, M., Daget, J. and D'Aubenton, F. (1955) 'Recherches hydrobiologiques dans le bassin du Moyen-Niger', *Bull. Inst. Fr. Afr. Noire (A. Sci. Nat.)*, **17**, 619–746. **3, 50, 73, 76, 97**

Blažka, P. (1958) 'The anaerobic metabolism of fish', *Physiol. Zool.*, **31**, 117–28. **104**

Blench, T. (1972) 'Morphometric changes', in *River Ecology and Man*. Proceedings of an International Symposium on River Ecology and the Impact of Man, held at the University of Massachusetts, Amherst, 20–23 June 1971, ed. R. T. Oglesby, C. A. Carlson and J. A. McCann. New York, Academic Press, pp. 287–308. **239, 247**

Bonetto, A. A. (1975) 'Hydraulic regime of the Paraná river and its influence on ecosystems', *Ecol. Stud.*, **10**, 175–97. **3, 17, 41, 50, 51, 60, 61, 62, 66, 68, 69, 75, 79, 100, 116, 152**

Bonetto, A. A. and Ezcurra, I. D. (1964) 'La fauna bentónica de algunas aguas rápidas del Paraná Medio', *Physis, B. Aires*, **24**, 311–16. **73**

Bonetto, A. A. and de Ferrato, A. M. (1966) 'Introducción al estúdio del zooplancton en las cuencas isleñas del Paraná Medio', *Physis, B. Aires*, **26** (72), 385–96. **68, 69**

Bonetto, A. A. and Pignalberi, C. (1964) 'Nuevos aportes al conocimiento de la migraciones de los peces en los ríos mesopotámicos de la República Argentina', *Commun. Inst. Nac. Limnol., Argent.*, **1**, 1–14. **91, 108, 110, 111**

Bonetto, A. A., Pignalberi, C. and Cordiviola, E. (1965) 'Contribución al conocimiento de las poblaciones de peces de las lagunas isleñas en el Paraná medio', *Ann. Congr. Latinoam. Zool. São Paulo*, **2**, 131–44. **267**

Bonetto, A. A., *et al.* (1969a) 'Limnological investigations on biotic communities in the Middle Paraná River Valley', *Verh. Int. Ver. Theor. Angew. Limnol.*, **17**, 1035–50. **45, 46, 49, 52, 55, 57, 58, 72, 76, 131**

Bonetto, A. A. *et al.* (1969b) 'Ciclos hidrológicos del río Paraná y las poblaciones de peces contenidas en las cuencas temporarias de su valle de inundación', *Physis, B. Aires*, **29**, 213–23. **98, 99, 100, 156, 167, 266**

Bonetto, *et al.* (1971) 'Informaciones complementarias sobre migraciones de peces en la cuenca de la Plata', *Physis, B. Aires*, **30**, 305–20. **91, 110, 111, 151, 251**

Botnariuc, N. (1967) 'Some characteristic features of the floodplain ecosystems of the Danube', *Hydrobiologia*, **8**, 39–49. **3, 14, 66, 70, 75**

Botnariuc, N. (1968) 'La conception de Gr. Antipa concernant la production biologique de la zone inondable du Danube, du point de vue des recherches actuelles', *Trav. Mus. Hist. Nat. Grigore Antipa*, **8**, 60–8. **3, 215**

Botswana Society (1976) *Proceedings of the Symposium on the Okavango Delta and its Future Utilization*. National Museum, Gabarone, Botswana, 30 Aug.–2 Sept. 1976. Gabarone, Botswana Society, 350 pp. **3**

Bowmaker, A. P. (1963) 'Cormorant predation on two central African lakes', *Ostrich*, **34**, (1), 2–26. **79**

Braga Adhemar, R. (1976) 'Ecologia e etologia de piranhas no nordeste do Brasil (Pisces-*Serrasalmus* Lacépède 1803)'. Tese. Instituto de Biociências de Universidade de São Paulo. Fortaleza, Ceará, Departamento Nacional de Obras contra as Secas (DNOCS), 268 pp. **196**

Braker, W. P. (1963) 'Black piranhas spawned at Shedd aquarium', *Aquarium, Philad.*, **32** (10), 12–4. **148**

Brandt, A. von (1972) *Revised and Enlarged Fish Catching Methods of the World.* West Byfleet, Surrey, Fishing News (Books), 240 pp. **184**

Braun, R. (1952) 'Limnologische Untersuchungen an einigen Seen in Amazonasgebiet', *Schwiez. Z. Hydrol.*, **14** (1), 128 pp. **49**

Brinkmann, W. L. and Santos U. de M. (1973) 'Heavy fish-kill in unpolluted floodplain lakes of central Amazonia, Brazil', *Biol. Conserv.*, **5**, 147–9. **52, 157**

Brown, M. E. (1957) *The Physiology of Fishes.* New York, Academic Press, 2 vols., 447 pp. **101, 104**

Bryson, R. A. (1974) 'A prospective on climatic change', *Science, Wash.*, **184**, 753–60. **38**

Butcher, A. D. (1974) 'A changing aquatic fauna in a changing environment', *IUCN Publ. (New Ser.)*, **9**, 197–219. **110, 249, 254**

Cabrera, S. E. (1962) *Crecimiento de pejerrey del Río de la Plata y algunos datos ecológicos sobre la especie Atherinidae: Basilichthys bonariensis (Cuv. et Val.)* Buenos Aires, Secretaría de Estado de Agricultura y Ganadería de la Nación, Dirección General de Pesca y Conservación de la Fauna, Departamento de Investigaciones Pesqueras, 53 pp. **91, 225**

Cabrera, S. E. and Candia, C. (1964) 'Contribución al conocimiento de la biología de sábalo (*Prochilodus platensis* Holmberg) del Río de la Plata', *Rev. Invest. Agropec. B. Aires*, **1** (4), 57–83. **91, 135**

Cabrera, S. E. *et al.* (1973a) 'Algunos aspectos biológicos de las especies de ictiofauna de la zona de Punta Lara (Río de la Plata) 2a Parte. Alimentación natural de Bagre Porteño (*Parapimelodus valenciennesi*)', *Publ. Serv. Hidrogr. Nav., Argent.*, **H1029**, 47 pp. **139**

Cabrera, S. E. *et al.* (1973b) 'Algunos aspectos biológicos de las especies de ictiofauna de la zona de Punta Lara (Río de la Plata) 1a Parte. Alimentación natural del pejerrey (*Basilichthys bonariensis*)', *Publ. Serv. Hidrogr. Nav., Argent.*, **H1028**, 29 pp. **91, 120**

Cadwalladr, D. A. (1965a) 'Notes on the breeding biology and ecology of *Labeo victorianus* Boulenger (Pisces: Cyprinidae) of Lake Victoria', *Rev. Zool. Bot. Afr.*, **72** (1–2), 109–34. **114**

Cadwalladr, D. A. (1965b) 'The decline in the *Labeo victorianus* Blgr. (Pisces: Cyprinidae) fishery of Lake Victoria and an associated deterioration in some indigenous fishing methods in the Nzoia river, Kenya', *East Afr. Agric. For. J.*, **30** (3), 249–56. **225**

Candia, C. R., Lourdes Baiz, M. de and Cabrera, S. E. (1973) 'Algunos aspectos biológicos de las especies de ictiofauna de la zona de Punta Lara (Río de la Plata) 3a Parte. Estudio de la edad y crecimiento del bagre porteño (*Parapimelodus valenciennesi*) con algunos datos sobre su reproducción', *Publ. Serv. Hidrogr. Nav., Argent.*, **H1030**, 33 pp. **91, 136, 138**

Canestri, V. (1972) 'El recurso icticola continental', *Regionalización ictiofaunística.* Caracas, Ministerio de Agricultura y Cria, Oficina Nacional de Pesca, 72 pp. **201**

Carey, T. G. (1967a) 'Some observations on distribution and abundance of the invertebrate fauna', *Fish. Res. Bull., Zambia*, **3**, 22–4. **75**

Carey, T. G. (1967b) 'Kafue river and floodplain research. Fish populations in lagoon and riverine environments', *Fish. Res. Bull., Zambia*, **3**, 9–12. **95**

Carey, T. G. (1968) 'Feeding habits of some fishes in the Kafue river', *Fish. Res. Bull., Zambia*, **4**, 105–9. **120**

Carey, T. G. (1971) 'Hydrological survey of the Kafue floodplain', *Fish. Res. Bull., Zambia*, **5**, 245–95. **36, 49, 50, 55, 58, 75**

Carter, G. S. (1953) *The Papyrus Swamps of Uganda.* Cambridge, Heffer, 25 pp. **52**

Carter, G. S. and Beadle, L. C. (1930) 'The fauna of the swamps of the Paraguayan Chaco in relation to its environment. 1. Physico-chemical nature of the environment', *J. Linn. Soc., Lond. (Zool.).* **37**, 205–58. **36, 50**

Carter, G. S. and Beadle, L. C. (1931) 'The fauna of the swamps of the Paraguayan Chaco in relation to its environment. 2. Respiratory adaptations in the fishes', *J. Linn. Soc., Lond. (Zool.)*, **37**, 327–68. **101**

Chanthepha, S. (1972) 'Nam Ngum fishery programme and fishery in Khone Falls

(Mekong river)'. Paper presented to SEADAG Seminar, Santa Barbara, 23 pp. (mimeo). **114, 189**

Chapman, D. W. (1967) 'Production in fish populations', in *The Biological Basis of Freshwater Fish Production*, ed. S. D. Gerking. Oxford, Blackwell Scientific Publications, pp. 3–29. **168**

Chevey, P. and Le Poulain, F. (1940) 'La pêche dans les eaux douces du Cambodge', *Mém. Inst. Océanogr. Indochine*, 5, 193 pp. **3, 132, 135, 180, 184, 187, 192, 194, 199, 209**

Chikova, V. M. (1974) 'Species and age composition of fishes in the lower reach (downstream) of the V. I. Lenin Volga Hydroelectric Station', in *Biological and Hydrological Factors of Local Movements of Fish in Reservoirs*, ed. B. S. Kuzin. New Delhi, Amerind Publishing Co., pp. 185–92. Translated from the Russian, published by Nauka Publishers, Leningrad (1968). **248**

Chitravadivelu, K. (1974) 'Growth, age composition, population density, mortality, production and yield of *Alburnus alburnus* (Linnaeus, 1758) and *Rutilus rutilus* (Linnaeus, 1758) in the inundation region of the Danube–Zofin', *Acta Univ. Carol. Biol.*, 1972, 1–76. **135, 136, 163, 166, 169, 218**

Christie, W. J. (1968) 'Possible influences of fishing in the decline of Great Lakes fish stock', *Proc. Conf. Great Lake Res. Int. Assoc.*, 11, 31–8. **222**

Chukajorn, T. and Pawapootanon, O. (1976) 'Annual catch statistics of freshwater fishes taken from seven reservoirs in northeastern Thailand'. Paper submitted to the IPFC Symposium on the Development and Utilization of Inland Fishery Resources, 1976. To be published in *Proc. IPFC*, 17 (in press).* **251**

Coche, A. G. (1967) 'Fish culture in rice fields, a world-wide synthesis', *Hydrobiologia*, 30 (1), 1–44. **48, 243**

Coche, A. G. (1968) 'Description of physico-chemical aspects of Lake Kariba, an impoundment in Zambia–Rhodesia', *Fish. Res. Bull., Zambia*, 5, 200–67. **48**

Coke, M. (1970) 'The water requirements of Pongolo floodplain pans'. Paper presented to the Republic of South Africa Water Year 1970 Convention: Water for the Future, 6 pp. (mimeo). **248**

Coke, M. and Pott, R. (1970) *The Pongolo Floodplain Pans: A Plan for Conservation.* Pietermaritzburg, Natal Parks Board, South Africa, 34 pp. **18, 256**

Committee for the Coordination of Investigations of the Lower Mekong Basin (1970) *Report on Indicative Basin Plan; A Proposed Framework for the Development of Water and Related Resources of the Lower Mekong Basin.* Manila, APO Production Unit for UN/ECAFE, E/CN.11/WRD/MKG/L.340, pp. var. **47, 225**

Congdon, J. C. (1973) 'Fish populations of channelized and unchannelized sections of the Chariton river, Missouri', *Spec. Publ. N.C. Div. Amer. Fish. Soc.*, 2, 52–62. **254**

Conroy, D. A. (1975) 'An evaluation of the present state of world trade in ornamental fish', *FAO Fish. Tech. Pap.*, 146, 128 pp. **220**

Cordiviola de Yuan, E. (1971) 'Crecimiento de peces del Paraná medio. 1. 'Sabalo' (*Prochilodus platensis* Holmberg)', *Physis, B. Aires*, 30 (81), 483–504. **136, 139**

Cott, H. B. (1961) 'Scientific results of an inquiry into the ecology and economic status of the Nile crocodile (*Crocodilus niloticus*) in Uganda and Northern Rhodesia', *Trans. Zool. Soc. Lond.*, 29 (4), 211–356. **78**

CTFT, (1957) *Notes et documents sur la pêche et la pisciculture (Dahomey, Vallée inférieure de l'Ouémé).* Série D.G. No. 2. Nogent-sur-Marne, Centre Technique Forestier Tropical, Sér. D.G. 2. **211, 226**

Daget, J. (1952) 'Mémoires sur la biologie des poissons du Niger. 1. Biologie et croissance des éspèces du genre *Alestes*', *Bull. Inst. Fr. Afr. Noire*, 14 (1), 191–225. **107, 114, 119, 121, 133, 135, 136**

Daget, J. (1954) 'Les poissons du Niger Supérieur', *Mém. Inst. Fr. Afr. Noire*, 36, 391 pp. **66, 94, 95, 97, 120, 151**

Daget, J. (1956) 'Mémoires sur la biologie des poissons du Niger moyen. 2. Recherches sur *Tilapia zillii* (Gerv)', *Bull. Inst. Fr. Afr. Noire*, 18 (1), 165–223. **133**

Daget, J. (1957a) 'Mémoires sur la biologie des poissons du Niger moyen. 3. Reproduction et croissance d'*Heterotis niloticus* Ehrenberg, *Bull. Inst. Fr. Afr. Noire,* **19,** 295–323. **48, 109**

Daget, J. (1957b) 'Données récentes sur la biologie de poissons dans le delta central du Niger', *Hydrobiologia,* **9,** 321–47. **135, 137**

Daget, J. (1960a) 'Les migrations de poissons dans les eaux douces tropicales africaines', *Proc. IPFC,* **8** (3), 79–82. **106**

Daget, J. (1960b) 'Effets du barrage de Markala sur les migrations de poissons dans le moyen-Niger', in *Proceedings of the Seventh Technical Meeting,* IUCN/FAO, Athens, Sept. 1958. Brussels, IUCN, vol. 4, pp. 352–6. **250**

Daget, J. (1966) 'Abondance relative des poissons dans les plaines inondées par la Bénoué à hauteur de Garoua (Cameroun)', *Bull. Inst. Fondam. Afr. Noire (A. Sci. Nat.),* **28,** 247–58. **90**

Daget, J. and Economidis, P. S. (1975) 'Richesse spécifique de l'ichtiofaune de Macédione orientale et de Thrace occidentale (Grèce)', *Bull. Mus. Natl. Hist. Nat., Paris (3° Sér.) (Ecol. Gén. 27),* (346), 81–4. **88**

Daget, J. and Ecoutin, J.-M. (1976) 'Modèles mathematiques de production applicables aux poissons subissant un arrêt annuel prolongé de croissance', *Cah. ORSTOM (Hydrobiol.),* **10** (2), 59–70. **140, 142, 163, 170, 172**

Daget, J., Planquette, N. and Planquette, P. (1973) 'Premières données sur la dynamique des peuplements de poissons du Bandama (Côte d'Ivoire)', *Bull., Mus. Natl. Hist. Nat., Paris (3° Sér.) (Ecol. Gén. 7),* **151,** 129–43. **163, 164, 165, 174, 267**

Dahl, G. (1971) *Los peces del Norte de Colombia.* Bogotá, D.E., Ministerio de Agricultura, Instituto de Desarrollo de los Recursos Naturales Renovables, INDERNEA, 319 pp. **108, 110**

Dansoko, F. D. (1975) 'Contribution à l'étude de la biologie des *Hydrocyon* dans le delta central du Niger'. Thesis. Mali, Bamako, Ministère de l'Education Nationale, 105 pp. **163**

Dansoko, F. D., Breman, H. and Daget, J. (1976) 'Influence de la sécheresse sur les populations d'Hydrococynus dans le delta central du Niger', *Cah. ORSTOM, (Hydrobiol.),* **10** (2), 71–6. **142, 155**

D'Aubenton, F. (1963) 'Rapport sur le fonctionnement d'un barrage mobile sur le Tonle-Sap'. Paris, Muséum National d'Histoire Naturelle, 38 pp. (mimeo). **46, 50**

Day, F. (1958) *The Fishes of India; Being a Natural History of the Fishes Known to Inhabit the Seas and Freshwaters of India, Burma and Ceylon.* London, W. Dawson, 2 vols. vol. 1, 778 pp.; vol. 2, pp. var. **108, 109**

Dehadrai, P. V. and Tripathi, S. D. (1976) 'Environment and ecology of freshwater airbreathing teleosts', in *Respiration of Amphibious Vertebrates,* ed. G. M. Hughes. London, Academic Press, pp. 39–72. **101, 105**

Delmendo, M. N. (1969) 'Lowland fishponds in the Philippines', *Curr. Aff. Bull. IPFC,* **54/55,** 1–11. **167, 244**

Desai, V. R. (1970) 'Studies on the fishery and biology of *Tor tor* (Hamilton) from river Narbada. 1. Food and feeding habits', *J. Inland Fish. Soc. India,* **2,** 101–12. **132**

Dickie, L. M. (1976) 'Predation, yield and ecological efficiency in aquatic food chains', *J. Fish. Res. Board Can.,* **33** (2), 313–6. **222**

Dubey, G. P. and Chatterjee, S. N. (1976) 'Case study of Gandhi Sagar reservoir Madhya Pradesh, India'. Paper presented at IPFC Symposium on the Development and Utilization of Inland Fishery Resources, 1976. To be published in *Proc. IPFC,* **17** (in press).* **251**

Ducharme, A. (1975) 'Informe tecnico de biología pesquera (Limnología)', *Publ. Proy. Desarr. Pesca Cont. INDERENA/FAO Colomb.,* **4,** 42 pp. **33, 44, 47, 52, 58**

Dudley, R. G. (1972) 'Biology of *Tilapia* of the Kafue floodplain, Zambia: predicted effects of the Kafue Gorge Dam'. Ph.D. Dissertation, University of Idaho, Moscow, USA, 50 pp. **136, 139, 141, 155, 273**

Dudley, R. G. (1974) 'Growth of *Tilapia* of the Kafue floodplain, Zambia: predicted effects of the Kafue Gorge Dam', *Trans. Am. Fish. Soc.,* **103,** 281–91. **141, 154**

Dudley, R. G. (1976) *Status of Major Fishes of the Kafue Floodplain, Zambia Five Years after Completion of the Kafue Gorge Dam.* Final report submitted to the National

Science Foundation Scientists and Engineers in Economic Development Program. Athens, Georgia, University of Georgia Grant No. OIP75-09239: 15 Mar. 1975–30 Apr. 1977, 71 pp. **154**

Durand, J. R. (1970) 'Les peuplements ichtyologiques de l'El Beid. Première note. Presentation du milieu et résultats généraux', *Cah. ORSTOM (Hydrobiol.)*, 4 (1), 3–36. **115, 116, 186, 221**

Durand, J. R. (1971) 'Les peuplements ichtyologiques de l'El Beid. 2e note. Variations inter et intraspécifiques', *Cah. ORSTOM (Hydrobiol.)*, 5 (2), 147–59. **115**

Durand, J. R. and Loubens, G. (1969) 'Croissance en longueur d'*Alestes baremoze* (Joannis, 1835) (Poissons, Characidae) dans le bas Chari et le Lac Tchad', *Cah. ORSTOM (Hydrobiol.)*, 3 (1), 59–105. **91, 136, 138**

Durand, J. R. and Loubens, G. (1970a) 'Variations du coefficient de condition chez les *Alestes baremoze* (Pisc. Charac.) du bas Chari et du Lac Tchad', *Cah. ORSTOM (Hydrobiol.)*, 4 (1), 27–44. **136**

Durand, J. R. and Loubens, G. (1970b) 'Observations sur la sexualité et la reproduction des *Alestes baremoze* du bas Chari et du Lac Tchad', *Cah. ORSTOM (Hydrobiol.)*, 4 (2), 61–81. **150, 152, 155**

Eckholm, E. P. (1976) *Losing Ground; Environmental Stress and World Food Prospects.* New York, W. W. Norton, 223 pp. **239**

Economic Commission for Europe (1971) *River Basin Management.* Proceedings of the Seminar Organized by the Committee on Water Problems of the United Nations Economic Commission for Europe and held in London (United Kingdom) 15–22 June 1970. New York, ST/ECE/WATER/3:E.70.II.E.17: 101 pp. **255**

Edwards, A. M. and Thorne, J. B. (1970) 'Observation on the dissolved solids of the Casiquiare and Upper Orinoco, April–June 1968', *Amazoniana*, 2 (3), 245–56. **41**

Egborge, A. B. M. (1971) 'The chemical hydrology of the River Oshun, Western State, Nigeria', *Freshwat. Biol.*, 1 (3), 257–72. **48, 49**

Egborge, A. B. M. (1974) 'The seasonal variation and distribution of phytoplankton in the River Oshun, Nigeria', *Freshwat. Biol.*, 4 (2), 177–91. **55**

EIFAC (1974) 'Report of the Symposium on Methodology for the survey, monitoring and appraisal of fishery resources in lakes and large rivers. Aviemore, Scotland, UK, 2–4 May 1974', *EIFAC Tech. Pap.*, 23, 33 pp. **266**

Eliseev, A. I. and Chikova, V. M. (1974) 'Conditions of fish reproduction in the lower reach (downstream) of the V. I. Lenin Volga Hydroelectric Station' in *Biological and Hydrological Factors of Local Movements of Fish in Reservoirs*, ed. B. S. Kuzin. New Delhi, Amerind Publishing Co., pp. 193–200. Translated from the Russian, published by Nauka Publishers, Leningrad (1968). **248**

Enăceanu, V. (1957) 'Contributiuni la determinarea productivităţii apelor piscicole', *Bul. Inst. Cercet. Piscic.*, 16 (2), 83–5. **75**

Enăceanu, V. (1964) 'Das Donauplankton auf rumänischen Gebiet (km 488 bis km 345)', *Arch. Hydrobiol. Suppl.*, 27, 442–56. **67**

Ertl, M. (1966) 'Zooplankton and chemistry of two backwaters of the Danube river', *Hydrobiol. Stud.*, 1, 267–95. **68, 69, 70**

Espinosa, V. de and Gimenex, C. B. (1974) 'Estudio sobre la biología y pesca del bocachico *Prochilodus reticulatus* (Valenciennes) en el Lago de Maracaibo', *Inf. Téc. Of. Nac. Pesca Caracas*, 63, 32 pp. **138, 201**

Everett, G. V. (1974) 'An analysis of the 1970 commercial fish catch in three areas of the Kafue floodplain', *Afr. J. Trop. Hydrobiol. Fish.*, 3 (2), 148–59. **180, 185, 186, 204**

FAO (1976) 'Yearbook of fishery statistics. Catches and landings, 1975', *FAO Yearb. Fish. Stat.*, 40, pp. var. **1, 212, 219**

FAO (1977) *Strengthening the Soil Survey Administration, the Sudan. Multitemporal Landsat-imagery Interpretation of the Flood Region Draining to the Sudd, Southern Sudan. Based on the work of E. F. de Pauw and Berna Spiers.* Rome, 1977, 27 pp. 3 figs., 2 maps. AG:DP/SUD/71/553, Technical Report 1. **269**

FAO/UN (1954) 'Report to the Government of Iraq on the development of inland fisheries. Based on the work of A. van den Eelaart', *Rep. FAO/UNDP(TA)*, 270, 38 pp. **108**

FAO/UN (1956) 'Report to the Government of Iraq on fishways at dams on the Tigris and Euphrates rivers', *Rep./FAO/UNDP(TA)*, 526, 20 pp. **250**

FAO/UN (1962) 'Rapport au Governement de la République du Niger sur la situation et évolution de la pêche au Niger. Basé sur le travail de M. Jacques M. A. Daget', *Rapp. FAO/PEAT*, 1525, 27 pp. **179, 180**

FAO/UN (1968a) *Multipurpose Survey of the Kafue River Basin, Zambia.* Vol. 4. *The Ecology of the Kafue Flats.* Part 1. 'Ecology and development', prepared by H. J. van Rensburg. Rome, FAO/SF:35/ZAM, 138 pp. **48, 61, 238**

FAO/UN (1968b) 'Report to the Government of Zambia on fishery development in the Central Barotse plain. Based on the work of D. W. Kelley, Inland Fishery Biologist', *Rep. FAO/UNDP (TA)*, 2554, 83 pp. **120, 130**

FAO/UN (1969a) 'Report to the Government of Zambia on fishery development in the Central Barotse floodplain. Second phase. Based on the work of D. Duerre', *Rep. FAO/UNDP(TA)*, 2638, 80 pp. **18, 48, 49, 69, 185, 238**

FAO/UN (1969b) 'Report to the Government of Nigeria on fishing technology relating to river and swamp fisheries of Northern Nigeria. Based on the work of William Reed, FAO/TA Fishery Technologist', *Rep. FAO/UNDP(TA)*, 2711, 90 pp. **187, 189, 211**

FAO/UN (1970a) 'Report to the Government of Nigeria on fishery investigations on the Niger and Benue rivers in the northern region and development of a programme of riverine fishery management and training. Based on the work of M. P. Motwani', *Rep. FAO/UNDP(TA)*, 2771, 196 pp. **17, 115, 116, 139, 151, 211**

FAO/UN (1970b) 'Report to the Government of Zambia on fishery development in the Central Barotse floodplain. Based on the work of G. F. Weiss', *Rep. FAO/UNDP(TA)*, 2816, 19 pp. **187**

FAO/UN (1971a) 'Rapport au Gouvernement du Dahomey sur l'évolution de la pêche intérieure, son état actuel et ses possibilités, établi sur la base des travaux de R. L. Welcomme, Spécialiste de la pêche', *Rapp. FAO/PNUD(AT)*, 2938, 97 pp. **17, 98, 167, 185, 211, 212, 226**

FAO/UN (1971b) 'Rapport au Gouvernement du Niger sur le développement et la rationalisation de la pêche sur le fleuve Niger, établi sur la base des travaux de N. Bacalbasa – Dobrovici, technologiste des pêches', *Rapp. FAO/PNUD(AT)*, 2913, 33 pp. **211**

FAO/UN (1973) *Kainji Lake Research Project, Nigeria. Pelagic Primary Production in Kainji Lake.* Report prepared for the Government of Nigeria by the FAO of the UN acting as executing agency for the UNDP, based on the work of S. G. Karlman. Rome, FI:SF/NIR 24. Technical Report 3, 59 pp. **58**

Fenerich, N. A., Narahara, M. Y. and Godinho, H. M. (1975) 'Curva de crescimento e primeira maturação sexual do mandi, *Pimelodus maculatus* Lac. 1803 (Pisces, Siluroidei)', *Bol. Inst. Pesca Santos*, 4 (1), 15–28. **136, 138, 139**

Fernando, C. H. (1976) 'Reservoir fisheries in South East Asia; past, present and future'. Paper presented at IPFC Symposium on the Development and Utilization of Inland Fishery Resources. To be published in *Proc. IPFC*, 17 (in press).* **227, 252**

Fily, M. and D'Aubenton, F. (1966) *Cambodge: Grand Lac–Tonle Sap. Technologie des pêches 1962–1963*, Paris, Ministère des Affaires Estrangères Service de Coopération Technique, 373 pp. **183, 185, 189, 205**

Fittkau, E. J. (1967) 'On the ecology of Amazonian rain-forest streams', in *Atas de Simposio sobre a Biota Amazônica*, Conselho Nacional Pesquisas, Rio de Janiero, vol. 3. *Limnologia*, pp. 97–108. **76**

Fittkau, E. J. (1970) 'Role of caimans in the nutrient regime of mouth-lakes of Amazon affluents (a hypothesis)', *Biotropica*, 2 (2), 138–42. **78**

Fittkau, E. J. (1973) 'Crocodiles and the nutrient metabolism of Amazonian waters', *Amazoniana*, 4 (1), 103–33. **78, 126, 130, 223, 236**

Fittkau, E. J. and Klinge, H. (1973) 'On biomass and trophic structure of the Central Amazonian Rain Forest ecosystem', *Biotropica*, 5 (1), 2–14. **78**

Fittkau, E. J. *et al.* (1975) 'Productivity biomass and population dynamics in Amazonian water bodies', *Ecol. Stud.*, **11**, 289–311.   **74, 75, 76**

Fontenele, O. (1953) 'Contribucão para o conhecimento da biologiá da Curimata pacu *Prochilodus argenteus* (Spix)', *Rev. Bras. Biol.*, **13**, 87–102.   **150**

Fox, P. J. (1976) 'Preliminary observations on fish communities of the Okavango Delta', in *Proceedings of the Symposium on the Okavango Delta and its Future Utilisation.* National Museum, Gabarone, Botswana, 30 Aug.–2 Sept. 1976. Gabarone, Botswana Society, pp. 125–30.   **137, 152, 167**

Frank, S. (1959) 'Zavislost rùstu nĕkterých druhù ryb na potravních podminkách v polabské tùni Poltruba', *Vestn. Cesk. Spol. Zool.*, **23**, 247–53.   **137**

Fraser, T. M. (1972) 'Fishermen of the Middle Mekong'. Paper presented to the SEADAG Mekong Development Seminar, Santa Barbara, Calif. 1972. Also submitted for publication in *Anthropologica.*   **195, 206**

Fryer, G. (1965) 'Predation and its effects on migration and speciation in African fishes: a comment', *Proc. Zool. Soc. Lond.*, **144**, 301–22.   **109**

Fryer, G. and Whitehead, P. J. P. (1959) 'The breeding habits, embryology and larval development of *Labeo victorianus* Boulenger (Pisces: Cyprinidae)', *Rev. Zool. Bot. Afr.*, **59** (1–2), 33–49.   **109, 154**

Gallais, J. (1967) 'Le Delta intérieur du Niger; étude de géographie régionale', *Mém. Inst. Fondam. Afr. Noire*, **79** (2 vols.), 619 pp.   **236, 238**

Gaygalas, K. S. and Blatneve, D. P. (1971) 'Growth characteristics and the structure and abundance of the bream (*Abramis brama* (L.)) stock in the watercourses of Summer Polders of the Nyamunas River Delta', *J. Ichthyol.*, **11** (5), 682–92.   **166, 254**

Geisler, R. (1969) 'Untersuchungen über der biochemischen Sauerst offbedarf und der Sauerstoffvenbranch von Fischer in einen tropischen Schwarzwasser (Rio Negro, Amazonien, Brasilien)', *Arch.-Hydrobiol.*, **66**, 307–25.   **46, 51**

Geisler, R., Knöppel, H. A. and Sioli, H. (1973) 'The ecology of freshwater fishes in Amazonia; present status and future tasks for research', in *Applied Sciences and Development*, vol. 2. Tübingen, Institute for Scientific Cooperation, pp. 144–62.   **77, 108, 126, 144**

Gessner, F. (1960) 'Limnologische Untersuchungen am Zusammerflus des Rio Negro und des Amazonas (Solimões)', *Int. Rev. Ges. Hydrobiol.*, **45**, 55–79.   **47**

Gibbs, R. J. (1970) 'Mechanisms controlling world water chemistry', *Science, Wash.*, **170**, 1088–90.   **40**

Gilmore, K. S. (1976) 'Development potential and constraints of a fishing industry in Okavango Delta', in *Proceedings of the Symposium on the Okavango Delta and its Future Utilisation.* National Museum, Gabarone, Botswana, 30 Aug.–2 Sept. 1976. Gabarone, Botswana Society, pp. 175–8.   **238**

Godoy, M. P. de (1959) 'Age, growth, sexual maturity, behaviour, migration, tagging and transplantation of the Curimbatá, *Prochilodus scrofa*, Steindachner, 1881, of the Mogi Guassu River, São Paulo State, Brazil', *An. Acad. Bras. Cienc.*, **31**, 447–77.   **91, 109**

Godoy, M. P. de (1975) *Peixes do Brasil Suborden Characoidei Bacia do Rio Mogi Guassu.* Piracicaba, Editora Franciscam, 4 vols. pp. var.   **3, 91, 108, 112, 113, 114, 131, 135, 202, 245, 248, 266**

Gomez, A. L. and Monteiro, F. P. (1955) 'Estudo da populacão total de peixes da represa da Estacão Experimental de Biologia e Piscicultura em Pirassununga São Paulo', *Rev. Biol. Mar. Valp.*, **6**, 82–154.   **167**

Gonzalez-Jimenez, E. (1977) 'The Capybara', *World Anim. Rev.*, **21**, 24–30.   **236**

Gosse, J. P. (1963) 'Le milieu aquatique et l'écologie des poissons dans la région de Yangambi', *Ann. Mus. R. Afr. Cont.*, **116**, 113–271.   **8, 48**

Granados, J. F. (1975) *Estimaciones de la captura, esfuerzo y población pesquera en los ríos Magdalena, Cauca y San Jorge 1974–1975.* Bogotá, INDERENA, 48 pp.   **185, 200**

Green, J. (1963) 'Zooplankton of the River Sokoto, the Rhizopod Testacea', *Proc. Zool. Soc. Lond.*, **141**, 497–514.   **68**

Green, J. (1970) 'Freshwater ecology in the Mato Grosso, Central Brazil. 1. The conductivity of some natural waters', *J. Nat. Hist. Lond.*, **4**, 289–99.   **41**

Green, J. (1972a) 'Freshwater ecology in the Mato Grosso, Central Brazil. 2. Associations of Cladocera in meandering lakes of the Rio Suiá Missú', *J. Nat. Hist. Lond.*, 6, 215–27. **14, 70**

Green, J. (1972b) 'Freshwater ecology in the Mato Grosso, Central Brazil. 3. Associations of Rotifera in meandering lakes of the Rio Suiá Missú', *J. Nat. Hist. Lond.*, 6, 229–41. **70**

Greenway, P. J. and Vesey-Fitzgerald, D. F. (1969) 'The vegetation of Lake Manyara national park', *J. Ecol.*, 57, 129–49. **65**

Greenwood, P. H. (1958) 'Reproduction in the East African lung-fish *Protopterus aethiopicus* Heckel', *Proc. Zool. Soc. Lond.*, 130, 547–67. **148**

Gunderson, D. R. (1968) 'Floodplain use related to stream morphology and fish populations', *J. Wildl. Mgmt.*, 32, 507–14. **238**

Gupta, S. D. and Jhingran, A. G. (1973) 'Ageing *Labeo calbasu* (Hamilton) through its scales', *J. Inland. Fish. Soc. India*, 5, 126–8. **138**

Hall, A., Valente, I. M. and Davies, B. R. (1977) 'The Zambezi River in Moçambique: The physico-chemical status of the Middle and Lower Zambezi prior to the closure of the Cabora Bassa Dam', *Freshwat. Biol.*, 7, 187–206. **48**

Hall, J. B. and Pople, W. (1968) 'Recent vegetational changes in the lower Volta river', *Afr. J. Sci.*, 8 (1–2), 24–9. **247**

Hammerton, D. (1972) 'The Nile river – a case history', in *River Ecology and Man*, ed. R. T. Oglesby, C. A. Carlson and J. A. McCann, New York, Academic Press, pp. 171–213. **48**

Harrel, R. C., Davis, B. J. and Dorris, T. C. (1967) 'Stream order and species diversity of fishes in an intermittent Oklahoma stream', *Am. Midl. Nat.*, 78, 428–36. **88**

Harrison, A. D. (1966) 'Recolonization of a Rhodesian stream after drought', *Arch. Hydrobiol.*, 62, 405–21. **76**

Hastings, R. E. (1972) *Interim Report 1970–1972. Fisheries Research Unit, Lower Shire.* Zomba, Malawi, Fisheries Department, July, unpag. **43, 48, 59**

Henderson, H. F. and Welcomme, R. L. (1974) 'The relationship of yield to Morpho-Edaphic Index and numbers of fishermen in African inland fisheries', *CIFA Occas. Pap.*, 1, 19 pp. **212, 251**

Hickling, C. F. (1961) *Tropical Inland Fisheries.* London, Longman, 287 pp. **x**

Holčik, J. (1972) 'Abundance, ichthyomass and production of fish populations in three types of water-bodies in Czechoslovakia (Man-made lake, trout lake, arm of the Danube river), in *Productivity Problems of Freshwaters*. Proceedings of the IBP-Unesco·Symposium on Productivity Problems of Freshwaters, held in Kazimierz Donly, Poland, 6–12 May 1970, ed. Z.,Kajak and A. Hillbricht-Ilkowska. Warsaw, Polish Scientific Publishers, pp. 834–55. **165**

Holčik, J. and Bastl, I. (1973) 'Ichtyocenoźy dvoch Dunajských ramien so zertelóm na zmeny v ich druhovom zioźeni a hustote vo vztaha ku kolisaniu hladiny v hlavnom toku' ('Ichthyoceneses of two arms of the Danube with regard to changes in species composition and population density in relation to the fluctuation of the water level'), *Biol. Pr.*, 19 (1), 106 pp. **166**

Holčik, J. and Bastl, I. (1975) 'Sampling and population estimation with small mesh seine as used during ichthyological research on Danubian backwaters', *EIFAC Tech. Pap.*, 23, Suppl. 1, 627–40. **267**

Holčik, J. and Bastl, I. (1976) 'Ecological effects of water level fluctuations upon the fish population in the Danube river floodplain in Czechoslovakia', *Acta Sci. Nat. Brno*, 10 (9), 1–46. **166, 215**

Holčik, J. and Bastl, I. (1977) 'Predicting fish yield in the Czechoslovakian section of the Danube river based on the hydrological regime', *Int. Rev. ges. Hydrobiol.*, 62 (4), 523–32. **215, 219**

Holden, M. J. (1963) 'The populations of fish in dry season pools of the river Sokoto', *Fish. Publ. Colon. Off.*, 19, 58 pp. **91, 98, 100, 142, 154, 167, 267**

Holden, M. J. and Green, J. (1960) 'The hydrology and plankton of the River Sokoto', *J. Anim. Ecol.*, 29, 65–84. **48, 50, 55, 67, 68, 69**

Holden, P. B. and Stalnaker, C. B. (1975) 'Distribution and abundance of mainstream fishes in the middle and upper Colorado River basins 1967–1973', *Trans. Amer. Fish. Soc.*, **104**, 217–31. **248**

Horton, R. E. (1945) 'Erosional development of streams and their drainage basins: hydrophysical approach to quantitative morphology', *Bull. Geol. Soc. Am.*, **56**, 275–370. **8**

Howard-Williams, C. and Lenton, G. M. (1975) 'The role of the littoral zone in the functioning of a shallow tropical lake ecosystem', *Freshwat. Biol.*, **5**, 445–59. **58, 66**

Huet, M. and Timmermans, J. A. (1963) 'La population piscicole de la Semois inférieure, Grosse rivière belge du type supérieur de la zone à barbeau', *Trav. Stn. Rech. Eaux For. Groenendaal. Hoeilaart (D)*, **36**, 31 pp. **165**

Hughes, J. M. (ed.) (1976) *Respiration of Amphibious Vertebrates*. London, Academic Press, 402 pp. **101. 102, 105**

Hurault, J. (1965) 'Les principaux types de peuplement du sud-est Dahomey; et leur représentation cartographique', *Etud. Photo-Interpret. Inst. Geogr. Natl., Paris*, **2**, 79 pp. **180, 238, 242, 261**

Husar, S. L. (1975) 'A review of the literature of the Dugong (*Dugong dugon*)', *Wildl. Res. Rep. U.S. Fish. Wildl. Serv.*, **4**, 30 pp. **80**

Husain, Z. (1973) 'Fish and fisheries of the lower Indus basin (1966–1967)', *Agric. Pak.*, **24** (3/4), 297–322. **204, 206, 207**

Hynes, H. B. N. (1970) *The Ecology of Running Waters*. Liverpool, Univ. Press, 555 pp. **x, 68, 72**

Hynes, J. D. (1975) 'Annual cycles of macro-invertebrates of a river in southern Ghana', *Freshwat. Biol.*, **5**, 71–83. **76**

Ihering, R. von (1930) 'La piracema ou montée du poisson', *C. R. Séanc. Soc. Biol., Paris*, **103**, 1336–8. **108, 150**

Imevbore, A. M. A. and Bakare, O. (1974) 'A preimpoundment study of swamps in the Kainji lake basin', *Afr. J. Trop. Hydrobiol. Fish.*, **3** (1), 79–94. **54**

INDERENA (1973) *Operación Subienda 1973. Investigación pesquera*. Bogotá, Colombia, Instituto de Desarrollo de los Recursos Naturales Renovables, 133 pp. **113, 114, 144, 151**

Indrasena, H. H. (1970) 'Limnological and freshwater fisheries development work in Ceylon', in *Proceedings of the IBP Section PF (Freshwater Productions) Meeting of Inland Water Biologists in Southeast Asia*, at Kuala Lumpur and Malacca (Malaysia) 5–11 May 1969. Sponsored by Unesco. Djakerta, Unesco Field Science Office for Southeast Asia, pp. 45–7. **212**

Islam, B. N. and Talbot, G. B. (1968) 'Fluvial migration, spawning and fecundity of Indus River Hilsa, *Hilsa ilisha*', *Trans. Am. Fish. Soc.*, **97**, 350–5. **109**

Ivlev, V. S. (1966) 'The biological productivity of waters', *J. Fish. Res. Board Can.*, **23**, 1727–59. **168**

Jackson, P. B. N. (1961a) 'The impact of predation, especially by the tiger fish (*Hydrocyon vittatus* Cast.) on African freshwater fishes', *Proc. Zool. Soc. Lond.*, **136**, 603–22. **109**

Jackson, P. B. N. (1961b) *The Fishes of Northern Rhodesia*. Lusaka, Zambia, Government Printer, 140 pp. **225**

Jhingran, V. G. (1968) 'Synopsis of biological data on *Catla catla* (Hamilton 1822)', *FAO Fish. Synop.*, **32**, Rev. 1, pp. var. **113**

Jhingran, V. G. (1975) *Fish and Fisheries of India*. Delhi, India, Hindustan Publishing Corporation, 954 pp. **3, 41, 204**

Johnels, A. G. (1954) 'Notes on fishes from the Gambia river', *Ark. Zool.*, **6** (17), 327–411. **135, 136, 137**

Johnels, A. G. and Svensson, G. S. O. (1954) 'On the biology of *Protopterus annectens*', Ark. Zool., 7, 131–44. **148**

Johnson, C. R. (1976) 'Diel variations in the thermal tolerance of *Gambusia affinis* (Pisces: Paeciliidae)', *Comp. Biochem. Physiol. (A. Comp. Physiol.)*, **55**, 337–40. **104**

Johnson, D. S. (1967) 'On the chemistry of freshwaters in southern Malaya and Singapore', *Arch. Hydrobiol.*, **63**, 477–96. **41, 42**

Johnson, D. S. (1968) 'Malayan blackwaters', in *Proceedings of the Symposium on Recent Advances in Tropical Ecology*, Part 1, ed. R. Misra and B. Gopal. Varanasi, India, International Society for Tropical Ecology, pp. 303–10. **41, 42**

Jonglei Investigation Team (1954) *The Equatorial Nile project, its Effects in the Anglo-Egyptian Sudan.* Report of the Jonglei Investigation Team. Vols. I–V. Khartoum, Sudan, Government Publication (restricted). **3**

Junk, W. (1970) 'Investigations on the ecology and production biology of the floating meadows (*Paspalo echinochloetum*) on the middle-Amazon. Part 1. The floating vegetation and its ecology', *Amazoniana*, **4**, 449–95. **64**

Junk, W. (1971) 'Primeiros resultados das investigacoes acerca a povoaçao animal em substrato flutuante identico em diferentes tipos de aguas da Amazonia', in II° Simpósio y Foro de Biología Tropical Amazónica, Florencia (Caqueta) y Leticia (Amazonas), Asociación pro Biología Tropical. Colombia, enero 1969. Bogotá, pp. 81–5. **73**

Junk, W. J. (1973) 'Investigations on the ecology and production-biology of the floating meadows (*Paspalo echinochloetum*) on the Middle Amazon. Part 2. The aquatic fauna in the Root Zone of floating vegetation', *Amazoniana*, **4**, 9–102. **44, 46, 47, 52, 53, 71**

Junk, W. J. and Honda, M. S. (1976) 'A pesca nu Amazonia; aspectos ecologicos e economicos', in *Anais do Premero Encontro Nacional sobre limnologia, Piscicultura e Pesca Continental*, ed. J. Israel Vargas, C. G. Cid Loureiro y R. Milward de Andrade. Fundacão João Pinheiro, Secretaria do Planjamento e Coordenaçao Geral, pp. 211–26. **202**

Kapetsky, J. M. (1974a) 'Growth, mortality and production of five fish species of the Kafue river floodplain, Zambia', PhD dissertation, University of Michigan, 194 pp. **140, 141, 159, 160, 163, 164, 170, 236, 273**

Kapetsky, J. M. (1974b) 'The Kafue river floodplain: An example of preimpoundment potential for fish production', in *Lake Kariba: A Man-made Tropical Ecosystem in Central Africa*, ed. E. K. Balon and A. G. Coche. The Hague, W. Junk, pp. 497–523. **140, 169**

Kapetsky, J. M. *et al.* (1976) *Fish Populations in the Floodplain Lakes of the Magdalena River: Second Report*, Bogotá, INDERENA-FAO, 30 pp. **98, 131, 167**

Kapetsky, J. M. *et al.* (1977) 'Some ecological aspects of the shallow lakes of the Magdalena floodplain, Colombia'. Paper presented to the Intertropical Synposium on Stability and Diversity in Tropical Communities, Panama, Mar. 1977. **72, 151, 167, 186**

Kapetsky, J. M. (in press) 'Fish population estimates in floodplain lakes', in *Guidelines for Sampling Fish in Freshwaters*. Rome, FAO. **267**

Keulder, P. C. (1970) 'Orange River research', *Rep. South Afr. IBP/PF Working Group*, **4**, 7–9. **48**

Khalil, L. F. (1971) 'Check list of helminth parasites of African freshwater fishes', *Tech. Commun. Commonw. Inst. Helminthol.*, **42**, 80 pp. **158**

Khan, H. A. and Jhingran, V. G. (1975) 'Synopsis of biological data on Rohu, *Labeo rohita* (Hamilton, 1822)', *FAO Fish. Synop.*, **111**, 100 pp. **113, 135, 154**

Kimpe, P. de (1964) 'Contribution à l'étude hydrobiologique du Luapula-Moero', *Ann. Mus. R. Afr. Cent. (Ser. 8 Sci. Zool.)*, **128**, 1–238. **108**

Knöppel, H. A. (1970) 'Food of central Amazonian fishes. Contribution to the nutrient ecology of Amazonian rain forest streams', *Amazoniana*, **2** (3), 257–352. **120**

Kok, L. T. (1972) 'Toxicity of insecticides used for Asiatic rice borer control to tropical fish in rice paddies', in *The Careless Technology – Ecology and International Development*, ed. M. T. Farvar and J. P. Milton. Record of Conference on Ecological Aspects of International Development, 1968: National History Press, Garden City, New York, USA, pp. 489–98. **244**

Konare, A. (1977) 'Collecte, traitement et commercialisation du poisson en plaines inondables', in *CIFA Working Party on River and Floodplain Fisheries*, contributions by members of the Working Party, pp. 32–45 (mimeo).† **211, 215**

Krykhtin, K. L. (1975) 'Causes of periodic fluctuations in the abundance of the non-anadromous fishes of the Amur river', *J. Ichthyol.*, **15** (5), 826–9.   **142, 152, 157, 218**

Kuehne, R. A. (1962) 'A classification of streams, illustrated by fish distribution in an eastern Kentucky creek', *Ecology*, **43**, 608–14.   **88**

Kushlan, J. A. (1976) 'Environmental stability and fish community diversity', *Ecology*, **57**, 821–5.   **131**

Lagler, K. E., Bardach, J. E., Miller, R. R. and May, D. R. (1977) *Ichthyology*. New York, Wiley and Sons, 2nd edn, 506 pp.   **104**

Lelek, A. and El Zarka, S. (1973) 'Ecological comparison of the preimpoundment and postimpoundment fish faunas of the River Niger and Kainji Lake, Nigeria', *Geophys. Monogr. Ser.*, **17**, 655–60.   **249**

Lellack, J. (1966) 'Influence of the removal of the fish population on the bottom animals of the five Elbe backwaters', *Hydrobiol. Stud.*, **1**, 323–80.   **75**

Leopold, L. B., Wolman, M. B. and Miller, J. P. (1964) *Fluvial Processes in Geomorphology*. San Francisco, W. H. Freeman, 522 pp.   **5, 233**

Le-Van-Dang (1970) 'Contribution to a biological study of the lower Mekong', in *Proceedings of the IBP Regional Meeting of Inland Water Biologists in Southeast Asia*, at Kuala Lumpur and Malacca (Malaysia) 5–11 May 1969 (sponsored by Unesco). Djakarta, Unesco Field Science Office for Southeast Asia, pp. 59–64.   **65, 97**

Lewis, W. M. (1970) 'Morphological adaptations of cyprinodonts for inhabiting oxygen deficient waters', *Copeia*, **1970** (2), 319–26.   **103**

Liebman, M. and Reichenbach-Klinke, H. (1967) 'Eingriffe des Menschen und deren biologische Auswirkung', in *Limnologie der Donau*, ed. R. Leipolt. Stuttgart, E. Schweizerbart'sche Verlagsbuchhandlung, pp. VI–VIII, 1–25 (Eng. summary, pp. 116–17).   **246**

Liepolt, R. (ed.) (1967) *Limnologie der Donau*. Stuttgart, E. Schweizerbart'sche Verlagsbuchhandlung, pp. var.   **3, 22**

Liepolt, R. (1972) 'Uses of the Danube river', in *River Ecology and Man*, ed. R. T. Oglesby, C. A. Carlson and J. A. McCann. New York, Academic Press, pp. 233–49.   **22, 205, 212, 247**

Livingstone, D. A. (1963) 'Chemical composition of rivers and lakes', in *Data of Geochemistry*, ed. M. Fleischer. Washington, DC, Government Printing Office, Ch. 4.   **48**

Loftus, K. H. (1976) 'Science for Canada's fisheries rehabilitation needs', *J. Fish. Res. Board Can.*, **33** (8), 1822–57.   **92**

Loubens, G. (1969) 'Etude de certains peuplements ichtyologiques par des pêches au poison (1re Note)', *Cah. ORSTOM (Hydrobiol.)*, **3** (2), 45–73.   **164, 165, 167, 267**

Loubens, G. (1970) 'Etude de certains peuplements ichtyologiques par des pêches au poison (2e Note)', *Cah. ORSTOM (Hydrobiol.)*, **4** (1), 45–61.   **90**

Lowe-McConnell, R. H. (1964) 'The fishes of the Rupununi savanna district of British Guiana, South America. Part 1. Ecological groupings of fish species and effects of the seasonal cycle on the fish', *J. Linn. Soc. (Zool.)*, **45**, 103–44.   **3, 79, 94, 95, 98, 108, 119, 131, 135, 136, 148, 154, 158**

Lowe-McConnell, R. H. (ed.) (1965) *Man-made Lakes*. Proceedings of a symposium held at the Royal Geographical Society. London, Academic Press, 218 pp.   **250**

Lowe-McConnell, R. H. (1967) 'Some factors affecting fish populations in Amazonian waters', in *Atas do Simpósio sobre a Biota Amazonia*, Conselho Nacional Pesquisas, Rio de Janeiro, Conservação de Natureza e Recursos Naturais, pp. 177–86.   **102, 138, 154**

Lowe-McConnell, R. H. (1975) *Fish Communities in Tropical Freshwaters*. London, Longman, 337 pp.   **x, 88, 95, 131, 147, 150, 154**

Lowe-McConnell, R. H. (1977) 'Ecology of fishes in tropical waters', *Inst. Biol. Stud. Biol.*, **76**, 64 pp.   **222, 260**

Mago-Leccia, F. (1970) 'Estudios preliminares sobre la ecología de los peces de los llanos de Venezuela', *Acta Biol. Venez.*, **7** (1), 71–102.   **3, 95, 96, 98, 121, 131, 135, 167**

Mann, K. H. (1965) 'Energy transformations by a population of fish in the River Thames', *J. Anim. Ecol.*, **34**, 253–75. **165, 168**

Mann, K. H. (1972) 'Case history: the River Thames', in *River Ecology and Man*, ed. R. T. Oglesby, C. A. Carlson and J. A. McCann. New York, Academic Press, pp. 215–32. **169**

Mann, R. H. K. (1971) 'The population, growth and production of fish in four small streams in Southern England', *J. Anim. Ecol.*, **40**, 155–90. **163**

Marlier, G. (1951) 'Recherches hydrobiologiques dans les rivières du Congo oriental. Composition des eaux. La conductibilité électrique', *Hydrobiologia*, **3**, 217–27. **48**

Marlier, G. (1967) 'Ecological studies on some lakes of the Amazon Valley', *Amazonian*, **1**, 91–115. **55, 57, 65, 69, 70, 72, 74, 122-3**

Marlier, G. (1973) 'Limnology of the Congo and Amazon rivers', in *Tropical Forest Ecosystems in Africa and South America: A Comparative Revue*, ed. B. J. Meggers, E. S. A. Ayensu and W. D. Duckworth. Washington, Smithsonian Institution Press, pp. 223–38. **31, 43**

Matthes, H. (1964) 'Les poissons du lac Tumba et de la région d'Ikela. Etude systématique et écologique', *Ann. Mus. R. Afr. Centr. Ser. 8vo (Ser. Zool.)*, **126**, 204 pp. **41, 42, 96, 121, 122, 151**

Matthes, H. (1977a) 'The problem of rice-eating fish in the Central Delta, Mali'. Contribution to FAO/CIFA Symposium on River and Floodplain Fisheries, Burundi, Nov. 1977, 26 pp. (Proceedings in press).† **130, 242**

Matthes, H. (1977b) 'Interim report on the Apure river basin (Venezuela) development with respect to fisheries', in *CIFA Working Party on River and Floodplain Fisheries*; Contributions by members of the Working Party. Rome, FAO, pp. 46–54 (mimeo). † **238**

McArthur, R. H. and Wilson, E. O. (1967) *The Theory of Island Biogeography.* Princeton, NJ, Princeton Univ. Press, 203 pp. **88**

McFadden, J. T. and Cooper, E. L. (1962) 'An ecological comparison of six populations of brown trout (*Salmo trutta*)', *Trans. Am. Fish. Soc.*, **91**, 53–62. **165**

Meschkat, A. (1972) Nuevas técnicas de pesca fluvial recomendadas para el Ecuador. Quito, Service Forestal y Piscicultura, 34 pp. **192**

Meschkat, A. (1975) 'Aquacultura e pesca em aguas interiores no Brasil', *Doc. Téc. SUDEPE*, **9**, 35 pp. **202**

Micha, J. C. (1973) *Etude des populations piscicoles de l'Ubangui et tentatives de sélection et d'adaption de quelques espèces à l'étang de pisciculture.* Nogent-sur-Marne, Centre Technique Forestier Tropical. **48**

Mikkola, H. and Arias, P. A. (1976) *Evaluación preliminar de la limnología y de las poplaciones de peces en el sistema del canal del Dique. Parte 1. Limnología.* Bogotá, Proyecto Pesca Continental, INDERENA–FAO, 65 pp. **44, 56, 57, 58, 70, 74**

Mizuno, T. and Mori, S. (1970) 'Preliminary hydrobiological survey of some Southeast Asian inland waters', *Biol. J. Linn. Soc.*, **2**, 77–117. **50**

Moghraby, A. I. el (1977) 'A study on diapause of zooplankton in a tropical river – The Blue Nile', *Freshwat. Biol.*, **7**, 77–117. **71**

Monakov, A. V. (1969) 'The zooplankton and the zoobenthos of the White Nile and adjoining waters in the Republic of the Sudan', *Hydrobiologia*, **33**, 161–85. **67, 69, 70, 72, 73, 74**

Mucha, V. (1967) 'Die Mikrobiologie der Donau', in *Limnologie der Donau*, ed. R. Liepolt. Stuttgart, E. Schweizerbart'sche Verlagsbuchhandlung, pp. V, 132–57 (Eng. summary pp. 103–5). **54**

Muncy, R. J. (1973) *A Survey of the Major Fisheries of the Republic of Zambia.* Rome, FAO, FI:DP 9/10 ZAM 511/3:69 pp. **216**

Muncy, R. J. (1977) 'Floodplain fishery of the Kafue river, Zambia, Africa'. Paper submitted to FAO/CIFA Symposium on River and Floodplain Fisheries, Burundi, Nov. 1977 (Proceedings in press).† **215, 216**

Nagaraja Rao, S. and Rajalakshmi, T. (1976) 'Investigations on the fisheries of River Godavari. Andhra Pradesh: India'. Paper presented to the IPFC Symposium on the Development and Utilization of Inland Fishery Resources, Colombo, Sri Lanka, 27–29 Oct. 1976. To be published in *Proc. IPFC*, **17** (in press).* **249**

Natarajan, A. V. (1976) 'Ecology and the state of fishery development in some of the man-made reservoirs in India'. Paper presented to the IPFC Symposium on the Development and Utilization of Inland Fishery Resources, Colombo, Sri Lanka, 27–29 Oct. 1976. To be published in *Proc. IPFC*, **17** (in press)* **251**

Natarajan, A. V. and Jhingran, A. G. (1963) 'On the biology of *Catla catla* (Ham.) from the river Yamuna', *Proc. Natl. Inst. Sci. India (B)*, **29** (3), 326–55. **135, 138**

Nelson, K. (1964) 'Behaviour and morphology in the glandulocaudine fishes (Ostariophysi, Characidae)', *Univ. Cal. Publ. Zool.*, **75** (2), 59–152. **149**

Nicolau, A. (1952) 'Vegetatia acuatică̦ factor important în determinarea conditiilor hidrobiologice din băltile regiunii inundabile a Dunării', *Bull. Inst. Cercercet. Piscis.*, **11** (4), 53–69. **62**

Nikolsky, G. V. (1937) 'On the distribution of fishes according to the nature of their food in the rivers flowing from the mountains of Middle Asia', *Proc. Int. Assoc. Limnol.*, **8**, 170–6. **132**

Nikolsky, G. V. (1956) *Ryby basseyna Amura (The Fishes of the Amur Basin)*. Moscow, Akademiia Nauk SSR, 551 pp. **154**

Norman, J. R. (1975) *A History of Fishes* (3rd edn, P. H. Greenwood). London, Ernest Benn, 467 pp. **101**

Novotna, M. and Korinek, V. (1966) 'Effect of the fish-stock on the quantity and species composition of the plankton of two backwaters', *Hydrobiol. Stud.*, **1**, 297–322. **70**

Obeng, L. (ed.) (1969) *Man-made Lakes: The Accra Symposium*. Proceedings of a symposium held at Accra. Accra, Ghana Univ. Press, 398 pp. **250**

Odum, E. P. (1967) 'The strategy of ecosystem development', *Science, Wash.*, **164**, 262–70. **260**

Oglesby, R. T., Carson, C. A. and McCann, J. A. (eds.) (1972) *River Ecology and Man*. New York, Academic Press, 465 pp. **x**

Ohya, M. (1966) 'Comparative study on the geomorphology and flooding in the plains of the Cho-Shui-Chi, Chao-Phya, Irrawaddy and Ganges', in *Scientific Problems of the Humid Tropical Zone Deltas and their Implications*. Proceedings of the Dacca Symposium, 1964. Paris, Unesco, pp. 23–8. **16, 36**

Okedi, J. (1971) 'Further observations on the ecology of the Nile perch (*Lates niloticus*) in Lake Victoria and Lake Kyoga', *Rep. E. Afr. Freshwat. Fish. Res. Organ.*, **1970**, 42–54. **150**

Oliva, O. (1960) 'Further contributions to the fish population composition in middle Bohemia', *Véstn. Cesk. Spol. Zool.*, **24**, 42–9. **166**

Opération Pêche (1977) *Rapport annuel 1976*. Mopti, Opération Pêche, 44 pp. **207**

ORSTOM (1969) *Annales hydrologiques 1964–1965*. ORSTOM, 431 pp. **33**

Osmera, S. (1973) 'Annual cycle of zooplankton in backwaters of the flood area of the Dyje', *Hydrobiol. Stud.*, **3**, 219–56. **68, 69, 70, 71**

Otobo, F. O. (1977) 'Commercial fishery in the middle river Niger, Nigeria'. Contribution to FAO/CIFA Symposium on river and floodplain fisheries, Burundi, Nov. 1977 (Proceedings in press).† **249**

Pantulu, V. R. (1970) 'Some biological considerations related to the lower Mekong development', in *Proceedings of the Regional Meeting of Inland Water Biologists in Southeast Asia*, at Kuala Lumpur and Malacca (Malaysia) 5–11 May 1969 (sponsored by Unesco). Djakarta, Unesco Field Science Office for Southeast Asia, pp. 113–19. **113**

Parameswaran, S., Selvaraj, C. and Radhakrishnan, S. (1970) 'Observations on the maturation and breeding season of carps in Assam', *J. Inland Fish. Soc. India*, **2**, 16–29. **152**

Pardo, G. (1976) 'Inventario y zonificación de la cuenca para fines hidroagrícolas', in *Conferencias del Foro. Seminario Foro Aprovechamientos de Propósito Multiple Protección Contra las Inundaciones*. Bogotá, Proyecto Cuenca Magdalena, Cauca Convenio Colombo Holandes, pp. D3–1 to D3–7. **17**

Patil, M. R. (1976) 'Pollutional effects of industrial wastes on riverine fisheries of India'. Paper presented to the IPFC Symposium on the Development and Utilization of Inland Fishery Resources, Colombo, Sri Lanka, 27–29 Oct. 1976. To be published in *Proc. IPFC*, **17** (in press).* **246**

Petr, T. (1968) 'Population changes in aquatic invertebrates living on two water plants in a tropical man-made lake', *Hydrobiologia*, **32**, 449–85. **72**

Petr, T. (1974) 'A pre-impoundment limnological study with special reference in fishes of the Great Ruaha River (Tanzania) and some of its tributaries (River Yovi and Little Ruaha) in and around the proposed impoundment areas'. Uppsala, Institute of Systemat Biology, 104 pp. (cyclostyled report). **48**

Phelines, R. F., Coke, M. and Nicol, S. M. (1973) 'Some biological consequences of the damming of the Pongolo river', in *Proc. 11ème Congrès des Grands Barrages*. Commission Internationale des Grands Barrages, pp. 175–90. **256**

Pillay, S. R. and Rosa, H. Jr. (1963) 'Synopsis of biological data on Hilsa, *Hilsa ilisha* (Hamilton, 1822)', *FAO Fish. Biol. Synop.*, **25**, pp. var. **110, 150, 154**

Poll, M. and Renson, H. (1948) 'Les poissons, leur milieu et leur pêche au bief supérieur du Lualaba', *Bull. Agric. Congr. Belg.*, **39** (2), 427–46. **212, 223**

Preston, F. W. (1962a) 'The canonical distribution of commonness and rarity. Part 1', *Ecology*, **43** (2), 185–215. **90**

Preston, F. W. (1962b) 'The canonical distribution of commonness and rarity. Part 2', *Ecology*, **43** (3), 410–32. **90**

Preston, F. W. (1969) 'Diversity and stability in the biological world', *Brookhaven Symp. Biol.*, **22**, 1–12. **90**

Prowse, G. A. and Talling, J. F. (1958) 'The seasonal growth and succession of plankton algae in the White Nile', *Limn. Oceanogr.*, **3**, 222–38. **54**

Quensière, J. (1976) 'Influence de la sécheresse sur les pêcheries du delta du Chari (1971–1973)', *Cah. ORSTOM Hydrobiol.*, **10** (1), 3–18. **156, 224**

Raimondo, P. (1975) 'Monograph on operation fisheries, Mopti', in Consultation on fisheries problems in the Sahelian Zone, Bamako, Mali, 13–20 Nov. 1974. *CIFA Occas. Pap.*, **4**, 294–311. **17, 181, 202**

Rao, N. G. S., Ray, P. and Gopinathn, K. (1972) 'Observations on the spawning of *Cirrhina reba* (Hamilton) in the Cauvery and Bhavani rivers', *J. Inland Fish. Soc. India*, **4**, 69–73. **152**

Rao, R. G. and Rao, L. H. (1972) 'On the biology of *Labeo calbasu* (Ham. Buch.) from the River Godavari', *J. Inland Fish. Soc. India*, **4**, 26–37. **138**

Reed, W. *et al.* (1967) *Fish and Fisheries of Northern Nigeria*. Zaria, Ministry of Agriculture, 226 pp. **110, 192, 221**

Regier, H. A. and Henderson, H. F. (1973) 'Towards a broad ecological model of fish communities and fisheries', *Trans. Am. Fish. Soc.*, **102** (1), 56–72. **222**

Regier, H. A. and Loftus, K. H. (1972) 'Effects of fisheries exploitation on salmonid communities in oligotrophic lakes', *J. Fish. Res. Board. Can.*, **29**, 959–68. **222**

Regier, H. A. (1976) 'Environmental biology of fishes: emerging science', *Environ. Biol. Fish.*, **1** (1), 5–11. **264**

Reiss, F. (1973) 'Zur Hydrographie und Makro benthosfauna tropischer laguner in der savanner des Território de Roraima, Nordbrasilien', *Amazoniana*, **4**, 367–78. **74**

Reiss, F. (1977) 'Qualitative and quantitative investigations on the macrobenthic fauna of Central Amazon lakes. 1. Lago Tupé, a black water lake on the lower Rio Negro', *Amazoniana*, **6** (2), 203–35. **75, 76**

Reizer, C. (1971) *Contribution à l'étude hydrobiologique du Bas-Sénégal. Premières recommandations d'aménagement halieutique*. Nogent-sur-Marne, Centre Technique Forestier Tropical, 142 pp. **48**

Reizer, C. (1974) *Définition d'une politique d'aménagement des ressources halieutiques d'un écosystème aquatique complex par l'étude de son environnement abiotique, biotique et anthropique. Le fleuve Sénégal Moyen et Inférieur*. Docteur en Sciences de l'Environnement. Dissertation Arlon. Fondation Universitaire Luxembourgeoise, 4 vols., 525 pp.   **10, 49, 59, 79, 109, 136, 143, 167, 186, 187, 190, 202, 203, 211**

Ricker, W. E. (ed.) (1971) 'Methods for assessment of fish production in fresh waters', *IBP Handb.*, 3, 348 pp.   **266**

Ricker, W. E. (1975) 'Computation and interpretation of biological statistics of fish populations', *Bull. Fish. Res. Board Can.*, **191**, 382 pp.   **267**

Ringuelet, R. A., Aramburu, R. H. and Aramburu, A. A. de (1967) *Los peces argentinos de agua dulce.* Buenos Aires, Librart SRL, 602 pp.   **150**

Roberts, T. R. (1973) 'Ecology of fishes in the Amazon and Congo basins', in B. J. Meggers, E. S. Ayers and W. D. Duckworth, *Tropical Forest Ecosystems in Africa and South America: A Comparative Review*, ed. B. J. Meggers and E. S. Ayers. Washington, Smithsonian Institution Press, pp. 239–54.   **1, 88, 96, 126, 151**

Roman, B. (1966) 'Aportación al estudio de la fauna ictiológica dulceacuícola de Río Volta'. Doctoral Thesis. Barcelona, Spain.   **151**

Russev, B. (1967) 'Das Zoobenthos der Donau', in *Limnologie der Donau*, ed. R. Liepolt. Stuttgart, E. Schweizerbart'sche Verlagsbuchhandlung, pp. V, 242–71 (Eng. summary, pp. 111–12).   **73, 75**

Ryder, R. A. *et al.* (1974) 'The morpho-edaphic index, a fish-yield estimator – review and evaluation', *J. Fish. Res. Board Can.*, **31** (5), 663–88.   **251**

Rzóska, J. (1974) 'The Upper Nile swamps, a tropical wetland study', *Freshwat. Biol.*, **4**, 1–30.   **18, 54, 58, 67, 72, 73, 75, 97, 236, 237**

Rzóska, J. (ed.) (1976) *The Nile: Biology of an Ancient River.* The Hague, Monographiae biologicae, vol. 20, 417 pp.   **236**

Rzóska, J. and Talling, J. F. (1966) 'Plankton development in relation to hydrology and reservoir regime in the Blue Nile', *Verh. Int. Ver. Theor. Angew. Limnol.*, **16**, 716–18.   **54**

Sabol, K. J. (ed.) (1974) *National Conference on Flood Plain Management, 1974.* League City, Texas, NACD (National Association of Conservation Districts), 261 pp.   **22, 244, 255**

Sagua, N. O. (1977) 'The effect of Kainji dam, Nigeria, upon fish production in the River Niger below the dam at Faku'. Contribution to FAO/CIFA Symposium on River and Floodplain Fisheries, Burundi, Nov. 1977, (Proceedings in press).†   **249**

Sánchez Romero, J. (1961) 'El paiche'. *Aspectos de su historia natural, ecología y aprovechamiento.* Lima, Servicio de Pesquería, 48 pp.   **43, 102, 148**

Sandon, H. and Tayib, A. (1953) 'The food of some common Nile fish', *Sudan Notes Rec.*, **34**, 205–23.   **131**

Sao-Leang and Dom Saveun (1955) 'Aperçu général sur la migration et la reproduction des poissons d'eau douce du Cambodge', *Proc. IPFC*, **5** (2–3), 138–62.   **91, 95, 97, 115, 151, 239**

Sarnita, A. S. (1976) 'Some aspects of fisheries and their development in man-made lakes in Indonesia with special reference to Lake Jatiluhur, West Java'. Paper presented to the IPFC Symposium on the Development and Utilization of Inland Fishery Resources, Colombo, Sri Lanka, 27–29 Oct. 1976. To be published in *Proc. IPFC*, **17** (in press).*   **251**

Sayer, J. A. and van Lavieren, L. P. (1975) 'The ecology of the Kafue lechwe population of Zambia before the operation of hydro-electric dams on the Kafue river', *E. Afr. Wildl, J.*, **13**, 9–37.   **234, 235**

Schmid, M. (1961) *Incidences possibles sur la végétation en bordure du Tonlé Sap de la construction d'un barrage conçu pour régulariser le régime du Bas-Mekong.* Report submitted to Committee for Coordination of Investigations of the Lower Mekong Basin, UN ECAF, 15 pp. (mimeo).   **61**

Schmidt, G. W. (1969) 'Vertical distribution of bacteria and algae in a tropical lake', *Int. Rev. Ges. Hydrobiol.*, **54**, 791–7.   **54**

Schmidt, G. W. (1970) 'Number of bacteria and algae and their interrelations in some Amazonian waters', *Amazoniana*, **2**, 393–400.   **54, 55**

Schmidt, G. W. (1972a) 'Amounts of suspended solids and dissolved substances in the

middle reaches of the Amazon over the course of one year (August 1969–July 1970)',
Amazoniana, **3**, 208–23. **47, 49**

Schmidt, G. W. (1972b) 'Seasonal changes in water chemistry of a tropical lake (Lago do
Castanho, Amazonia, South America)', *Verh. Int. Ver. Theor. Angew. Limnol.*, **18**,
613–21. **49**

Schmidt, G. W. (1973a) 'Primary production of phytoplankton in the three types of
Amazonian waters. 2. The limnology of a tropical floodplain lake in Central Amazonia
(Lago do Castanho)', *Amazoniana*, **4** (2), 139–203. **44, 50, 52, 57**

Schmidt, G. H. (1973b) 'Primary productivity of phytoplankton in a tropical floodplain
lake of Central Amazonia, Lago do Castanho, Amazonas, Brazil', *Amazoniana*, **4**,
379–404. **56, 57**

Schmidt, G. W. (1976) 'Primary production of phytoplankton in the three types of
Amazonian waters. 4. The Primary Productivity of Phytoplankton in a bay on the lower
Rio Negro (Amazonas, Brazil)', *Amazoniana*, **5** (4), 517–28. **46, 51, 57**

Schneberger, E. and Funk, J. L. (eds.) (1971) *Stream Channelization, a Symposium.*
Special Pub. No. 2. N. Central Div., AFS, 83 pp. **254**

Sénégal, Direction des eaux, forêts et chasses (1976) 'La pêche continentale: préparation
du Ve plan de développement économique et social'. Dakar, 10 pp. (mimeo). **215**

Shepherd, C. J. (ed.) (1976) *Investigation into Fish productivity in a Shallow Freshwater
Lagoon in Malawi 1975/76.* London, Ministry of Overseas Development, 90 pp. **41,
56, 58, 72, 74, 79, 215, 238**

Shiraishi, Y. (1970) 'The migration of fishes in the Mekong river', in *Proceedings of the
IBP Regional Meeting of Inland Water Biologists in Southeast Asia*, Kuala Lumpur
and Malacca (Malaysia) 5–11 May 1969 (sponsored by Unesco). Djakarta, Unesco
Field Science Office for Southeast Asia, pp. 135–40. **110, 113**

Sidthimunka, A. (1970) 'A report on the fisheries survey of the Mekong river in the vicinity
of the Pa Mong dam site', *Tech. Pap. Dep. Fish. Thailand*, **8**, 75 pp. **47, 67, 68, 69, 74,
75, 164, 165, 167**

Sidthimunka, A. (1972) 'Fisheries in relation to impoundment in the Mekong basin –
experience in Thailand', in *Proceedings of the SEADAG Seminar on the Impact of
Development on the Fisheries of the Lower Mekong River*, 3–5 Feb. 1972. **152, 252**

Sioli, H. (1964) 'General features of the limnology of Amazonia', *Verh. Int. Theor. Angew.
Limnol.*, **15**, 1053–8. **61**

Sioli, H. (1968) 'Principal biotypes of primary production in the waters of Amazonia', in
Proceedings of the Symposium on Recent Advances in Tropical Ecology, ed. R. Misra
and B. Gopal. Varanasi, India, International Society for Tropical Ecology, pp.
591–600. **41**

Sioli, H. (1975a) 'Amazon tributaries and drainage basins', *Ecol. stud.*, **10**, 199–213. **3,
17, 75, 76**

Sioli, H. (1975b) 'Tropical river: the Amazon', in *River Ecology*, ed. B. A. Whitton.
London, Blackwell Scientific Publications, pp. 461–88. **3**

Smart, M. (ed.) (1976) *Proceedings of the International Conference on the Conservation
of Wetlands and Waterfowl.* Slimbridge, International Waterfowl Research Bureau,
492 pp. **236**

Smith, P. A. (1976) 'An outline of the vegetation of the Okavango drainage system', in
Proceedings of the Symposium on the Okavango Delta and its Future Utilization.
National Museum, Gaborone, Botswana, 30 Aug.–2 Sept. 1976. Gaborone, Botswana
Society, pp. 93–112. **61**

Soulsby, J. J. (1959) 'Status of the Lake Mweru fishery', *Rep. Jt. Fish. Res. Organ.*, **8**
(1958), 30–8. **48, 225**

Sparks, R. E. and Starret, W. C. (1975) 'An electrofishing survey of the Illinois river
1959–1974', *Ill. Nat. Hist. Bull.*, **31** (8), 317–80. **253**

Sreenivasan, A. (1976) 'Fisheries of the Stanley reservoir (Mettur dam) and three other
reservoirs of Tamilnadu, India – a case history'. Paper presented to the IPFC
Symposium on the Development and Utilization of Inland Fishery Resources,
Colombo, Sri Lanka, 27–29 Oct. 1976. To be published in *Proc. IPFC*, **17** (in
press).* **251**

Sritingsook, C. and Yoovetwatana, T. (1976) 'Induced spawning of Pla yee-sok, *Probarbus jullieni* Sauvage'. Paper presented to the IPFC Symposium on the Development and Utilization of Inland Fishery Resources, Colombo, Sri Lanka, 27–29 Oct. 1976. To be published in *Proc. IPFC*, **17** (in press).* **108, 225**

Starret, W. C. (1972) 'Man and the Illinois river', in *River Ecology and Man*, ed. R. T. Oglesby, C. A. Carlson and J. A. McCann. New York, Academic Press, pp. 131–69. **253**

Stauch, A. (1966) 'Le bassin Camerounais de la Bénoué et sa pêche', *Mém. ORSTOM*, **15**, 152 pp. **192, 212**

Strahler, A. N. (1957) 'Quantitive analysis of watershed geomorphology', *Trans. Am. Geophys. Union*, **38**, 913–20. **8**

Svensson, G. S. O. (1933) 'Freshwater fishes from the Gambia river (British West Africa). Results of the Swedish expedition, 1931', *K. Svensk. Vetenskskopsabad. Handl.*, **12**, 13 pp. **8, 35, 36, 92, 148, 187**

Swingle, H. S. (1954) 'Fish populations in Alabama rivers and impoundments', *Trans. Am. Fish. Soc.*, **83** (1953), 47–57. **165**

Szemes, G. (1967) 'Das Phytoplankton der Donau', in *Limnologie der Donau*, ed. R. Liepolt. Stuttgart, E. Schweizerbart'sche Verlagsbuchhandlung, pp. V, 158–79 (Eng. summary pp. 105–7). **57**

Tait, C. C. (1967a) 'Hydrological data', *Fish. Res. Bull., Zambia*, **3**, 26–8. **49, 52**

Tait, C. C. (1967b) 'Mass fish mortalities', *Fish. Res. Bull., Zambia*, **3**, 28–30. **157**

Talling, J. (1957) 'The longitudinal succession of water characteristics in the White Nile', *Hydrobiologia*, **9** (1),73–89. **48, 55**

Talling, J. and Talling, I. B. (1965) 'The chemical composition of African lake waters', *Int. Rev. Ges. Hydrobiol.*, **50** (3), 421–63. **48**

Talling, J. F. and Rzóska, J. (1967) 'The development of plankton in relation to hydrological regime in the Blue Nile', *J. Ecol.*, **55**, 637–62. **67**

Tang Cheng Eng *et al.* (1973) *A Report on Paddy and Paddy Field Fish Production in Krian Perak*. Malaysia, Ministry of Agriculture and Fisheries, p. 57. **180, 243**

Thailand, Department of Fisheries, Inland Fisheries Division, Statistics Unit (1974) 'Fish farm and pond production for 1973'. Bangkok, Ministry of Agriculture, 64 pp. (mimeo). **244**

Thompson, K. (1976) 'The primary productivity of African wetlands, with particular reference to the Okavango Delta', in *Proceedings of the Symposium on the Okavango Delta and its Future Utilisation*. National Museum, Gabarone, Botswana, 30 Aug.–2 Sept. 1976. Gabarone, Botswana Society, pp. 67–79. **65**

Thornton, I. W. B. (1957) 'Faunal succession in umbels of *Cyperus papyrus* L. on the upper White Nile', *Proc. R. Entomol. Soc. Lond. (A)*, **32**, 119–31. **72**

Timmermans, J. A. (1961) 'La population piscicole de l'Eau Blanche. Petite rivière du type supérieur de la zone à Barbeau', *Trav. Stn. Rech. Eaux Fôr. Groenendaal-Hoeilaart (D)*, **30**, 16 pp. **165**

Trefethen, P. (1972) 'Man's impact on the Columbia river', in *River Ecology and Man*, ed. R. T. Oglesby, C. A. Carlson and J. A. McCann. New York, Academic Press, pp. 77–98. **249**

Tongsanga, S. and Kessunchai, P. (1966) 'Fish populations and ecological studies of flood water fisheries in Pra Nakorn Sri-Ayuthaya province', *Occas. Pap. IPFC*, **6**, 38 pp. **107, 146, 148, 185, 189, 192, 204**

Toynbee, A. (1976) *Mankind and Mother Earth*. London, Oxford Univ. Press, 641 pp. **2**

Turner, J. L. (1977) 'Changes in the size structure of Cichlid populations in Lake Malawi resulting from bottom trawling', *J. Fish. Res. Board Can.*, **34**, 232–8. **222**

Tweddle, D., Hastings, R. E. and Jones, T. (1977) 'The development of a floodplain fishery: Elephant Marsh, Malawi'. Paper submitted to FAO/CIFA Symposium on River and Floodplain Fisheries, Burundi, Nov. 1977. (Proceedings in press).† **208**

UN (1966) 'Economic Commission for Asia and the Far East. A compendium of major international rivers in the ECAFE region', *UN Water Resourc. Ser.*, **25**, 75 pp. **33**

UN (1969) *Report of the United Nations Interregional Seminar on Flood Damage Prevention Measures and Management.* New York, United Nations, ST/FAO/SER.C/ 144, 117 pp. **245, 255**

Unesco (1969–71) *Discharge of Selected Rivers of the World. 1. General and Regime Characteristics of Stations Selected. 2. Monthly and Annual Discharges Recorded at Various Selected Stations (From Start of Observations up to 1964). 3. Mean Monthly and Extreme Discharges (1965–1969).* Paris, Unesco, vol. 1, 70 pp., vol. 2, 194 pp., vol. 3, 98 pp. **33**

Ungemach, H. (1971) 'Chemical rain water studies in the Amazon region', II° Simposio y Foro de Biología Tropical Amazónica, Florencia (Caquata) y Leticia (Amazonas) Columbia, enero 1969, Asociación pro Biología tropical, Bogotá, pp. 354–8. **43**

Ungemach, H. (1972) 'Die Ionenfracht des Rio Negro, Staat Amazonas, Brasilien nach Untersuchungen', *Amazoniania*, 3, 175–85. **42**

University of Idaho *et al.* (1971) *Ecology of Fishes in the Kafue River.* Report prepared for FAO/UN acting as executing agency for UNDP. Moscow, Idaho, University of Idaho, FI:SF/ZAM 11: Tech. Rep. 2, 66 pp. **3, 49, 50, 79, 115, 116, 136, 216**

University of Michigan *et al.* (1971) *The Fisheries of the Kafue River Flats, Zambia, in Relation to the Kafue Gorge Dam.* Report prepared for FAO/UN acting as executing agency for UNDP. Ann Arbor, Michigan, University of Michigan, FI:SF/ZAM 11: Tech. Rep. 1, 161 pp. **3, 163, 167, 168, 174, 216, 267, 273**

Vaas, K. F. (1953) 'Fisheries in the lake district along the River Kapuas in West Borneo', *Proc. IPFC*, 4 (2), 192–207. **122**

Van der Leeden, F. (1975) *Water Resources of the World, Selected Statistics.* New York, Water Information Center, 568 pp. **34, 39**

Vesey-Fitzgerald, D. M. (1970) 'The origin and distribution of valley grasslands in East Africa', *J. Ecol.,* 58, 51–75. **59**

Vidal, J. C. (1964) *Un caso de mortandad de peces en el Río Parana.* Buenos Aires, Argentina, Dirección General de Pesca, 26 pp. **43**

Vidal, J. C. (1967) 'Contribución al estudio biológico del Sabalo de los Ríos Parana y Uruguay. (Prochilodus platensis *Holmberg*). Buenos Aires, Argentina, Dirección General de Pesca y Conservación de la Fauna, 51 pp. **91, 121, 150, 202, 208**

Vidal, J. C. (1969) *Actividades pesqueras en Rosario.* Rosario, Estación Hidrobiológica de Rosario, 41 pp. **135, 207**

Visser, S. A. (1974) 'Composition of waters of lakes and rivers in East and West Africa', *Afr. J. Trop. Hydrobiol. Fish.,* 3, 43–60. **41**

Viswanathan, N. and Sundararaj, B. I. (1974) 'Seasonal changes in the hypothalamo-hypophyseal-ovarian system in the catfish, *Heteropneustes fossilis* (Bloch)', *J. Fish. Biol.,* 6, 331–40. **152**

Volker, A. (1966) 'Surface hydrology of deltaic areas', in *Scientific Problems of the Humid Tropical Zone Deltas and their Implications.* Proceedings of the Dacca Symposium. Paris, Unesco, pp. 143–9. **36**

Vranovsky, M. (1974a) 'Zooplankton baciaskeho systemu Ramien pred vyustenim do Llavneho toku a Jeho Vyznam preformovanie zooplanktonu v Dunaji' ('Zooplankton of the side arms of Baka ahead of its confluence with the main stream on its importance for the forming of zooplankton of the River Danube'). *Biol. Pr. Slov. Akad. Vied,* 7 (20), 77 pp. **68, 70**

Vranovsky, M. (1974b) 'Zur Kenntnis der Verteilung, Biomasse und Drift des Zooplanktons im tschechoslowakisch–ungarischen Donau-abschnitt' ('Contribution to the knowledge of the distribution, biomass and drift of the zooplankton in the Czechoslovak–Hungarian stretch of the Danube'). *Arch. Hydrobiol.,* Suppl. 44 (3), 360–3. **68**

Wassink, E. C. (1975) 'Photosynthesis and productivity in different environment – conclusions', in *Photosynthesis and Productivity in Different Environments,* ed. J. P.

Cooper. International Biological Programme 3. London, Cambridge Univ. Press, pp. 675–87. **66**

Weiss, H. W. and Midgley, D. C. (1975) 'Mathematical floodplain modelling, Vol. 1', *Rep. Univ. Witwatersrand Hydrol. Res. Unit*, 7/75, pp. var. **37**

Weiss, H. W. and Midgley, D. C. (1976) 'Mathematical floodplain modelling, Vol. 2', *Rep. Univ. Witwatersrand Hydrol. Res. Unit*, 3/76, pp. var. **37**

Welcomme, R. L. (1964) 'The habitats and habitat preferences of the young of the Lake Victoria *Tilapia* (Pisces-Cichlidae)', *Rev. Zool. Bot. Afr.*, **40** (1–2), 1–28. **103, 104–5**

Welcomme, R. L. (1967) 'The relationship between fecundity and fertility in the mouth-brooding cichlid fish *Tilapia leucosticta*', *J. Zool. Lond.*, **151**, 453–68. **150**

Welcomme, R. L. (1969) 'The biology and ecology of the fishes of a small tropical stream', *J. Zool. Lond.*, **158**, 485–529. **48, 116, 151**

Welcomme, R. L. (1970) 'Studies on the effects of abnormally high water levels on the ecology of fish in certain shallow regions of Lake Victoria', *J. Zool. Lond.*, **160**, 405–36. **46**

Welcomme, R. L. (1972a) 'The inland waters of Africa', *CIFA Tech. Pap.*, 1, 117 pp. **41, 48**

Welcomme, R. L. (1972b) 'An evaluation of the acadja method of fishing as practised in the coastal lagoons of Dahomey (West Africa)', *J. Fish. Biol.*, **4**, 39–55. **192, 195**

Welcomme, R. L. (1975a) 'The fisheries ecology of African floodplains', *CIFA Tech. Pap.*, 3, 51 pp. **98, 216**

Welcomme, R. L. (ed.) (1975b) 'Symposium on the methodology for the survey, monitoring and appraisal of fishery resources in lakes and large rivers. Aviemore, Scotland, 2–4 May 1974. Panel reviews and relevant papers'. *EIFAC Tech. Pap.*, 23, Suppl. 1, 2 vols., 747 pp. **266**

Welcomme, R. L. (1976) 'Some general and theoretical considerations on the fish yield of African rivers', *J. Fish. Biol.*, **8**, 351–64. **1, 8, 47, 210, 219**

Welcomme, R. L. and Hagborg, D. (1977) 'Towards a model of a floodplain fish population and its fishery', *Environ. Biol. Fish.*, 2 (1), 7–24. **140, 160, 161, 170, 172, 218, 222, 256**

Welcomme, R. L. and Henderson, H. F. (1976) 'Aspects of the management of inland waters for fisheries', *FAO Fish. Tech. Pap.*, **161**, 36 pp. **224**

Westlake, D. F. (1963) 'Comparison of plant productivity', *Biol. Rev. Camb. Philos. Soc.*, **38** (3), 385–425. **65**

Westlake, D. F. (1975) 'Primary production of freshwater macrophytes', in *Photosynthesis and Productivity in Different Environments*, ed. J. P. Cooper. International Biological Programme 3. London, Cambridge Univ. Press, pp. 189–206. **62, 65**

Whitehead, P. J. P. (1958) 'Indigenous river fishing methods in Kenya', *East Afr. Agric. J.*, **24**, 111–16. **188**

Whitehead, P. J. P. (1959a) 'The anadromous fishes of Lake Victoria', *Rev. Zool. Bot. Afr.*, **59**, (3–4), 329–63. **108, 113**

Whitehead, P. J. P. (1959b) 'The river fisheries of Kenya. Part 1: Nyanza province', *East Afr. Agric. J.*, **24**, 214. **186**

Whitehead, P. J. P. (1960) 'The river fisheries of Kenya. Part 2: The lower Athi (Sabaki) River', *East Afr. Agric. For. J.*, **25** (4), 259–65. **167**

Whiteside, B. G. and McNatt, R. M. (1972) 'Fish species diversity in relation to stream order and physicochemical conditions in the Plum Creek drainage basin', *Am. Midl. Nat.*, **88**, 90–101. **88**

Whitley, J. R. (1974) 'Some aspects of water quality and biology of the Missouri river', *Trans. Miss. Acad. Sci.*, 7–8, 60–72. **247, 248, 249**

Whitton, R. B. (ed.) (1975) *River Ecology*. London, Blackwell, 725 pp. **x, 14**

Whyte, S. A. (1971) 'The ecology of Chironomids in a small tropical man-made lake. The Danfa Reservoir'. M.Sc. Thesis, University of Ghana. **76**

Williams, N. V. (1960) 'A review of the Kafue River fishery', *Rhodesia Agric. J.*, **57**, 86–92. **206**

Williams, R. (1971) 'Fish ecology of the Kafue River and floodplain environment', *Fish. Res. Bull. Zambia*, 5, 305–30. **107, 113, 115, 116, 158**

Willoughby, N. G. and Tweddle, D. (1977) 'The ecology of the commercially important species in the Shire Valley fishery, Southern Malawi', in CIFA Working Party on River and Floodplain Fisheries; Contributions by members of the Working Party, pp. 1–19 (mimeo).† **135, 150, 204**

Willoughby, N. G. and Walker, R. S. (1977) 'The traditional fishery of the lower Shire Valley, Malawi, Southern Africa', in *CIFA Working Party on River and Floodplain Fisheries*; Contributions by members of the Working Party, pp. 20–31 (mimeo).† **134, 185**

Wimpenny, R. S. (1943) 'The fisheries of Egypt', *Sci. Prog. Lond.,* **29** (114), 210–27. **142, 154, 215**

Winstanley, D. (1975) 'Rainfall and river discharges in the sub-Sahara zone (10°–20°N) of Africa', in Consultation on Fisheries Problems in the Sahelian Zone, Bamako, Mali, 13–20 Nov. 1974. *CIFA Occas. Pap.,* **4**, 97–114. **38**

Wolverton, B. and McDonald, R. C. (1976) 'Don't waste waterweeds', *New Sci.,* **71**, 318–20. **62**

Wourms, J. P. (1972) 'The developmental biology of annual fishes. 3. Pre-embryonic and embryonic diapause of variable duration in the eggs of annual fishes', *J. Exp. Zool.,* **182**, 389–414. **105**

Zambia (1965) *Fisheries Research Bulletin 1963–64.* Lusaka, Game and Fisheries Department, *Fish. Res. Bull. Zambia,* **1963–64**, 211 pp. **211**

Zambia, Central Statistical Office (1971) *Fisheries Statistics (Natural Waters) 1970.* Lusaka, Central Statistical Office, 140 pp. **211**

Zambia, Department of Fisheries (1974) *Annual Report 1974,* 39 pp. **211**

Zambriborshch, F. S. and Nguen Tan Chin (1973) 'The descent of fish larvae into the sea through the Kiliya arm of the Danube', *J. Ichthyol.,* **13** (1), 90–5. **108, 254**

Geographical index

Africa, 1, 18, 73, 88
  floodplains of, 25–7
  general references, 41, 42, 219
Akosombo reservoir, 247; see also
  Volta L.
Aljab L. (lagoon of Nile Sudd, Sudan),
  69
Amaravathy reservoir (India), 251
Amazon R. (South America), 3, 8, 13,
  14, 17, 24, 25, 33, 39, 41, 47, 49,
  54, 55, 61, 73, 88, 89, 92, 96, 108,
  126, 144, 151, 157, 225
Amu Darya R. (Central Asia), 22, 132,
  227
Amur R. (Asia), 22, 142, 152, 154, 157,
  218
Aouk R. (tributary of Chari R., Chad),
  21, 26
Apure R. (tributary of the Orinoco,
  Venezuela), 17, 21, 24, 33, 52, 66,
  96, 97, 98, 116, 167, 201, 237
Arauca R. (Venezuela), 17, 24, 66, 97,
  237
Asia, 1
  floodplains of, 27–30
  general references, 219
Atar L. (lagoon of Nile Sudd, Sudan),
  69
Atrato R. (Colombia), 17, 22
Austria, 57
Ayame Reservoir (Ivory Coast), 25
Ayapel (lagoon of Magdalena flood-
  plain, Colombia), 12, 44

Bahr Aouk, 21, 26; see also Aouk R.
Bahr el Ghazal R. (Sudan), 26
Baka (arm of Danube R., Europe), 68,
  70
Bandama R. (Ivory Coast), 48, 89, 163,
  164, 165
Bangala swamp (floodplain on Zaire
  R.), 27
Bangladesh, 27–9, 181, 184, 197
Bangula lagoon (part of Shire

floodplain, Malawi), 41, 56, 58, 72,
  73, 74, 215, 238
Bangweulu L. (Zambia), 79
Bani R. (Mali), 38
Barito R. (Borneo), 30
Barotse plain: (floodplain of Zambezi
  R., Zambia), 18, 25, 185, 186, 211,
  222
Benin, 17, 25, 180
Benue R. (West Africa), 17, 25, 39, 89,
  90, 116, 211
Bhavani R. (India), 152
Bhavani Sagar reservoir (India), 251
Biskupicke (backwater of Danube R.),
  166
Borneo, 30
Brahmaputra R. (India), 27, 29, 32, 39,
  89, 204, 219, 239
Branco R. (Brazil), 24, 74
Brazil, 52

Calado L. (lagoon of Amazonian
  Várzea, Brazil), 46, 52, 53
Cambodia (= Kampuchea), 180
Canal del Dique (canal between
  Magdalena R. and sea, Colombia),
  22
Candaba swamps (floodplain of
  Pampanga and Angat R., Phillip-
  pines), 167, 244
Capanaparo R. (Venezuela), 24
Carabali (lagoon of Magdalena R.
  floodplain, Colombia), 57
Carcaraña R. (Paraná system,
  Argentina), 250
Castanho L. (lagoon of Amazonia
  Várzea, Brazil), 44, 45, 54, 56, 57
Catatumbo R. (Venezuela), 17, 22, 200
Cauca R. (tributary of Magdalena,
  Colombia), 13, 22, 47
Cauvery R. (India), 152, 204, 249
Central African Empire, 26
Central America, 17, 22
Central Delta (floodplain of Niger R.,

Taxonomic index

General index

Actinomycetes, 54
Adaptation to survive extreme
    conditions
    invertebrates, 70, 76
    fish, 101–6
Aerial photography, 268
Aestivation, 76, 105
Agriculture
    dry, 240–2
    wet, 242–4
Air breathing in fishes, 101–4, 206
Allochthonous sources of nutrients and
    food, 67, 77, 78, 119, 120, 122,
    126–30
Alluvial deposits, 1
Anabranch of river, 7
Anadromous fish, 86
Animal communities associated with
    aquatic vegetation, 71–2
Annual fishes, 105–6, 152
Aquaculture, 230, 257
    in rice field (rice-fish culture), 243–4
Artificial islands for housing fishermen
    or cattle, 181
Ash, 66
'Aufwuchs', 58, 66, 120
Autochthonous sources of food, 67,
    119, 120

Backswamps, 5, 9, 15
Backwaters, 54, 55, 68, 96, 126
    standing stock in, 165–6
Bacteria, 53–4
Bankfull level or stage, 31, 37
Benthos, 73–7
Biochemical oxygen demand, 53
Biomass
    of animal communities associated
        with vegetation, 71–2
    of benthos, 74
    of emergent vegetation, 65–6
    of fish (ichthyomass), 162–8
    of floating vegetation, 62–3
    of primary producers, 57–8
    of zooplankton, 68–70

Blackfishes, 82, 91, 100, 107, 144, 148,
    153, 177
Blackwaters, 41, 42, 49, 75, 76, 78
    blackwater rivers and lakes, 66, 73
Blooms of algae and zooplankton, 55,
    67, 68, 80
Boats, 183–4
Bottom substrate
    influence on distribution, 100
    influence on standing stock, 167
Brackish waters, 9
Brackish-water species of fish, 86
Braided channels, 7
Burning of floodplain vegetation, 65–6

Canonical distribution of abundance of
    species, 90
Carnivorous fishes, 121
Catadromous fish, 86
Catch
    composition of, 199–205
    differences between years, 215–19
    in different rivers, 211–12
    influence of fishermen on, 212–13
    of freshwater fish, 1
Cattle occurrence on floodplain, 41, 65,
    236–8
Channelisation – effect on fish, 254–5
Channels of rivers, 5, 7–9, 19, 94
    benthos in, 73
    ichthyomass in, 163–4
    primary production in, 55
    thermal conditions in, 43–5
    zooplankton in, 67–8
Chemistry of river water, 40–53
Cienagas, 22; *see also* lagoons
Clearwater rivers, 13
Closed seasons, 227
Coastal deltas, 21, 25, 36
Competition for food, 132
Condition factor (K), 133, 136
Conductivity of water, 41, 47–9, 55, 80
Creeks, 9
Creeping flow, 31